Alexander Kemp

Hand-book of the Presbyterian Church in Canada

1883

Alexander Kemp

Hand-book of the Presbyterian Church in Canada
1883

ISBN/EAN: 9783337206154

Printed in Europe, USA, Canada, Australia, Japan

Cover: Foto ©Andreas Hilbeck / pixelio.de

More available books at **www.hansebooks.com**

HAND-BOOK

OF THE

Presbyterian Church in Canada.

1883.

EDITED BY

Rev. A. F. KEMP, LL.D., *Editor Digest Minutes of Synod Pres. Church of Canada, &c.*

Rev. F. W. FARRIES, *Minister of Knox Church, Ottawa.*

AND

J. B. HALKETT, *Of the Marine and Fisheries Department.*

J. DURIE & SON, OTTAWA, PUBLISHERS.

PRINTED AND BOUND BY A. S. WOODBURN, OTTAWA

PREFACE.

THE Editors make no apology for the publication of this little book. It was felt by them, and many others, that the Church, by its several unions, had grown to such dimensions that it was difficult for the best informed, and impossible for the most part of its members, by any means within their reach, to obtain any conception of the extent of its field of operations, of its great schemes of Missions and Benevolence, and of the Legislative, Judicial and Advisory actings of its General Assembly. It therefore occurred to them that no better way could be devised by which to represent the Church as a grand organization for the preaching of the everlasting Gospel, and the extension of Christ's Kingdom within the wide Dominion of Canada, than by preparing, with their best ability, the Hand-book now published.

It embraces the leading features of our Presbyterian Church as a living power in the country, sets forth the covenants and conditions of our last glorious Union, and details, to an extent commensurate with the information available, the *personel* of our Ministry. The novelty of this last feature has, doubtless, prevented many brethren from replying to our queries, and left us only the items provided in our published records. But the interest of these biographical notices will, probably, when another edition of the Hand-book is called for, induce a larger number to furnish the personal items required. Advantage has also been taken of public sources of information, to furnish fuller particulars than required by the schedules of those of our ministers, whose labors are worthy of special recognition.

We have endeavored to present in collected form the judicial decisions of the Assembly since the Union. Its administration of justice and discipline is certainly one of its highest functions. The collective wisdom and learning of the Church, guided by the Spirit of Christ, is presumed to be afforded in these solemn determinations. They embrace subjects of faith, morals, and practical Christian life, than which there is surely nothing of more importance to the Church. In most instances the decisions are, happily, such as commend themselves to the conscience and intelligence of Christian men. If any defect may be noted, it is that, in many instances, neither the facts of the cases, nor the reasons for the decisions are recorded—no uncommon defect in the judicial records of Church Courts. In some cases it may, no doubt, be expedient to omit details in matters of discipline, but in most cases, a careful statement of facts and reasons is desirable, and would give our Assembly's decisions all the weight of legal precedents.

We have given also as full an account of our Colleges as our space would permit, and think that, from the facts furnished, together with the historical statements, inquirers may gather from our pages a fair knowledge of the high status and work of our University and Theological Schools. They cover our field from East to West, and are well worthy of the Church's liberality and esteem. They are as trees planted by the River of God, which yieldeth fruit in their season, and whose leaf fadeth never.

Of our great Mission and Benevolent schemes we present an ample account. In a compacted form our little book exhibits what the Church is doing at Home and Abroad—from which it will be apparent that, while we have no reason to boast of our labors or our liberality, we yet need not be ashamed of our endeavours. No part of the Church's duty is altogether neglected. From year to year our work is expanding into greatness in our hands. A dispensation of grace is evidently committed to us. Our record since the Union may well awaken devoutest gratitude to Christ our Head, for abundant blessings bestowed, and stimulate our faith, zeal, and liberality to yet greater achievements.

It was intended to give some special account of the Literature of the Church, which, although not extensive, is yet fully up to the mark of what may be expected in a young country. In the biographical notices will be found references to the published productions of our ministers, and the indications are that fruit of learning in Science and Theology is now growing which will ripen in due season. Meanwhile encouragement should be given to every endeavor to use the Press for the defence and dissemination of the truth.

It is not the purpose of the Editors to publish an annual volume of the Hand-book. If our present effort meets with approval, a new edition may, in two or three years, be projected, and which experience may enable them to publish in a form more worthy of acceptance.

TABLE OF CONTENTS.

ERRATA.

Page 383--add 6. The Presbytery of British Columbia in connection with the Church of Scotland, 1 Minister and 4 Churches.

Agents of the Church Duties, p. 381.

THE CHURCH—ITS CONSTITUTION.

June 15th, 1875.

I. ITS UNION.

MINUTES 1875, p. 3.—At Montreal, and within the Victoria Hall there :—

Which day the General Assembly of the Canada Presbyterian Church, the Synod of the Presbyterian Church of Canada in connection with the Church of Scotland, the Synod of the Presbyterian Church of the Lower Provinces, and the Synod of the Presbyterian Church of the Maritime Provinces in connection with the Church of Scotland, met according to appointment for the purpose of consummating the union of their respective Churches.

The Rev. George M. Grant, M. A., Moderator of the Synod of the Presbyterian Church of the Maritime Provinces in connection with the Church of Scotland, gave out the hundredth psalm, which was sung. The Rev. Principal Snodgrass, D. D., Moderator of the Synod of the Presbyterian Church of Canada in connection with the Church of Scotland, read appropriate passages of Scripture, and the Rev. Principal Caven, D. D., Moderator of the General Assembly of the Canada Presbyterian Church, engaged in prayer.

The minute, adopted by each Synod, agreeing to the consummation of union and instructing its Moderator to sign the articles of union, was read by the Clerks of the respective Supreme Courts in succession This minute in the case of the Canada Presbyterian Church, dated the fifteenth day of June, is as follows :—

The General Assembly of the Canada Presbyterian Church, at its meeting in the month of November last year, having, after taking the necessary constitutional means for ascertaining the mind of the Church on the subject, resolved to unite with the Presbyterian Church of Canada in connection with the Church of Scotland, the Presbyterian Church of the Lower Provinces, and the Presbyterian Church of the Maritime Provinces in connection with the Church of Scotland, on the ground of the articles of union agreed upon by the Supreme Courts of the negotiating Churches; and having by the help of God completed all preliminary arrangements, does now—whilst recounting with fervent gratitude all the goodness and mercy vouchsafed to his Church in the past—humbly trusting that the Divine sanction will be given to the solemn and important step about to be taken—and earnestly praying that the Holy Spirit in all his quickening and sanctifying influences may descend largely on the united Church—RESOLVE, and hereby does record its resolution, to repair forthwith as a constituted Assembly to the VICTORIA HALL, the appointed place of meeting, for the purpose of consummating the Union with the aforesaid Churches, and of forming one General Assembly, to be designated and known as the General Assembly of the Presbyterian Church in Canada,—and does at the same time declare that the united Church shall be considered identical with the Canada Presbyterian Church, and shall possess the same authority, rights, privileges, and benefits to which this Church is now entitled.—And further, with the view of ratifying the act of Union, the General Assembly does empower its Moderator to sign in its name the Preamble and Basis of Union, and also the Resolutions adopted in connection therewith.

The Minute, adopted by the Synod of the Presbyterian Church of the Lower Provinces and the Synod of the Presbyterian Church of the Maritime Provinces in connection with the Church of Scotland, is of the same date, and couched in the same terms, the names of the Churches being simply transposed. That, adopted by the Synod of the Presbyterian Church of Canada in connection with the Church of Scotland, is dated Monday, the fourteenth day of June, and varies from the foregoing only in the following particulars, in addition to the transposition of names, viz:—Instead of the words "to repair forthwith as a constituted Assembly," insert "to repair on the adjournment of the Court to-morrow morning." Also, after the words "and benefits to which this Church is now entitled," add "excepting such as have been reserved by Acts of Parliament."

The Preamble, Basis and accompanying Resolutions, which form the Articles of Union, were read by the Rev. William Reid, M. A., one of the Joint Clerks of the General Assembly of the Canada Presbyterian Church. These are as follows:—

PREAMBLE.

Page 4.—The Presbyterian Church of Canada in connection with the Church of Scotland, the Canada Presbyterian Church, the Presbyterian Church of the Lower Provinces, and the Presbyterian Church of the Maritime Provinces in connection with the Church of Scotland, holding the same doctrine, government and discipline, believing that it would be for the glory of God and the advancement of the cause of Christ, that they should unite and thus form one Presbyterian Church in the Dominion, to be called the "Presbyterian Church in Canada," independent of all other Churches in its jurisdiction and under authority to Christ alone, the Head of His Church, and Head over all things to the Church, agree to unite on the following Basis, to be subscribed by the Moderators of the respective Churches in their name and in their behalf.

BASIS OF UNION.

1. The Scriptures of the Old and New Testament, being the Word of God, are the only infallible rule of faith and manners.

2. The Westminster Confession of Faith shall form the subordinate standard of this Church; the Larger and Shorter Catechisms shall be adopted by the Church, and appointed to be used for the instructions of the people; it being distinctly understood that nothing contained in the aforesaid Confession or Catechisms, regarding the power and duty of the Civil Magistrate, shall be held to sanction any principles or views inconsistent with full liberty of conscience in matters of religion.

3. The government and worship of this Church shall be in accordance with the recognized principles and practice of Presbyterian Churches, as laid down generally in the "Form of Presbyterian Church Government" and in "The Directory for the Public Worship of God."

ACCOMPANYING RESOLUTIONS.

1. RELATIONS TO OTHER CHURCHES.

Page 5. 1.—This Church cherishes Christian affection towards the whole Church of God, and desires to hold fraternal intercourse with it in its several branches, as opportuni y offers.

2. This Church shall, under such terms and regulations as may from time to time be agreed on, receive Ministers and Probationers from other Churches, and especially from Churches holding the same doctrine, government and discipline with itself.

2. MODES OF WORSHIP.

With regard to modes of Worship, the practice presently

followed by Congregations shall be allowed, and further action in connection therewith shall be left to the legislation of the united Church.

3. FUND FOR WIDOWS AND ORPHANS OF MINISTERS.

Steps shall be taken, at the first meeting of the General Assembly of the united Church, for the equitable establishment and administration of an efficient Fund for the benefit of the Widows and Orphans of Ministers.

4. COLLEGIATE INSTITUTIONS.

The aforesaid Churches shall enter into union with the Theological and Literary Institutions which they now have, and application shall be made to Parliament for such legislation as shall bring Queen's University and College, Knox College, the Presbyterian College, Montreal, Morrin College, and the Theological Hall at Halifax, into relations to the United Church similar to those which they now hold to their respective Churches, and to preserve their corporate existence, government and functions, on terms and conditions like to those under which they now exist; but the united Church shall not be required to elect Trustees for an Arts' Department in any of the Colleges above named.

5. LEGISLATION WITH REGARD TO RIGHTS OF PROPERTY.

Such legislation shall be sought as shall preserve undisturbed all rights of property now belonging to congregations and corporate bodies, and, at the same time, not interfere with freedom of action on the part of congregations in the same locality desirous of uniting, or on the part of corporate bodies which may find it to be expedient to discontinue, wholly or partially, their separate existence.

6. HOME AND FOREIGN MISSIONARY OPERATIONS.

Page 6.—The united Church shall heartily take up and prosecute the Home and Foreign Missionary and Benevolent operations of the several Churches, according to their respective claims; and with regard to the practical work of the Church and the promotion of its Schemes, whilst the General Assembly shall have the supervision and control of all the work of the Church, yet the united Church shall have due regard to such arrangements, through Synods and Local Committees, as shall tend most effectually to unite in Christian love and sympathy the different sections of the Church, and at the same time to draw forth the resources and energies of the people in behalf of the work of Christ in the Dominion and throughout the world.

7. GOVERNMENT GRANTS TO DENOMINATIONAL COLLEGES.

In the united Church the fullest forbearance shall be allowed as to any difference of opinion which may exist respecting the question of State grants to Educational Establishments of a Denominational character.

Subscription and Declaration.

These Articles of Union were then subscribed, in the name and by the appointment of the Supreme Courts of the several Churches entering into union, by their respective Moderators. Whereupon the Rev. P. G. McGregor, Moderator of the Synod of the Presbyterian Church of the Lower Provinces, solemnly, declared as follows:—

The Moderators of the Synod of the Presbyterian Church of Canada in connection with the Church of Scotland, of the General Assembly of the Canada Presbyterian Church, of the Synod of the Presbyterian Church of the Lower Provinces and of the Synod of the Presbyterian Church of the Maritime Provinces in connection with the Church of Scotland, having signed the terms of Union in name of their respective Churches, I declare that these Churches are now united and do form one Church, to be designated and known as the "Presbyterian Church in Canada."

The Moderators of the four Courts gave each other the right hand of fellowship, after which Psalm cxxxiii was sung.

The General Assembly of the united Church was then constituted with prayer by the Rev. P. G. McGregor.

The rolls of the Supreme Courts of the four Churches was read by the Clerks of the respective Courts, and these were declared to constitute the Roll of the first General Assembly of the Presbyterian Church in Canada.

1. Of those belonging to the Canada Presbyterian Church there answered 217 Ministers and 79 Elders.

2. Of those belonging to the Presbyterian Church of Canada in connection with the Church of Scotland, there answered 75 Ministers and 43 Elders.

3. Of those belonging to the Presbyterian Church of the Lower Provinces, there answered 121 Ministers and 28 Elders.

4. Of those belonging to the Presbyterian Church of the Maritime Provinces, there answered 13 Ministers and 7 Elders.

8. MODERATOR OF THE ASSEMBLY.

Page 9.—It was moved by Dr. Taylor, seconded by Dr. Bayne, and carried by acclamation, that the Rev. John Cook, D. D., Minister of St. Andrew's Church, Quebec, be Moderator of this Assembly for the current year. Dr. Cook was conducted to the chair, thanked the House for the honor thus conferred, and addressed the Assembly in suitable terms.

9. INTERIM CLERKS.

It was moved by Dr. Topp, seconded by Dr. Jenkins, and passed unanimously, that the Clerks of the several Supreme Courts, which have merged into and constitute this Court, be *interim* Clerks of this Assembly.

10. COMMITTEE ON BUSINESS.

Page 10.—The Moderator nominated a Committee to prepare the business for to-morrow, composed of the following members, viz: the Moderators of the hitherto existing Supreme Courts who have just retired from office, the Clerks, the Conveners of the late Committees on Union of the several Churches, Dr. Jenkins and Dr. McVicar; Dr. Topp, Convener.

It was agreed to hold the future sederunts of this Assembly in Erskine Church.

An invitation given to a social entertainment to be given this evening in this place by the Members of the Church in Montreal, for the purpose of celebrating the consummation of Union, was accepted.

It was unanimously resolved to hold a diet of prayer this afternoon at four o'clock in St. Paul's Church

The Assembly adjourned to meet in Erskine Church to-morrow morning at eleven o'clock, of which public intimation was made, and this sederunt was closed with praise and prayer.

11. CONCERNING STANDING ORDERS.

It was agreed to adopt the following Resolution: That until rules for regulating the business of the Courts of the

Church are adopted, these shall be governed by the well-understood principles and practice of Presbyterian Churches; it being understood that no rule or precedent of any one of the four Churches just united, inconsistent with the principles or practice of any of the other Churches, shall be of binding force, until it has been re-affirmed by the Assembly.

II.—COURTS OF THE CHURCH.

1. THE GENERAL ASSEMBLY.

Page 13—The Assembly appointed a Committee, Professor Gregg, *Convener*, to prepare and report a measure for the constitution of the General Assembly as a Representative Body.

Constitution of the General Assembly as finally approved, by Presbyteries and adopted 1876, p. 73, 1877 p. 22.

1. The General Assembly shall consist of one-fourth of the whole number of Ministers on the Rolls of the several Presbyteries with an equal number of acting Elders.

2. If the number on the Roll of any Presbytery be incapable of division by four, then the fourth shall be reckoned the fourth of the next higher number divisible by four.

3. Each Presbytery shall elect its representatives at an ordinary meeting held at least thirty days before the meeting of the General Assembly; and, in the event of any of these repreeentatives resigning their commissions, or being unable to attend the Assembly, it shall be lawful for the Presbytery to elect others in their place at any subsequent meeting previous to the meeting of the General Assembly.

4 Each Presbytery Clerk shall forward to the Clerks of the General Assembly, so as to be in their hands at least eight days before its meeting, commissions in favor of the Ministers and Elders elected as representatives; and from such commissions the Clerks shall prepare the Interim Roll, to be called at the opening of the Assembly; which, being amended, if necessary, shall be confirmed as the Roll of Assembly.

5 Any twenty-five of these Commissioners, of whom at least thirteen shall be Ministers, being met on the day and at the place appointed, shall be a quorum for the transaction of business.

2. THE BARRIER ACT.

MINUTES 1876, p. 72, 1877, p. 22.—1. No proposed law or rule relative to matters of doctrine, discipline, government, or worship, shall become a permanent enactment until the same has been submitted to Presbyteries for consideration. Such consideration shall be given by each Presbytery, at an ordinary meeting, or a special meeting held for the purpose; and an extract minute of the Presbytery's judgment shall be sent to the Clerks of the General Assembly, before the next meeting of that Court.

2. The Assembly, if it sees cause, may, by a majority of two-thirds of those present, pass such proposed law or rule into an Interim Act, which shall possess the force of law until the Presbyteries have, as herein required, reported their judgment upon it to the next General Assembly.

3. If a majority of the Presbyteries of the Church express their approval, the Assembly may pass such proposed law or rule into a standing law of the Church. If a majority of the Presbyteries express disapproval, the Assembly shall reject such proposed law or rule, or again remit it to the Presbyteries.

3. OFFICERS OF THE ASSEMBLY.

1. *Moderators, their Election and Status.*

MONTREAL, 1876, p. 41 —*Resolved,* That the Moderator of Assembly be elected by open nomination and vote of the Assembly, with the understanding that Presbyteries shall have the right to nominate.

Page 79.—The Assembly resolved that the Moderator for the year shall, during his term of office, be *ex officio* a member of all Boards or Committees with the exception of those Boards, the number of whose members is prescribed by the Acts of Parliament incorporating them.

2. *List of Moderators.*

Montreal 1875.—Rev. John Cook, D.D., St. Andrew's Church, Quebec.

Toronto, 1876.—Rev. Alexander Topp, D.D., Knox Church, Toronto.

Halifax, 1877.—Rev. Hugh McLeod, D.D., Sidney, C. B.

Hamilton, 1878.—Rev. John Jenkins, D.D., St. Paul's Church, Montreal.

Ottawa, 1879.—Rev. William Reid, D.D., Clerk of Assembly, Toronto.

Montreal, 1880.—Rev. Donald Macrae, D.D., St. Stephen's Church, St. John, N. B.

Kingston, 1881.—Rev. D. H. McVicar, L.L.D., Principal, Montreal College.

St. John, 1882.—Rev. William Cochrane, D.D., Zion Church, Brantford.

3. *Clerks of General Assembly.*

1876, p. 45.—1. That the Rev. Wm. Reid, M.A., and the Rev. Professor J. H. McKerras, M.A., be Joint Clerks of the General Assembly, and that the salary of each be two hundred and fifty dollars per annum, exclusive of incidental expenses.

2. That, in consideration of the long and faithful services of the Rev. W. Fraser, he be appointed one of the Clerks of the General Assembly, with his former salary of one hundred and fifty dollars per annum.

II.—RECONSTRUCTION OF SYNODS AND PRESBYTERIES.

1875, page 11, I.—*Synod of the Maritime Provinces.*—That it would not be advisable to divide the Lower Provinces into two Synodical districts, and that in the meantime these should be constituted into one Synod, to be called the Synod of the Maritime Provinces, that this Synod be divided into the following Presbyteries:—

1. SYDNEY– To be the same as the present Presbytery of Cape Breton.

2. VICTORIA AND RICHMOND—To be bounded on the present Presbytery of that name.

3. PICTOU—To include the congregations in the Counties of Antigonish, Guysboro' and Pictou, except those of River John and West Branch River John.

4. WALLACE—To include the congregations in River John, West Branch River John, Earltown, Tatamagouche, New Annan, Wallace, Pugwash, Goose River, Amherst and Springhill.

5. TRURO—To be bounded as the Presbytery of that name in connection with the Presbyterian Church of the Lower Provinces.

6. HALIFAX—To be bounded as the present Presbytery of Halifax in the Presbyterian Church of the Lower Provinces, except Newfoundland.

7. LUNENBURG AND YARMOUTH—To be bounded as the present Presbytery of that name.

8 ST. JOHN—To include the same territory as the Presbytery of that name in connection with the Presbyterian Church of the Lower Provinces.

9. MIRIMACHI—To include the present Presbyteries of that name and Restigouche.

10. PRINCE EDWARD ISLAND—To include the Province of that name.

11. NEWFOUNDLAND—To include the Island of Newfoundland.

II.—*Synod of Montreal and Ottawa*—To comprise all the Province of Quebec, with the exception of the territory occupied by the congregation of New Carlisle of the Canada Presbyterian Church which is transferred to the Synod of the Maritime Provinces and united with the Presbytery of Miramichi, the Presbyteries of Ottawa and Brockville of the Canada Presbyterian Church, and the Presbyteries of Glengarry, Ottawa, Perth, and of the Presbyterian Church of Canada in connection with the Church of Scotland.

Page 12. III.—*Synod of Toronto and Kingston*—To be coterminous with the present Synods of Toronto of the Canada Presbyterian Church, and to include also the boundaries of the present Presbyteries of Guelph and Durham of the aforesaid Church and the Presbytery of Kingston.

IV.—*Synod of Hamilton and London*—To be coterminous with the present Synods of Hamilton and London of the Canada Presbyterian Church, with the exception of the territory embraced by the Presbyteries of Guelph and Durham of the aforesaid Church.

V.—*Synod of Manitoba, consisting of the Presbytery of Manitoba.*—To embrace the Province of Manitoba, all the Territories of the North-West and the Province of British Columbia. The Synod of Manitoba to meet in the Presbyterian Church, Wini peg, on the second Wednesday of July, at ten o'clock in the forenoon, to define the boundaries of Presbyteries and attend to all other competent business. Mr. Black to be Moderator.

Instructions to Synods concerning Presbyteries and Records.

That it be remitted to Synods to prescribe the boundaries of Presbyteries in the Western portion of the Church, subject to the following general instructions:—

1. That, being duly convened, the first item of business shall be the definition of the boundaries of Presbyteries.

2. That each Presbytery, with the Ministers and Churches within its limits, be defined as to boundaries by geographical lines, or with respect to the most convenient lines of travel.

3. That the formation of small Presbyteries be discouraged.

4. That when two or more congregations, on different sides of a Synodical or Presbyterial line, are under one Pastoral charge, they shall for the time belong to that Presbytery with which the Minister is connected, but only so long as such congregational relation continues.

5. That the Synods and Presbyteries heretofore existing, which shall lose their present organization by consolidation under these arrangements, shall be considered and designated as continuing their succession in that Synod now defined, or Presbytery to be constituted, which includes the largest portion, counting both Ministers and Churches, of said Body, as existing at the date of Union, to attend as may be found necessary to its business and interests.

6. That the Clerks of all Ecclesiastical Judicatories, except Kirk Sessions, procure new Minute Books, in which to record their proceedings from and after the date at which the Union takes effect in such Judicatories; that all newly-arranged Presbyteries be instructed to place the Records of their predecessors in safe keeping until the General Assembly acquire a secure and fire-proof building or apartment in which to deposit them; and that the Assembly take immediate steps to obtain such a building or apartment in connection with the Agency of the Church.

The Synods, thus constituted, were instructed to meet for

organization this afternoon at three o'clock in the following places, viz.:—The Synod of the Maritime Provinces in Stanley Street Church; the Synod of Montreal and Ottawa in Erskine Church; the Synod of Toronto in St. Paul's Church; and the Synod of Hamilton and London in Knox Church. In each case the oldest ordained Minister present shall preside as Moderator.

III.—REPORTS OF SYNODS.

1. *Synod of Montreal and Ottawa.*

MINUTES 1875, *Appendix* p. 2.—The Clerk of the Synod gave in the report of this Synod. It was moved and seconded and passed, that the arrangement of Presbyteries within the bounds of this Synod, proposed by that Body, be confirmed by the General Assembly.

Boundaries of its Presbyteries.

App. P. 2.—This Synod shall be divided into five Presbyteries, viz:—Quebec, Montreal, Glengarry, Brockville, Ottawa.

1. The Presbytery of Quebec shall comprise the following congregations:—St. Andrew's, Quebec; Chalmers' Church, Quebec; Valcartier; Three Rivers; Point Levi; St. Sylvester; Leeds; Inverness; Danville; Richmond; Melbourne; Sherbrooke; Lingwick; Winslow; Hampden; Lake Megantic; Kennebec Road; Rivière du Loup, and Métis.

2. The Presbytery of Montreal shall comprise the following congregations, viz:—St. Andrew's; St. Paul's; Knox Church; Erskine Church; Stanley Street Church; St. Joseph Street Church; St. Matthew's, Nazareth Street; St. Mark's; Crescent Street Church; St. Gabriel Street Church; Chalmers' Church, St. John's, in the City of Montreal; Côte des Neiges; Lachine; Beauharnois; Chatham; Grenville; Dundee; Elgin P.Q.; Athelstane; Huntingdon; Ormstown; Georgetown; Beachridge; Russeltown; Hemmingford; Laprairie; St. Louis de Gonzigue; Valleyfield; Laguerre; Rockburn; Gore; English River, Howack; Chateauguay Basin; St. Andrew's; Henry's Church, Lachute; First Church, Lachute; Mille Isles, Harrington; Ste. Thérèse; Grande Fresnière; St. Eustache; New Glasgow; Farnham Centre, and Covey Hill.

3. The Presbytery of Glengarry shall comprise the following

congregations, viz:—Lancaster; Williamstown; Martintown; Indian Lands; Kenyon; Lochiel; Vankleekhill; Alexandria; Dalhousie Mills; Cote St. George; Cornwall; Roxbrough; Finch; Osnabruck; East Hawkesbury.

4. The Presbytery of Brockville shall comprise the following congregations:—Waddington; Brockville; Prescott; Spencerville; Edwardsburg; Bell's Corners; Morrisburgh; Williamsburg; Dunbar; Matilda; West Winchester; Morwood; South Gower; Mountain; Kemptville; Oxford Mills; Merrickville; Burritt's Rapids; North Augusta; Fairfield; Yonge; Lyn; Newboro'; Westport; Bishop's Mills; Oxford; Smith's Falls; Perth; Lanark: Middleville.

5. The Presbytery of Ottawa shall comprise the following congregations, viz:—Adamston; Douglas; Grattan; Pembroke; Almonte; McNab; Wakefield; Fitzroy; Torbolton; Beckwith; Russell; Gloucester; Pakenham; Aylwin; Alice; Pettawawa; Ramsay; Metcalfe; Osgoode; Nepean; Bell's Corners; Carleton Place; Litchfield; Arnprior; Coulonge; Westmeath; L'Orignal; Hawkesbury; Buckingham; Cumberland; Chelsea; Huntley; Ross; Bristol; Richmond; Plantagenet; St. Andrew's Church, Ottawa; Knox Church, Ottawa; Bank Street Church, Ottawa; Daly Street Church, Ottawa; New Edinburgh; Rochesterville; Hull; and Aylmer.

2. *Synod of Toronto and Kingston.*

App. p. 3. 4.—The report of the proceedings of this Synod was given in by the Clerk of that Court. It was moved, seconded and passed unanimously, that the report, defining the boundaries of Presbyteries within the Synod of Toronto and Kingston, together with the Overture unanimously adopted by the Synod respecting the name of the Synod, to wit, that it be designated the "Synod of Toronto and Kingston," be and hereby is adopted with the exception of the recommendation respecting the congregations of Walkerton and Brant.

Boundaries of its Presbyteries.

1. The Presbytery of Kingston shall include the territories formerly occupied by the late Presbyteries respectively, of the same name, of the Canada Presbyterian Church, and the Presbyterian Church of Canada, in connection with the Church of Scotland.

2. The Presbytery of Peterborough shall have the same bounds as those of the Presbytery of the Canada Presbyterian Church, formerly designated the Presbytery of Coburg.

3. The Presbytery of Whitby shall extend from Pickering in the west to Clark in the east inclusive, and northwards, as far as Claremont, Utica, Port Perry and Williamsburg.

4. The Presbytery of Lindsay shall include that portion of the County of Ontario not comprised within the limits of the Presbytery of Whitby, as well as that part of the County of Victoria not comprehended within the bounds of the Presbytery of Peterborough.

5. The Presbytery of Toronto shall have the same boundaries as those of the late Presbytery of Toronto, of the Canada Presbyterian Church, but excluding the Northern half of the Township of Melancthon.

6. The Presbytery of Barrie shall comprise the boundaries of the late Presbytery of Simcoe, of the Canada Presbyterian Church, including, also, the Township of Mulmur and the south line of Osprey.

7. The Presbytery of Owen Sound.—The bounds thereof be the same as those of the late Presbytery of Owen Sound, in the Canada Presbyterian Church, with the exception of the western, which shall be coterminous with the county-line between Grey and Bruce, as far north as the gravel road leading westward to Southampton, and then along said gravel road to Lake Huron, and further, that the congregation of Tara, which is situated south of the gravel road, be included in this Presbytery.

8. The Presbytery of Guelph shall have the same bounds as those assigned to the Presbytery of Guelph by the Synod of the late Canada Presbyterian Church, in the year one thousand eight hundred and sixty-one, with the exception of Harriston, Rothsay, Palmerston, South Luther and Little Toronto, Arthur, Cotswold, and the Townships of Amaranth and Luther.

9. The Presbytery of Saugeen shall comprise the same bounds as those of the late Presbytery of Durham of the Canada Presbyterian Church, with the addition of the congregations of Harriston, Palmerston, Rothsay, Arthur, Teviotdale, South Luther, and Little Toronto.

3. *Synod of Hamilton and London.*

App. pp. 5-6.—The Clerk read the report of this Synod. It was moved, duly seconded and passed, that the report be received, and that the arrangement of Presbyteries, together with the recommendations therein, be confirmed.

Boundaries of its Presbyteries.

1. Hamilton Presbytery.—That this Presbytery be coterminous with the boundaries of the Hamilton Presbytery of the Canada Presbyterian Church.

2. Paris Presbytery.—That this Presbytery be coterminous with the boundaries of the Paris Presbytery of the Canada Presbyterian Church.

3. London Presbytery.—That thebounds of this Presbytery be as formerly under the Canada Presbyterian Church.

4. Chatham Presbytery.—That the boundaries of this Presbytery be coterminous with those of this Chatham Presbytery of the Canada Presbyterian Church.

5. Stratford Presbytery.—That the boundaries of the Presbytery be coterminous with those of this Stratford Presbytery of the Canada Presbyterian Church.

6. Huron Presbytery.—That the boundaries of this Presbytery be coterminous with those of the Huron Presbytery, as under the Canada Presbyterian Church.

7. Bruce Presbytery.—That the boundaries of this Presbytery be coterminous with those of the Bruce Presbytery, as under the Canada Presbyterian Church; but that the two congregations of Walkerton, and the Congregation of Brant belong to the Presbytery of Bruce.

4. *Synod of the Maritime Provinces.*

Minutes, p. 17—The Clerk of this Synod reported that, as instructed, they had met yesterday and ratified the arrangement of Presbyteries referred to in yesterday's minutes. The Assembly confirmed the action of the Synod.

IV.—CHANGES IN PRESBYTERIES.

Toronto, 1876, p. 73.—The Assembly resolved—

1. To separate Calvin Church, Rothsay, from Palmerston,

and connect it with Moorefield—the united charge to be within the bounds and under the jurisdiction of the Presbytery of Guelph.

2. To transfer the congregation of Colquhoun's Settlement from the Presbytery of Glengarry to that of Brockville.

3. To transfer the congregation of Free St. John's, Walkerton, and that of North and West Brant from the Presbytery of Bruce to that of Saugeen.

4. To allow the congregation of Tara to remain within the bounds of the Presbytery of Bruce.

5. To defer until next meeting of Assembly the defining of the boundaries of the Presbyteries of Toronto and Barrie, and instruct these Presbyteries to confer, with a view to supply in the meantime the debateable district with religious ordinances.

6. To allow to lie on the table until the next meeting of Assembly the following recommendations of the Committee, viz. :—

(*a*) The transference of the Congregation of Fenelon Falls and Somerville, as well as that of Haliburton, from the Presbytery of Peterborough to that of Lindsay.

(*b*) The erection of a new Presbytery, to be designated the "Presbytery of Lanark and Renfrew," and to include all the congregations and mission-stations within the Counties of Lanark, Renfrew and Pontiac, the congregation of Kitley in the County of Leeds, and the Palmerston mission-stations in the County of Frontenac.

Page 83.—The Presbytery of Chatham craved and obtained leave to transfer the congregation of St. Anne, Illinois, to the Chicago Presbytery of the Presbyterian Church in the United States, provided the congregation desire it and the Presbytery deem it advisable.

Page 82.—The Presbytery of Saugeen craved and obtained assessors to assist the Presbytery in a case of difficulty.

HALIFAX, 1877, p. 26.—The congregation of Fenelon Falls and Somerville were transferred from the Presbytery of Peterborough to that of Lindsay.

Page 29.—The erection of the new Presbytery of Lanark and Renfrew was remitted to Montreal and Otatwa, with the Synod of power to take action thereon.

HAMILTON, 1878, p. 26.—The Clerk produced and read an Extract Minute of the Presbytery of Ottawa memorializing the Assembly to detach the congregations within the bounds of the County of Pontiac, and annex them to the Presbytery of Lanark and Renfrew, which the Synod of Montreal and Ottawa had agreed to constitute and establish, as it was empowered to do by last Assembly. It was unanimously agreed to grant the prayer of the memorial.

HAMILTON, 1878, p. 25.—There was read an Extract Minute of the Synod of Hamilton and London, transmitting the petition of certain members of the Presbyteries of Huron and Bruce, requesting the formation of a new Presbytery.

It was moved and seconded and carried, That the petition lie on the table until next meeting of Assembly, and that the Presbyteries interested, viz.: those of Huron, Bruce, Stratford and Saugeen, be instructed to transmit to next Assembly their judgment as to the proposed new Presbytery.

Page 24.—The Clerk produced and read an Extract Minute of the Synod of Toronto and Kingston, transmitting Extract Minutes of the Presbyteries of Owen Sound and Barrie, craving the transference of Parry Sound Mission and Collingwood Mountain Station from the former to the latter Presbytery. The transference was unanimously agreed to.

OTTAWA, 1879, p. 23.—The Committee appointed to consider changes in the bounds ot Presbyteries recommended and the Assembly agreed.——

1. To transfer Knox Church, Embro, from the Presbytery of London to that of Paris.

2. To transfer the congregation of West Brant from the Presbytery of Saugeen to that of Bruce, with a view to union with the congregation of Pinkerton, that these may form one pastoral charge under the supervision of the Presbytery of Bruce.

3. To transfer from the Presbytery of Saugeen to that of Bruce, the following charges, viz.:—North Brant and West Bentinck; St. John's, Walkerton; Balaklava; and Hanover and North Normanby.

PRESBYTERY OF MAITLAND.

That the petition for the erection of the said Presbytery be granted, and that it be composed of the following charges, viz.:—Ashfield, Dungannon and Port Albert, St. Helen's and Whitechurch, Wingham, Belgrave, Bluevale and Eadie's, Melville Church, Brussels, Knox Church, Brussels, Cranbrook and Ethel, Walton, East Ashfield Mission Station, Wroxeter and Fordwich, St. Andrew's Church, Lucknow, South Kinloss and Lucknow, Langside, Knox Church, Ripley, Huron, Pine River, Knox Church, Kincardine, St. Andrew's Church, Kincardine, and Chalmer's Church, Kincardine Township.

It was further agreed that the Presbytery thus formed be within the bounds and subject to the jurisdiction of the Synod of Hamilton and London.

Page 24.—5. With reference to the Palmerston group of Stations, it was moved seconded and carried, that said group be transferred to the Presbytery of Kingston in accordance with the terms of the Memorial.

6. The Assembly further agreed to transmit to the Synod of Hamilton and London for consideration the recommendation of the Committee to the effect that a portion of the Mission field of the Presbytery of Bruce be assigned to the new Presbytery of Maitland.

Montreal, 1880, p. 29.—The Committee on boundaries of Presbyteries handed in a report, and the Assembly resolved in terms of its recommendations.

1. To transfer the Mission Stations of Moreton and Seeley's Bay from the Presbytery of Kingston to that of Brockville.

2. To re-transfer the Mission Station of Blairton from the Presbytery of Kingston to that of Peterborough.

3 To sanction the transference of Honeywood from the Prestery of Barrie to that of Toronto, with a view to its union with Horning's Mills in the latter Presbytery.

4. To implement the recommendation of the Synod of Toronto and Kingston, by transferring Burns' Church, Rocky Saugeen, from the Presbytery of Saugeen to that of Owen Sound, for the purpose of uniting it with the congregation of Latona, and forming them into a pastoral charge, under the jurisdiction of the Presbytery of Owen Sound.

5. To annex the township of Amaranth to the Presbytery of Saugeen, except the portion of said township in the north-east corner belonging to the congregation of Shelburn, and such part of the south-east corner of the township as belongs to the congregation of Orangeville; and that both of these charges continue, as heretofore, under the jurisdiction of the Presbytery of Toronto.

6. To defer for a year the resolution of the Presbytery of London, praying that said Presbytery be divided, and a new Presbytery be formed within its present bounds.

7. To assign all matters affecting the boundaries of Presbyteries already existing, and the transference of congregations from one Presbytery to another, within the bounds of the several Synods, to the said Synods, respectively, as part of their work.

PRESBYTERY OF SARNIA.

TORONTO, 1881, p. 26.—The Committee appointed on Applications for the Division of Presbyteries, submitted and read a report on the petitions for the division of the Presbytery of London, stating in substance that the Committee had considered the petition for division from the said Presbytery, and also a petition from the Session of Strathroy, and had heard parties and after due deliberation, recommended that a new Presbytery be formed, in accordance with the petition to that effect, to be called "THE PRESBYTERY OF SARNIA," to consist of the following congregations:—1. St. Andrew's Church, Sarnia; 2. Knox Church, Camlachie; 3. Forest and McKay's; 4. Knox Church, Thedford, and Lake Road; 5. Parkhill and McGillivray; 6. Nairn and Beechwood; 7. West Williams and N.E. Adelaide; 8. Point Edward; 9. Burns' Church and Moore Line; 10. Brigden and Bear Creek; 11. Alvinston and Napier; 12. Petrolia; 13. Mandaumin; 14. Wyoming and South Plympton; 15. Watford and Main Road; 16. Adelaide and Arkona. *Mission Stations*—Corunna and Mooretown; Oil Springs. The Assembly received the report, and decerned and ordered in terms of its recommendation.

ST. JOHN, N. B., 1882, p. 25.—The Committee on Bills recommended, and the recommendation was adopted, that the application of the Presbytery of Sarnia, respecting the transference of the congregation of Strathroy to its bounds, be referred to the

Synod of Hamilton and London; and that the applications of the Presbyteries of Sarnia and Chatham be granted, that the station of Sombra be transferred to the Presbytery of Sarnia.

PRESBYTERY OF FREDERICTON.

1881, p. 34.—The Committee on Applications for the Division of Presbyteries, handed in a report setting forth that they had had before them and considered an overture from the Presbytery of St. John, asking for the erection of a new Presbytery, to be formed out of the said Presbytery, to be called the Presbytery of Fredericton, together with a dissent and complaint against the action of Presbytery in transmitting the overture, and recommending the Assembly to refer the case to the Synod of the Maritime Provinces, with power to grant the prayer of the overture should it seem wise to that Court to do so.—Carried unanimously: That the report be received and its recommendations adopted

REGULATIONS ANENT THE RECORDS OF CHURCH COURTS.

1. The pages shall be numbered in words at length as well as in figures.

2. Every page shall be signed by the Clerk, and the Record of each sederunt by the Moderator and Clerk. In case of the death or removal of the Moderator or Clerk, the Record shall afterwards be signed by the then acting Moderator or Clerk, *cum nota* of the cause, in presence of the Court.

3. The time and place of meeting shall be minutely stated in words.

4. Every page shall have a suitable margin, on which the items of recorded business, etc., shall be indexed.

5. The place and date of each meeting shall be shortly indicated on the margin at the top of the page.

6. Church Courts shall take special care that their records are carefully and correctly written. All erasures or other changes in the Record shall be noted on the margin, with the initials of the Clerk's name.

7. All sums of money shall be given in words as well as in figures.

8. No unnecessary vacant spaces shall be left between the minutes of sederunt.

ARCHIVES OF THE CHURCH.

OTTAWA, 1879, p. 58.—Overture regarding the preservation of all records and *retenta* from the origin of Presbyterianism in Canada to the present time. It was proposed, seconded and carried, The General Assembly having heard and considered the Overture on the preservation of the records and *retenta* of the Superior Courts of the several Churches now united under the name of the Presbyterian Church in Canada, and the collection of other books and papers that may be of value in connection with the history of the said Churches, recognizing the importance of the subject brought before it in the overture, and believing there should be no delay in carrying out the subject it has in view—resolve, as they hereby do, to appoint a Committee, Mr. John Gray (Orilla), Convener, with instructions, 1st, to inquire as to the present custody of the said records and *retenta*; to take possession of the same in the name of the Church; and, in the meantime, to deposit those that belonged to the Presbyterian Church of Canada in connection with the Church of Scotland, in Queen's College, Kingston; those that belonged to the Canada Presbyterian Church (including the records and *retenta* of the Superior Courts of the Presbyterian Church of Canada and the United Presbyterian Church in Canada), in Knox College, Toronto, or the Presbyterian College, Montreal, as the Committee may direct; and those that belonged to the Presbyterian Churches of the Provinces of New Brunswick and Nova Scotia, in the Presbyterian College, Halifax; 2nd, to collect, as they may be able, such other books and documents as may be of historical value in connection with any of the Presbyterian Churches of the Dominion; and 3rd, to report their diligence in the premises to the next General Assembly.

MONTREAL, 1880, *App.* p. 229—The Committee have to report that, in obedience to the instructions of the last General Assembly, they have taken steps to collect such documents and works as may seem calculated to throw light on the early history of the Presbyterian Church throughout the Dominion. For this purpose a circular was issued, with directions in regard to the persons to whom documents, etc., should be sent; and in response thereto several books and other papers have been deposited. The places selected as depositories are Halifax, Presbyterian College, Montreal Presbyterian College, Queen's College, and Knox College; and the persons to whom all papers and documents are requested to be sent are Dr. MacGregor, Professor Campbell, Principal Grant, Dr. Gregg, Mr. H. S. McCollum, St. Catharines, and the Convener of this Committee.

It is of very great importance that anyone possessing documents bearing on the history of Presbyterianism in this land should secure their safety by transmitting them to any of the persons named above.

III. ORDINATION, INDUCTION AND LICENSE.

1. QUESTIONS AT ORDINATION OR INDUCTION OF MINISTERS.

MINUTE 1876, p. 70.—1. Do you believe the Scriptures of the Old and New Testaments to be the word of God, and the only infallible rule of faith and manners?

2. Do you believe the Westminister Confession of Faith, as adopted by this Church in the Basis of Union, to be founded on and agreeable to the Word of God, and in your teaching will you faithfully adhere thereto?

3. Do you believe the Government of this Church by Sessions, Presbyteries, Synods and General Assemblies, to be founded on and agreeable to the Word of God, and do you engage as a Minister of this Church to maintain and defend the same?

4. Do you own the purity of worship at present authorized by this Church, and will you conform thereto?

5. Do you promise to give a dutiful attendance in the Courts of this Church, to submit yourself in the spirit of meekness to the admonitions of this Presbytery to be subject to it and the superior judicatories, to follow no divisive course, but maintain according to your power the unity and peace of the Church?

6. Are zeal for the glory of God, love to the Lord Jesus Christ, and desire of saving souls, so far as you know your own heart, your great motives and chief inducements to enter the office of this ministry?

7. Have you directly or indirectly used any undue means to procure this call?

8. Do you engage, in the strength and grace of our Lord Jesus Christ, to live a holy and circumspect life, to rule well your own house, and faithfully and diligently to discharge all the duties of the ministry to the edification of the body of Christ?

2. QUESTIONS TO CANDIDATES FOR LICENSE.

Numbers 1, 2, 3, 4, as above

5. Do you engage, in the strength and grace of our Lord Jesus Christ, to live a holy and circumspect life, and faithfully to preach the gospel, as you may have opportunity?

6. Do you promise to submit yourself in the Lord to the several judicatories of this Church?

3. QUESTIONS AT ORDINATION OF ELDERS.

Numbers 1, 2, 3, 4, (omitting "in your teaching" in No. 2, and substituting in No. 3, "Ruling Elder" for "Minister.")

5. In accepting the office of Elder do you engage, in the strength and grace of the Lord Jesus Christ, faithfully and diligently to perform the duties thereof; watching over the flock of which you are called to be an overseer, and in all things showing yourself to be a pattern of good works?

4. QUESTIONS AT ORDINATION OF DEACONS.

Numbers 1, 2, 3, 4, (*Mutatis mutandis*).

5. In accepting the office of Deacon do you engage, in the strength and grace of our Lord Jesus Christ, faithfully and diligently to perform the duties thereof?

5. FORMULA TO BE SIGNED BY ALL OFFICE-BEARERS.

"I hereby declare that I believe the Westminister Confession of Faith, as adopted by this Church in the Basis of Union, and the government of the Church by Sessions, Presbyteries, Synods and General Assemblies, to be founded on and agreeable to the Word of God; that I own the purity of worship at present authorized by this Church; and that I engage to adhere faithfully to the doctrine of the said Confession, to maintain and defend the said government, to conform to the said worship, and to submit to the discipline of this Church, and to follow no divisive course from the present order established therein."

IV.—ADMISSION OF MINISTERS FROM OTHER CHURCHES

1. ACT FOR THE RECEPTION OF MINISTERS.

MONTREAL, 1880, p. 52. The draft Act for the reception of ministers, having been approved by a majority of Presbyteries, in terms of the Barrier Act, was enacted as a standing law of the Church, in terms following:—

1. Any minister who is a settled pastor in a Church which holds the same doctrines, government and discipline as this Church, and who is regularly called by a congregation of the Church, may be received by a Presbytery on presenting a Presbyterial certificate; but the Presbytery if it sees cause may refer the case to the Assembly.

2. Ministers and licentiates expressly designated or commissioned by the Churches in Great Britian and Ireland, may, on producing their commissions, be admitted by Presbyteries as ministers or probationers of this Church.

3. In all cases, in which an applicant for admission does not come in the manner provided above, but with a Presbyterial certificate only, he cannot be received into full standing as a minister or probationer of this Church without permission of the General Assembly.

4. The Presbytery shall, at an ordinary meeting, hold private conference with the applicant, for the purpose of ascertaining his doctrinal views, literary attainments and other particulars. If satisfied, the Presbytery shall record its judgment, and transmit the application, with extracts of its proceedings thereon, and relative documents, to the next General Assembly; and the Clerk of the Presbytery shall forthwith issue circular letters to the other Presbyteries of the Church.

5. The Presbytery, if unanimous in transmitting the application, may in the meantime avail itself of the applicant's services.

6. If the Assembly grants permission to receive the applicant, the Presbytery shall on his satisfactorily answering the questions to be put to ministers or probationers, and on his signing the formula, receive him as a minister or a probationer of this Church.

7. When the Church to which the applicant belonged is not a Presbyterian Church, the applicant must apply to the Presbytery within whose bounds he resides, and produce documentary evidence of his good standing as a minister in the Church to which he belonged. The Presbytery, if satisfied with such evidence, shall proceed to confer with him, and answers must be obtained to the following questions, viz:—

(1.) What course of study has he passed in Arts and Theology?

(2.) When, where and by whom was he ordained to the ministry?

(3.) Has he ever been connected with any other Church than that from which he brings documents, and if so, in what capacity?

(4.) What are his reasons for applying for admission to this Church, and what has led to his change of views?

(5). How long has he resided within the bounds of the Presbytery?

8. The Presbytery, if satisfied with the answers to these questions, shall further inquire as to the degree of success which has attended the previous ministry of the applicant. If satisfied as to the probability of his usefulness in the Church, and as to his Christian character and good report, the Presbytery shall record its judgment on the whole case and apply for leave to admit him. The answers given and the information obtained must be embodied in a report, transmitted to the General Assembly, along with extracts of the Presbytery's proceedings and other documents.

9. The applications, sent forward by the various Presbyteries of the Church, shall be considered and disposed of as the General Assembly may from time to time determine.

10. If the Assembly grants permission to receive the applicant, the Presbytery shall proceed as hereinbefore mentioned in section *sixth*.

11. All applicants for admission to the Church, other than those referred to in section *first* and *third*, must appear personally before the General Assembly.

2. MINISTERS RECEIVED.

TORONTO, 1876, p. 81. Messrs. J. Russell Kean, William Stephenson, D. M. McGregor, Daniel W. Cameron, Thomes D. Johnston, John Dobbin West, James Ballantine, John Nicholls, William Hawthorne, David Mann, Charles Brouillette, and W F. Clarke, as Ministers.—Messrs. William C. Armstrong and William Frizzell as Licentiates of this Church.—Mr. Joseph A. Andrew to the status of a Student of Divinity of the First year.—Remit M. Ouriere to the care of the Presbytery of Montreal for the purpose of employing him in such work in connection with French Evangelization as he may be fitted for, and of prescribing such course of study as may specially qualify him for such work.

HALIFAX, 1877, p. 44. Messrs. Abraham Beamer, James Campbell, J. L. Robertson, and R. D. Duclos as Ministers.—Remit to the Synod of the Maritime Provinces the application of Mr. James Fitzpatrick a Licentiate of the Presbyterian Church in the United States of America, to be received as a Probationer. —Remit Mr. Camerle to the care of the Presbytery of Montreal for a year, with a view to the direction of his studies; but require that Presbytery to make a fresh application to the Assembly before they admit him to the status of a Minister.—Receive Mr. B. Ouriere, as a Minister of this Church; but, considering that there is a diversity of opinion on the question of Roman Catholic ordination, agreed that this act is not to be regarded as a precedent decisive of the question.

HAMILTON, 1878, p. 52.—Messrs. George Coull, M.D., Joseph H. Paradis, E. Roberts, B. J. Brown, Robert Scrimgeour, and O. Camerle, (ex-priest) as Ministers.

Malcolm Cameron, Alexander W. McLeod, Samuel T. Warrender as Licentiates.

Mr. Laing dissented from the reception of Mr. Camerle as an ordained minister.

OTTAWA, 1879, p. 34.—Messrs. D. R. Crockett and J. A. R. Dickson, as Ministers.

Permit Mr. Hoskin to resume his position as a Minister.

In regard to the reception of M. Antonio Internoscia (formerly a priest of the R. C. Church) it was moved and carried, That M. Internoscia, ex-priest, be admitted as a minister. Mr. Laing, and others craved leave to enter a dissent.

MONTREAL, 1880, p. 26.—Remit the application on behalf of Mr. James Christie to the Presbytery of Truro, with instructions to restore him to the ministry should all the circumstances in his case seem to them to justify such action.

Receive Mr. F. W. Archibald as a Licentiate.

Recognize the full status of Mr. William Doak as a minister.

Defer the case of Mr. Christopher Smith, in its present state and in the absence of all the necessary information.

Receive Mr. Dugald McGregor as a minister of this Church.

KINGSTON, 1881, p. 42. The Assembly granted leave to the Presbyteries applying to receive as Ministers of the Church, Mr. James McElory, from the Presbyterian Church, in Ireland; Mr. W. D. Rees, from the Baptist Church; Mr. G. H. Edmunds, from the Methodist Episcopal Church; Mr. G. A. Smith, from the Cumberland Presbyterian Church; Mr. James Howie, from the Congregational Church; Mr. John Ferris, from the Church, of Scotland; Mr. Andrew Love, if his papers are satisfactory, and Mr. John A. Cairns as a Licentiate.

SPECIAL CASES.

1881, p. 43.—J. A. Andrew, formerly a Minister of the Methodist Church, having attended the required classes in Queen's College, receive him as a Minister.

Mr Peter Fleming, place under the care of the Presbytery, with instructions to prosecute his studies in Greek and Hebrew, with a view to his being received as a Minister at the next Assembly.

Mr. Henry Norris, a minister of the Methodist Episcopal Church, advised to attend one of the Theological Colleges two years, with a view to his reception as a Minister the Examining Board to decide what classes he shall attend.

Mr. Anthony Couboue, an ex-priest of the Church of Rome, who, it was stated, had attended one session at the Montreal College, was received as a missionary to labour under the Board of French Evangelization.

Mr. Alexander McKenzie.—The Assembly, after hearing relative papers read, granted leave to the Presbytery of Toronto to receive him as a Minister.

Mr. Archibald Lees, formerly a Minister of this Church, but now under sentence of deposition, the Assembly resolved, that should he see proper to apply to the General Assembly of the Free Church of Scotland for the removal of the sentence of deposition, the General Assembly of this Church will place no barrier in the way. And further, instructs the Presbytery of Kingston to furnish Mr. Lees with any documents that may be necessary in his case.

Page 43—The Assembly ordered that, henceforth, Presbyteries on making application to the Assembly for leave to receive Ministers, forward at the same time full extracts from their Minutes of all proceedings in regard to such application.

St. John, N. B., 1882, p. 12.—Application from the Presbytery of London, on behalf of Dr. Charles Elliott, formerly Professor of Divinity in the Theological College of the North-West, of the Presbyterian Church in the United States. It was granted at once, and the Presbytery of London had leave, as requested, to admit Dr. Elliott as a Minister.

Page 26.—The Assembly agreed to receive Messrs. Andrew Hudson, Wm. Henry Jamieson, Daniel Blue, G. A. McLachlin, Thomas McAdam, Peter Fleming, Godfrey Shore as ministers, and Mr. J. G. Henderson as a Licentiate.

Page 27.—On the application of the Presbytery of Ottawa, on behalf of Messrs. Joseph Vessot and J. A. Vernon, the Assembly resolved, that it was inexpedient to receive them as ministers, although recognizing their services in connection with the Board of French Evangelization, and not desiring to interfere with their present position.

On the application on behalf of Mr. P. S. Vernier, transmitted by the Presbytery of Ottawa, the Assembly resolved that Mr. Vernier be placed under the oversight of the Presbytery of Ottawa, with instructions to the Presbytery to supervise his education, by examination and otherwise, and to report to the next Assembly.

The application of the Presbytery of London, on behalf of Mr. Geo. Crombie, be not granted in the meantime, but that they have leave to employ him as a catechist.

Defer in the meantime, consideration of the applications on behalf of Messrs. Lees and Charbonnel.

V. JUDICIAL CASES.

1. REFERENCE CONCERNING AN ORGAN.

TORONTO, 1876, p. 27.—The Presbytery of Wallace transmitted a reference concerning an application from the congregation of Amherst for permission to use an Organ in public worship.

After consideration it was moved and carried by a majority of 220 to 47. That the Presbytery of Wallace be instructed to intimate to the congregation of Amherst that they are at liberty to introduce instrumental music in public worship, provided the harmony of the congregation be not thereby distracted.

From this finding Messrs. Robb, Thomas Macpherson, John McTavish, John Fraser, Peter Crurie, George Sutherland; William Heron, Arnold Ross, John McAlpine, Hector McCrimmon dissented, for reasons to be given in in due time. (No reasons published.)

2. REFERENCE AS TO CERTAIN NAMES ON PRESBYTERY ROLLS.

Page 28.—There was produced and read a Reference from the Presbytery of Wallace, craving direction as to the course to be pursued with reference to the names of certain Ministers formerly belonging to the Synod of the Presbyterian Church of the Maritime Provinces in connection with the Church of Scotland, who have not entered the United Church, whether or not they should remain on the Roll of the Presbytery. Mr. Thomas Sedgwick was heard in support of the Reference. Whereupon it was unanimously agreed

—Sustain the reference and authorize the Presbytery to retain or remove their names, as they may see cause.

Mr. Mackinnon made a statement as to a like state of things in connection with the Roll of the Presbytery of Picton. The same was held to be a Reference, and the Presbytery of Pictou was instructed in the same terms in which the reference from the Presbytery of Wallace has just been disposed of.

3. REFERENCE *in re* HOUSTON—PRESBYTERY OF ST. JOHN.

Page 28.—The Assembly next took up a Reference from the Presbytery of St. John, craving instructions as to the manner in which they should deal with the following case brought before them by an Extract Minute of the Presbytery of Miramichi in these terms: "The Clerk read certain papers put into his hands "by the Rev. Samuel Houston, late of Calvin Church, St. John, "and now of St. Luke's Church, Bathurst, a Minister within the "bounds, libelling certain parties who are elders of a congrega- "tion under the jurisdiction of the Presbytery of St. John, and "making request that this Presbytery instruct the Clerk to for- "ward the same to the Presbytery of St. John in order that they "put said parties on their trial for said offence. Mr. Houston "further makes request that the Presbytery authorize him to "prosecute the matter before the Presbytery of St. John. These "requests the Presbytery granted, and the Clerk was instructed "accordingly."

The following motion was passed unanimously, Sustain the Reference and remit to the Presbytery of St. John to proceed and deal with the case.

4. REFERENCE *in re* SIMPSON—PRESBYTERY OF PARIS.

There was produced and read a Reference from the Presbytery of Paris in regard to Mr. John H. Simpson, a local preacher in the Methodist Church of Canada, at present engaged in teaching a school at Waterford, who desires to be received under the care of the Presbytery with a view to the Ministry in the Presbyterian Church. Mr. Lowry was heard in support of the Reference. Whereupon it was resolved, Instruct the Presbytery to correspond with the authorities of the College which Mr. Simpson proposes to attend, with a view to have him entered on terms that may be most advantageous to the applicant, and at the same time preserve the integrity of the course.

5. REFERENCE *in re* REV. D. J. MACDONNELL.

(1.) *Deed of Reference—first finding.*

TORONTO, 1876, p. 33.—From the Presbytery of Toronto, arising out of the action of the Presbytery in regard to a sermon preached last September by the Rev. D. J. Macdonnell, B.D., Minister of St. Andrew's Church, Toronto, on the eternity of the future punishment of the wicked. On the 4th November last, the Presbytery dealt with Mr. Macdonnell on account of this sermon, and, as part of their judgment, required him to report to that Court as to his agreement with the teaching of the Confession of Faith on the doctrine in question, not later than the last regular meeting before the next General Assembly. On the 18th April, and at subsequent dates, Mr. Macdonnell laid before the Presbytery, or a Committee of that Court, a succession of statements of his views on the points in question, which were deemed unsatisfactory. On the 30th May last, the following statement was presented by Mr. Macdonnell, viz: "Notwithstanding diffi-"culties which I have regarding the eternity of future punishment, "I continue my adhesion to that doctrine as implied in my "assent to the Confession of Faith, formerly given." On this the following action by a majority of the Presbytery was taken, viz: "That the statement, handed in by Mr. Macdonnell, be "transmitted to the General Assembly with an expression of the "hope that the Assembly may find it a satisfactory basis for the "settlement of the case; and that the whole matter be now refer-"red to the General Assembly with the request that that Vener-"able Court would finally issue it."

This constituted the Deed of Reference. Parties having been heard and after much reasoning the judgment of the Assembly by a majority of 263 to 161 was as follows:—Sustain the Reference for judgment; find that in statements made before this Assembly Mr Macdonnell has declared that he does not hold the doctrine of everlasting punishment in the sense held by this Church and formulated in the Confession of Faith, nevertheless that he has adopted no doctrinal views contrary to the Confession of Faith; therefore resolved: I. That the above twofold statement is not satisfactory to this Assembly ; 2. That a Committee be appointed to confer with Mr. Macdonnell in the hope that they may be able to bring in a report as to Mr. Macdonnell's views which may be satisfactory to this Assembly.

(2.) *Dissent.*

From this decision Dr. Snodgrass dissented for the following reason, viz.: "Because Mr. Macdonnell has this evening fully "and clearly stated his views to the Assembly, and because the "course which the Assembly has resolved to take is not fitted, "unless by undue constraint, to bring his views into full accord "with the accepted doctrine of the Church." 84 Ministers and 20 Elders joined in the Dissent.

A Committee was accordingly appointed by the moderator, Dr. Bayne, convener.

(3.) *Report of Committee.*

1876, p. 53.—The Assembly went into Committee of the Whole on the report of the Committee on the Reference from the Presbytery of Toronto, as follows:—

Page 53. The Committee beg leave to report to the General Assembly that Mr. Macdonnell met with them and stated that, while he was desirous to meet the wishes of the Assembly in regard to conference with the Committee, he respectfully referred them to the statement made on Thursday evening before the Assembly, as clearly defining his position, and that the report of that statement, which was published in the daily *Mail* of the 16th inst., is substantially correct.

After mature deliberation the Committee agreed to lay before the Assembly the following minute, for the adoption of the Court.

Considering (1) that this General Assembly has already declared that the statements of his views, made by Mr. Macdonnell before it, are not satisfactory: (2.) That, on meeting with the Committee appointed by the Assembly to confer with him, he signified that he has at present no further statement to make, by which his position towards the doctrine in question might be modified: (3.) That the doctrine of the eternity or endless duration of the future punishment of the wicked, as taught in the

Confession of Faith, is a doctrine of Scripture, which every Minister of this Church must hold and teach: The General Assembly feels under obligation to continue its care in this matter.

But, inasmuch as Mr. Macdonnell has expressed his regret for having preached the sermon which gave occasion for these proceedings, has intimated that his mind is at present in an undecided state as regards the doctrine in question, and has engaged, while seeking further light, not to contravene the teachings of the Church; the Assembly, in the hope that Mr. Macdonnell may soon find his views in accord with the Standards on the subject in question—

Resolve, that further time be given him carefully to consider the matter; and that he be required to report, through his Presbytery, to the next General Assembly, whether he accept the teaching of the Church on the subject.

The Assembly would commend their brother to the guidance of the Spirit of Truth, praying that, with the Divine blessing upon further study of the Word of God, all difficulties as to the Scriptural evidence of the momentous doctrine concerned may speedily cease to perplex his mind.

Resolved, by a majority of 127 to 71, that the report as it stands be adopted.

The Committee rose, the Moderator resumed, and the Chairman reported the resolution of the Committee of the Whole, whereupon, a vote being taken, it was carried by 127 to 64: "That the resolution reported by the Committee of the Whole House, become the finding of the Assembly."

(4.) *Dissent and Reasons.*

From this decision Principal Snodgrass, in his own name, and in the name of all who may adhere to him, craved leave to dissent, for the following reasons, viz :—

1. Because the Committee, in considering the position of Mr. Macdonnell, do not appear to have attached due weight to the full statement of his views submitted by him to the Assembly on the evening of Thursday last.

2. Because the report gives an exaggerated representation of Mr. Macdonnell's attitude towards the doctrine in question.

3. Because the deliverance of the Assembly is not fitted, except by undue constraint, to result in the removal of Mr. Macdonnell's difficulties.

Forty members adhered to this dissent, and concurred in all the reasons.

Three dissented and concurred in the third reason.

Nine dissented without reasons.

A Committee was appointed to answer the aforesaid reasons.

(5) *Answers to Reasons of Dissent.*

Page 69. The Convener of the Committee reported answers to the reasons of dissent presented by Principal Snodgrass and others, as follows, viz.:

1. In answer to the first reason, your Committee reply that a due consideration of the statement made by Mr. Macdonnell on Thursday last, shows that the more favorable expressions therein employed are neutralized by others, indicative of his inability to assent to the views of the Church, and especially by his direct definition of the attitude of his mind towards the doctrine in question as one of *doubt*, as distinguished from belief on the one hand, and denial on the other. And your Committee add that they fail to discover evidence of any substantial change of opinion from that held by Mr. Macdonnell, when he was last before the Presbytery of Toronto, or when he addressed the Assembly on Monday night.

2. In answer to the second reason, your Committee reply that they are wholly at a loss to discover the foundation on which it rests. The only statement contained in the report respecting Mr. Macdonnell's attitude towards the doctrine is that "he has intimated that his mind is at present in an undecided state as regards the doctrine in question," which surely cannot be viewed as an exaggerated representation. And your Committee further observe that, inasmuch as all the motions submitted to the Assembly approved of that portion of the report, which contains the alleged exaggeration of Mr. Macdonnell's attitude, the dissentients, voting as they did for these motions, have seriously weakened the ground on which their dissent proceeds.

3. This reason rests on two assumptions, neither of which seems to your Committee to be well founded. *First:* That the

chief end aimed at by the Assembly in the action complained of is to bring Mr. Macdonnell's views into accord with the doctrine held by the Church; whereas that end is secondary, and not primarily aimed at. The granting of time for consideration was the result of a desire to deal tenderly and leniently with a brother, as there seemed still reason to hope that on a more full consideration he would be able so to define his position as to make further dealings unnecessary; and the fixing of the limit at one year arose from the circumstance that it was the shortest possible time in which a report can be presented to the Supreme Court. And *secondly:* if your Committee understand this reason, it proceeds upon the assumption that the fixing of a time-limit, within which Mr. Macdonnell is to report, tends to hinder his mind from acting freely and fairly. This, your Committee affirm, cannot be, since men are constantly called upon to decide important questions of truth and duty within very definite time-limits. Your Committee would further add that the absence of such a time-limit as is complained of would leave it open for a minister to remain permanently in the Church, whose avowed mental attitude towards an important doctrine of God's Word is not such as this Church demands of her accredited teachers.

(6.) *Report of Mr. D. J. Macdonnell and finding.*

Halifax, 1877, p. 11.—The Clerk produced and read an Extract Minute of the Presbytery of Toronto, transmitting a report from the Rev. D. J. Macdonnell, B.D., as required by last Assembly, as follows, viz :—

"The General Assembly of 1876 having required me to report through the Presbytery of Toronto to this Assembly, whether I accept the teaching of the Church on the eternity of the future punishment of the wicked, I beg respectfully to state that I hold no opinion at variance with that teaching."

Page 15. The Assembly having discussed the answer at length, on motion by a majority of 174 to 82 it was resolved:—

The General Assembly, having heard the statement of Mr. D. J. Macdonnell, given in as his reply to the injunction of last Assembly, whereby he was required to report through his Presbytery whether he accepts the teaching of the Church on the subject of the eternity or endless duration of the future punishment of the wicked, as taught in the Confession of Faith and as a doctrine of Scripture, finds that, while representing that he holds no opinion at variance with that teaching, he has failed to state that he accepts it, and accordingly requires him to give in writing, addressed to the Moderator, before ten o'clock on Monday forenoon, a categorical answer to the said question in terms of the deliverance of last Assembly.

(7.) *Reasons of Dissent.*

From this finding Principal Snodgrass craved leave to dissent in his own name and in the name of all who may adhere to him, for the following reasons, viz.:—

1. Because Mr. Macdonnell has already reported an answer in a form as categorical as can fairly and constitutionally be required of a Minister, who adheres to the Confession of Faith.

2. Because the Assembly has no constitutional right, at this stage of the proceedings in the matter before it, to require Mr. Macdonnell to give his answer in any particular form.

To this dissent and for these reasons forty members adhered.

A Committee was appointed to answer the aforesaid reasons.

(8.) *Answer to Reasons of Dissent.*

1877, p. 17. 1. It is replied to the first reason—

(1.) That the statement of Mr. Macdonnell cannot be regarded as in any sense an answer to the question which the Assembly in the exercise of its constitutional rights put to him.

(2) To justify the answer of Mr. Macdonnell by the statement that it is all that can be constitutionally required of a Minister who adheres to the Confession of Faith is to present a false issue, inasmuch as the adherence of Mr. Macdonnell to the Confession of Faith in regard to the doctrine of the endless duration of future punishment is the very point in question before the Court; and, so far from the dissentients having the right to affirm his adherence in the present instance, Mr. Macdonnell in his last statement before the previous General Assembly expressed his inability at that time to give it.

2. That the Assembly has certainly a constitutional right in such a case as the present, for the maintenance of the truth of God, to require an answer in whatever form it deems best fitted

to satisfy itself of his acceptance of the doctrine involved (*vide* "Rules and Forms of Procedure of the Presbyterian Church of the Lower Provinces," pp. 103, 104, and "Hill's Practice in the Church Courts," p. 54.)

(9.) *Reply of Mr. D. J. Macdonnell.*

Page 16. The Clerk produced and read a communication which the Moderator had this morning received from Mr. Macdonnell, in response to the requirement embodied in the motion, which on Saturday had become the judgment of the House. Said communication is in the following terms, viz.:—

"I herewith submit in writing what I said on Saturday last, when it was announced that the amendment proposed by Dr. Topp had become the judgment of the Assembly.

"I hold that I have already given an answer to the question embodied in that resolution as categorical as a Minister within the Church, who has declared his adherence to the Confession of Faith, and who still adheres to it, can fairly or constitutionally be required to give on a point on which he is confessedly in difficulty.

"If that answer be not deemed sufficient, I request, as I have a constitutional right to do, that the Presbytery of Toronto be instructed to frame a libel and deal with the matter according to the laws of the Church."

It was moved and passed unanimously, that Mr. Macdonnell's statement, now read, be received; that the consideration of the same be taken up at ten o'clock to-morrow morning; and that meantime the statement be printed and copies placed in the hands of members.

Page 21. The Assembly proceeded to the consideration of Mr. Macdonnell's answer given in yesterday morning. Soon after the debate had commenced, a motion was submitted and carried, that, before the Assembly proceeds further in considering what future action should be taken in this case, a Committee be appointed to meet and deliberate with the view of presenting a basis for a satisfactory adjustment of the case, and that the debate be in the meantime suspended. A Committee in terms of this motion was accordingly appointed with instructions to report at the afternoon sederunt.

(10.) *Conclusion of the Case.*

1877, p. 23. Dr. Jenkins, Convener of the Committee appointed to meet and deliberate with the view of presenting a basis for a satisfactory settlement of the matter relating to Mr. Macdonnell, reported—

That they have ascertained from Mr. Macdonnell, through a sub-Committee, that, in intimating in his last statement to the General Assembly his adherence to the Confession of Faith, he intends to be understood as saying:—

"I consider myself as under subscription to the Confession of Faith in accordance with my Ordination vows, and I therefore adhere to the teaching of the Church as contained therein on the doctrine of the eternity or endless duration of the future punishment of the wicked, notwithstanding doubts or difficulties which perplex my mind."

The Committee therefore unanimously recommend that this statement be accepted as satisfactory, and that further proceedings be dropped.

On motion the Assembly unanimously resolved, that the report now read be received and adopted, and that the Assembly decern in terms thereof.

The House joined in singing Psalm cxxii. 6-9, and engaged in prayer.

6—(1.) REFERENCE AND APPEALS FROM THE PRESBYTERY OF ST. JOHN.

1877, p. 11. There were produced and read Extract Minutes of the Presbytery of St. John, N. B., transmitting—

(1.) Complaint and appeal:—the Rev. Samuel Houston vs. Mr. James A. Tufts.

(2.) Complaint and appeal:—the Rev. Samuel Houston vs. the Rev. David Maclise, D. D.

(3.) Reference anent a libel instituted by the Rev. Samuel Houston against certain Trustees of Calvin Church, St. John.

(2.) *Appointment of a Judicial Committee.*

Whereupon it was moved and passed unanimously, that, in accordance with the recommendation of the Committee on Bills and Overtures, these papers and all relative documents be referred for consideration to a Committee, with power to call for parties and papers and frame a deliverance in the matter.

(3.) *Report of Committee.*

1877, p. 48.—The Committee appointed to recommend a deliverance on these cases, gave in the following :—

1. With reference to the first case, viz.:—an appeal by the Rev. Samuel Houston from the finding of the Session of Calvin Church, St. John, on the matter of a libel by him against John Logan and others, elders in said Calvin Church.

At the suggestion of the Committee, the respective parties agreed to withdraw the charges and imputations on the one side and on the other, which were the subject of libel and appeal, and accordingly subscribed in presence of the Committee the following documents, viz :—

"The undersigned, having written a letter in the 'New York Evangelist,' over the signature of 'Erigena,' making certain references to the affairs of Calvin Church, St. John, and having also written other letters on the same subject, hereby disclaims all intention in the said letters of imputing fraud or dishonesty to the officers of that Church, and hereby expresses his regret at having used any language which may have been deemed offensive."

(Signed) SAMUEL HOUSTON.

"The undersigned, having written certain letters, some of which were published in the newspapers of St. John and elsewhere, affecting the character and standing of the Rev. S. Houston, formerly Minister of Calvin Church, St. John, and now Minister of St. Luke's Church, Bathurst, hereby withdraw all injurious imputations contained in such letters or any of them, and express our regret for having written the same."

(Signed) JAMES LOGAN. ALEXANDER STEWART.

Page 49. The latter of the above documents was agreed to by Mr. Logan and Mr. Stewart, as well on their own behalf as on behalf of Messrs. Tufts and McLaughlin, for whom they were duly authorized to act, setting their authority before the Committee.

2. With reference to the second case, viz.:—An appeal by Mr. Houston against the finding of the Presbytery of St John upon a libel by him against Mr. Tufts, an Elder of Calvin Church ; also a dissent and appeal from the same finding by the Rev. Dr. Waters.

At the suggestion of the Committee, the parties agreed to the following deliverance, viz.:—

"Mr. Tufts having in writing withdrawn all injurious imputations upon the character and standing of the Rev. Samuel Houston in the letter referred to by Mr. Tufts in his letter to Dr. Duncan, and having expressed regret at having imputed the same, we are of opinion that further action in this case be stayed, believing that there was warrant for the libel taken upon said letter to Dr. Duncan and for dealing with Mr. Tufts in reference thereto."

3. With reference to the third case, viz.:—a libel by Mr. Houston against the Rev. Dr. Maclise, the parties appeared before the Committee and, after opening the case, Dr. Maclise, in presence of the Committee, made the following statement, viz.:—

"That he does not know facts which would drive Mr. Houston from the Ministry; that he does not believe he used the words; and that, if he did use the words, he did not mean to use them, and now withdraws them."

With the above statement Mr. Houston expressed himself satisfied.

The Committee, therefore, recommend that no further proceedings be had or taken on the several cases, and that the parties be urged henceforth to study the things that make for peace.

The Assembly unanimously agreed to decern in terms of the report.

7. COMPLAINT—PRESBYTERY OF BARRIE *vs.* SYNOD OF TORONTO AND KINGSTON.

1877, p. 26.—The Assembly took up a Dissent and Complaint—the Presbytery of Barrie *vs.* the Synod of Toronto and Kingston anent a complaint of Mr. Marples. Dr. Robb, on the part of the aforesaid Synod, objected *in limine* that reasons in support of the dissent had not been furnished by the appellants within ten days of the time when the dissent was taken, as required by the laws of the Church, and accordingly claimed that the complaint should not be entertained by the Assembly. Mr. Gray, on behalf of the appellants, was heard on this point. The Moderator sustained Dr. Robb's objection, and the matter was thus dismissed.

8. JUDICIAL COMMITTEE.

(1.) *Appointment.*

Hamilton, 1878, p. 15.—In accordance with a recommendation of the Committee on Bills and Overtures, the Assembly unanimously resolved to appoint a Committee, to be known as "The Judicial Committee," to consider all causes that may come before the Court, with power to hear parties and prepare findings, and with instructions to report, it being understood that members of the Committee shall not take part in any cause or causes in which, as parties, they have an interest.

(2.) *Causes Remitted.*

The Clerk read the papers and called the parties in the following causes :—

1. Appeal :—Presbytery of Sydney *vs.* the Synod of the Maritime Provinces.

2. Appeal :—Æneas McMaster *vs.* the Synod of Montreal and Ottawa.

3. Dissent and Complaint :—Mr. J. J. Cameron *vs.* the Presbytery of Stratford.

4. Appeal :—Mr. D. McLellan *vs.* the Synod of Hamilton and London.

5. Reference :—The Synod of Hamilton and London in the case of Mr. Andrew Watson.

The papers in all these causes were referred to the Judicial Committee, and the parties were instructed to appear before that Committee.

(3.) *Report of Judicial Committee.*

Hamilton, 1878, p. 31.—The Convener presented and read a report, and in accordance with its recommendations, the Assembly adopted the following as their deliverances in the several causes referred to.

1. The Presbytery of Sydney *vs.* the Synod of the Maritime Provinces.

Sustain the appeal ; and, inasmuch as the Presbytery of

Sydney, in erecting the Stations of Victoria and Lingan, and continuing them as such, acted in accordance with its constitutional rights, hereby confirm the said action of that Presbytery.

2. Mr. J. J. Cameron *vs.* the Presbytery of Stratford.

Dismiss the dissent and complaint, and confirm the judgment of the Presbytery.

3. Mr. Donald McLellan *vs.* the Synod of Hamilton and London.

Dismiss the appeal, inasmuch as the Kirk Session of McNab Street Church, Hamilton, acted in the exercise of a constitutional right in seeking an expression of the views of the congregation as to the use of additional hymns.

4. Reference from the Synod of Hamilton and London anent the reception of Mr. Andrew Watson, as a Minister of this Church, by the Presbytery of London.

Sustain the Reference and declare the action of the Presbytery to be null and void, inasmuch as the Presbytery received Mr. Watson as a Licentiate and Minister of this Church without a certificate of Licensure and Ordination, and without referring the case to the General Assembly.

Parties were called in all these causes and judgment was intimated.

5. In regard to the Appeal :—Æneas McMaster *vs.* the Synod of Montreal and Ottawa, inasmuch as new papers in the cause have been received by the Clerk, the absence of which hitherto was satisfactorily explained, the Assembly agreed to remit this cause to the Committee, as these papers may form an element in coming to a judgment on the matter.

(4) *Supplemental Report.*

Page 44. The Convener of the Judicial Committee presented and read a supplementary report, which the Assembly adopted as their deliverance in the Appeal—McMaster *vs.* the Synod of Montreal and Ottawa.

Considering that it had not been shown that the congregation of Hampden, as such, was liable for any part of the arrears of stipend due to Mr. Macdonald, the General Assembly dismiss the appeal ; find that the Presbytery of Quebec erred in directing

Mr. Macdonald to retain in his hands moneys held by him as a Trustee for the benefit of said congregation; and consequently confirm the action of the Synod of Montreal and Ottawa in reversing the decision of said Presbytery.

(5.) *Memorial from Brooksdale, Zorra.*

Hamilton, 1878, p. 37. The Assembly took up a Memorial from certain petitioners, representing that previous to the Union they were Members of the Presbyterian Church in Zorra in connection with the Church of Scotland—that they were organized by the Presbytery of London many years ago—that, believing themselves to be placed by the arrangements made at the time of the Union under the care of the Presbytery of Stratford, they applied to that Presbytery for supply of religious ordinances, but that the Presbytery of London claims that they are within its jurisdiction. The petitioners prayed the Assembly definitely to enact that the Brooksdale congregation, to which they belong, be placed under the jurisdiction of the Stratford Presbytery.

(6.) *Report on Brooksdale case.*

Hamilton, 1878, p. 48. The Convener of the Judicial Committee presented and read a report regarding the Memorial from Brooksdale, Zorra. In terms of its recommendations, the Assembly decerned as follows, viz:—

Receive the Memorial; appoint a Commission, with Assembly powers to issue the case, to meet at Stratford at an early date, and summon to appear for their respective interests the Petitioners, the Presbyteries of London and Stratford, the congregations of Harrington, Embro, Thamesford and Burns' Church, East Zorra; Dr. Topp, Convener.

(7.) *Decision of Commission.*

Ottawa, 1879, p. 26. The Convener of the Commission with Assembly powers, appointed by last Assembly to meet at Stratford and settle the matters referred to in the Memorial from Brooksdale, Zorra, gave in a report, which was received and adopted, and the papers were ordered to be printed in the Appendix to the Minutes.

Ottawa, 1879, App. p. 235. At Stratford, and within Knox Church there, the eleventh day of July, one thousand eight hundred and seventy-eight, the Commission appointed by the General Assembly in the matter of a petition from Brooksdale, praying to be placed within the bounds of the Presbytery of Stratford, met and was constituted. Dr. Topp, Convener.

The Minute of Assembly appointing the Commission was read. The petition referred to the Commission by the Assembly was also read.

The Convener stated that, in accordance with the instruction of Assembly, he had cited the Presbytery of London, the Presbytery of Stratford, and the congregations of Harrington, Embro, Thamesford, and Burns' Church, East Zorra.

There were read extract minutes of the Synod of Hamilton and London, instructing petitioners to apply to the General Assembly to be placed within the bounds of the Presbytery of Stratford.

The Commission heard parties, and several questions being asked and answered, the Commission after deliberation unanimously resolved, "That the parties claiming to belong to the Presbyterian Church of Zorra, formerly in connection with the Church of Scotland, and now before this Commission as memorialists, be declared, and they are hereby declared, to be properly within the bounds of the Presbytery of Stratford, and are now placed under the ecclesiastical jurisdiction of that Presbytery."

The several parties acquiesced and craved extracts which were granted.

9—(1.) JUDICIAL CAUSES AND COMMITTEE WITH INSTRUCTIONS.

Ottawa, 1879, p. 10. The Assembly next took up :—

1. A Complaint :—Ralph Dodds, an elder of Knox Church, Perth, vs. the Presbytery of Lanark and Renfrew.

2. A Protest and Appeal :—James Haliday, a member of the aforesaid congregation, vs. the Presbstery of Lanark and Renfrew, in regard to the introduction of an organ as an aid in conducting the praise in said congregation of Knox Church, Perth,

Papers in the cause were read, and it was, on motion, agreed to refer these to a Judicial Committee, hereafter to be appointed.

Page 18. That it be an instruction to the Committee that, when parties have been heard and a finding arrived at, that finding shall be intimated to the parties, so that they may have an opportunity, if they see fit, of availing themselves of the right to be heard by the Assembly before the report of the Committee is finally disposed of. The Committee was appointed, Dr. Topp, Convener.

(2.) *Report of Committee.*

Ottawa, 1879, p. 46. Dr. Topp, Convener of the Judicial Committee, presented a report in the causes :—

Dodds vs. the Presbytery of Lanark and Renfrew, Haliday vs. the Presbytery of Lanark and Renfrew. Parties were called and the report was read, a majority of ten to seven adopting the following finding, viz :—

"That the complaint and appeal be dismissed. At the same "time the Assembly express the hope that in any further proceed- "ings which may be taken in this matter the Presbytery will "have careful regard to the maintenance of the peace of the con- "gregation."

Messrs. Dodds and Haliday, having intimated non-aquiescence in the proposed finding, and having expressed a desire to be heard by the House, stated their case and presented their objections to the report of the Committee. Dr. Mann and Dr. Bain were heard for the Presbytery and Mr. Haliday in reply. Whereupon it was moved and seconded and carried that the report be received and adopted.

10—(1.) PETITION—PRESBYTERY OF LANARK AND RENFREW.

Montreal, 1880, p. 33. The Assembly took up a petition from the Presbytery of Lanark and Renfrew, setting forth in substance that difficulties had arisen in the congregation of Knox Church, Perth, which they—the Presbytery—found it beyond their power to remove, and praying the General Assembly to appoint a Commission to proceed to Perth, to meet the congregation of Knox Church, and endeavor to ascertain the causes of the strifes and troubles referred to, and decern—giving to all parties such counsels and instructions as in their wisdom may seem proper. On motion the Assembly agreed to grant the prayer of the petition and appointed the Commission, with Assembly powers, in terms thereof. Professor McLaren, Convener.

(2) *Report and Decision of Commission.*

Kingston, 1881, App. 249–250. The Commission met in Knox Church, Perth, on Thursday, 19th day of August, 1880. Mr. W. McLaren, Moderator. The minute of Assembly appointing the Commission was read. There were also read the petition of the Presbytery of Lanark and Renfrew, and extract minutes of the decision of the Synod of Montreal and Ottawa.

The Presbytery of Lanark and Renfrew, in accordance with the request of the Commission, appeared before the Commission.

It was agreed to hear, first, the Presbytery in explanation of the reasons which led them to petition the General Assembly for the appointment of a Commission; and accordingly Messrs. Crombie and Wilson were heard on the part of the Presbytery.

The Commission then called for statements from that part of the congregation who have hitherto been opposed to the use of instrumental music, when Mr. J. Haliday addressed the Commission, after which several questions were asked and answered. Messrs. R. Dodds and W. J. McLean were also heard, and various questions were asked and answered.

The Commission then proceeded to hear statements from those in favor of instrumental music in public worship. Mr. F. B. Allan addressed the Commission, also Mr. Sheriff Thompson and Mr. Cromwell. Mr. James Allan, who said that he had not taken any part either for or against the use of instrumental music, then addressed the Commission. Mr. Burns also made a statement with reference to the history and position of the question in the congregation. The Commission adjourned to meet to-morrow at ten o'clock, a. m.

An opportunity was given to any one who had not previously made any statement to do so now, but no one came forward.

The Commission then agreed that each party in the congregation should select five of their number to confer with the Commission with the view of arriving at a settlement that might be satisfactory to all. Five members were accordingly selected by each party, and a conference was held by the Commission with these parties so appointed. Thereafter the Commission unanimously adopted the following deliverance:—

The Commission having met with the congregation of Knox Church, Perth, and the Presbytery of Lanark and Renfrew, and heard lengthened statements from all the parties interested, finds:

1. That in reference to the cause of the strifes and troubles at present prevailing in Knox Church, Perth, while there appears to have been imprudence in urging the introduction of instrumental music in public worship, in the divided state of feeling upon that question existing in the congregation, the troubles have assumed a form in which the abandonment of instrumental music as an aid in the service of praise would not restore harmony to the congregation.

2. That the present unhappy state of matters in the congregation does not appear to be due to any acts or courses of conduct on the part either of the Minister or of the office-bearers of the Church, which should have occasioned the existing state of feeling, but is largely due to an apparent tendency to give heed to idle rumors, and to magnify into grave offences trivial mistakes and omissions, which proper church feeling would have passed over as unworthy of serious regard.

3. That the Presbytery of Lanark and Renfrew is instructed to proceed as early as practicable to hold an election of elders in Knox Church, Perth, but that in view of the present circumstances of the congregation the Commission directs that no person shall be held as elected unless he has a majority of three-fourths of the votes cast, and in conducting the election the Presbytery is instructed to follow the ordinary usage of the Presbyterian Church, and not the rules laid down in the constitution of Knox Church; and further, that the number of elders to be elected in the meantime shall not be more than five in addition to the one already in office.

4. That whereas there is nothing which has been brought to light of such a nature as should prevent the restoration of the harmony between the different sections of the congregation and the pastor and people; the Commission would therefore earnestly counsel them to cultivate a spirit of brotherly kindness and Christian forbearance, and to avoid everything which may tend to revive past alienations.

Mr. Crombie craved extracts on behalf of the Presbytery of Lanark and Renfrew, which were granted.

11. APPEAL *in re* BROOKSDALE CASE.

(1.) *Case called and remitted.*

Montreal, 1880, p. 10. The Assembly proceeded to take up an appeal of the Presbytery of Stratford, from action of the Synod of Hamilton and London, in the case of the congregation of Brooksdale. Parties were called, and compeared.

The Assembly agreed to refer this appeal, with all the papers in the case, to a Committee.

(2.) *Judicial Committee Appointed.—Dissent.*

1880, p. 15. The Assembly proceeded on the recommendations of the Committee on Business to consider the expediency of appointing a Judicial Committee, to consider causes of a judicial character which may be by the Assembly referred to such Committee, with the same instructions as those given to the Committee of last year. (See Minutes, 1879. p. 18.)

It was moved by Dr. Grant, seconded by Mr. Laing, that a Judicial Committee be now appointed, and that the members recommended by the Committee of Bills and Overtures compose said Committee; and that such Committee be amalgamated with the Committee on the Brooksdale Case to form one Judicial Committee. Principal Caven, Convener.

It was moved in amendment by Dr. Kemp, seconded by Mr. Archibald Matheson, that the Judicial Committee be not appointed, and that Judicial business be considered according to the constitution and usages of the Church as heretofore. A vote being taken, the motion of Dr. Grant was carried against the amendment of Dr. Kemp by a large majority, and the motion became the judgment of the House.

Dr Kemp craved that his dissent from this decision be marked in the Minutes.

(3.) *Report of Committee and Decision.*

1880, p. 216. Dr. Caven submitted and read a report from the Judicial Committee on the Brooksdale Case, representing that the case came before the Committee in the form of an appeal of the Presbytery of Stratford against a finding of the Synod of Hamilton and London, anent the Brooksdale Station. The report was received and the recommendations were adopted.

1. Sustain the decision of the Synod of Hamilton and London, in finding that the motion offered by Mr. Gordon, in the Presbytery of Stratford, was not incompetent.

2. With a view of determining the whole question as to how the Presbytery shall deal with the parties claiming to belong to the Presbyterian Church of Zorra, formerly in connection with the Church of Scotland, the Assembly, by request of appellant and respondent, and also of the appellant to the Synod, appoint a Commission, Principal Caven, Convener, with full power to determine the matter—the Commission to meet at Knox Church, Stratford, on Wednesday, the seventh day of July next, at half-past one o'clock in the afternoon,—and instruct the Clerk of the Presbytery of Stratford to notify all parties who were notified to attend the Commission of Assembly in 1878.

(4) *Decision of Commission.*

Kingston, 1881, p. 16. Dr. Reid laid before the Assembly the record of the proceedings of the Commission of Assembly appointed last year, in the matter of appeals from decisions of the Presbytery of Stratford, and of the Synod of Hamilton and London, in the matter commonly known as the Brooksdale Case. (See Minutes, 1880, pp. 10, 26). Also, the record of proceedings of the Commission on the case of Knox Church, Perth. (See Minutes, 1880, pp. 33, 45). The Assembly ordered these records to be printed in the Appendix to its Minutes.

1881, App. p. 249. At Stratford, and within Knox Church there, on the 7th day of July, 1880, the Commission appointed by the General Assembly for the purpose of determining the question as to how the Presbytery of Stratford should deal with the parties claiming to belong to the Presbyterian Church of Zorra, formerly in connection with the Church of Scotland, met and was constituted. Dr. Caven, Moderator.

The minute of Assembly appointing this Commission was read. Parties were called and appeared. All parties connected with the case were fully heard. Thereupon the Commission resolved as follows:—

1. The parties claiming to belong to the Presbyterian Church of Zorra, formerly in connection with the Church of Scotland, to whom supply of service has been given for some time by the Presbytery of Stratford, are recognized, though imperfectly organized, as the congregation of Zorra, which was reported by the Presbytery of London in connection with the Church of Scotland, at the time of the Union of the Churches.

2. In the opinion of the Commission it is desirable that services should continue to be held at Brooksdale.

3. The Presbytery of Stratford is instructed to make such arrangements for supply of service at Brooksdale as shall not imperil the interests of the congregation of Harrington.

The meeting of Commission was then closed

12. REFERENCE—SYNOD OF TORONTO AND KINGSTON *in re* MRS. PHILLIPS.

(1.) *Report of Judicial Committee.*

Montreal, 1880, pp. 50, 51. Principal Caven brought up a report from the Judicial Committee, in the matter of the Reference from the Synod of Toronto and Kingston and in this case; and requested that while the report was being read the Assembly should sit with closed doors. It was moved and carried, that the request be complied with. Strangers were then requested to retire.

The Hon. Mr. Morris, Messrs. D. J. Macdonnell, C. B. Pitblado, and J. Middlemiss, craved that their dissent from the action of the Assembly, in closing the doors, be marked in the Minutes.

The report is as follows:—

The Committee having maturely considered the references from the Synod of Toronto and Kingston for advice with regard to a reference to them by the Presbytery of Saugeen, of a reference from the kirk session of Arthur, anent the church standing of two members of that congregation, as affected by their marriage in the Province of Ontario, after one of them, Maria Jane

Buschter, who it would appear had been previously married in said Province on the 10th of August, 1870, to one Henry Lewis, and had, after a residence of eighteen months in the State of Illinois, on the 24th day of March, 1879, obtained a decree of divorce from her said husband in the District Court of the State of Illinois, on the grounds, as stated in the judgment of said Court, in the cause of Maria Jane Lewis *versus* Henry Clay Lewis, viz.:—"That the defendant has been guilty of habitual drunkenness, and had wilfully absented himself from the said complainant, without any reasonable cause, for more than the space of two years before the filing of the complaint thereon."

The Committee, in pursuance of their duty, submit the following statement to the Assembly :—

1. It appears that after the obtaining of the said decree, the said Maria Jane Buschter returned to Ontario, and on the 27th of May, 1879, was married to one Thomas Phillips, who was a member of the congregation of Arthur, as Mrs. Lewis had been previously to her departure to Illinois.

2. That after the solemnization of the marriage by the Rev D. Stewart, minister of Arthur, the question of the marriage was then taken up by the Kirk Session of Arthur, in consequence of the expressed dissatisfaction of a member of the congregation with regard to the said marriage, and the Session agreed after deliberation to ask the advice of the Presbytery, "1st, as to whether Mr. Stewart was justified, under the circumstances, in marrying the said parties; and, 2nd, as to whether the said Thomas Phillips and Mrs. Phillips are entitled to the privilege of church membership."

3. The Presbytery, on the 16th of September, 1879, considered the reference, and, after reasoning, sent the question back to the Session of the Arthur congregation to proceed formally in the case, and appointed Assessors to act with the Session thereon.

4. The Session accordingly met on the 6th of October last, and entered upon consideration of the case. The Session had before them the decree of divorce granted in the State of Illinois. The Session took declarations of certain witnesses that the said Lewis had been guilty of adultery, and had admitted the same.

5. The Presbytery considered the evidence and decree, and remitted the case to the Synod of Toronto and Kingston for ad-

vice, who directed the Presbytery of Saugeen to prepare a full statement of the case for submission to the General Assembly for advice.

6 From the Presbytery's statement it would appear that about two years ago, after the marriage of Mr. and Mrs. Lewis, they parted in February, 1872, specially on the ground that the said Lewis had committed adultery. Mrs. Lewis then went to her father's house, and supported herself and child by teaching music. Mrs. Lewis corresponded, they relate, with Lewis in different letters about obtaining a divorce from him, and informed him that she intended to apply in the proper manner to secure it. They also state that about two years after their separation Lewis wrote his wife that she could do what she liked in the matter, and that after having lived a separate life and supported herself and child for several years, Mrs. Lewis then repaired to the United States and lived in the State of Illinois for one year and six months, when she obtained, as before stated, a divorce from the said Lewis.

(2.) *Decision Recommended.*

The Committee, having given this statement of the facts of this case, beg leave to report to the Assembly as follows:—

Inasmuch as marriage is a civil contract as well as a religious ordinance, due regard to the law of the land and to the interests of public morality require that the Church should not lend her sanction to divorces or re-marriages which our law, in this matter conformable to Scripture, does not recognize.

Whilst in the case before us there is evidence that divorce might have been sued for on the ground recognized by Scripture, and the law of Canada, as adequate, yet the party whose relation to the Church is in question, obtained, in a foreign country, a divorce which the law of this country does not hold to be valid; the divorce, therefore, and the marriage which followed, should not, by any action of the General Assembly, be regarded as having fully satisfied the requirements which Christian duty enjoins us to respect.

In these circumstances, the judgment of the General Assembly is that the party should be instructed and encouraged to seek divorce from Henry Lewis in the way provided by the law of Canada and without questioning the good faith of the party in the steps which she has taken—expressing also sympathy with her in the painful and trying position in which she has been placed—the Assembly deems it necessary, to avoid all offence, that she should not be regarded as in full communion with the Church until the requirements of the civil law have been duly complied with.

In regard to the conduct of the Rev. D. Stewart in marrying to Thomas Phillips the person above referred to, the General Assembly find that they have no evidence before them upon which to pronounce any judgment.

(3.) *Minority Report.*

Mr D. J. Macdonnell here read a paper purporting to be a report of the minority of the Judicial Committee, in terms following: "The minority of the Judicial Committee, while concurring in the historical statement prepared by the Committee in the case of Mrs. Phillips, and in the deliverance proposed down to the word '*placed*,' desire to have the following words substituted for the remaining portion of the finding:—'Considering the acknowledged difficulty of obtaining divorce in Canada even on the grounds recognized in Scripture; considering, further, that there were sufficient grounds in this case for obtaining divorce according to the law of Canada; the General Assembly does not deem it necessary, in the present position of the matter, to disturb the church standing of the parties. (Signed) D. J. Macdonnell, John J. A. Proudfoot, G. D. Matthews, John McMillan, George Bell, LL. D., John Gray, D. McCurdy."

It was then resolved, that the report be received, and that the finding contained therein, together with the paper read by Mr. Macdonnell, be printed for the use of members of the Assembly, and the consideration of the report made the first order of business for to-morrow morning.

The case was resumed next morning and the decision recommended by the Committee was adopted by a majority of 57 to 16.

13. REFERENCE—PRESBYTERY OF PARIS *in re* CHAMBERS.

1880, p. 55. There was taken up a reference from the Presbytery of Paris, containing an application of Mr. Robert Chambers, a minister of this Church, now a missionary in Eastern Turkey, under the American Board of Commissioners for Foreign

Missions, requesting that his ministerial status as a minister of this Church be preserved to him in the foreign field. The Assembly resolved as follows: Sustain the reference from the Presbytery of Paris; agree to recognize Mr. Robert Chambers as a minister of this Church, and that his name be entered on the roll of the Presbytery of Paris; and, further, cordially sanction his acceptance of employment as a missionary, in Turkey, of the American Board of Commissioners for Foreign Missions, and earnestly bid him God-speed in his work.

14. APPEAL—PRESBYTERY OF SYDNEY *vs.* SUTHERLAND.

1880, p. 26. Dr. Caven read another report from the Judicial Committee, in a case of appeal of the Presbytery of Sydney against a decision of the Synod of the Maritime Provinces in the matter of a reference from the said Presbytery to the said Synod in the case of Mr. Sutherland, of Gabarus, and containing a resolution for adoption by the Assembly. On such recommendation of the Committee the Assembly resolved:—That the action of the Synod be not reviewed, and that the decision appealed against be allowed to stand.

15.—JUDICIAL COMMITTEE AND CASES.

Kingston, 1881, pp. 15, 16. The General Assembly appointed a Judicial Committee to consider and report on Judicial Causes which may be referred by the Assembly to the said Committee. Mr. T. W. Taylor, Convener.

(1.) *Petitions--Presbytery of Sydney in re Sutherland.*

The Assembly took up the appeal of said Presbytery from the action of the Synod of the Maritime Provinces, in the matter of Mr. Sutherland, of Gabarus, disposed of by the Assembly last year, praying the Assembly to give the Presbytery's Commissioner an opportunity of being heard in support of said appeal, to consider appeals before the Synod, and to give final judgment. The Commissioner of the Presbytery of Sydney—Mr. G. L. Gordon—was heard, assigning reasons for entertaining said petition. The petition was referred to the Judicial Committee.

(2.) *Petition—Rev. J. Fraser in re Synod of Toronto and Kingston*

There was taken up and read said memorial and petition. containing recitals regarding proceedings of the Synod of Toronto and Kingston, bearing hardly upon his character and standing as a Minister of the Gospel, and praying the Assembly to take the whole case into their consideration, and to set aside the finding of the said Synod at their late meeting at Bowmanville, and re-affirm the decision of the Presbytery of Kingston, of March last. Remitted to the Judicial Committee.

(3.) *Appeal—Presbytery of Stratford vs. Synod of Hamilton and London.*

The Assembly took up and read this appeal in the matter of the transference of the congregation of Molesworth from the Presbytery of Stratford to that of Maitland. All the papers were read and the parties called and the case was remitted to the Judicial Committee.

(4.) *Report of Judicial Committee.*

1881, p. 34. Mr. T. W. Taylor, from the Committee reported,

1.—On the appeal of the Presbytery of Stratford from the decision of the Synod of Hamilton and London, in the case of Molesworth congregation, stating that the Committee had read the papers, and had heard parties, and recommended to the Assembly that the action of the Synod of Hamilton and London be approved of, and the appeal of the Presbytery of Stratford dismissed. On motion made, and duly seconded, the Assembly decerned in terms of the same.

2.—On the appeal of the Presbytery of Sydney from decisions of the Synod of the Maritime Provinces, in the case of the Gabarus Congregation, that the Committee had heard the the Commissioner for the Presbytery of Sydney, and the Commissioners for the Synod of the Maritime Provinces on the question of re-opening the case, and thereafter resolved: "That the Committee re-open the case on its merits, on the ground that the appellants were not able to be present at last Assembly, and that, in their absence, the action of the Synod against which appeal was taken was not reviewed." Thereupon the papers were read, and parties heard, and the Committee recommended to the Assembly the following deliverance :—

(1.) The Presbytery of Sydney having, after the adoption of the report of a Committee which formulated certain findings, referred the case for final judgment to the Synod of the Maritime Provinces, it was competent for the Synod to hear the whole case and decide it.

(2.) Allow the appeal from the decision of the Synod as regards the election of trustees, in relation to which irregularity seems to have occurred.

Page 35. (3.) Allow the appeal from the decision of the Synod on the fourth appeal, as to the inquiry by the Presbytery into the regularity of the election and ordination of elders.

(4.) Dismiss the appeal from all the other decisions of the Synod on the various charges and appeals; but in doing so the General Assembly do not endorse or adopt all the reasons assigned by the Synod for its proceedings, or approve of all the language in which these reasons are expressed. The Assembly, on motion made and duly seconded, decerned and ordered in terms of the deliverance contained therein.

3.—On the petition of the Rev. Joshua Fraser, the Committee—having read and considered the petition and accompanying papers, and having also examined the record of the Synod of Toronto and Kingston as to the action taken by that Synod in connection with the case of Mr. Fraser, at its meetings in the years 1880 and 1881,—respectively recommend the following resolution for the adoption of the General Assembly:—That it being alleged that the decision of the Synod of Toronto and Kingston, complained of, was come to in the absence of Mr. Fraser, and without notice to him, the decision and all proceedings thereunder be suspended until the next meeting of the Synod, that Mr. Fraser may have an opportunity, if he shall see fit, on giving notice to the Presbytery of Kingston, and the Rev. Andrew Wilson, for applying to the Synod to rescind or vary the said decision, and to be heard in regard thereto. The report was received, and the Assembly decerned and ordered in terms thereof.

16. JUDICIAL COMMITTEE AND CASES.

St. John, N.B., 1882, p. 10.—A Judicial Committee to consider and report on all cases of a judicial nature which may be referred to the same, was appointed. Rev. John Laing, Convener.

(1.) *Reference Anent Appeal of Dr. Barclay.*

Page 16. There was taken up a Reference from the Synod of Toronto and Kingston in regard to this appeal from action of the Presbytery of Toronto respecting a claim for money alleged to be due to appellant from the congregation of St. Andrew's Church, Toronto. Extract Minutes of the said Synod were read, referring the whole case to the Assembly, and praying the Assembly to appoint a Commission with Assembly powers to deal with the said Appeal, and to dispose finally of the same. Prsfessor McLaren and Mr. Andrew Wilson, appointed to support the Reference, were heard. It was moved and agreed to,—That in accordance with the request in this Reference from the Synod of Toronto and Kingston, respecting certain claims of the Rev. Dr. Barclay against the congregation of St. Andrew's, Toronto, the General Assembly appoints a small Commission to investigate the case, with power finally to issue it. Rev. Dr. Cook, Convener.

(2.) *Appeal—Rev. A. Bell and Session vs. Synod of Toronto and Kingston.*

Page 16. There was taken up an appeal of Mr. Bell, minister of St. Andrew's Church, Peterborough, on behalf of himself and the Session of said Church, against action of the Synod of Toronto and Kingston, in the matter of appeal by Mr. Bell and said Session from a decision of the Presbytery of Peterborough, in the case of an appeal to said Presbytery by Mr. Daniel Pentland, from action of the Session of the church aforesaid in refusing him a certificate of Church membership.

(3.) *Appeal—Presbytery P. E. I in re Rev. S. G. Lawson.*

The Assembly ordered that the papers and parties in this case be referred to the Judicial Committee.

(4.) *Report of Judicial Committee in re Lawson.*

Page 31, Mr. J. Laing, Chairman, brought up and read a first report, containing the finding of the Committee on the appeal of the Presbytery of Prince Edward Island from action of the Synod of the Maritime Provinces, in the case of the Rev. S. G. Lawson, in terms following:—

That the General Assembly sustain the appeal, express strongly their sense of the injury done to religion by the conduct and spirit of Mr. Lawson, and resolve that he be rebuked at the bar of the Assembly by the Moderator.

The Assembly, being deeply concerned that the ministry be not dishonoured, would solemnly warn Mr. Lawson that any repetition of the offence proved would necessarily incur censure still graver.

It was moved, seconded and carried by a large majority, that the report be received and adopted, and the Assembly decerned and ordered in terms of the recommendations of the report.

Mr J. C. Smith craved that his dissent from this decision of the Assembly be marked in the Minutes, for reasons to be afterwards given in.

Mr. Lawson here handed in a statement, expressing his submission to the decision of the Assembly, and requesting that it be engrossed in the Minutes. The Assembly granted Mr. Lawson's request, and ordered accordingly. The statement is as follows:—"Whilst firmly believing that if I had a new trial, where all matters could be considered—matters which were not before the Commission—my sentence would not have been so severe, yet I bow with all submission to the decision of this venerable Court. (Signed) S. G. Lawson."

In accordance with the decision foregoing, Mr. S. G. Lawson was called to the bar, and was solemnly rebuked by the Moderator.

(5.) *Report of Judicial Committee—Appeal Rev. A. Bell, et al.*

Page 48. The Chairman of the Judicial Committee, presented a second report embodying a finding in this case in terms following:—

The Judicial Committee have to report that they have carefully considered this case, and recommend that the following be the finding of the Assembly:—

The General Assembly, without either sustaining or dismissing the appeal, and in view of all circumstances of the case, instruct the Session of St. Andrew's Church, Peterborough, to give Mr. Pentland a certificate of his actual standing in the Church at the time of his first application, November 26, 1880. From this decision Mr. Laing dissented.

The parties being recalled, acquiesced.

Dr. Jardine, for the Committee, explained at length the grounds upon which they based the decision to which they had come. It was then moved and resolved: That the Assembly adopt the finding of the Committee, and the Assembly decerned, and ordered in terms thereof.

Mr. Thomas Sedgwick craved to have his dissent from this decision marked in the Minutes.

(6.) *Reasons of Dissent—Mr. J. C. Smith.*

Page 36. Mr. J. C. Smith, of Guelph, dissented from the action of the Assembly in the matter of the appeal of the Presbytery of Prince Edward Island from a decision of the Synod of the Maritime Provinces in the case of the Rev. S. G. Lawson, for the reasons following:—

1. Because the facts of the case, so far as brought out on the floor of the Assembly, do not, in my opinion, warrant the decision came to.

2. Because in a matter involving consequences of such gravity both to individuals and to the cause of religion generally, every legitimate means ought to be resorted to prior to the recording of any final judgment.

3. Because the party placed under the censure of the General Assembly signified his willingness to submit to the sentence of the Supreme Court *in the face of a written conviction on his part, and read in open Court,* to the effect that he solemnly believed that a commission, if appointed to examine further into the merits of the case, would, in all probability, see its way to a finding of less severity, and in more obvious harmony with the interests of justice.

The Assembly appointed a Committee to answer the reasons of dissent given in by Mr. Smith. Mr. Middlemiss, Convener.

(7.) *Answers to Reasons of Dissent.*

Answers were handed in and read by Mr. Middlemiss and the Assembly received the same and ordered them to be engrossed in the Minutes.

1. It is to be presumed that, in the opinion of those who voted in favor of the decision come to, the said decision was warranted by the facts as presented to the Assembly.

2. The Assembly's Committee having been put in possession of all the necessary facts of the case as between Mr. Lawson and the Presbytery against whose decision he appealed, it did not appear that there was any call to appoint a Commission, especially as they were fully convinced that it was in the interests of religion that the matter should be finally disposed of by this Assembly.

3. Mr. Lawson's statement of his conscientious convictions however solemnly made, after the decision of the Assembly was arrived at, cannot be a reason why that decision should not have been come to on the merits of the case as they are actually presented.

VI. PROCEDURE IN CHURCH COURTS.

1.—GENERAL RULES.

1. The Moderator takes the chair at the hour to which the Court stands adjourned, calls the members to order, and constitutes with prayer.

2. At the first assembling of a Court the roll is called, and the sederunt recorded; and members coming in afterwards have their names noted on reporting themselves to the clerk.

3. After the calling of the roll, the minutes of last ordinary meeting, and of all other meetings held in the interval, are read and sustained. In the case of the General Assembly, the minutes are read at the opening of each sederunt.

4. The Court then calls for all reports and other papers referring to business before it. It then prepares a docket, consisting of: (1) Business arising out of the minutes; (2) New business.

5. A member of a Church Court ought not to retire from a meeting without leave of the Moderator, or withdraw from attendance without the consent of the Court.

6. The Moderator names all Committees of the Court, unless their appointment be otherwise provided for by motion or rule; and, unless a Convener is specially named, the first named member of the committee is Convener. In case of his absence, or inability to act, the second named member takes his place.

7. The Courts of the Church—excepting the Session—are open Courts; but it is competent, on motion made, to sit with closed doors.

8. It is not competent for an inferior Court to erase or alter any part of its records, unlsss when ordered by a superior Court.

9. The Moderator takes care that the minutes correctly record the proceedings of the Court.

10. A Court for the greater freedom of discussion may resolve itself into a Committee of the Whole, when the Moderator leaves the chair, and a chairman is appointed. A separate minute of the proceedings is taken. When the Court resumes the Moderator takes the chair, and the chairman reports.

11. Clerks of Courts are entitled to charge for extracts of minutes, or copies of papers furnished to individuals, at the rate of ten cents for each hundred words, or fraction thereof.

2.—GENERAL STANDING ORDERS.

1. Every motion or amendment is presented in writing, as soon as it has been made to the Court.

2. A motion or amendment is not discussed until it has been duly seconded, and it cannot be altered or withdrawn without the permission of the Court.

3. When a motion and amendment are under discussion, it shall not be competent to introduce another motion, except as an amendment to the amendment; and the question of adopting or

rejecting such second amendment shall be decided before any other amendment is admissible. Action on amendments shall precede action on the original motion.

4. If a motion under debate contains two or more parts it shall, on the call of two members, at any time before the vote is finally taken, be divided and the question taken on each part.

5. A motion for adjournment is always in order.

6. When a subject is under debate no motion is competent, except to adjourn the debate, to lay on the table, to postpone, to commit, to amend, or to take an immediate vote on the motion or motions before the Court.

7. A motion to adjourn, to lay on the table, or to take an immediate vote, shall be decided without debate.

8. When the time for taking up an order of the day, or for adjournment, has arrived, the Moderator shall intimate the same, and a member who may then be addressing the Court shall have the right to the floor when the business interrupted is resumed

9. It is not competent for a Court to alter a decision, unless one-fourth of the members present during the sederunt at which the decision was given, vote in favor of reconsideration; and a motion for reconsideration is not in order if proposed by one who voted in the minority; and notice of it must be given at the sederunt preceding that at which it is to be proposed.

10. A member shall not speak more than once on any motion or amendment, unless with permission of the Court, or in explanation, or to correct mistakes.

11. A speaker is not to be interrupted unless upon a call to order. When so interrupted, he shall cease speaking until the point of order is decided. The member calling to order shall state the grounds on which the call has been made; but no other member is entitled to speak to the point of order, unless with the permission or at the request of the Moderator, with whom the decision on the point rests.

12. When a member, in speaking, utters language which another member regards as offensive and censurable, the latter may require that the words of the speaker be taken down; in

such case nothing further can proceed until either the speaker has withdrawn or satisfactorily explained the words complained of, or the words have been taken down by the clerk; the speaker shall then be allowed to proceed. Words thus taken down may afterwards be considered by the Court, on the complaint so made, as a matter of business, and the speaker, if found censurable, is dealt with as the offence may require; but the business of the Court, in hand when the words were uttered, may not at the time be interrupted beyond having the words taken down. A party in a cause, not being a member of the Court, may in similar circumstances claim like protection.

13. When a member arises to address the Court, the Moderator announces his name; and when two or more members rise at the same time, he decides which of them shall speak.

14. Any member who is dissatisfied with a decision of the Moderator may appeal to the Court; and the question on such appeal shall be decided without debate.

15. When the Court is ready for a vote, if there is only one motion before it, the Moderator shall put the question, "Shall this motion pass, 'yea' or 'nay'?" If a motion and amendment are before the Court he shall put the question, "Shall the motion be amended as proposed?" And afterwards the motion, or the motion as amended, as the case may be, shall be put "'yea' or 'nay'?" Before a vote is taken the doors are closed.

16. Ordinarily, a vote is taken by the members rising in their places, on the call of the Moderator. It is competent for two members to require the vote to be taken on a main motion by calling the roll, or to have the state of any vote recorded.

17. It is not competent for any committee to sit during the time when the Court is sitting, without leave.

18. The clerk of a higher Court, on the receipt of papers sent up from a lower Court, endorses thereon the date of receipt, numbers the papers and authenticates the same by his signature or initials.

18. The Clerks of Church Courts shall send a copy of all documents printed by the authority of their courts to the library of each college connected with the Church.

3.—STANDING ORDERS OF THE ASSEMBLY.

1. Reports of ordinations, inductions, licensure, deaths, demissions, suspensions, depositions of ministers, and of the erection or dissolution of congregations within the respective Synods, shall be sent up by the clerks of these Courts so as to be in the hands of the clerk of Assembly at least eight days before the Assembly meets.

2. A large portion of the second sederunt, and such portion of other diets as the Moderator of Assembly may think proper, shall be spent in devotional services.

3. The clerks of the Assembly, together with those of Synods and Presbyteries who may be commissioners, are to meet as a Committee on Business, and arrange all such business as may be requisite previous to the first diet of the annual meeting of the Assembly. This committee, together with such members as may be appointed by the Assembly, constitute the Committee on Bills and Overtures, which acts also as the Committee on Business, to arrange from time to time the order of business to be brought before the Court.

4. After the arrangement of business has been reported by the Committee on Bills and Overtures, and sanctioned by the Assembly, the clerks of the Assembly shall cause a docket of business to be printed, for the information of members.

5 All papers shall be transmitted to one of the clerks of Assembly at least eight days before the meeting of Assembly, and all such papers shall pass through the Committee on Bills and Overtures before presentation to the Assembly.

6. In order that all documents coming before the Assembly may be preserved in a form convenient for reference, reports, overtures, references, appeals, extracts of minutes, and all other matters whatsoever, intended to be submitted to the Assembly, shall be written on foolscap paper on one side only, and with a margin on the left hand of not less than two inches. For the sake of securing fully the ends of justice, parties who have causes to bring before the Assembly, are recommended to print copies of all papers in the cause in numbers sufficient for the use of members, and in a shape suitable for binding along with the printed minutes of the Assembly.

7. The conveners of standing committees shall give in their annual reports to the Committee on Bills and Overtures, not later than the second sederunt of the meeting of the Assembly. These must be in printed form, in a shape suitable for binding along with the printed minutes of Assembly.

8. The Assembly shall appoint a committee, of not less than two from each Synod, and not more than four from any one Synod, to nominate members for the standing committees of the Assembly.

THE CHURCH—ITS COLLEGES.

UNION RESOLUTION.

MONTREAL, 1875, p. 5. The aforesaid Churches shall enter into union with the Theological and Literary Institutions which they now have; and application shall be made to Parliament for such legislation as shall bring Queen's University and College, Knox College, the Presbyterian College, Montreal, Morrin College, Quebec and the Theological Hall at Halifax into relations to the United Church similar to those which they now hold to their respective Churches, and to preserve their corporate existence, government and functions, on terms and conditions like to those under which they now exist; but the United Church shall not be required to elect Trustees for an Arts' Department in any of the Colleges above-named.

I. QUEEN'S UNIVERSITY AND COLLEGE.

(Kingston, Ontario.)

1. HISTORICAL STATEMENT.

The Presbyterian Church in connection with the Church of Scotland at its first organization in Canada, was solicitous for the education of candidates for the Ministry. In 1832 an Overture was presented to the Synod urging that an application be made to the Government of Upper Canada to found a professorship of Theology in connection with the projected King's University, or, in the event of refusal or delay, that the Synod should itself adopt a permanent measure for the education of Ministers. For three years efforts were earnestly made to secure this object by memorials both to the Home and Imperial Governments, to all of which courteous and diplomatic answers were given but no real inclination shown to grant the request. The Church of England meanwhile strove to secure for itself the entire control of the large endowments set apart for University Education.

Despairing of any benefit from King's University, a Committee of Synod reported five reasons for immediate action: 1, that Ministers educated in the Colony would have advantages over strangers; 2, that some young men are seeking to enter the University whom a Scottish education would debar; 3, the scanty supply of Ministers from Scotland necessitated an immediate commencement; 4, that the sooner a College is planted the more rapidly it will grow; and 5, no other Church exacts a British education for its Ministers. It was therefore urged that a College should at once be created suitable for present wants and capable of expansion, and that an effort be made to raise an endowment of $20,000. A committee was appointed to mature a scheme for the foundation of a Collegiate Institution for Theological Education which resulted in an appeal to the mother Church for advice and aid, an injunction to Presbyteries to procure subscriptions for an endowment, and to assist in the education of young men who might offer themselves for the Ministry.

In 1837 a further effort was made to secure a Theological professorship in King's University, a delegate was even sent to England for the purpose, but all proved in vain. Finally the Synod declared that they could not, considering the extreme urgency of the case, delay any longer to undertake the education of candidates for the Holy Ministry in these provinces, and appointed a committee to report a plan by which the declaration might be carried into effect. A plan was accordingly transmitted to the Presbyteries for this purpose, but the Commission of 1838 seem to have been discouraged by the troubled condition of the country, and deemed it inexpedient to prosecute the work further. In 1839 the Colonial Society of Scotland while deprecating any further application to the government, recommended voluntary effort and offered £1,000 sterling to aid. As yet the views of the Canadian Church were limited to a Theological Institute, under an apprehension that funds for anything more could not be obtained. It was nevertheless thought by many that all the departments of clerical education should be aimed at under the control of the Synod. An Act of incorporation was accordingly sought, and an elaborate plan published of twenty-three sections embracing courses of Literary, Philosophical and Theological Education, more extensive than even the curricula of the Scottish Colleges, and providing for frequent examinations of students by Presbyteries. Before following out this enlightened scheme, another effort was made to secure the endowment of a Theological chair in King's University which had no result. An application was made to the Legislature for an Act of incorporation for a College under the corporate name of the "Trustees of St Andrew's College of Canada," with power to apply funds "for the sustentation of a Bursar of Divinity in the University of King's College as soon as a Theological professorship shall be established therein for the Church of Scotland." This Bill, was however dropped. Meanwhile a Committee of the Assembly in Scotland offered $150 per annum to each of five young men to be educated in Scotland who should be recommended by the Canadian Synod and receive a similar amount from them. This offer while gratefully acknowledged was not approved of, but a Bill was prepared for the establishment of an Institution in Kingston to be known as "the Scottish Presbyterian College" and it was resolved to prosecute the collection of subscriptions with the two-fold object of educating Ministers and providing a liberal education for other professions commencing with two professors and two tutors. The Commission of Synod pledged itself to raise £5,000 within six months as an endowment for one professor, the parent Church was expected to contribute another £5,000, and the Church at large £30,000, for buildings library, &c. This scheme called forth great enthusiasm and much liberality. The aim was "to establish a University in which, while one of its important objects should be the training of Ministers of the Gospel to supply the long crying destitution of this land, there would also be given to our youth the fullest access to the cultivation of all the branches of a literary and scientific education. The University to be a Presbyterian University, to belong to the Presbyterian Church, and its education to be based on religious principles." In 1839, a Bill was accordingly presented to the Legislature entitled: "An Act for the establishment of a College at Kingston by the name and style of the University of Queen's College." This Act bound the Institution to the doctrines of the Confession of Faith and to the Presbyterian Church with powers to appoint Professors and Tutors and to grant degrees. A doubt existing as to the propriety of granting the name without the prior consent of Her Majesty, the title was changed to the "University at Kingston." A Royal Charter was, however, graciously granted in 1841, and the University received its present honored name.

It was now agreed to raise £5,000 in Canada, which, with another £5,000 from the parent Church, would be sufficient to begin with. The Colonial Committee of the Church of Scotland, having received authority by the charter to do so, appointed the Rev. Dr. Liddell, of Lady Glenorchy's Church, Edinburgh, as the first Principal, even more promptly than was expected in Canada. He arrived in Kingston at the end of December, 1841, and although disappointed at finding that no preparations had been made—no building, no students, no anything, but a charter, not, however, discouraged, he resolved to commence immediately. A house was rented, the Rev. P.C. Campbell, of Brockville, was appointed classical professor, and on the 7th March, 1842, a commencement was made, with ten advanced students, and as many more in the Arts. After the first session the College removed to more commodious premises, though nothing better than a dwelling house opposite St. Andrew's Church; when, also, the venerable Professor Williamson was added to the staff, as teacher of Mathematics. In 1842 the Synod appointed that every Professor in Queen's College being an ordained Minister of the Church, should be a constituent member of the Presbytery of Kingston, and as such, entitled to sit in all meetings of the Synod. So closely, too, was the Institution related to the Church that each of its congregations had power to nominate members from whom Trustees should be elected. Tenacious, however, of their promised interest in King's University, since become the University of Toronto, the Synod in 1843 proposed the transfer of Queen's to Toronto, and to unite with King's, so as to form one University for Ontario. Happily the scheme failed, and Queen's became, as it is now, the University of the Presbyterian Church of Canada. In 1846, Principal Liddell resigned his position and returned to Scotland, and Dr. Machar was appointed in his place, and discharged its duties along with the pastorate of St. Andrew's Church for the next ten years. At the same time, Professor Campbell, accepted a charge in Scotland, and subsequently became Principal of the University of Aberdeen. Professor George Romanes and Dr. Urquhart were, however, added to the staff. The University question was still unsettled, and hopes were entertained that the claims of the Church of Scotland would not be overlooked; but the tendency of political feeling was not favorable, and in 1849 the Bill establishing the present University of Toronto crushed all expectations that any part of the University endowments would be assigned to educational institutions belonging to any of the churches of the province. Henceforth the friends of Queen's resolved to place the University College on a more efficient footing. In 1850, the Commission of

Synod issued a vigorous address to the Church and country in its behalf, and resolved that henceforth it should be one of the permanent schemes of the Church, and supported by an annual collection. This address took bold grounds of objections to the University College, as not meeting the wants and just expectations of the Church and country, declared it to be the imperative duty of the Presbyterian Church to maintain Queen's College and University as an Institution vital to the welfare of both Church and country; that there might be in this great Province at least one University where literary and sicentific instruction should be combined with religion. A new interest was thus awakened in Queen's, and in 1854 the Summer Hill property on which the College now stands was purchased for £6,000. On the resignation of Dr. Machar in 1856, Dr. Cook, of Quebec, accepted the position of Principal and Professor of Theology for a time, and Professors Weir, Lawson and Mowat were subsequently added to the staff. In 1859, the Rev. Dr. Leitch was secured as Principal, and under his care the College enjoyed a growing prosperity. Another vigorous attempt was, however, made to share in the surplus revenues of University College, but this also failed, and henceforth the Institution cast itself on the liberality of its constituents. Not deterred by difficulties, the faculties of Theology, Arts, Medicine and Law, originally contemplated by its founders were instituted, and met with gratifying prosperity; the revenues were found adequate, its bursaries liberally increased, and its literary curriculum was assimilated to the Colleges of Scotland. In 1864, Dr. Leitch in the midst of his usefulness died at Kingston, in the 49th year of his age, deeply regretted. The Rev. Dr. Snodgrass, then Minister of St. Paul's Church, Montreal, was appointed his successor. In 1865, Professor Murray, in the department of Logic; and in 1866, the late and lamented Professor Mackerras in Classics, were added to the staff, and the curriculum in Arts was extended to four years. At this time, also, the Royal College of Physicians and Surgeons having obtained a charter was affiliated with Queen's and its own medical faculty was given up. In 1867 the College suffered a severe loss by the suspension of the Commercial Bank, by which its endowments were reduced from $32,000 to $10,700, and its income from $1,950 to $856, from this source, following upon which was the withdrawal of the annual parliamentary grant of $5,000. In these circumstances an earnest appeal to the Church and the country was made and a resolution adopted to maintain the University at all hazards and to meet its losses by raising an endowment of $100,000. The Church so earnestly responded to this appeal that in 1873 an endowment was obtained nearly equal to the whole lost revenue, and the permanency and prosperity of the University secured. The staff was subsequently enlarged, the faculties maintained with efficiency, and the number of students augmented.

Then came the Union carrying the College with it. Legislation was readily obtained from the Provincial Assembly in 1875, and from the Dominion Parliament in 1881, which placed Queen's University and College, into relation with the United Church similar to that which it held to the Church by which it was founded and fostered. In 1877, after a period of thirteen years, of arduous and successful labor for which he received the thanks of the Church, Principal Snodgrass, resigned his office and accepted an important charge in Scotland. To the vacant position Rev. Geo. M. Grant, M. A., D. D., was appointed, under whose wise and vigorous administration the present splendid buildings have been erected and the endowments largely increased. The curriculum of Arts has also been skillfully adapted to the requirements of modern scholarship, its classes and honors opened to ladies, and its faculties well equipped with teachers of eminence in their several departments.

The Presbyterian Church, of Canada, has thus obtained by the auspicious Union an University of its own which cannot fail to exert a powerful influence for good on the higher education of the Dominion.

2. UNIVERSITY OFFICERS.

Board of Trustees.

C. F. IRELAND, Esq., Kingston, Secretary-Treasurer.

Chancellor.

SANDFORD FLEMING, Esq., C.E., C.M.G.

Principal and Vice-Chancellor.

VERY REV. GEORGE MUNRO GRANT, M.A., D.D.

Vice-Principal.

REV. JAMES WILLIAMSON, M.A., L.L.D.

Registrar.

REV. GEORGE BELL, B.A., L.L.D.

College Staff.

I.—In Divinity.

The Principal.................... *Primarius Professor of Divinity*
Rev. John B. Mowat, M.A..... *Professor of Hebrew and Biblical Criticism.*
Rev. James Carmichael, (King). *Lecturer on Church History.*
Rev. Donald Ross, B.D.......... *Lecturer on Apologetics.*
——————— .... *Watkins Lecturer on Elocution.*

II.—In Arts.

Rev. J. Williamson, M. A., LL.D. *Professor of Astronomy.*
Rev. John B. Mowat, M. A..... *Professor of Hebrew*
Nathan F. Dupuis, M. A., F. B. S., Edin..................... *Professor of Mathematics.*
George McGowan................ *Professor of Chemistry.*
Rev. George D. Ferguson, B. A.. *Professor of History and English Language and Literature*
John Watson, M.A., L.L.D..... *Professor of Logic, Mental and Moral Philosophy and Political Economy.*
John Fletcher, B. A., Oxon.... *Professor of Classical Literature*
L. H. Marshal, M.A., F.R.S.C.. *Professor of Physics.*
Rev. Alex. B. Nicholson, B. A.. *Lecturer on Modern Languages and Assistant to Professor of Classics.*
Rev. James Fowler, M A....... *Lecturer on Natural Science.*
Rev. R. Campbell, M. A. (Renfrew)... .. .. *Lecturer on Political Economy.*

Registrar of University Council.

Archibald P. Knight, M. A.

Observatory Board.

The Principal, Professor Williamson, M. Flanagan, Esq.

Director of Observatory.

Professor of Astronomy.

Curators of the Library.

The Principal, Professors Mowat and Fletcher.

Librarian.
REV. G. BELL, L.L.D.

Curators of Museum.
Lecturer on Natural Science and DR. BELL.

Examiners in Gaelic.
EVAN MACCOLL, Esq., R. M. ROSE, Esq., Rev. A. B. NICHOLSON, B. A

3. UNIVERSITY COUNCIL.

The Council consists of the Chancellor, the Trustees, the members of the Senate, and thirty-three elective members.

The Chancellor is elected by the Council, except when two or more candidates are nominated, in which case the election is by registered graduates and alumni. He holds office for three years, and, as highest officer of the University, presides at meetings of Council and Convocation, and at Statutory meetings of Senate. In his absence he is represented by the Vice-Chancellor.

Of the elective members seven retire annually, except in every fifth year, when only five retire. Successors are elected by registered graduates and alumni. Retiring members may be re-elected.

The Council has power to discuss all questions relating to the College and its welfare, to make representations of its views to the Senate or the Board of Trustees, to decide on proposals for affiliation, and to arrange all matters pertaining to the installation of Chancellor, its own meetings and business, the meetings and proceedings of Convocation, and the fees for membership, registration and voting.

Convocation for the conferring of degrees, etc., is held upon the last Wednesday of April, in each year.

4. REGULATIONS AFFECTING STUDENTS.

1. Every Student shall, before Matriculation, produce a certificate of character from his Minister, or some respectable person competent to grant such certificate, and at the time of his Matriculation shall subscribe the following declaration:—

"I, ———, being now admitted a Student of Queen's College, do hereby sincerely and solemnly declare and promise that I shall at all times render due respect and obedience to the Principal, Professors, and other authorities of the

University, and strictly observe the Laws and Statutes thereof; that I shall give a regular attendance at my classes, and shall apply myself diligently to the studies in which I am engaged, and perform to the utmost of my power the exercises prescribed; that I shall conduct myself in a courteous and p aceable manner towards my fellow Students; and that I shall always maintain and defend the rights and privileges of the University, and never seek, in any way or manner, the hurt or prejudice thereof."

2. All Students must have their names and other particulars entered annually in the University Register, and when presenting themselves for Registration must produce the Treasurers receipt for fees.

3. On registering, Students shall receive tickets admitting them to the Classes which they propose to attend,

4. The ticket for each Class must be presented to the Professor before the Student can have his name entered in the roll book

5. This ticket must be presented to the Professor at the close of his course of lectures, when it will be exchanged for a certified class ticket.

6. Graduates and Under-graduates in Arts, when attending prayers, their several classes, or any College meeting, shall wear the academic costume prescribed by the College Senate.

7. At five minutes past the hour of meeting the door of the class-room shall be locked, after which the roll shall be called.

8. Students absenting themselves from any class-meeting must explain the cause of their absence to the Professor in writing.

9. The use of tobacco in any form, and unnecessary noises during class hours, within the College Building, shall not be allowed.

10. Insubordination, immoral conduct either in or out of College, gross neglect of study, refusal to perform the appointed exercises, breach of College regulations, injury to College property, and all offences of a similar kind, shall render a Student liable to the infliction of a penalty proportionate to the offence. The penalties which the College Senate may inflict shall be such as the following:—

(1). Fines not exceeding, in any one case, ten dollars.

(2). A note of disapprobation in the class certificate.

(3). Rustication for a definate period.

(4). Degradation from the rank of Under-graduate.

(5), Forfeiture of right to a degree.

(6). Expulsion.

11. Students who do not attend four-fifths of the whole number of class-meetings in a session, shall not be regarded as having attended a full session, unless the Senate, for sufficient reasons, record a decision to the contrary.

12. When applying for examination in any subject the Student must present to the Senate his certified class ticket.

13. After the Pass Examinations the Registrar shall certify on the back of the class-ticket the University standing of the Student. The Candidate for Graduation must present to the Senate the ticket so certified.

14. All intending Candidates must, at such time as the Senate shall appoint, intimate in writing to the Secretary of the Senate the particular examinations at which they propose to appear, and the Honours, if any, for which they mean to compete; and before taking their places at the examination they must pay to the Secretary of the Senate the examination fee specified in the Calendar.

15. No Candidate shall be allowed to bring any book or paper to the examination.

16. No communication of any kind, by conversation, exchanging of notes, or any other means, shall be allowed to pass from one Candidate to another during the examination. Each Candidate is expected to take particular care not to distract in any way the attention of other Candidates.

17. In each of the departments of examination written questions shall be set, to which written answers shall be given in presence of the Examiners.

18. The asking of information from Examiners respecting the contents of Examination Papers placed in the hands of Candidates shall be discouraged, and any Examiner may intimate his entire disallowance of it. An explanation considered necessary shall not be made to one Candidate without being made in the same terms to all.

19. If any Candidate be found consulting a book or note,

copying another Candidate's paper. or using any other unfair means of answering the questions proposed, he shall be required at once to leave the room, and shall not be permitted to appear at any remaining part of the examination, nor shall any papers which he may have before given in be sustained. Cases of this nature shall be reported to the Senate, and the Senate shall deal with them as very grave offences.

Scholarships.

20.—The Senate shall award all Scholarships in the Arts, Law and Theological Faculties, by examinations, subject only to the conditions of the founders and the regulations of the Board of Trustees.

21. The subjects of examination and all special conditions of award shall be published annually in the Calendar, and shall be strictly adhered to.

22. The minimum qualification for holding a Scholarship shall be the obtaining of one-half of the whole number of marks allotted to the subject or subjects upon which the Scholarship is awarded. All Candidates who are not Intrants, must be Pass men of the last preceding session of their course.

23. No Student shall hold two Scholarships.

24. When a Student gains several Scholarships of unequal amounts he shall hold the most valuable one, and the rest shall be awarded to the other competitors in the order of merit.

25. Suitable mention shall be made in the Calendar of the honour of gaining more Scholarships than one.

Library.

26.—No Student is entitled to borrow or consult books until he produces his registration ticket.

27. A Student having deposited his registration ticket with the Librarian is entitled to borrow books. The owner may redeem his ticket at any time by returning all books borrowed and paying all fines or charges incurred. All tickets must be redeemed before the close of the session.

28. A Student may have in his possession at any one time only three volumes, unless the Librarian, for sufficient reasons, may see fit to allow him to borrow more.

29. A volume can be retained only 14 days, and it must invariably be returned at the expiration of that period. But it may be re-borrowed after remaining in the Library for one day, if not asked for in the meantime by some other person than the former borrower.

30. A Student desiring a volume already loaned shall leave the usual check for the same, and he shall then have the first claim upon the volume. Such volume, when returned, shall be charged to his account for three days, when, if he fails to claim it, it shall be loaned to the first applicant thereafter.

31. For every volume retained beyond the stipulated time the borrower shall pay a fine of three cents per day for every day it is so retained. But for every volume so retained, after having been notified by the Librarian, he shall pay a fine of fifty cents per day for each day it is retained after the notification.

32 Sickness or absence may be a reason for relaxing a fine, at the judgment of the Librarian.

33. If a volume become due upon a holiday it shall be held to be due on the first class day thereafter.

34. Graduates, who are not Students, may obtain the privileges of the Library upon the payment of three dollars per annum.

35. Dictionaries, Gazetteers, Encyclopedias, Atlases and other works of reference, may be consulted in the Reading Room, but cannot be taken out of the building.

36. Writing or marking in a borrowed book, unless for the purpose of correcting typographical errors, is strictly forbidden, and it will render the offender liable to have his Library privileges cancelled.

37. No borrowed book shall be taken into class to be used as a class-book.

Reading Room.

38.—The Registrar shall, for a fee of twenty-five cents, issue, to any registered Student applying, a check entitling him to take out books for consultation in the Reading Room. The holder, when he applies for a book for consultation is to deposit his check with the Librarian, and is to redeem it by the return of the volume consulted.

39. Any person, as determined by the judgment of the Librarian, may be allowed to consult books in the Reading Room, upon the payment of one dollar per annum.

40. A book received for consultation in the Reading Room is not to be taken away unless by the consent of the Librarian.

41. All noise in the Reading Room is strictly prohibited.

42. Any person violating the two preceding regulations renders himself liable, upon the first offence, to such fine, not exceeding fifty cents, as the Librarian may see fit to impose, and for subsequent offences, to having his Reading Room ticket cancelled.

43. Attendance at Church.—All Students must attend the Churches to which they profess to belong, and produce certificates of attendance from their clergymen when required.

44. Boarding.—No Student is allowed to board or lodge in any house not approved of by the Senate, except by permission of parents or guardians given in writing. Information as to approved houses may be obtained from the Registrar. The expense of suitable boarding is moderate.

45. Fees.—The following fees payable strictly in advance—class fees on University Day (16th October); graduation fees before Convocation Day :—

The classes of Chemistry and Physics, each per session		$12 00
Any other class, any number of sessions		6 00
Registration and Library, per session		4 00
Apparatus, per session		2 00
Matriculation Examination		1 00
Pass Examination		2 00
Doctor of Science (D. Sc.) Graduation Fee		50 00
Bachelor of Arts (B.A.)	"	10 00
Bachelor of Laws (LL.B.)	"	10 00
Doctor of Medicine (M.D.)	"	30 00
Master of Arts (M.A.)	"	20 00
Bachelor of Divinity (B.D.)	"	20 00
Admission *ad eundem gradum*, B.A.		10 00
" " " M.A.		20 00

5. FACULTY OF THEOLOGY AND CURRICULUM.

Matriculation and pass examination begin on 1st November.

The prescribed order of classes must be observed by all Students who are candidates for the degree of Bachelor of Divinity.

(1.) *Divinity.*

Lectures on the Evidences of Religion natural and revealed, including the canonicity, authenticity, genuineness and credibility of the Biblical Records; the Inspiration and Authority of the Scriptures; Systematic Theology; the Pastoral Office; and Homiletics—with prelections and examinations on Hill's Lectures in Divinity, Butler's Analogy, and Greek Testament for Doctrinal Exegesis. Students have opportunities of conducting devotional exercises, practising pulpit elocution, and performing missionary work. The course extends over three sessions, that of 1881-82 being the first in order.

(2.) *Hebrew and Chaldee.*

First year.—Wolfe's Hebrew Grammar. Gen. XIV—XVIII. Josh. VIII—X. Job, I., II. 1 Sam. I., IV. Ps. XXXV—L. Translations into Hebrew.

Second year.—Gesenius' Hebrew Grammer. Exod. XXXII—XXXIV. Num. XI., XII. Jer. XII—XIV. Ps. L—LXVII. Is. XL., XLI. Prov. XXX., XXXI. Translations into Hebrew.

Third year.—Gesenius' Hebrew Grammar. Winer's Chaldee Grammar. Ps. CX—CXIX. Isaiah XL—LI. Dan. II., III. Ezra. IV , V.

(3.) *Biblical Criticism.*

Hebrews, James, I., II., III., John in Greek. Biblical Hermeneutics Lectures.

(4.) *Apologetics.*

Lecturer for the session.

(5.) *Church History.*

Council of Nice to the Reformation. Lecturer for the session.

The Church requires the following discourses to be delivered during the course:—Homily; Lecture and Greek Exercise; Sermon and Hebrew Exercise.

(6.) *Matriculation Examination.*

Westminster Confession; Hill's Lectures, Bk. I.; Gospel by Mark in Greek and English; Examination in Hebrew on Regular Verbs and Pronouns, and Genesis, ch. I., with analysis of the Regular Verbs and Pronouns contained in it.

(7.) *Pass Examinations.*

On the work of the session.

6. DEGREE OF BACHELOR OF DIVINITY.

(1) *Regulations.*

1.—Candidates for the Degree of Bachelor of Divinity (B.D.,) must be graduates in Arts of this University, or of a University whose degrees are recognized for this purpose by the Senate.

2.—The degree shall not be conferred until the Candidate has completed his Theological Curriculum, with a view to the ministry in the Church to which he belongs, and has passed a satisfactory examination in the branches of Theology taught in this University.

3.—The subjects of examination shall be in two departments, the *first* embracing—(1) Hebrew and (2) the Evidences of Religion and the Inspiration of Scripture; and the *second* embracing —(1) Church History, (2) Biblical Criticism, and (3) Systematic Theology.

4.—Candidates who have completed their Theological course may be examined in either of these departments, and may defer their examination in the other department, provided there be not a greater interval than two years between their two examinations.

5.—Students who have completed all the sessions but one of their Theological course, may be admitted to examination in the first department.

6.—A Candidate may, subject to the preceding regulations, appear at any University examination in Theology, provided he gives two weeks' notice of his intention to the Registrar.

7.—When a Student who is a candidate for the degree, shall obtain at a pass examination on any subject two-thirds of the marks allotted to the subject, he may, on recommendation of the examiner, be exempted from further examination on that subject.

(2.) *Subjects of Examination.*

First Department.—1. Evidences of religion, and Inspiration of Scripture.

2. Hebrew, Isaiah, xl—lxvi. Chaldee, Daniel, ii., iii.

Second Department.—1. Church History—Centuries, i—iii; the Reformation; the Church in Scotland.

2. Biblical Criticism—Epistle to Romans in Greek; Biblical Hermeneutics; Hammonds' Textual Criticism of New Testament. Introduction to Pentateuch and Gospel of John.

3. Systematic Theology—Person of Christ, Doctrine of Sin, Doctrine of the Atonement, Justification, Work of the Holy Spirit.

The following books may be consulted:—Paley's Evidences. Butler's Analogy, Tulloch's Burnett Prize on Theism, Moxley's Bampton Lectures on Miracles, Trench on the Miracles (preliminary essay); Westcott on the Canon of the New Testament; Lee on Inspiration; Dorner on the Person of Christ; Liddon's Bampton Lectures on our Lord's Divinity; Tulloch on the Christian Doctrine of Sin; Crawford on the Atonement; Grotius de satisfactione Christi; Hill's Lectures in Divinity; Christian Dogmatics, (Van Oosterzee's and Martensen's); Keil on the Old Testament, and Bleek on the New Testament; Killen's Old Catholic Church; Fisher's History of the Reformation; Biblical Hermeneutics (Elliott and Harsha.)

STUDENTS' MISSIONARY ASSOCIATION.

This Association holds a weekly meeting on Saturday morning, in the Divinity class-room. In addition to devotional exercises and the ordinary business of the Association, reports are read by members from time to time, respecting the fields occupied by them during the preceding summer under the Home Mission Board of the General Assembly. A Sabbath morning prayer meeting is held in the classical room under the management of the Association. The Association also assists the Convener of the Presbytery's Home Mission Committee in filling appointments for Sabbath day services in the neighborhood of Kingston.

7. SCHOLARSHIPS IN ARTS.

(1.) *Conditions.*

Scholarships in Arts have *endowment nominations* connected with them, securing exemption from class fees for *one* session, and thereby adding from $18 to $24 to the given value of each.

Any student who passes in English is eligible for a scholarship; but scholarships marked *close* can be held only by students having in view the ministry of the Presbyterian Church, being given by their founders upon that condition.

Scholarships awarded upon matriculation examinations are tenable during the first session, and those awarded upon sessional examinations are tenable during the following session, except open scholarships, gained by students in the last year of their course in Arts, which are paid at once.

Successful candidates for scholarships must make *at least* two-thirds the number of marks allotted to the subject or subjects upon which the scholarship is awarded.

(2.) *Junior Matriculation.*

Mackerras' Memorial.—Value, $100. Awarded upon the marticulation examinations in Latin and Greek.

Gunn.—Value, $100. Awarded upon the matriculation examination for General Proficiency.

Watkins.—Value, $80. Awarded upon the matriculation examination in Classics, Mathematics and English, and tenable only by candidates who have spent one year at the Kingston Collegiate Institute.

Grant.—Value, $60. Awarded to the matriculant who passes the best examination in English Composition.

Leitch Memorial No. 1.—Value, $57. Awarded upon the matriculation examination in Mathematics.

Rankine. (Close.)—Value $55. Awarded upon the matriculation examination in English.

Mowat.—Value, $50. Awarded to the best candidate at a special oral examination on Arithmetic. Competition will take place on 2nd October.

Marion Stewart McDonald.—Value, $100. Given to a deserving student or students from Glengarry Co., Ont., and awarded after the matriculation examination.

M. C. Cameron.—Value, $60. Given to the best Gælic scholar, reader or speaker. The examination takes place after the matriculation examinations.

(3.) *Awarded on Sessional Examinations.*

St. Andrew's Church, Toronto. (Close).—Value, $50. Awarded upon the sessional examination in Senior Greek.

Toronto. (Close.)—Value, $60. Awarded upon the sessional examination in Junior Physics.

Class Memorial. (Close)—Value, $35. Awarded upon the sessional examination in Junior Mathematics.

McIntyre. (Close.)—Value, $50. Awarded upon the sessional examination in Senior Mathematics.

Church, No. 1. (Close.)—Value, $65. Awarded upon the sessional examination in Junior Greek.

Church, No. 2. (Close.)—Value, $60. Awarded upon the sessional examination in Rhetoric and English Literature.

Buchan, No. 1. (Close.)—Value, $50. Awarded upon the sessional examination in Senior Philosophy (Mental and Moral). Tenable during the first year in Theology.

Buchan, No. 2. (Close.)—Value, $100. Awarded upon the sessional examination in Senior Physics. Tenable during the first year in Theology.

McNab and Horton. (Close.)—Value, $50. Awarded upon the sessional examination in Senior Chemistry.

McGillivray.—Value, $50. Awarded upon the sessional examination in Junior Latin.

Grant.—Value, $60. Awarded upon the sessional examination in Junior Chemistry.

Nickle.—Value, $50. Awarded upon the sessional examination in Natural Science.

Cataraqui.—Value, $50. Awarded upon the sessional examination in History.

Kingston. Ladies—Value, $35. Awarded upon the sessional examinations in Senior French and German.

8. SCHOLARSHIPS IN THEOLOGY.

(1.) *Matriculation.*

David Strathern Dow.—Value, $100.

Dominion.—Value, $80. Open to students belonging to any Presbyterian Church in the Dominion,

Buchan, No. 3.—Value, $75.

Church of Scotland, No. 1.—Value, $60.

Church of Scotland, No. 2.—Value, $50.

(2.) *Awarded at Close of Session.*

Anderson.—Value, $50. Awarded upon the sessional examination of the first year,

Hugh McLennan.—Value, $25. Awarded upon the best sessional examination in Church History.

Church of Scotland, No. 3.—Value, $50. Awarded upon the sessional examinations of the first year.

Mackerras' Memorial Prize.—Value, $25 in books. Awarded upon the sessional examination in Greek Testament Exegesis.

Leitch Memorial, No. 2.—Value, $80. Awarded upon a sessional examination, and tenable through three successive years, should the successful candidate, after the completion of his Theological curriculum at this University attend a Scottish University. Candidates must have the degrees of B.A. The next competition will take place in April, 1884 or 1886. Subjects of examination:—the Epistles to Romans and Hebrews, Butler's Analogy, and the Theological Lectures of the session.

Spence.—Value, $60. Awarded upon the sessional examinations at the close of the first year in Theology. The next competition will take place in 1884.

(3.) *Church Bursaries.*

These are awarded to deserving students, who have not obtained scholarships, and who are preparing for the ministry of the Presbyterian Church in Canada. Recipients must sign a written obligation to repay the money should they change their intention with regard to the ministry. Recommendations accompanying contributions for the benefit of particular students, whether matriculants or not, are duly observed.

9. UNIVERSITY PRIZES.

These are prizes in money for literary articles, essays, etc., as specified under each particular prize. The prizes are given at Convocation.

Conditions of Competition.

1. Competitive papers (except for Thorburn, which see) must be given in to the Secretary of the Senate not later than the 2nd November.

2. Each paper is to bear a motto, instead of the author's name, and to have attached to it a sealed envelope, bearing the same motto and containing a written declaration over the author's signature, to the effect that it is his unaided composition.

3. The envelopes attached to successful papers shall be opened and the writers' names made known at the closing Convocation of the session.

4. The best productions must be reported by the examiners to be of sufficient merit.

5. All successful productions shall be the property of the University, and shall be at the disposal of the Senate.

Lewis.—Value $25. Given for the best lecture on Luke xviii., 9-14 inclusive. Open to students of Theology.

Macpherson—Value $25. For the best essay on the Influence of Britain on India. Open to registered students.

Carmichael—Value $25. For the best essay on the Spectroscope and Spectrum Analysis. Open to registered students of the present or preceding session.

MacLennan.—Value $25. For the best essay on Recent English Psychology. Open to registered students of the present or preceding session.

Two prizes, each of the value of ten dollars in books, will be annually offered for competition among under-graduates, for the best composition in Latin and Greek prose respectively, on subjects prescribed.

Chancellor's Essays.—Two prizes of $50 each ; to be awarded for the best English essays on subjects prescribed. To be sent in to the University Registrar on or before University Day. If the essays be not of sufficient merit, the prizes will be open for another competition:

Thorburn.—Value $40. Historical. To be prescribed.

10. MEDALS.

No Gold Medal will be awarded to any candidate who fails to obtain three-fourths of the whole number of marks. No Silver Medal will be awarded to any candidate who fails to obtain at least two-thirds of the whole number of the marks.

Prince of Wales' Gold Medal in Classics.—For the best examination on the honour work in Latin and Greek. Open to all registered students.

Carruthers' Gold Medal in Mathematics.—For the best examination on the honour work in Mathematics. Open to all registered students.

Carruthers' Gold Medal in Chemistry.—For the best examination on the honour work in chemistry. Open to all registered students.

The Mayor's Gold Medal in Mental and Moral Philosophy.—For the best examination on the honour work in Mental and Moral Philosophy, as prescribed for the session. Open to all under-graduates or graduates taking the honour work in those subjects.

Chancellor's Gold Medal in History, and English Language and Literature.—For the best examination on the honour work in those subjects, with an essay on Representative Government. Open to undergraduates or graduates taking the honour work.

Graduates' Gold Medal in Political Economy.—For the best examination on the honour work in Political Economy. Open to students attending classes in Arts, Law, Medicine or Theology.

Prince of Wales' Silver Medal in Modern Languages.—For the best examination on the honour work in French and German. Open to under-graduates or graduates taking the honour work in that subject.

Prince of Wales' Silver Medal in Natural Science.—For the best examination in the honour work in Natural Science. Open to under-graduates or graduates taking the honour work in that subject.

Prince of Wales' Silver Medal in Classics.—For the candidate who stands second in the examination on the honour work in Latin and Greek.

11. EXTRACTS—REPORT TO ASSEMBLY, 1882.

Legislation.

St. John, N.B.: App p. 10.—As soon as the decision of the Privy Council in the Temporalities Fund was known, application was made to the Dominion Parliament for remedial legislation. So warm and universal was the sympathy felt for the University, that the Bill passed through the House of Commons and the Senate without a single voice against it, and is now fortified by the triple brass of royal charter, the Provincial Legislature and the Dominion Parliament.

Preparatory Department.

The Preparatory Department, which existed for three years, has been abolished, with the sanction of the Church, and to the great satisfaction of the Professors. Evidently the benefits of university and theological training can be fully enjoyed only by those who have been well grounded in elementary studies, and nowhere can this drill be given so well as in High Schools and Academies.

12. STATISTICS.

Students, 1881.

The number of students registered for the season of 1881 and 1882 in Arts and Divinity is two hundred and sixty-one, of whom sixty are studying for the ministry. An increase of students in twelve years from 99 to 261, sufficiently illustrates the growth of Queen's, and its importance to the Church and the country.

Students, 1881-82.

In Arts, 174; in Theology, 16; in Law, 3; in Medicine, 68. Total, 261.

Graduates from 1841 *to* 1882.

LL.D., 16; D.D., 35; B.D., 8; B.Sc., 3; LL.B., 5; B.A., 314; M.A., 82; M.D., 351; Fellows R.C.P.S.K., 16; Licentiates R.C.P.S.K., 62. Total, 892.

Special Finances.

1882 App. p. 102.—The establishment by the Assemblyof

1881 of a Common Fund for its Theological Colleges in Ontario and Quebec, has been nobly responded to by the Church, from which $4000, the least sum required for the Theological Department, is likely to be received. Special subscriptions for the Library Fund, amounting to $1000, have also been received. For an additional chair in Arts, and the long-desired third chair in Theology, an appeal was made to the friends of the University, resulting in subscriptions of $7,500 a year for five years.

Ordinary Revenue.

Receipts	$20,904 58
Expenditure	21,269 95
Deficit	365 37

Scholarships and Prize Essays.

Receipts	$3,835 08
Disbursements	1,929 38
Balance on hand	1,905 70

Assets and Liabilities.

$311,092 56.

*** The Calendar, with full information respecting the faculties of Theology, Arts, Law, and Medicine can be obtained on application to the Registrar. The royal charter of Queen's College, conferring University powers; the Ontario Union Act, 38 Vict., Cap. 76, assented to December 21st, 1874, creating besides the Chancellor and Vice-Chancellor, defining the powers and mode of election of the former; creating also a "Council," with *ex officio* and elective members; together with the "Statutes, Rules and Ordinances of Queen's University and College," amended up to October 26th, 1875, are printed in full in "Taylor's Public Statutes relating to the Presbyterian Church in Canada." The Ontario Act having been declared *ultra vires* by the Privy Council, a Dominion Act, intituled "An Act respecting Queen's College at Kingston," 45 Vic., Cap. 123, was passed and assented to in 1881, and simply confirms the Ontario Act and all the acts of the Corporation and Council done under its provisions.

II.—KNOX COLLEGE.

I.—HISTORICAL STATEMENT.

This eminent seat of Theological learning is said to have commenced its career in an upper room at the residence of one of its professors in James Street, Toronto, in 1844, immediately after the great ecclesiastical revolution in Scotland in the notable year 1843. The Presbyterian Church of Canada was then formed, in sympathy, although not in connection, with the Free Church of Scotland, and among its earliest acts was the creation of an institution for the education of its ministers. A temporary habitation was secured for the College in hired rooms now forming part of the Queen's Hotel. An arrangement was made with the Rev. Mr. King, then a minister of the Free Church, afterwards settled in Halifax, N. S, and with the Rev. Henry Esson, of St. Gabriel Street Church, Montreal, to give instructions to such students in Theology and Literature as might offer themselves for the Ministry. The Rev. Dr. Burns of Paisley having accepted the pastorate of Knox Church, Toronto, agreed at the same time to devote himself to the work of instructing students. As the result of this movement fourteen students were enrolled in various stages of literary progress and arranged into classes. The Synod which met at Hamilton in 1846 gave the institution the name of "Knox College." This same year the Rev. R. McCorkle of St. Nimans, Scotland, gave temporary services as Professor of Divinity and the Rev. Wm. Rintoul of Streetsville in the departments of Hebrew and Biblical Criticism. An Academy for secular learning, and as a preparatory school, was also associated with the College, at the head of which the Rev. Mr. Gale was placed. The Synod of 1847, judging that the increase of students required the undivided services of the Professor of Theology, separated the professorship from the pastorate of Knox Church, at the same time warmly thanking Dr. Burns for his valuable services to the College for two successive sessions. The same Synod instructed Dr. Bayne, of Galt to proceed to Scotland, and in conference with the Colonial Committee of the Free Church, to secure a permanent Professor of Divinity. This led to the appointment of the Rev. Michael Willis, D.D., to the vacant office which he held as professor and principal for twenty-three years, resigning in 1870; and as Emeritus professor till his decease in 1879. In 1849 the Boarding House for students was established. For several years efforts were also made to prepare a Constitution and an Act of Incorporation for the College. The Academy was finally given up in 1852, and interim arrangements were made for the preliminary training of students. On the decease of the Rev. H. Esson in 1853, the Rev George Paxton Young, LL.D., then Minister of Knox Church, Hamilton, was appointed "Second professor of Divinity in Knox College," to whom also was assigned "the departments of Logic, Mental and Moral Philosophy and the Evidences of Natural and Revealed Religion." He held this position till 1868, when he took charge of the Preparatory Department; resigning connection with the College in 1872 on accepting the Chair of Metaphysics and Ethics in the University College, Toronto. In 1854 the Rev. John Laing resigned his tutorship having accepted the charge of the Church in Scarborough, and Mr. Smith was appointed to take charge of the preparatory classes of English, Latin, Greek and Mathematics, and to superintend the Boarding House. In 1855 a literary curriculum was devised, consisting of a preliminary class for preparatory studies and a subsequent three years' course in the advanced departments of Collegiate learning. The same year the Synod after much debate decided in favor of deeding the College property to the principles of the Church as defined in the Standards, the property to be held by Trustees elected annually by the Synod. A Committee was appointed to obtain such a deed, to receive subscriptions, to get plans and estimates for a new building, and to report to a special meeting of Synod if necessary. In the meantime Elmsly Villa, once the official residence of the Governors of Upper Canada was purchased at a fair price, and with the addition of a wing, was prepared as a College and resident Boarding House, and so used for nineteen years. In 1856 it was found desirable to establish a third theological chair for the departments of Evidences and Church History, to which the Rev. Dr. Burns was appointed and relieved from the pastorate of Knox Church, which position he held till the resignation of the professorship in 1864 and as Emeritus till his decease in 1869. In 1866 Professor Caven was appointed to the Chair of Exegetical Theology to include the departments of Evidences, Biblical Criticism and Interpretation of Scripture, and in 1873 was appointed Principal. In 1867 Dr. Proudfoot was appointed Lecturer on Homiletics, and his services have been continued from year to year. Dr. Ure was appointed at the same time but resigned in 1870. In 1871 the Rev. Dr. Inglis was appointed to the Chair of Systematic Theology, but resigned in 1873 to accept a pastorate in Brooklyn, N.Y.; and in the same year the Rev. Wm. McLaren, then of Knox Church, Ottawa, was appointed his successor. In 1872 the Rev. Dr. Gregg, then Minister of Cooke's Church, Toronto, was appointed Professor of Apologetics.

A vigorous and successful effort was made in 1873-74 for the erection of more convenient and commodious premises. A fine site was procured at the head of Spadina Avenue, subscriptions to the amount of $122,000 obtained, and in 1874 the present handsome College was occupied. Its massive proportions and aspiring pinnacles worthily represent the Church to which it belongs and the purpose to which it is consecrated. It has a frontage of 250 feet, wings running back 150 feet, a tower rising over the front entrance 130 feet. It contains spacious Corridors, Lecture Rooms, Private Rooms, Dormitories and Dining Hall, with all the conveniences and comforts of a first-class residence and represents a cost of not less than $150,000.

The Act of Incorporation of "Knox College" was obtained from the United Parliament of Upper and Lower Canada in 1858. It defines the powers and privileges of the College in the usual terms, and gave the Synod the special and peculiar power to define for itself the Theological doctrines and principles which shall be taught in the College and to declare in what books and documents these principles and doctrines are contained not afterwards to be revocable by the Synod. This peculiar form of Act arose from an aversion on the part of the friends of the Church in Parliament to Legislate in any way on matters of religion, deeming the name of the Church in the Act a sufficient security for the faithful administration of the Trust. The Synod having, however, a different opinion insisted unanimously that the principles of the Church to be taught in the College should be explicitly stated in the Act and accepted the compromise offered of the power to legislate on this point for itself. The Union Act of 1874 confirmed without altering the provisions of the Act of 1858. The only amending legislation that has been found necessary is the short Act of 1880 granting to "Knox College," as was at first intended, but for special reasons deferred, the power of conferring the degrees of B.D. and D.D.

DECLARATION OF PRINCIPLES.

"The Synod in accordance with the terms of the Act for the incorporation of Knox College, at its first session after the passing of the Act, resolved and declared,—

That the principles and doctrines to be taught in Knox College by the professors and tutors, or other persons who shall from time to time, and at all times hereafter, be employed or appointed in giving instruction in the said College, shall be such and such only as are consistent with and agreeable to the 'Confession of Faith,' the 'Larger and Shorter Catechisms,' and the 'Form of Church Government,' all which are called 'The

Westminster Standards,' and shall comprise all theological learning consistent with said Standards; Provided always, that the said 'Confession of Faith,' be understood and taken with the explanatory note thereto, agreed upon by the Synod of the Presbyterian Church of Canada, met at Toronto in the year of our Lord 1854: Provided also, that the said 'Westminster Standards' be taken and understood with such other, or further directions and rules as to Church government, discipline, or worship, as may from time to time be prescribed or ordained by the Synod of the said Presbyterian Church of Canada, with the concurrence of a majority of the Presbyteries of the said Church, to be ascertained in such manner as the Synod shall prescribe, and that such regulations and rules be duly recorded in the minute book of the said Synod, and signed by the Moderator and clerk for the time being of such Synod.

The Synod further instruct their Clerk to register this resolution and declaration in the records of the Synod and in the public Records of the City of Toronto."

2. OFFICERS OF THE COLLEGE.

Board of Management.

W. M. CLARK, ESQ., Chairman.

Senate.

THE REV. PRINCIPAL CAVEN, D.D., President.

College Staff.

REV. PRINCIPAL CAVEN, D.D , Professor of Exegetics and Biblical Criticism.

REV. WILLIAM GREGG, D.D., Professor of Apologetics and Church History.

REV. WILLIAM McLAREN, Professor of Systematic Theology.

REV. J. J. A. PROUDFOOT, D.D., Lecturer in Homiletics, Church Government and Pastoral Theology.

Hebrew by PROFESSOR HIRSCHFELDER, in University College.

Elocution by PROFESSOR J. W. TAVERNER and R. LEWIS.

D. M. RAMSAY, B.A., and J. S. McKAY, B.A., Classical Tutors.

3. ADMISSION OF STUDENTS.

1. Young men desiring to enter upon study with a view to

the Ministry are required to make application to some Presbytery of the Church; which, being satisfied regarding their moral and religious character, their motives, and their general fitness to study for the Ministry, will certify them to the Board of Examiners. This regulation applies to entrants upon the Preparatory Course in Knox College, as well as to students who, having taken their Literary Course in the University of Toronto or elsewhere, seek to enter the College as Students of Theology. All Art Students in order to be eligible for Home Mission Work require to be approved by a Presbytery as Candidates for the Ministry.

2. According to the law of the General Assembly, Students are required, each Summer, after entering the College, to appear before the Presbytery within whose bounds they are labouring or residing, and to render a written Exercise prescribed to them; on which, they will be certified to the College Senate for the subsequent year.

3. The Board of Examiners will meet in the College on Thursday, the 5th of October, at 9 o'clock a.m., when Students entering on Theology are required to appear and furnish the evidence of standing referred to under the head *Theological Curriculum*

4. THEOLOGICAL CURRICULUM.

Students entering upon the Course in Divinity shall present a Presbyterial Certificate, together with the evidence of having obtained the degree of B.A. at the University of Toronto; or at McGill College, Montreal; or at Queen's College, Kingston; or at Victoria College, Cobourg; or at one of the National Universities of Great Britain or Ireland, or other University recognized by the Senate; or, instead of said Degree, a certificate of having satisfactorily passed the final examination in the Preparatory Course in Knox College; or of having completed a three years' curriculum in some approved College, and having passed the examinations connected therewith; but in all cases Students must present evidence of having attended at least one Session, a class in Hebrew, or otherwise they must undergo an elementary examination in that language.

Only by permission of the General Assembly can any Student who has not fulfilled these conditions be admitted to Theology.

The Theological course extends over three Sessions of Six months.

Classes.

First year.—Exegetics, Biblical Criticism, Apologetics, Church History, Systematic Theology.

Second year.—Exegetics, Apologetics, Church History, Systematic Theology, Homiletics, &c.

Third year.—Exegetics, Church History, Systematic Theology, Homiletics, &c.

Exercises.

Students of the first year are required to prepare a Homily; of the second year, a Lecture and a Critical Greek Exercise; and of the third year, a Sermon and a Hebrew Critical Exercise.

Certificates.

In addition to such examinations as may be held by the Professors during the Session, the Board examines the Classes at the close of it, and, if the Examination proves satisfactory, certifies the Students to their Presbyteries accordingly.

The Senate gives a general certificate to Students who have completed their Theological Course, in order to their being taken by Presbyteries on preliminary trials for license. A Diploma from the College is also given.

5. SCHOLARSHIPS.

The Discourses prescribed in the several years must be handed in before the Closing Examinations, in order to qualify for holding any Scholarship awarded in connection with them:

First Year in Theology.

Bayne, $50, for proficiency in Hebrew: Examination on entering Theology.

James McLaren, $60, General Proficiency in Closing Examination.

Alexander, (I.), $50, for Systematic Theology: Closing Examination.

Goldie, $50, for Exegetics: Closing Examination.

Gillies, (I.), $40, for Church History: Closing Examination

Dunbar, $50, for Apologetics: Closing Examination.

Gillies, (II.), $40, for Bible Criticism: Closing Examination.

Second Year.

J. A. Cameron, (I.), $60, General Proficiency in Closing Examination.

Knox Church, Toronto, (I.), $40, Church History: Closing Examination.

Loghrin, $50, Systematic Theology: Closing Examination.

Alexander, (II.), $50, Exegetics: Closing Examination.

Knox Church, Toronto, (II.), $40, Apologetics: Closing Examination.

Heron, $40, for best average Examination by Student who has not gained another Scholarship.

Third Year.

Bonar-Burns, $100, General Proficiency; Closing Examination.

Fisher, (I.) $60, Systematic Theology: Closing Examination.

Fisher, (II.), $60, Exegetics: Closing Examination.

Cheyne, $40, for best average Examination by Student who has not gained another Scholarship.

Second and Third Years.

Boyd, $40, Homiletics: Closing Examination.

Smith, $50, Essay—(prescribed.)

First, Second and Third Years.

Clark Prize I—(Lange's Commentary) New Testament, Greek: Closing Examination.

Clark Prize II.—(Lange's Commentary) Old Testament, Hebrew: Closing Examination.

Gaelic Scholarship—$40, for Proficiency: may be held by a Student who has taken another.

First and Second Years.

Prince of Wales Prize—$60, (for two years) Essay prescribed, to be given on 31st October.

6. DEGREE OF BACHELOR OF DIVINITY.

By the Act 44 Victoria, Chapter 81, passed in 1881, by the

Legislative Assembly of Ontario, Knox College, was invested with the power of Conferring Degrees in Divinity, B.D., and D.D., the enacting clauses of which are as follows:

Her Majesty, by and with the advice and consent of the Legislative Assembly of the Province of Ontario, enacts as follows:

1. The Senate of Knox College, shall have power to confer the degrees of Bachelor of Divinity and Doctor of Divinity upon graduates in Arts of such University as the said Senate shall recognize for that purpose, as well as upon such Students of the said College as are now taking the regular course of study therein, or have, before passing of this Act, completed the said course, and are now ordained Ministers of the Presbyterian Church in Canada, subject, however, in either case, to such regulations as to examination or otherwise as may, from time to time, be prescribed by by-law of the said Senate.

2. The said Senate shall also have power to confer the honorary degree of Doctor of Divinity, and may make by-laws and regulations touching any matter or thing pertaining to the conditions on which said degree may be conferred.

Senate Regulations.

Degree of Bachelor of Divinity (B. D.):

1. Candidates for this degree must be graduates in Arts of some approved University; but Students who have already completed the Literary Course in Knox College, and are now in the Ministry of the Presbyterian Church in Canada, and also Students who are now taking the regular course in Knox College, may become candidates.

2. Candidates must have completed a course of Theological study in this College, or in some Theological School approved by the Senate.

3. This degree cannot be conferred earlier than one year after the completion of the ordinary Theological Course.

4. The subjects of examination shall be arranged into **two** departments, as follows:

First Department.

(1) *Latin*—Augustini, de Doctrina Christiana, Lib. I. (2) *Greek*—Gospel of

Luke and Epistle to Romans (3) *Hebrew*—Genesis, chs. 1-5 (inclusive); Psalms 2, 8, 19, 45, 72, 110. (4) *Apoolgetics*—Rawlinson's Historical Evidences; Farrar's Critical History of Free Thought; Flint's Anti-theistic Theories. (5) *Church History and Church Government*—Killen's Ancient Church. (6) *Systematic Theology*—Westminster Confession of Faith; Bannerman on Inspiration. (7) *Textual Criticism and Canon*—Scriviner's Introduction to the Criticism of the New Testament; Westcott's History of the New Testament Canon.

Second Department.

(1) *Greek*—Justin Martyr, Apol. I. (2) *Hebrew and Chaldee*—Isaiah, chs. 1-6 Daniel, chs. 3-5. (3) *Church History*—Fisher's Reformation. (4) *Systematic Theology*—Turrettini, Tom. II.; Locus, Decimus Quartus, Quaest. I., II., X.—XIV.; Cunningham's Historical Theology, Vol. I. (5) *Exegetics*—Fairbairn's Hermeneutics; Ellicott on Galatians. (6) *Homiletics and Pastoral Theology*—Consult Shedd's Homiletics and Van Oosterzee's Practical Theology.

5. Candidates may take, at one examination, the whole of the work in both departments, but not earlier than the month of March after the completion of the ordinary Theological Course.

6. The examination in the two departments may be taken at different times In this case the examination in the First Department shall not usually be taken earlier than the month of March next following the completion of the ordinary theological course; but students who shall have averaged not less than sixty per cent. of the maximum number of marks in the examinations of the preceding year shall be allowed to take this examination at the close of their ordinary course. The examination in the Second Department cannot be taken earlier than the March following or later than two years from that date.

7. Candidates are required to communicate their names, together with attestations of their qualifications, as specified in the foregoing regulations, to the Secretary of the Senate, at least two months before the day appointed for the examination.

8. The fee for the Degree of B. D. shall be ten dollars ($10) to be paid to the Secretary previously to its being conferred.

7. SCHOLARSHIPS FOR UNIVERSITY STUDENTS.

To encourage Students to take a University Course, a limited number of Scholarships is offered for competition to Undergraduates of the University of Toronto who are prosecuting their studies with a view to the Ministry of the Presbyterian Church in Canada. In order to hold any of these Scholarships, it is necessary to give attendance on the Lectures of the year in University College.

1. For Students who have passed their Matriculation:

1. St. James' Square Church, Toronto..........................$60
2. Knox Church, Stratford.......................................50

2. For Students of the Second Year:

1. Alexander, 1st..$60
2. Mulholland...40

3. For Students of the Third Year:

1. Central Church, Hamilton.....................................$60
2. Charles Street Church, Toronto..............................40

4. For Students of the Fourth Year:

1. Brantford, Zion Church..$50
2. Alexander, 2nd...40

These Scholarships are tenable for one year only, but the Scholars for one year may compete for the Scholarships of the succeeding year. A Student holding a University Scholarship may compete for these, but in the event of being successful, he will receive only the third part of the Scholarship, the remainder being awarded to the Student not holding any other Scholarship who would be next entitled to it. The Board will not award those Scholarships unless a certain standard is reached. Students holding them must sign a declaration of their intention to become Ministers of the Presbyterian Church in Canada. Intending competitors must intimate their purpose to the Rev. J. Laing, M. A., Dundas, before the 8th September. For subjects of Examination see the Calendar.

8. PREPARATORY LITERARY COURSE.

Classical tuition is provided in Knox College for such Students as are unable to take a full University Course, or in whose case it is thought that the Curriculum of the University may with advantage be modified.

Students availing themselves of this tuition are required to give three years' attendance on certain classes (as indicated below) in University College, and to pass the terminal examination in these classes.

Classes.

First Year:—Latin, Greek and Mathematics—Knox College. English Literature and History—University College.

Second Year:—Latin and Greek—Knox College. Logic, Rhetoric, Junior Mental Philosophy, Natural History or Chemistry—University College.

Third Year:—Latin and Greek—Knox College. Mental Philosophy, Moral Philosophy and Hebrew—University College.

9. RESIDENCE OF STUDENTS.

The Students rooms are furnished by the Church. The rate of board is three dollars per week, all charges for attendance, etc., included. Where it is preferred, Students are allowed to reside in the College on payment to the Steward of seventy-five cents per week, finding board elsewhere. In the case of Students, all applications for rooms must be made to the Principal, and these are appropriated in the order in which applications are received; academic seniority, however, entitling Students to a preference in the choice of rooms. Students can retain their rooms from one Session to another, irrespective of the rule as to seniority, by giving notice before the beginning of the Session that they wish to do so.

The classes admitted to board in the College are as follows, viz:—

(*a*) Students in their Theological Course.

(*b*) Students preparing for their Theological Course, whether in Knox College, in the University of Toronto, or in some other Educational Institution in Toronto.

(*c*) In the event of the rooms not being all occupied by Students, Ministers or Probationers of the Church, who may be temporarily resident in Toronto, may be admitted to board; but their residence, if longer than a week, must be sanctioned by the Principal.

Residence in the College is, of course, optional on the part of Students; but the Board of Management hopes that the arrangements of the establishment will prove such as to make residence desirable and highly advantageous.

10. SUMMARY OF BY-LAWS.

(1.) *The Board.*

Minutes 1860, page 26.—A Board of Management of thirty-five ordained ministers and elders annually appointed by the

General Assembly to meet at least three times a year, shall have the whole management of the financial affairs of the College, and shall receive annual reports from the Senate of all the departments and transmit the same to the Assembly with an audited balance sheet, co-operate with the Senate in maintaining discipline, take charge of the boarding department, appoint and dismiss all servants, appoint an acting sub-committee; the chairman of the Board to have charge of corporation seal.

(2.) *The College Senate.*

It shall consist of the Principal and Professors with seven members of the Assembly annually appointed, and shall have a general superintendance and control, examine students at the close of each session and present to the Board annually a report of the studies of the Classes and all matters under its supervision.

(3.) *The Principal.*

He shall summon and preside at all meetings of the Senate, shall have only a casting vote, preside at the opening and closing of the College, conduct all official correspondence, and shall under the Senate, have a general superintendence of the Students.

(4.) *Professors and Tutors.*

All Professors shall be ordained Ministers of the Church and Tutors, members in full communion, and both shall sign the prescribed formula. They shall be appointed by the General Assembly by open vote of the majority present. They may resign to the Assembly or be removed, suspended or deposed by it.

(5.) *Sessions, Admissions and Attendance of Students.*

1. The Session or Academical Year shall commence on the first Wednesday of October and end on the first Wednesday of April, with recess at the end of December.

2. Students must be certified to the Senate by some Presbytery, must sign the Album of the College and agree to submit to its discipline.

3. At the close of the Session Students must apply to their Professors for a certificate to be presented to the Presbytery or Board of Examiners, and before License obtain a certificate from

the Senate, signed by the Principal attesting that he has attended all the classes and performed all the duties required by the Church.

4. Cases of an urgent or peculiar nature of attendance or absence shall be adjudged by the Senate according to the circumstances of each case.

11. STATISTICS.

Students.

Theological, 1881-82.—First year, 13; second year, 13; third year 11; total, 37.

Preparatory—First year, 6; second year, 7; third year, 9; total, 22. This does not include University Students who have the Ministry in view, nine of whom received special Knox College Scholarships.

Graduates.—From 1873 to 1882 inclusive, 124; and since the College was established, 344, not including many who have received partial training in the Institution.

Finances, 1882.

(1.) *Ordinary Fund.*

Receipts	$11,527 13
Expenditures	12,604 46
Deficit	1,071 33

(2.) *Building Fund.*

Receipts	$5,3 7 00
Expenditures	3,644 72
On hand	1,692 87

(3.) *Endowment Fund.*

Receipts	$44.502 98
Expenditures	32,288 79
On hand	12,214 19
The total amount	52,592 10

This does not include the subscriptions of the present year which already approximate $100,000.

(4.) *Debt Account.*

On Building	$20,000 00
On Ordinary Fund	11,195 51

(5.) *Bursary Fund.*

Investment	$8,000 00
Receipts	1,722 12
Expenditures	1,712 99

(6.) *Assets.*

Buildings, Ground and Furnishings	$120,000 00
Endowment Fund, (invested and subscribed) about	150,000 00
Library and Museum	10,000 00
Scholarships	8,000 00
Total, about	288,000 00

11. RESOLUTION OF THE ASSEMBLY.

St. John, N. B., 1882, p. 23—Receive the Report of Knox College; express approval of the purpose of the Board of Management to take steps, without delay, for largely increasing the Endowment Fund, and enjoin the constituency of the Colleges placed upon the common fund, unitedly and heartily to contribute to that Fund, according to the estimates sanctioned by the General Assembly, so that the revenue for theological education may be made equal to the necessary expenditure in each of the Colleges. The General Assembly, moreover, having in view the widely-extended field which the Church is being called at once to occupy, would earnestly remind ministers and Presbyteries of the duty of encouraging, in all proper ways, such young men as may have their attention suitably turned towards the ministerial office.

*** The Calendar of the College containing full information for the ensuing Session of 1883-84 can be obtained on application to the Rev. Principal Caven, D.D., at the College, Toronto, Ont.

III. PRESBYTERIAN COLLEGE, MONTREAL.

(*Affiliated to McGill University*).

1. HISTORICAL STATEMENT.

This College obtained its Charter in the year 1865. For two years after there was, however, nothing but the charter—no endowments, no buildings, no library, no professors, no students. It now has about sixty students, four regular professors, a library of ten thousand volumes, fine buildings and permanent endowments, to the value of one hundred and twelve thousand dollars. The buildings, which have recently been greatly enlarged through the munificence of David Morrice, Esq , occupy a large extent of ground in one of the most favorable and healthy positions in the city, and are admirable for elegance and completeness. They include commodious class rooms, convocation hall, library, dining hall, studies and dormitories for resident students. The work of instruction, was begun in the winter of 1867-68, by the Rev. Dr. Gregg now of Knox College, Toronto; and the Rev. William Aitkin then of Smiths' Falls, acting as lecturers. A little company of Students gathered around them in the lecture rooms of Erskine Church, generously granted free of expense. In the fall of 1868, the Rev. Dr. MacVicar, the present Principal, entered upon his duties as the first, and for some time, the only permanent professor. The work continued to grow until the winter of 1873, when the original College building was opened. The most valuable assistance was rendered to the College in several departments of learning, by the Rev. Dr. Gibson now of London, England, the Rev. Professor McLaren now of Knox College, Toronto, and others acting as temporary lecturers. In 1873, the Rev. John Campbell, M. A., was appointed Professor of Church History and Apologetics; in 1880, the Rev. Daniel Coussirat, B.A., B D., accepted the French Professorship of Theology; and in 1882, the Rev. John Scrimger, M.A. after some years of temporary service, was appointed permanent Professor of Hebrew and Greek Exegesis. The Rev. William J. Dey, M.A. also became Dean of Residence, taking charge of the library and of the preparatory courses in classics and mathematics. The College has thus a regular staff of four professors of Theology and a Dean of Residence, and in addition to these five special lecturers in various departments: making ten in all who are actively engaged in the work of teaching.

The regular course of instruction in Theology, extends over three sessions of six months each, embracing all the subjects usually found in a Theological Curriculum. Special features of this course, however, not found elsewhere in any Protestant College on this Continent, are the lectures given in French and on the Gaelic language. A considerable number of the Students, being of French origin, and preparing themselves for the work of French Evangelization, it has been found necessary that one professor should lecture wholly in this language; while the need which still exists for Gaelic services in certain parts of the Church has made it desirable that some instruction should also be given in that tongue.

In addition to the ordinary subjects taught in the clasess as prescribed for each year an optional honor course, is provided in which attendance at lectures is not required but to which certificates of honor, scholarships, medals, and fellowships are attached. There is also provision for a post-graduate course of one year.

By its Charter, the College possesses authority to confer the degrees of B.D. and D.D., either upon its own Students, or upon others who may comply with the prescribed conditions. The degree of B.D., is conferred upon those who successfully pass an examination on the subjects contained in the honor and post-graduate courses. These Scholarships are upon a fairly liberal scale varying in value from twenty to one hundred dollars, besides a number of prizes, and are offered in the several years to those standing highest in the prescribed subjects; and a fellowship of the value of five hundred dollars ($500), is awarded annually to the Student standing relatively highest in all the years, to enable him to take an additional session abroad.

The College already in its brief career of sixteen years has seventy-eight graduates, nearly all of whom are filling positions of honor and usefulness in different parts of the Church Of this number twenty-six or one-third of the whole, are able to conduct services in two languages. The College has many external advantages arising from its situation. The City of Montreal, the largest in the Dominion, is a great Presbyterian centre, contain ing in addition to the College, sixteen Presbyterian Churches, thirteen of which are under the General Assembly. Every facility is thus afforded for becoming acquainted with Church work, for the study of pulpit eloquence, for active Christian benevolence, and for the enjoyment of Christian hospitality. Students desirious of acquiring a practical acquaintance with the French language, find in the city the amplest opportunities. In addition to McGill University with which the College is affiliated, there are three Protestant schools of Theology as well as various Scientific and Art Institutions that are available for general culture. Students also preparing for the foreign mission fields, may find the best facilities for the study of medicine in connection with the medical faculty of McGill University.

The Act of incorporation and by-laws are almost identical in terms with those of Knox College, the only difference being that "members in full communion" with the Church as well as Ministers and Elders may be placed on the Board of Management.

2 —COLLEGE OFFICERS.

Board of Management.

DAVID MORRICE, Esq., Chairman.
JOHN STIRLING, Esq., Secretary.
REV. R. H. WARDEN, Treasurer.

The Members are annually appointed by the General Assembly.

Senate.

REV. D. H. MACVICAR, D.D., LL.D, President.
REV. PROFESSOR CAMPBELL, M.A., Secretary.

The Members are annually appointed by the General Assembly.

Principal.

REV. D. H. MACVICAR, D.D., LL.D.

Registrar.

REV. JOHN CAMPBELL, M.A.

Dean of Residence and Librarian.

REV. W. J. DEY, M.A.

Staff.

REV. D H. MACVICAR, D.D., LL.D., Principal, and Professor of Systematic Theology, Homiletics and Church Government.

REV. JOHN CAMPBELL, M.A., Professor of Church History and Apologetics.

REV. D. COUSSIRAT, B.D., B.A., French Professor of Theology.

REV. JOHN SCRIMGER, M.A., Professor of Old and New Testament Exegesis.

Rev. A. B. Mackay, Lecturer in sacred Rhetoric and Elocution.

Rev. Neil MacNish, B.D., LL.D., Lecturer in the Gaelic Language and Literature.

Rev. D. Coussirat, B.D., B.A., Lecturer in Oriental Language (in McGill College).

Rev. W. J. Dey, M.A., Lecturer in Classics and Mathematics.

A. C. Hutchison, Esq., Lecturer in Ecclesiastical Architecture.

John McLaren, Esq., Lecturer in Sacred Music.

3.—REGULATIONS AFFECTING STUDENTS.

1. Students who desire to enter upon a course of Theological Study in this College, other than those who have completed their course of three years in its Literary Department, must present to the Registrar for transmission to the Senate, before the 5th of October:—

(1.) A Presbyterial Certificate;

(2.) Evidence of having obtained the degree of B. A. at Queen's University, McGill University, the University of Toronto, Dalhousie College, or other recognized institution;

(3.) A certificate of having passed at least one examination in Hebrew.

2. Regular Students in the preparatory department, who have passed the sessional examination of the third year in that department, are not again required to stand an examination for entrance into theology, but are entitled to take their place in the Theological Classes on presenting the usual Presbyterial certificate, together with that of the Senate to their having passed the said examination.

3. Divinity Students who have already taken a part of their Theological course in other recognized institutions will be admitted on the presentation of regular certificates of good standing and dismission from the authorities of such institutions, to their standing in this College.

4. Occasional students may be admitted to attendance upon courses of lectures on presenting a Presbyterial order to that effect, or on payment of the fee of four dollars for each course,

or of ten dollars for all the courses. Such occasional Students are not required to pass the terminal or sessional examinations, nor are they eligible for the scholarships and other rewards open to regular students. Should they, however, desire to take the sessional examinations, certificates of their proficiency may be given them by the Professors whose lectures they have attended. The Senate may remit the fees in special cases.

4. THEOLOGICAL CURRICULUM.

The course of instruction in Theology extends over three sessions of six months each. In addition to the ordinary subjects taught in the classes of the various Professors as prescribed for each year, in which every student must pass an examination at the close of the session, an honor course is provided, which is optional, and in which no lectures are given, but to which certificates of honor, scholarships and medals are attached.

Ordinary Course.

FIRST YEAR.—*Department I.—Systematic Theology* (1.) Theology proper; Nature and attributes of God—the Trinity; the Divinity of Christ; the Holy Spirit; Decrees of God—Creation—Providence. (2.) Anthropology; Origin, Nature and Original State of Man; Covenant of works; the Fall; Nature of Sin; Free Agency.

Department II.—Apologetics (1.) Natural Theology, including Foundations of Natural Religion; History of Religion and of Natural Theology; Arguments for the Being and Attributes of God, a Future State, etc.; Refutation of Anti-Theistic systems. (2.) Connection of Natural and Revealed Religion. (3.) Evidences of Christianity, including the Genuineness, Credibility and Divinity of the Old and New Testament Scriptures.

Department III.—Church History. (1.) Old Testament History. (2) History of the Jews from the Restoration to the Birth of Christ. (3.) New Testament History, including a Harmony of the Gospel narratives. (4) The Connection of Sacred and Profane History. (5) Geography and Antiquities of the Bible.

Department IV.—Sacred Literature. (1.) Introduction to the Old and New Testaments. (2.) Bible Criticism, Restoration of the Text of the Old and New Testaments. (3.) Principles of Hermeneutics; Inspiration; Canon. (4.) Readings in Biblical Hebrew and Greek.

Department V.—Homiletics. (1.) Historical Introduction. (2.) Principles of Homiletics. (3.) Structure of Sermons and Art of Preaching. Homiletical Exercises, including Criticism, etc.

Department. VI.—Théologie Française. (1.) Vie de Jésus. (2.) Théorie de la prédication. (3.) Exercises homilétiques.

Department VII.—Sacred Rhetoric and Elocution.

Students of the first year are required to prepare and deliver before the close of the Session a Homily, the subject of which will be prescribed by the Principal.

Honor Course and First Examination for degree of B. D. to Students in course.

The books of the Honor Course in each year are generally selected from among those to which attention has been directed, and a partial analysis of which has been given in the classes.

1.—Westminster Confession of Faith. 2.—Rawlinson's Historical Evidences. 3.—Davidson's Introduction to the New Testament. 4.—Book of Genesis, Chaps. 1-4 (Hebrew). 5.—Gospel according to Mark (Greek). 6.—Killen's Ancient Church, Vol. 1.

Ordinary Course.

SECOND YEAR.—*Department I.—Systematic Theology.* (1.) Soteriology (begun) Plan of Redemption—Covenant of Grace; Person of Christ. (2.) Soteriology; Offices of Christ; the Atonement; Grace; Regeneration; Faith; Justification; Santification.

Department II.—Apologetics.—(1.) History of Unbelief and of Christian Apologetics, with a review of the principle objections to Christianity and Divine Revelation in the past. (2.) Analysis and refutation of the leading systems of Unbelief in the present.

Department III.—Church History. (1.) History, Literature, Constitution and Cultus of the Church in the Apostolic, Patristic and Scholastic periods. (2.) History of the Jews and of Christian Missions during the same periods. (3.) Progress of Error, and Witnesses for the Truth before the Reformation.

Department IV.—Sacred Literature, including Exegetics. (1.) Exegetical Exercises in Old Testament (Hebrew). (2.) Exegetical Exercises in New Testament (Greek).

(The portion of Scripture to be read, with appropriate Commentaries, will be made known at the commencement of the Session).

Department V.—Theologie Francaise. (1.) Vie de St. Paul. (2.) Théologie pastorale. (3.) Exercices homilétiques.

Department VI.—Sacred Rhetoric and Elocution.

Department VII.—Sacred Music. (Optional).

Students of the second year are required to prepare and deliver before the close of the Session a Lecture, the subject of which will be prescribed by the Professor of Church History and Apologetics.

Honor Course and Second Examination for degree of B. D. to Students in course.

1.—Jacob's Ecclesiastical Policy. 2.—Farrar's Critical History of Free Thought. 3.—Shedd's Homiletics. 4.—Fairbairn's Hermeneutics. 5.—Book of Ruth (Hebrew). 6.—Epistle to Romans (Greek).

Ordinary Course.

THIRD YEAR.—*Department I.—Systematic Theology.* 1.—The Decalogue; Means of Grace; The Sacraments. 2.—Eschatology; State of the Soul after Death; Second Advent; Resurrection—Final Judgment; the End of the World Books: Hodge, Turretine, Calvin, Thornwell, Bartlet, Reid.

Department II.—Church History. (1.) History of the Reformation. (2.) History of the Protestant Church since the Reformation, with special reference to the Reformed Churches of Great Britain and Ireland, and their branches in America. (3.) History of Christian Missions and of the Jews. (4.) History of the Romish and Greek Churches since the Reformation. (5.) Review of existing denominations.

Department III.—Exegetics. (1.) Exegetical Exercises in Old Testament Hebrew. (2.) Exegetical Exercises in New Testament Greek.

(The portions of Scripture to be read, with appropriate Commentaries, will be made known at the commencement of the Session).

Department IV.—Church Government. (1.) Historical View of Forms of Church Government. (2.) Development of Scriptual Form, and Refutation of Errors. (3.) Church Polity—Forms of Process, etc.

Department V.—Pastoral Theology. (1.) Personal Qualifications and Duties of the Minister. (2.) Social and public duties. (3.) The care of Souls in general. (4.) Special Pastoral Work.

Department VI.—Théologie Francaise. (1.) Apologétique. (2.) Dogmatique de Martensen ; étude critique. (3.) Exercises homilétiques.

Department VII.—Ecclesiastical Architecture.

Students of the third year must prepare a Popular Sermon, and Greek and Hebrew Exercises with additions, and deliver the Sermon. The Subjects of the exercises will be prescribed—that of the Popular Sermon by the Professor of Church History; and of the Exercises and Additions by the Professor of Exegetical Theology.

Honor Course and Third Examination for degree of B.D. to Students in course.

1.—Augustine, De Doctrina Christiana, Lib. I. (Latin). 2.—Calvin's Institutes, Book IV. 3.—Lightfoot's Commentary on the Philippians. 4.—Hodge on the Atonement. 5.—Bungener's History of the Council of Trent. 6.—Psalms i., ii., xxiii., xlii., li., ciii., cx. (Hebrew).

Post-Graduate Course (Optional).

FOURTH YEAR. *Department I.—Systematic Theology.*—Martensen. *Department II.—Church History.*—Hagenbach. *Department III.—Apologetics.*—Christlieb. *Department IV—Canonicity.*—Westcott. *Department V.—Hebrew and Chaldee.*—Daniel. Psalms and Vulgate. *Department VI.—Patristic Greek and Latin.*—Vulgate and Chrysostom.

This course embraces the work of the Final Examination for degree of B.D. to Students in Course.

The Lectures of the fourth year are few in number, students thus being left free to pursue in private any special course of Theological study, in doing which they are assured the assistance and direction of the Faculty. Except in the case of Resident

Fellows, no exercises are required from those taking the Post-Graduate Course.

French Theological Department.

All French Students, and Students preparing for French work, are required to attend the Lectures in Théologie Française, and English Students who understand French are urged to do the same. Students taking this course, and passing examination in it, are exempted from examination in the Biblical History and Homiletics of the first year, the Apologetics and Sacred Rhetoric of the second, and the Exegesis and Architecture of the third. In the honour work they may also take the examinations in Latin, Greek and Hebrew authors, and Calvin, Martensen, Bungener and Christlieb in French instead of English. In the First year they may exchange Killen for De Pressensé, "Histoire des trois premièrs Siècles;" in the Second year, Farrar and Shedd for Abbadie, "Traité de la Verité de la Réligion Chrétienne" and Vinet; and in the Post-Graduate course, Westcott for Reuss, "Histoire du Canon du Nouveau Testament." Students intending to exercise these options must give notice to the Principal or French Professor, at least three weeks before the sessional examinations.

French Students are not required to give more than one of their College Exercises in English, and at least two of them must be in French. These French Exercises will be prescribed by the French Professor.

While French Students are eligible for all the Scholarships and other rewards of the Theological course, in consideration of the disadvantage at which they are placed by pursuing their studies in both languages, two scholarships are offered for competition to them exclusively. In addition to the ordinary work of their years the following subjects are prescribed to competitors:

Bungener's Histoire du Concile de Trente; Grammaire Historique de la Langue francaise, par Auguste Brachet.

5. DEGREES IN DIVINITY.

Regulations of Senate.

1.—Those entitled to become candidates for the dergree of B.D. must have completed a course of Theological study in this, or some other recognized institution.

2.—They must be Graduates in Arts of some recognized University.

Note.—Applications to be examined for the degree, by those who have completed a course of Theological study without having taken a degree in Arts, will, until further notice, be received by the Senate and entertained according to the merits of each individual case.

3.—The final examination for B.D. cannot be passed nor the degree conferred until the Session following that in which the candidate has completed his ordinary course in Theology, unless by special permission of the Senate.

4.—The curriculum contains the following subjects: *Latin:* Biblia Vulgata—Book of Psalms; Augustine—De Doctrina Christiana, L. I. *Greek:* Testamentum Græcum—Mark and Romans; Lightfoot's Commentary on the Philippians; Chrysostom—De Sacerdotio, L. I. *Hebrew and Chaldee:* Genesis, ch. i.-iv.; Ruth; Psalms i., ii., xxiii., xlii., li., ciii., cx.; Daniel i.-iv. *Introduction, etc.:* Davidson's Introduction to the New Testament; Westcott on the Canon; Fairbairn's Hermeneutical Manual. *Apologetics:* Rawlinson's Historical Evidences; Farrar's Critical History of Free Thought; Christlieb's Modern Doubt. *Dogmatics:* Westminster Confession of Faith; Hodge on the Atonement; Martensen's Dogmatics. *Church Government:* Jacobs' Ecclesiastical Polity of the New Testament; Calvin's Institutes, Book IV. *Homiletics:* Shedd. *Church History:* Killen's Ancient Church, Vol. I.; Bungener's History of the Council of Trent; Hagenbach's History of the Church in the 18th and 19th Centuries.

5.—Candidates may proceed to the degree of B.D. in one of three methods:

(1.) They may take at one examination the whole of the work prescribed for the degree.

(2.) They may divide the work into two portions, passing the examination in the first portion at any period of study and the second after an interval of not more than three years as follows:

First Examination.—*Greek:* Gospel according to Mark and Epistle to the Romans. *Hebrew:* Genesis i.-iv.; Ruth. *Introduction, etc.:* Davidson and Fairbairn. *Apologetics:* Rawlinson and Farrar. *Dogmatics:* Confession of Faith. *Church Government.* Jacobs. *Homiletics:* Shedd. *Church History:* Killen.

Second Examination.—*Greek:* Lightfoot and Chrysostom. *Hebrew and Chaldee:* Psalms and Daniel. *Latin:* Psalms and Augustine. *Introduction:* Westcott. *Apologetics:* Christlieb. *Dogmatics:* Hodge and Martensen. *Church Government:* Calvin. *Church History:* Bungener and Hagenbach.

(3.) Students of this College may spread the work over the three years of their Honor Course and the final examination for B.D. See Honor Course page 109.

6.—Students and others who have already begun their studies for the degree of B.D., on the basis of former Calendars may, prior to the final examination of 1884 take as their subjects of examination the Honor books of the three years as set forth in these Calendars with the following additional subjects: *Greek:* Gospel according to Mark; Epistle to the Romans; Book of Genesis, Septuagint *Latin:* Book of Psalms, Vulgate. *Hebrew and Chaldee:* Daniel i.—iv. *Dogmatics:* Martensen.

7.—Candidates who have already passed examinations in any part of the prescribed Honor Course will not be subjected to re-examination in the same.

8.—Candidates who have not passed such examinations may divide the work into two examinations, taking the Honor books of the First and Second Years for the subjects of the First Examination, and those of the Third Year with the additional subjects for the Second.

9.—The examinations will be held in the months of March and September of each year, and the degree will be conferred at the College Convocation, on the first Wednesday of April, or on such other occasions as the Senate may direct.

10.—Candidates for examination must send notice of their intention to present themselves, together with such fee and certification as may be necessary, to the Registrar, not later than the fifteenth day of January or September.

11.—The fee for examination for the degree of B.D. to candidates who have not passed examinations during their ordinary course in the College shall be five dollars; which fee must be paid to the Registrar at the time of application. Candidates who fail to pass may present themselves again without further fee.

12.—The fee for the degree of Bachelor of Divinity shall be ten dollars, which must be paid to the Registrar prior to the conferring of the degree.

13.—The hood of the Bachelor of Divinity of this College, shall be of black corded silk lined with blue silk and bordered with gold braid.

6. FELLOWSHIPS, MEDALS, CERTIFICATES OF HONOR, ETC.

FELLOWSHIP.

To all Students in Theology.

The Senate are empowered to offer for competition the Morrice Travelling Fellowship, of the value of five hundred dollars, tenable for one year.

To Students of the Third Year.

1.—The Hugh Mackay—$60. 2.—The Anderson—$30. For General Proficiency in the pass subjects, of the Sessional Examination.

Medals.

1.—A Gold Medal. 2.—A Silver Medal. For general Proficiency in all the subjects, pass and honor, of the Sessional Examination of the Third Year.

To Students of the Three Years.

The Alumni Scholarship of Fifty Dollars for Proficiency in Oriental Studies, presented by the Alma Mater Society. This Scholarship is open to competition by Divinity Students in all the years, but cannot twice be held by the same person. To be eligible for this scholarship, candidates must take first class in the ordinary work of their year, and the same in the following special subjects: Hebrew Grammar (Rudiger's Gesenius), Elements of Chaldee Grammar (Bagster's Manual), The Book of Daniel.

To French Students of the Three Years.

The Hamilton (McNab Street)—$40. The Guelph (Chalmer's Church)—$40. For General Proficiency in the pass work of their year and in the special subjects mentio .ed on page 110.

To Gaelic-speaking Students.

The MacLennan Scholarship of $40. The subjects of Examination are: 1.—Parsing extracts from the Gaelic version of Job, Chap. 38-42. 2.—Translation from English into Gaelic. 3.—A critical examination of Smith's Sean Dana; Tiomna Ghuil and Diarmaid. MacDonald: Birlinn Chlann Raonuill. Clarsach na Coille: A'choille Ghruamach.

The MacLennan prize of $10 in books selected by the successful competitor, appropriately bound and bearing the College Stamp, will be awarded for proficiency in reading the Gaelic Scriptures and metrical version of the Psalms. The selections from Ecclesiastes. Psalms 50-80 (metrical version). Colossians.

Gaelic Students are requested to prepare one of their exercises in Gaelic, the subject to be prescribed by the Gaelic Lecturer.

To Competitors for Scholarships.

No Student shall be entitled to rank in the first class in Honors or to receive a Scholarship who has not obtained two-thirds of the maximum of marks at which the examination is valued.

The first Scholarship of the First and Second years and the Gold Medal shall be awarded to the student who stands first in the first class in Honors in the respective years, provided always that the candidate for the Gold Medal has obtained three-fourths of the result of the examination.

The second Scholarship of the First and Second years and the Silver Medal shall be awarded to the student who stands next in rank in the first class in Honors.

The Medalists of the Third year are equally eligible with other Students of that year for the Hugh Mackay and Anderson Scholarships.

The third Scholarship of the First year and the third and fourth Scholarships of the second year shall be awarded to the Students who, not having taken a higher Scholarship, shall stand first in the pass work of their year, provided they obtain two-thirds of the result of the examination.

The Scholars of the Three years are equally eligible with other competitors for the Alumni Scholarship.

The holders of the French Scholarships are eligible for the ordinary awards in the Theological course.

Certificates of Honor Standing will be given to Students who have been placed in the first class, but have failed to obtain Medals or Scholarships.

Sacred Rhetoric, Music and Ecclesiastical Architecture will not be taken into account in awarding the Scholarships, as special prizes are connected with these subjects, but no Student shall be eligible for academic rewards who has not passed in these as prescribed for the respective years. The French Theological course will be reckoned at the same value as the English subjects with which it may be exchanged in the various years.

Prizes in Rhetoric, Music and Architecture.

The following prizes will be given annually for proficiency in Sacred Rhetoric, Music and Ecclesiastical Architecture, the prizes to consist of books selected by the successful competitors, appropriately bound and bearing the College Stamp:

For proficiency in Sacred Rhetoric, 1st prize $15, 2nd $10; in Music, 1st prize $10, 2nd $5; in Ecclesiastical Architecture, 1st prize $10, 2nd $5.

The first prize in each subject is open only to Students to whom the work is part of their course. All regular Students Literary and Theological attending the classes are eligible for the second prizes.

7. LITERARY CURRICULUM.

The General Assembly strongly recommends all Students to graduate in Arts, but prescribes for such as may not do so three sessions of six months each, in the subjects mentioned below, after their passing the following entrance examination:

Examination for Admission.

Latin.—Grammar and Caesar, de Bello Gallico, Book I. *Greek.* Grammar and Xenophon, Anabasis, Book I ch. 1-5 *Mathematics.*—Arithmetic; Euclid, Book I; Algebra, first four rules. *English.*—Grammar and Composition. (Correct English indispensable.) *History, etc.*—Outlines of English History; Geography.

Terminal Examination of the first year.

Latin.—Grammar and Virgil, Æneid, Book II. *Greek.* Grammar and Xenophon, Anabasis, Book I, ch 6-10. *Hebrew.* Grammar. *Mathematics.* Euclid, Books II and III; Algebra to simple equations. *English.* Orthographical, Etymological and Rhetorical Forms. *Natural Science.*—Outlines of Chemistry.

Terminal Examination of the Second year.

Latin.—Virgil, Æneid, Book VI. *Greek.*—Homer, Iliad, Book I. *Hebrew.*—Reading and Translation. *Mathematics.*—Euclid, Book IV; Algebra, Quadratic Equations and Progressions. *English.*—History of English Literature. *History.*—Outlines of Modern History. *Natural Science.*—Outlines of Botany or Zoology. *Philosophy.*—Logic and Psychology, as in McGill College.

Terminal Examination of the Third year.

Latin.—Cicero, in Catilinam Orat. I; Horace, Odes, Book I; Virgil, Æneid, Book VI. *Greek.*—Homer, Iliad, Book I or III; Epistle to Galatians. *Hebrew.*—Grammar; Genesis, ch. 1-5; Psalms 1-5. *Natural Science.*—Outlines of Geology. *Philosophy.*—Moral Science, and History of Philosophy, as in McGill College.

Applications by, or on behalf of, Students desiring to be admitted to the Literary Examinations and Classes, must be sent to the Registrar of the College on or before the first day of October, and such Students must appear, to pass their examinations on the first Thursday of the same month.

The College provides instruction in the Departments of Classics and Mathematics for Students who pursue the above special course and do not intend to graduate in Arts; but such Students are required to take the Hebrew, English, History, Natural Science and Philosophy, of the respective years at McGill College, and to present to the Senate, certificates from the University Professors of their having passed Sessional examinations in these subjects. *No literary Student will be granted his standing who does not pass examination in these departments, either in the manner specified, or for special reasons, before the Senate.*

Instead of the subjects at McGill College, French Students will take their Literature and Philosophy in the classes of Professor Coussirat.

Scholarship for Literary Students.

A Scholarship of the value of Forty Dollars will be open for competition to English Students, and to French Students not holding any other Scholarship, in the work of the third year; two-thirds marks being required.

Affiliation with McGill University.

The attention of Students is directed to the special advantages afforded them in virtue of the affiliation of the College with McGill University. They have thereby access to the Library, Museum and Lectures of that Institution, which stands in close proximity. By Scholarships which are in the gift of benefactors they may enjoy exemption from College Fees. In addition to these there are thirteen Exhibitions and Scholarships of from $100 to $125 each, annually offered for competition to Students in Arts, and at the close of the curriculum, gold medals, prizes and certificates of honor, are awarded to successful competitors.

While it is desirable that Students should complete their literary studies before entering upon their Theological course, the terms of affiliation allow them to combine these, exemptions in the University curriculum being granted to Students of affiliated Theological Colleges. Considerable extensions in the matters of options and exemptions have recently been introduced into the regulations of the University. (See McGill College Calendar for 1883-84).

McGill College Training.

The Senate of the Presbyterian College, having full knowledge of the nature of the training given, and the religious influence exerted on Students in the McGill University, confidently recommend parents to send their sons to it, whether they are designed for the Christian Ministry or for any other learned profession.

Scholarships for Students taking University Course.

In order to encourage Students intending to enter Theology to proceed to a degree in McGill University, the following Scholarships are offered:

The George Stephen—$50 for General Proficiency in the work of the First Year in McGill College. The Stirling—$50 for the same in the Second Year. The Drysdale—$50 for the same in the Third Year. A Scholarship—$50 for the same in the Fourth Year.

Scholarships for French Students and Students taking the French Course.

1. The following are open for competition to Students of the Three Years in the Literary course, provided that they have passed satisfactory examinations in the work of their respective years:—

The Paris (Dumfries St).—$40 for General Proficiency in the pass work of their year, and in the following additional subjects: Jouffroy, Cours de Droit Naturel; Duruy, Abrégé d'Histoire Universelle.

A Scholarship—$40 for the same.

2. A Special Scholarship of $60 by the Sabbath School of Knox Church, Montreal, is open to English Students taking the French Course, for the following exercises, in addition to the class work :—Reading in French, writing from dictation, answering questions in French Grammar, translating from French into English and from English into French; writing a French Essay, l'Infaillibilité du Pape.

The Nor'-West Scholarship.

This endowed Scholarship, the value of which for the present year is $50, will be awarded annually to a Student of this College coming from Manitoba and the North-West Territory, or preparing for Missionary labor in that field, on such conditions as the Senate may from time to time appoint.

Presbyterial and other Certificates.

All regular Students, whether in the Literary or Theological courses, must be certified to the College Senate by the Presbytery within the bounds of which they reside.

The Senate will certify Students to the Presbytery to which they may belong or to which they may be transferred after the annual examination at the close of the session.

The Senate gives a certificate of Academic standing to every student in Divinity at the close of each Academic year, and a diploma on parchment at the termination of the Theological Curriculum. Other certificates may be given by individual Professors.

Church Membership.

All Students connected with the College are required during the period of their studies to unite in membership with one of the congregations of the Church in the city or its immediate vicinity. This regulation in not intended to interfere with their liberty to visit other Churches.

Residence.

The original College Building is a stone edifice, elegant and commodious, pleasantly situated on the rising ground above the City, commanding a view of the University grounds, the City and the scenery of the St. Lawrence. To this has been added during the present year by the large hearted generosity of the Chairman of the College Board, an elegant and much more extensive series of stone buildings, designated by the Board as the Morrice Hall, including Convocation Hall and Library, Dining Hall, Dormitories and Offices, forming with the original building three sides of a large quadrangle. In external equipment the College is thus inferior to no Theological Institution on the continent.

Resident Students are furnished with rooms, heating and light, free of expense; but the Refectory and attendance of servants are in the hands of the Steward, whose fee will in no case exceed twelve dollars per month, and who is responsible to the Board of Management for the efficiency of his service.

Applications for vacant rooms must be made to the Dean of Residence, and these will be granted in the order in which applications are received. But in the choice of such vacant apartments, Students having academic seniority will be entitled to a preference.

Personal applications, complaints, etc., must be made to the Dean, solely, within the office hours that shall be indicated at the commencement of the session.

Students (resident or non-resident) in attending lectures are expected to wear gowns appropriate to their academic standing.

Library and Reading Room.

The Library, to which additions are constantly made, embraces all the Greek and Latin Fathers and Ecclesiastical writers, with some rare fac-simile codices and standard and recent works in Theology and cognate subjects. It is under the charge of the College Librarian, from whom books may be obtained, subject to the rules.

8. STATISTICS.

Students 1881-82.

On the Roll—Total 59, of whom there are B.A's 12, M.A. 1 B.C.L's 2, post-graduate 1.

Graduates from 1868 to 1882.

Bachelors of Divinity, 3.—Graduates in Theology, 78.

FINANCES.

Ordinary Fund, 1882.

Receipts....................................	$8,881 08
Expenditures..................................	8,852 11
On hand..	28 97

Endowment Fund.

Receipts..	$110,476 17
Interest from Investments................	1,762 38

Scholarship, Endowment and Ordinary Fund.

Receipts..	$2,985 49
Expenditures..................................	1,071 01
On hand..	245 24

Library Endowment and Ordinary Fund.

Receipts..	$496 45
Expenditures..................................	102 94
On hand..	64 51

Assets and Debts.

Building and Investments.................	$250,000 00
Debt on Building.............................	21,687 75

Calendars containing full particulars can be obtained on application to the Principal.

IV.—MORRIN COLLEGE, QUEBEC.

(In Affiliation with McGill University.)

I.—HISTORICAL STATEMENT.

This Institution owes its existence to the late Dr. Joseph Morrin of Quebec, who in September 1860 executed a Deed of Trust making over to parties therein named certain immovable properties and sums of money "for the establishment of a University or College within the City of Quebec for the instruction of youth in the higher branches of learning, and especially of young men for the Ministry for the Church of Scotland in the Province of Canada." To carry out this benevolent intention and deed, an Act of Incorporation, 24 Vic Cap. 109, of the Legislative Council and Assembly of Canada, assented to in 1861, was obtained, the preamble of which recites that "the said Joseph Morrin was desirous of leaving some permanent memorial of his regard for the City of Quebec of which he has been a citizen for more than fifty years, and over which he has twice had the honor of presiding as Chief Magistrate, and at the same time marking his attachment to the Church in which he was reared and to which he has always belonged, and considered that none could be more suitable for both purposes than a provision for increasing and rendering more perfect the means of obtaining for the youth generally, and especially those who may devote themselves to the Ministry of the said Church, the means of obtaining a liberal and an enlightened education." The Act according provides for the continuance of the Trust, and confers on the Governors the ordinary powers of legal incorporation. Among other things it provides that the Governors "shall be members of the Presbyterian Church of Canada in connection with the Church of Scotland or in the event of the union of that Church with any other Presbyterian body or bodies, then members of the United Church." In furtherance of the purpose of the Act a memorial was presented by the Governors of the College to the Synod of 1861 of the aforesaid Church, praying that the Synod in terms of the Act would appoint two Governors and ordain that as soon as there is a competent staff of Professors for common and theological education the certificates of such Professors shall be received by Presbyteries and the Synod as equally valid with those of Queen's College and the Scottish Universities. The Synod expressed thankfulness that Dr. Morrin, an Elder of the Church, should have devoted $50,000 for the purposes named, and cordially acceded to the prayer of the petition. In 1863 application was made to the Synod to have its course of Arts and Theology recognised by the Church which was granted as soon as the College shall possess Professors; (1) of Classics; (2) of Mathematics and Natural Philosophy; (3) of Logic, Metaphysics and Moral Philosophy; and if, in addition to the Professor of Divinity appointed by the Act, there be also a Professor (4) of Hebrew and Church History; provided the time of attendance be in accordance with the Laws of the Church and the Theological Professors be Ministers or Probationers of the Church. About this time the College was received into affiliation with McGill University, Montreal, its Curriculum in Arts assimilated to that College and its Students entitled to all the privileges and honors of that University. In 1870 the Governors obtained a College building and three houses situated in the centre of the City and immediately adjoining St Andrew's Church, in which also was placed the valuable Library of the Historical Society available for Professors and Students, together with its own Aylwin Library and ample Theological Collections. The last report of the General Assembly speaks in encouraging terms of the progress and usefulness of the College, and the great need of such an institution in the French and Roman Catholic City of Quebec. In 1881 the Staff was enlarged by the addition of two more Professors in Systematic Theology and Church History. Along with the other Colleges of the Church it obtained from the local legislature the power of conferring the degrees of B.D. and D.D.

2.—Officers of the College.

Governors.

The Rev. John Cook, D.D., LL.D., Chairman, and ten Members.

Registrar.

The Rev. Geo. Weir, M.A., LL.D.

Faculty of Theology.

The Principal, Apologetics and Homiletics.
Rev. G. D. Mathews, D.D., Systematic Theology.
Rev. Wm. B. Clark, M.A., Church History.
Rev. Geo. Weir, M.A., LL.D., Sacred Languages and Exegetics.

Faculty of Arts.

THE PRINCIPAL, Mental and Moral Philosophy.
REV. GEO. WEIR, M.A., LL.D., Classics and Logic.
REV. A. MACQUARRIE, B.A., Mathematics, Physics, and English Literature.
M. MILLER, Modern Languages.
G. G. GALE, M.D., Lecturer in Chemistry.

3.—THEOLOGICAL DEPARTMENT.

Regulations.

1. Students who desire to enter the Theological Department of Morrin College, with the view of studying for the Ministry, must forward to the Registrar on or before November 1st of each year:

(1.) A Presbyterial certificate of Church membership, and also recommending them to the Senate for admission.

(2.) Evidence that they are graduates of some University recognized as such by the Presbyterian Church in Canada, or that they have completed their attendance on the first three years' course of study in such University, or in Morrin College.

2. Divinity Students who have attended other Theological Seminaries will, on presenting Presbyterian certificates of standing and recommendation, be admitted *ad eundem gradum*.

3. The course of study throughout, is that recommended by the General Assembly of the Presbyterian Church in Canada, and similar to that of the other Colleges of the Church.

Scholarships and Prizes.

Scholarships—First class of $100, and Second class of $75—will be awarded to Students attending the Theological Department for superior answering at examinations held at the commencement of each Session, on the following subjects:

Students of the First year: *Latin.*—Cicero, De Senectute. *Greek.*—New Testament. Acts of the Apostles. *Theology.*—Confession of Faith. Chs 1-7 *Church History.*—The Apostolic Church.

Students of the Second year: *Latin.*—Cicero, De Officiis. Bk. I. Chs. 1-25. *Greek.*—New Testament. Gospels. *Theology.*—Confession of Faith. Ch. 8-17. Butler's Analogy. Part I. *Church History.*—Rise and Progress of Monastic Institutions.

Students of the Third year: *Latin.*—Cicero, De Officiis. Bk. I. Ch. 26 to end. *Greek.*—New Testament, Epistle to the Romans. *Theology.*—Confession of Faith. *Ecclesiology.*—Worship and Government of the Church. *Church History.*—History of the Church in Scotland. *Hebrew.*—Psalm 100-105.

Hebrew Scholarships.

A Prize of $10 will be awarded for best answering in Hebrew, by a Student entering his First year in Theology. Subject: Arnold's First Hebrew Book.

A Prize of $10 will be awarded for best answering in Hebrew, by a Student entering his Second year in Theology. Subjects: Grammar. Gen. Chaps. I. II. and Psalms I.–X.

The examinations will be held on November and the Scholarships may be held in addition to any other Class Scholarships or Prizes.

Degrees in Divinity.

By an Act of the Legislature of the Province of Quebec, Morrin College has been authorized to grant Degrees in Divinity. The regulations in respect of the B.D. degree are being prepared and may be ascertained on application to the Registrar.

Advantages.

Morrin College offers special advantages to young men in the Province of Quebec who may seek a Collegiate education. Being affiliated to McGill University, Montreal, attendance at its classes ranks as equal to attendance at Montreal, and as the course of study pursued in either Institution is identical, a Student may, at any time, if he desire it, pass from one College to the other without loss, while at the completion of his course in Morrin, he can obtain his Degree in Arts from the University. By the Will of the Founder, the Governors must belong to the Presbyterian Church, but in all other respects this College is undenominational. Its educational advantages and scholarships are open to Students of any religious persuasion.

Quebec is a singularly healthy city, while the grandeur of its situation, the quaintness of the old French town, and the historic importance of many of the events connected with it, invest it with an interest far beyond that pertaining to any other city on this continent. Protestant Churches of all communions are numerous, while the social advantages open to the Morrin College Students are very many.

Good board may be obtained in either English or French families at rates ranging from $3.50 to $4.00 a week.

4. ARTS DEPARTMENT.

Students attending Morrin College, purposing to graduate, have, in addition to attendance on the regular classes, to undergo three important examinations; the *Matriculation* or Entrance; the *Intermediate*, at the close of their second year's course; and the *Final*, or Degree, at the close of their fourth year.

The Matriculation Examination is the same as for McGill College Montreal, as also are the subjects for the four years' course. The Sessions begin about the middle of September and close about the end of April.

Scholarships in Arts, &c.

Written examinations will be held at the commencement of each Session, when Scholarships, *First* Class of $50 each, and *Second* Class of $25 each, will be awarded for superior answering on the subjects prescribed for Students in each of the four years of the Course.

An examination will be held at the close of the Session, when Prizes, *First* Class, $25, and *Second* Class, $15, will be awarded, according to answering on the whole work of the class.

Special prizes will also be given; one of $15 and two of $10, for Essays, the subjects of which will be prescribed and open to all Students attending Morrin College.

The Fee for each Session in Arts is $20, but Theological Students and Students in Arts studying for the Ministry pay no Fees.

Statistics.—Students, &c.

The Report to the General Assembly of 1882 gives 20 Matriculated Students in Arts and 31 occasional Students; total 51. In Theology there are 3 regular Students and 2 others. The number of Graduates are given in the Calendar of McGill University.

Finances.

The original Endowment was $50,000; the Gibb bequest $20,000; and by the generosity of Members of the Church a sum of $1,200 a year has been since 1881, added to the income of the College, the whole of which the Governors purpose to expend in Scholarships. Further to increase the funds of the Institution the General Assembly of 1882 resolved that "without assuming responsibility for the support of a Theological Department in

Morrin College, yet recognizing the valuable service rendered by said College, in training candidates for the Ministry of this Church allow the Presbytery of Quebec, as its congregations may see fit, to bestow their contributions on behalf of Morrin College."

* The Calendar with full information may be obtained from the Registrar at the College, Quebec.

5. PRESBYTERIAN COLLEGE, HALIFAX, N. S.

1. *Historical Statement.*

That branch of the Presbyterian body formerly known as the Presbyterian Church of Novia Scotia, for many years received a preparatory training for her theological students in the Pictou Academy, which was ably conducted by the late Rev. Thomas McCulloch, D.D., for upwards of twenty years who was also the Synod's Theological Professor. At his death the Rev. John Keir, of P. E. Island, was appointed Professor of Systematic and Pastoral Theology, and Rev. James Ross, D D., now Principal of Dalhousie College, Halifax, was subsequently called to the chair of Exegesis and Biblical Literature. After the close of the Pictou Academy aspirants to the ministry had no facilities for receiving an Arts' course, and as a necessary consequence the operations of the Theological Hall were for a season suspended for want of students. Having learned by experience to place no dependence upon any external source for the supply of her pulpits, the church founded an Institution at West River, Picton, in which young men might be prepared for entering the Hall, known as the West River Seminary. It was placed under the care of the Rev. Professor Ross, who, though single handed for six years conducted the classes with marked success. Opening with twelve students in the autumn of 1848, it continued in session for eight months. In the following year it received fresh accessions, so that at the close of the term of 1852, twenty-eight students were in attendance sixteen of whom entered the Hall in the Autumn. In 1854. the late Mr. Thomas McCulloch, was appointed Professor of Natural Philosophy and Mathematics, and increased the efficiency of the Institution. In 1858 the Seminary was transferred to Truro, where a commodious building had been erected for its classes. Here the attendance of the students at one time arose to 52, a large proportion of whom had the ministry in view. The Theological Hall continued in session six weeks in the autumn of each year, Rev. John Keir being Professor of Systematic and Pastoral Theology, and Rev. James Smith, of Stewiacke, being Professor Ross's successor in the chair of Exegesis and Biblical Literature. Excepting the income arising out of the Church's invested funds, which at that time were quite limited, the annual expenditure was met by the free will offerings of the people, whose sympathies the Institution had deeply enlisted. Friends in Scotland generously contributed also, in money and books about $3,500.

The Free Synod of Nova Scotia, encouraged by the Colonial Committee of the Free Church of Scotland, began to take steps with a view to the education of young men for the ministry, in 1861. Next year a plan for raising an endowment fund was adopted, the Colonial Committee undertaking to pay the salaries of the Professors for some years, till the fund could be collected; and during the succeeding winter a class of five students was taught by the Rev. A. Forrester, who at the same time supplied the congregation in Halifax, as a deputy from the Free Church of Scotland. In October, 1848, Professors King and McKenzie arrived from Scotland, and on the 2nd of November, the College was opened with an attendance of fifteen students, three of them in Theology. This session, Mr. Forrester, now settled in Halifax, gave a course of lectures in Natural Science. Rev. D. Honeyman taught Hebrew. Next session the attendance increased to nineteen, but one of the students died in the course of the winter. A still heavier blow fell on the College, in the death of Professor McKenzie. The following year (1860-1) Professor Lyall succeeded to the chair of Professor McKenzie, a d the attendance rose to twenty-two. In 1851 the Rev. John Stewart, of New Glasgow, visited Scotland, and collected $4,675 for a College Building. St. John's Church, in Gerrish Street, was purchased, and adapted for the purposes of the College and Academy. This last Institution was a necessary appendage to the College, as good classical schools were scarce in those days. It was a distinct organaiztion, though under the control of the same Board; and received a Provincial Grant of $1,000 per annum. The new premises were occupied in the winter of 1852. About this time Mr. Honeyman left Halifax, and Hebrew was added to the other departments taught by Professor King, till Mr. McKnight was sent out by the Colonial Committee to relieve him of it, in January, 1855. The Staff of the Free Church College remained without further change till the union with the Presbyterian Church of Nova Scotia in 1860.

At the union Professor Lyall was transferred to Truro. When the church entered into the scheme of re-organizing Dalhousie College, Professors Ross, McCulloch and Lyall received chairs in that Institution, and the Truro Seminary was closed in 1863.

Previously to the re-organization of Dalhousie College in the year 1863, the Synod of the Maritime Provinces in connection with the Church of Scotland had taken no part in the work of Collegiate Education. All its ministers, numbering at that time about forty, had been sent out by the Colonial Committee, and were ordained ministers of the Church of Scotland. From 1853 to 1863 the Synods of Nova Scotia and New Brunswick had been sending to Scotland promising young men to be educated for the Colonial Ministry. These were supported during their Collegiate course by annual bursaries supplied by the church. This plan having been found insufficient it was proposed to co-operate in the re-orgrnization of Dalhousie College, whose endowment funds had for some years been lying without being applied to their original and legitimate purposes. The Synod agreed to nominate to Dalhousie College one professor, and to raise t e endowment required for his support. Within three years from the re-commencement of Dalhousie College, in 1863, the Synod of the Maritime Provinces, in connexion with the Church of Scotland, was enabled by the liberality of the people to raise, in addition to the sum necessary for the support of the chair during that time, the capital sum of $20,000 as an endowment Professor McDonald, having been nominated by the Synod, and appointed by the Governors, to the Chair of Mathematics, entered upon his duties in the autumn of 1863, and continues to occupy the Chair of Mathematics up to the present time.

Dr. Keir died in 1858, and after the union of 1860 Professors King and McKnight, aided by Professor Smith, conducted the Hall of the united body in Gerrish Street, Halifax. Dr. Smith died in 1868, and Professor McKnight taught Exegetics as well as Hebrew for the next three sessions. On Dr. King's retirement, in 1871, Professor McKnight was transferred to the Chair of Theology and Church History, and Professor Currie was appointed to the Chair of Hebrew and Exegetical Theology.

Shortly before the union of 1875 the Synod of the Maritime Provinces unanimously resolved to request the Colonial Committee of the Church of Scotland to undertake the support of one chair in the Theological Hall in Halifax, and recommended the

Rev. Allan Pollok, D.D., to be appointed to the chair—the support asked to be continued until the necessary endowment could be raised. The Church of Scotland responded liberally to this request, and Professor Pollok's appointment by the church having been approved of by both Synods in the Maritime Provinces, he entered upon his duties as Professor of Church History and Pastoral Theology in the autumn of 1875—the year of union The Church of Scotland in 1878 has intimated its desire that it may be relieved from the support of this chair within two years, which has been done.

There are now six professors in the service of the church of the Maritime Provinces—three in Dalhousie College, and three in the Theological Hall, at Pine Hill. Professor McCulloch died in the opening of 1865; and the three Professors in arts at present supported by the Synod are Principal Ross, Dr. Lyall and Professor McDonald.

2. OFFICERS OF THE COLLEGE.

Board of Management.

The REV. R. F. BURNS, D.D., Chairman.
The REV. P. G. MCGREGOR, D.D., Secretary and Treasurer.
(*Thirty other Members.*)

Senate.

The REV. ALEXANDER MCKNIGHT, D.D., Chairman.
The REV. JOHN CURRIE, Clerk.
(*Eight other Members.*)

Board of Examiners.

The REV. R. LAING, M. A., Convener.
(*Five other Members.*)

Staff.

The REV. ALEXANDER MCKNIGHT, D.D., Principal and Professor of Theology.

The REV. JOHN CURRIE, Professor of Hebrew and Biblical Literature.

The REV. ALLAN POLLOK, D.D., Professor of Church History and Pastoral Theology.

3. CURRICULUM.

First Year.—Junior Hebrew, Apologetics, Exegetics and Church History.

Second and Third Years.—Systematic Theology, Senior Hebrew, Exegetics and Church History.

4. GENERAL REGULATIONS.

1, *Preparatory Course.*

Before entering the Hall, students are required to take a regular course in Arts, at Dalhousie College or some similar Institution. Dalhousie College has a staff of eight professors, three of whom are appointed and supported by the Synod of the Maritime Provinces. Full information respecting the course of study will be found in the College Calendar, which may be obtained by application to Principal Ross. The subjects embraced in the course are the following:—

First Year.—Latin, Greek, Mathematics and Rhetoric.

Second Year.—Latin, Greek, Mathematics, Chemistry and Logic.

Third Year.—Latin, Physics, Metaphysics, French or German, and Greek or Chemistry.

Fourth Year.—Latin, Ethics, History, French or German, and Mathematical Physics or Greek.

Students intending to study for the ministry are recommended to take the full course, and graduate as Bachelors of Arts. Those who, for special reasons, desire a shorter course, are required to take the following classes: Rhetoric, Latin (two sessions), Greek (three sessions), Mathematics (two sessions), Logic, Metaphysics, Physics and Ethics. This course may be overtaken in three winter sessions of six months each. Such Students are required to submit to the regular examinations in the several classes at the close of each session.

Presbyteries are authorized to accept a degree of B A. (Ethics and Metaphysics being included in the course) or *pass* certificates of attendance or proficiency in all the classes required, as sufficient evidence of literary qualification.

When a Student does not produce the *pass* certificates of one or more of the required classes, he shall be examined on th sub·jects taught in these classes, by the Board of Examiners, who shall have power, if they think it necessary, to defer his admission to the Hall. Exceptional cases, in which a Presbytery may recommend the admission of a student who cannot satisfy the Board of Examiners, must be brought before Synod or Assembly.

The Board of Examiners meet, at the call of the Convener, during the week immediately preceding the commencement of the Session. Students who which to appear before them must give intimation to the Convener at least a week before the 1st November.

2. *Presbyterial Superintendence.*

1. It is prescribed in the Rules of Procedure that Ministers pay particular attention to young men who are prosecuting a liberal education with a view to the Christian Ministry, obtain accurate information respecting their natural abilities, prudence and piety, and watch assiduously over their intellectual and spiritual improvement.

2. Applicants for admission to the Hall are nominated to the Presbytery of the bounds by their respective ministers, who shall produce the necessary University cetificates, and testimonials of Church membership; and the Presbytery, having examined the applicants specially on their religious knowledge, and motives in studying for the Ministry, and being satisfied, shall certify those who are graduates, or having obtained *pass* certificates in the necessary classes, to the Senate, and all others to the Board of Examiners.

3. Students of Divinity are required to appear every year before the Presbyteries within whose bounds they reside, and to give in a written exercise on a subject previously prescribed. A Presbyterial certificate should be produced by every student at the commencement of each session.

4. Every student is required, at the commencement of each session, to present a certificate of Church membership to the minister of some Presbyterian Congregation in Halifax; and should he leave Halifax at the close of session, to take with him a certificate of Church membership, to be presented to the Session or Presbytery within whose bounds he may reside during the summer.

3. *Work of the College.*

1. The College meets annually on the first Wednesday of November at 7.30 P. M., and closes on the last Thursday of April.

2. There are three Professorships of Theology, viz: one of Oriental Languages and Exegetical Theology, including Biblical Criticism and Hermeneutics; and one of Church History and Pastoral Theology, including Homiletics.

3. The Professor of Pastoral Theology is directed to take an opportunity, during the course of his lectures, of bringing before the minds of the students the claims of Foreign Missions, the qualifications necessary for missionary labor, and the best modes of discharging the missionary office.

4. Besides attending the classes and preparing the ordinary class exercises, each student is required to deliver the following discourses, viz: in the first year, an Apologetical thesis and a critical exercise on a passage of the Greek Testament; in the second year, a Polemical thesis and a Lecture; in the third year, a critical exercise on a passage of the Hebrew Bible and a Sermon. Students of the second and third years are expected to prepare these discourses during the recess, and give them as early in the session as possible:—not later than January.

5. At the end of the session each Professor shall furnish to every student in his class a certificate of attendance and conduct. Students shall, at the earliest opportunity after the close of tha Session, present their certificates to the Presbytery, within whose bounds they reside.

4. *Degree of B. D.*

1. Students preparing for the degree B.D., are required to make an average of at least 70 per cent. in each department, and a general average of at least 50 per cent. at the six regular pass examinations held during their three years course.

2. Other candidates are required to undergo a special examination in lieu of these and to make at least 50 marks per cent. on each paper, and an average of at least 70 per cent. on all the papers taken together, at such special examination.

3. Both classes of candidates are required, after fulfilling provisions 1 and 2 respectively, to pass a *final* examination on the various subjecis of theological study. Specimens of Patristic Greek and Theological Latin, shall be included among the subjects for this examination.

4. Special and final examinations will not be necessarily limited to the contents of particular books; but a list of books will be given in the Calendar as a general guide and help in preparing for them.

5. Special and final examinations will be held, when needful, at the close of the Session; notice to be given by candidates to the Clerk of Senate in the month of January preceding.

6. Fee for B. D., $10—also $5 for special examination.

Books recommended for Special Examination.

Greek.—Whole New Test. *Hebrew.*—Genesis; and Ps. i.-xx. *Exegetics, &c.*—Barrow's Sacred Geography and Antiquities. Keil's Introduction to the Old Testament. Westcott on the Canon of the New Testament, or Introduction, pp. i.-cvii. of

Charteris's Canonicity. Hammond's Textual Criticism of the N. T., or Scrivener. *Church History.*—Kurtz and Gieseler. *Theology and Apolegetics.*—Hodge's Systematic Theology. Isaac Taylor's Transmission of Ancient books. McKnight's Historical Evidence. Chapters on the Internal and Experimental Evidence in Haldane or Chalmers. Schaff on the Person of Christ.

Subjects for Final Examination.

Greek.—Septuagint, last ten Chapters of Genesis; Celsus—Quotations in Charteris's Canonicity, pp. 369-378. *Latin.*—Vulgate, Ps. xxxviii., l., lxv., lxvi., lxx., lxxx., lxxxix., xciv., xcix., cxiv., cxv., cxxvi., cxxvii., cxlviii. Luc. i., ii. Turrettini Theologia Elenctica, Locus ix., Qu. ix.-xii. inclusive. *Chaldee,* Daniel ii.-vii. Charteris on the Authenticity of John's Gospel, introduction to page cviii.

Library.

There is a Library of about 9,000 volumes, to which the students have free access. It is furnished with some of the leading reviews and magazines. No fee is charged. Students are not allowed to remove any books from the premises until entered in the Librarian's register.

Residence.

The premises at Pine Hill, contain accommodation for resident students. The building is elegant and commodious. The salubrity of the air, the beauty of the scenery, and the vicinity of the Public Park and North West Arm, make the locality attractive; and the rooms are convenient and comfortable. The fee for board—heating and light included—is reduced to two dollars per week—payable monthly in advance. The boarding arrangements are under the immediate charge of a competent person. Applications for rooms are to be addressed to Professor Currie, Secretary to the Senate, on or after the third Tuesday of October. Rooms will be allocated in the order of application after that date.

Class Prizes.

The class prizes have been awarded according to the results of eight examinations held during the Session upon the combined work of all the classes.

S. Davids, S.S. Prize $40; two of $20; two of $15; two of $10.
The McMillan of $25, in Theology.

The Pollok of $25, in Church History.
The Foot Massey of $25, in Hebrew and Exegetics.
The St. Matthew's of $25, in New Testament.
The Wiswell of $6, in Reading of Scripture.
The Forest Book Prizes, in Rules and Forms of Procedure.

Bursaries, 1882.

By the Bursary Committee to Boarding 15 Students $356; two Students in Dalhousie College $50; Newfoundland Bursary $200; New Glasgow Bursary $60.

Bursars must (1) be members of the Presbyterian Church in full communion; (2) attend Institutions within the bounds of the Synod; (3) present satisfactory testimonials; and (4) labor at least two years after they have finished their College course within the bounds of the Presbyterian Church in Canada. Bursars who fail to implement this engagement are expected to return the money. The Convener of the Sub-Committee on Bursaries is the Rev. John McMillan, Truro, to whom application should be made before the commencement of the Session.

5. Statistics.

Students, 1881–82.

First year, 7; Second, 5; Third, 5; Total, 17.

Graduates and Alumni 1875—1882.

Graduates 159; partial Students 26; Total 185.

Finances.

Ordinary Fund.

Receipts	$8,157 88
Expenditure	9,536 27
Deficit	1,378 39
Total Debt	3,069 59

Bursary Fund.

Receipts	$843 50
Expenditures	852 00
Debt	191 46

Endowment Fund.

This important work advances, but not with such progress as the Board desires. Last year the whole sum collected of the proposed $100,000 was $62,000, of which sum nearly $28,000 had been expended in the Pine Hall buildings and premises, including furnishing and other unavoidable expenses, besides nearly $6,000 for the Robic Street land and building plans, leaving about $27.000 invested, part of it permanently and part drawing bank interest. By a good deal of effort on the part of the Chairman and other friends of the College, $7,000 and upwards have been gathered in, so that the $69,000 have been passed, of which sum $27,000 are invested permanently, and $6,000 temporarily.

There are also the following permanent endowments for Bursaries. Hunter Fund $2,000; Mrs. Matheson's Legacy $1,000; George Kerr's $800; City Debentures $1,000.

* Calendars obtained on application to the Registrar.

VI. THE COLLEGE OF MANITOBA.

(Winnipeg.)

1. HISTORICAL STATEMENT.

This College was begun in 1871 in a country which but a year before had emerged from a state of disorder and had just been placed under responsible government; during a period, too, in which the country was passing through the ordeal of the reception of a heterogenecus immigration. Much caution and anxious thought was consequently required to pilot the College into a secure and permanent position. The wish of its promoters has evidently been to adapt the institution to the people of the country. While maintaining its religious character, at the same time it was desirable that none of its requirements should debar any student from its privileges. It originally begun in Kildonan, in connection with the congregation of the venerable Dr. Black, where a building costing about $5,000 was provided for it, its first three sessions were conducted there. But the growth of Winnipeg and the fact of its becoming the Capital of the Province justified, in the estimaticn of its friends, the removal of the College to that City. A rented building was there used for one year, and in 1875 a wooden erection was purchased for $4,000 both unsightly and unsuitable. The Board taking advantage of the increase in the value of property sold it for $7,000 after a use of six years. Foreseeing that a building of a different character would soon be required, a site thought suitable was purchased for $500 but damaged by the proximity of railways it was sold for $4,000 making a total of $11,000 as a nucleus for a new building. An appeal was then made to the citizens which met with a most favorable reception from influential members of all denominations. The City Council without a division passed a resolution granting the College exemption from all taxation, on account of its being a public benefit, an Act which the Legislature confirmed without opposition. A liberal subscription was soon obtained from the citizens and friends abroad, and a sum of not less than $22,000 became available for building purposes. A block of four and a half acres was immediately purchased from the Hudson Bay Company in the western part of the City, in a line with the Government buildings, for $6,000. Plans were advertised for a building to hold at least forty residents, and to contain class-rooms, museum, library and laboratory, steam heating, &c., with rooms for a Resident Principal or Professor, part only of which should be erected at first. A College has consequently been provided worthy of the Church which it represents and promises greatly to promote its welfare. The time is certainly coming when the demand for Collegiate education in this rising Province will require and secure not only the completion of the present plan but also its enlargement.

The College is happily confederated with other Colleges in a Provincial University in which all have an equal interest and share, and is now able to afford the highest form of education, with its appropriate honors and degrees, to the people among whom its lot is cast.

To its faculty of Arts it has added a faculty of Theology. The Presbytery of Manitoba at its formation memorialized the General Assembly of the Canada Presbyterian Church the year before the Union to be allowed to take charge of the education of Students for the Ministry. This was cautiously granted, the Assembly not committing itself to the immediate authorative of a Theological Faculty. But the progress of the Church and Country render this inevitable, so that now there is an acknowledged Staff of Theological Professors equal to the requirements of a thorough Theological Curriculum. The Staff is also representative in its *personel.* Professor Bryce was sent out in 1871 by the Canada Presbyterian Church, and Professor Hart in 1872 by the Church in connection with the Church of Scotland, with instructions from the Synod "to take part with Professor Bryce in the work of the Manitoba Presbyterian College and to engage likewise in Ministerial labor at such places as he might find suitable." He thus became the harbinger of the Union happily consummated in 1875 and which promises to yield such blessed results to the cause of true religion throughout the Dominion.

A Charter of Incorporation of date 36 Vict. cap. 33 was obtained from the Legislature and assented to in March, 1875, granting the usual powers and privileges to the "College of Manitoba," vesting the power of appointing and removing Professors and Tutors in the General Assembly, with the power of creating a Theological Faculty and "of declaring the doctrines and principles which said faculty shall teach." After the example of the Charter of Knox College; and that in the event of a union with any other body of Presbyterians the bases of such union should form part of the declaration of theological principles. The Board of Management consists of fifteen members and is annually appointed by the General Assembly of the United Church. The Home Mission no longer contributes to the maintenance of the College but it now rests on the liberality of the whole Church by which, considering its importance to the vast regions of the North-West it cannot fail to be liberally supported.

2. OFFICERS OF THE COLLEGE.

Board of Management.

A. G. B. Bannatyne Esq., Chairman; Rev. Professor Hart, M. A., Secretary, and D. MacArthur Esq., Treasurer.

Senate.

Rev. D. M. Gordon, B. D., Chairman.

Principal.

The Rev. George Bryce, M. A., LL. B.

Committee of Theological Superintendence.

Rev. C. B. Pitblado, Convener.

Staff of Instructors.

Rev. George Bryce, M. A., LL. B., Professor of Science and Literature, and Lecturer on Systematic Theology.

Rev. Thomas Hart, M. A., B. D., Professor of Classics and French, and Lecturer on Biblical Exegesis.

Mr. A. M. Campbell, B. A., Resident Tutor and Tutor in Mathematics.

Mr. N. McCallum, B. A., Tutor in Higher Mathematics.

Mr. J. C. Elliott, B. A., Assistant in Classics.

Privileges of Affiliation.

To elect seven representatives on the University Council of twenty-seven members; to nominate two of the eight members of the Board of Studies of the University; to have the College examinations counted as equivalent to the University Preliminary; to have the entire management of its own internal affairs, studies, worship and religious teaching; to grant, with the sanction of the General Assembly, the degrees of Bachelor of Divinity and Doctor of Divinity, which degrees shall entitle the holders to all rights and privileges as if granted by the University.

3. CURRICULUM.

1. *Preparatory Course.*

Hitherto Manitoba College has been dependant on its own preparatory department to fit its students for University, or proper College work. The fact that there were no Secondary Schools in the country made this imperative. The Board has always looked forward to the time when High Schools should be established by the Government, and it should be freed from this work.

2. *Theological Instruction.*

The General Assembly has from time to time put students for Theology under the care of the Presbytery of Manitoba, and authorized the Presbytery to supervise their studies, while attending Manitoba College. For this purpose the following resolutions were unamiously adopted by the Presbytery, in 1882:

1. That the large demand on the Church in Manitoba and the North-West for supply necessitates the obtaining of as great a number of laborers as possible, and at as reasonable an expense as as may be, especially for the large amount of summer work by students, which has been an important means of Church extension in Canada in the Presbyterian Church.

2. That the Presbytery, in view of this, deems it wise to call on Christian young men of good gifts to devote themselves to the ministry, and also to counsel parents to aim at the entrance of such of their sons as the Lord may leau into the work of the Gospel Ministry, that a native ministry by this means may be reared.

3. That the Presbytery, in accordance with the ancient rights of Presbyteries, and the expressed permission and approval of the General Assembly, take charge of such students as desire to pursue their studies, and appoint a standing committee for the superintendence of theological students, to prescribe subjects, to arrange for instruction, conduct examinations, and report to Presbytery at its meeting in May.

4. That the Committee on Theological Superintendence issue an address in the name of the Moderator of the Presbytery, presenting the object of these resolutions to the people.

5. That the persons already mentioned form the Committee on Theological Superintendence, and that the examinations be hold in conjunction with the final College Examinations.

Regulations for Students.

1. That students for the ministry be taken in charge by the Presbytery on their passing their Previous (2nd University) Examination, by the Committee of Theological Superintendence.

2. That their course be guided by having their attention specially directed to subjects in Classics and Mental and Moral Philosophy.

3. That until their B.A. course has been completed (or in those cases concerning which the Committee may decide that a course of study equivalent thereto has been passed), the only subjects of the Theological course that students may pursue as part of their curriculum shall be Hebrew, such works in Apologetics as may be included in the University course, and New Testament Greek, except that students may be allowed to attend the classes in Systematic Theology, for the purpose of fitting them for their Missionary work during the summer months; such attendance, however, will not be accounted as any part of their Theological course.

4. That on passing their B.A. Examination, or what may be deemed equivalent thereto by the Committee of Theological Superintendence, the students shall then enter upon their Theological course of study, which shall extend over a course of three years, the Theological Term of each year beginning on the first Wednesday of November and ending on the third Wednesday of April.

5. That the subjects of Theological study be those required by the General Assembly's Regulations, viz.:—Apologetics, Systematic Theology, Exegetics, Biblical Criticism, Church History, Homiletics and Pastoral Theology; as also a Homily, Popular Sermon, Lecture, and a Greek or Hebrew Critical Exercise.

6. That while the foregoing embraces the deliberate opinion of the Presbytery, as to the course to be pursued by students for the ministry, the Presbytery, according to the practice followed by the Church generally, would not be understood to discourage any person whose case should be made exceptional, from making application to the Presbytery with a view of pursuing a special course of study.

4 MEDALS, BURSARIES AND PRIZES—1882—83.

A bursary, the interest of £100 sterling, established by an old resident of Red River, will be awarded as the result of the Regular Terminal Examinations.

The proceeds of the first half-year's investment of $250, the "John Black Bursary."

Prizes in books are also awarded to successful students at the College Examinations.

The *Governor-General's* Medal will be presented to the best student of the College, who passes most successfully the December and March Examinations of the College, and has the highest number of marks at the Preliminary Examination of the University.

Students of Manitoba College, going up to the University Previous Examination or University Final Honor Examination are eligible for the Silver and Bronze Medals presented by the Governor-General to the University of Manitoba.

Fees.

Regular Course $9 per Term in advance. Caution money $5 per Session. Board $4.50 per week.

Residence Regulations.

Students are under the careful superintendence of the Resident Head of the College, and are not allowed to leave the Residence at night without his special permistion. Study hours are from 9.20 a.m. to 12.30 p.m.; 2 to 3.20 p.m; from 7 to 9.30 p.m. for Juniors; from 7 to 11 p.m. for Seniors. Morning worship is at 9; evening worship at 9.30. Religious instruction of a non-sectarian kind is given to all students of the College, unless objected to by parents or guardians. Resident students are expected to attend morning and evening Sabbath service, and afternoon Bible Classes in Knox or St. Andrew's Churches, Winnipeg, unless other arrangements are made by parents or guardians.

University students are required to provide themselves with College cap and gown, and are required to appear in their classes and at examinations with proper costume.

Theological Session from the first Wednesday in November to the third Wednesday in April.

V. STATISTICS.

Students, 1882.

Final, 5; University Preliminary Examination, 14; Preparatory second year, 6; first year, 23; Others, 2; total 55. Preparing for the Ministry 10.

Finances.

Receipts, including Building Fund	$58,052.41
Disbursements	56,414.96
On hand	1,637.45
Mortgage on College Building	24,000.00

⁂ The calendar containing full information can be obtained from the Rev. Professor Bryce, Winnipeg Manitoba.

LADIES' COLLEGES.

I. OTTAWA LADIES' COLLEGE AND CONSERVATORY OF MUSIC.

1. *Historical Statement.*

This College was established and incorporated by an Act of Parliament in 1869, in order to meet the desire expressed by many earnest Protestant gentlemen, to have a first-class education put within the reach of the young women of the eastern portion of the Dominion, based on decidedly religious and Protestant principles, and the better to secure these ends they have sought and cordially obtained affiliation and recognition from the General Assembly of the Presbyterian Church in Canada, by whom the institution is recommended to the confidence of the Church, and the Protestant community at large.

A thorough training is afforded in all the branches of an English, a Classical and Scientific Education; and in the Modern Languages and Fine and Useful Arts to those who desire these accomplishments. The studies of each pupil are carefully watched, and so regulated as not to be an undue burden and not to interfere with health.

Ottawa City, the Capital of Canada, one of the most attractive cities in the Dominion, is centrally situated and easily accessible by railway, has an invigorating climate, and is fast becoming an educational centre.

The College Buildings are situated on a bluff in the western part of the city. The beautiful and extensive grounds of the Public Buildings are in close proximity to the College, and at all times available for healthy recreation, and the use of the Library of Parliament can readily be obtained.

The studies of the Senior Class are available either for those who wish to graduate or who may prefer taking a portion of the branches. For young ladies who have completed the usual English course of instruction either in private or in public schools they are of great value. For the most part they are University studies and an important part of a liberal education, both as branches of knowledge and a means of intellectual culture.

2. *Courses of Instruction.*

The Courses of Instruction comprise all the branches of a solid English and Classical Education.

Preparatory Course.

This includes the Junior Department embracing English elementary studies. To enter, pupils must be able to read and count. To enter any other department, it is only necessary to have made fair progress in the regular branches of the lower departments.

Collegiate Course.

This generally extends over a period of three years. Pupils who are able to pass a satisfactory examination in the branches of this course, may graduate and receive a diploma.

First Year.—Arithmetic, advanced; Algebra, to simple Equations; Geometry, Euclid, books I. & II.; Natural Philosophy; Natural Science; English Grammar and Composition; History, British; Geography, civil and physical; English Literature, with works of distinguished authors; Latin; Scripture, History and Geography; Elocution. Elective Studies.—Latin, French, German, Italian, Drawing, Painting and Music.

Second Year.—Arithmetic; Book-keeping; Algebra, advanced; Geometry, advanced; Natural Philosophy, Sound and Light; English Literature, Shakespeare; Composition; Latin; History, European; Evidences of Christianity, Lectures; Scripure. Elective Studies.—Latin, French, German, Italian, Drawing and Book-keeping.

Third or Senior Year.—Rhetoric; Composition; Logic, Mental Philosophy; Natural Science.—Botany, Geology, Chemistry, Astronomy; French; Evidences of Christianity. Elective Studies.—Latin, German, French, Italian, Chemistry, Book-keeping, Drawing and Music.

Students who have completed the usual course of study in High Schools, Collegiate Institutes, or other Schools, would find the studies of this year highly profitable, even if they did not contemplate the full curriculum of the College. In any year of the course full value will be given to any of the studies taken by those who have passed the "Intermediate Examination."

For Graduation, the branches above mentioned, with not less than two books of Euclid, and a thorough knowledge of one language, are necessary; but for students who prefer special subjects, embracing all the departments, a special certificate will be given, if not less than three-fourths of the whole subjects are taken. To pass, fifty per cent. of the whole marks is required, and not less than forty in each study. Those who obtain ninety per cent. of the marks in any study will be marked as passing with honor.

Art Studies.

Drawing with pencil and crayon, from models and other examples, water color and oil painting with painting on porcelain and other fabrics are taught thoroughly by professional artists. Class instruction is also given in perspective drawing and in sketching from nature.

3. CONSERVATORY OF MUSIC.

All departments of the Conservatory are under the general supervision of the Director, J. W. Harrison, Esq., who gives the entire instruction to the senior organ and piano pupils, and to those studying musical theory. In consequence of the same method being used in all departments the progress of pupils is not interrupted when advancement takes place from lower to higher grades.

Mr. C. Reichling, the well known violinist of Montreal, having arranged to visit Ottawa weekly, the Conservatory is enabled to offer his important instruction on the violin. This instrument has been of late years much studied by ladies, for whom it is eminently adapted, and it is hoped that such a class may be formed as to render the performance of concert music a feature in the Conservatory.

Graduation.

The Standard of Graduation requires that the students should be able to perform in an artistic and satisfactory manner representative pieces selected from the classical works of the most eminent English and foreign composers, and should have a competent knowledge of musical theory.

For the graduating course in vocal music the same high standard will be required, and the songs will be chosen according to the voices of the candidates, and given out during the Session.

Honors and Prizes.

These are awarded for decided excellency for general efficiency and high standing in each of the studies of the regular course, and consist of gold and silver medals, and books, and diplomas of graduation.

The fees are moderate, the College building airy, healthy, well heated and furnished, the staff eminent in their several departments and the College rendered as much as possible a pleasant home.

Special terms are offered to the daughters of ministers.

Calendars giving full particulars obtained on application.

BOARD OF MANAGEMENT.

H. F. BRONSON, ESQ., President.
SHERIFF SWEETLAND, M.D., 1st Vice-President.
REV. WM. MOORE, D.D., 2nd Vice-President.

Principal.

REV. A. F. KEMP, M.A., L L. D.

Musical Director.

J. W. F. HARRISON, ESQ.

Instructor in Art.

PHILIP MONSON, ESQ.

2 YOUNG LADIES COLLEGE.

(Brantford, Ont.)

1. HISTORICAL STATEMENT.

The College established in 1874, in connection with the Presbyterian Church in Canada, has met with a gratifying measure of success. It now occupies a high position among the educational institutions of the country, and maintains its reputation for the thoroughness of the education imparted. The General Assembly of the Presbyterian Church in Canada, with which it is in connection by an Act of Incorporation, has for a series of years warmly commended the institution to the confidence and support of the church at large.

The location of the College is all that could be desired as a home for young ladies. The building is admirably adapted for College purposes, and presents an aspect at once elegant and home-like in all its arrangements. The grounds extend to three and a half acres, and everything provided that can conduce to the health and comfort of the pupils.

2. COURSE OF INSTRUCTION.

Preparatory Department.

Classes are organized to correspond with the 3rd and 4th forms of the Public School programme. Pupils will be able at an early age to begin the study of music and the modern languages at comparatively little cost. The time required in this department will depend on the maturity and application of the student.

Collegiate Department.

Candidates for admission to this department must be at least twelve years of age, and must pass the examination prescribed in the preparatory course, or must show such standing as will entitle them to enter the junior class or any other class more advanced. The High School Entrance Examination, or the Intermediate Examination will be accepted in the course for the subjects they embrace, and will admit to the junior and senior classes respectively.

In arranging the course of study pains will be taken to meet the diversified wants of students without sacrificing the regularity and system so essential to progress. Parents who intrust the training of their daughters to this institution are expected to allow sufficient time for the healthy unfolding and discipline of their minds before entering on the severer parts of the Collegiate course.

In the middle and senior years the subjects are arranged to meet the requirements of young ladies who may desire to prepare for the High School Intermediate Examination, with a view to teaching. Also in the department of Modern Languages, Literature and History there will be found a conformity to the Univerity subjects, in order to prepare for the Local Examinations for Women held annually in the College in accordance with the University regulations.

Regular Course.

First Year—Mathemetics, History, Political Geography and French.

Second Year—English, Mathematics, History, Geography, Civil and Physical, Science, French, Latin.

Third Year—English, Mathematics, History and Geography Ancient and Modern, French, German, Latin, Science, Philosophy and Logic.

Examinations.

The examinations as far as practicable are conducted by outside examiners.

1. On subjects which extend over the year, the final examination is held at the close of the College, but on all other subjects the final examination is held at the close of the term during which the subject has been read.

2. Students who have completed the entire course of study, and passed satisfactory examinations will be awarded diplomas.

3. Every candidate who passes the University Examination in one or more groups, and who has also passed successfully in the honor subjects of the group, will be entitled to a University Examination in one or more groups, and who has also passed successfully in the honor subjects of the group, will be entitled to a University certificate of her standing.

Art Department.

The full course of instruction embraces the following: copying from models with pencil or crayon, drawing from real objects, blocks, flowers, buildings, &c.; painting in water colors and in oil; sketching from nature; decoration, specially upon china and pottery; Lessons in perspective, and the general principles of art and design, are given at every stage of progress.

Students who take a three years' course in Drawing, and Oil or Water Color Painting, and have shown proficiency in the Art, will be entitled to a Certificate in Art.

Music.

The instruction given in this department embraces all the branches essential to a complete musical education. 1. Theory of Music—Embracing Harmony, Composition and History. 2. Singing—Embracing chorus-singing in classes, solo-singing, and voice culture. 3. Piano-forte playing—Embracing elementary and technical exercises, training in style, expression and artistic conception.

Special Diplomas are granted to those who take a full course, and pass the necessary examinations qualifying them to become teachers of vocal and instrumental music.

3. OFFICERS OF THE COLLEGE.

Board of Directors.

A. Robertson, Esq., Chairman; William Buck, Esq., Vice-Chairman; H. B. Fleming, Esq., Secretary.

Principal.

T. M. MacIntyre, M.A., LL.B.

Musical Director.

J. Edmond Aldous, B.A

Instructor in Art.

Henry Martin, Esq., A.R.S.A.

.*. Calendars with full information can be obtained from the Principal, Brantford, Ont.

THE CHURCH—ITS MINISTERS.

I. ROLLS OF SYNODS.

Synod of the Maritime Provinces.

Rev. P. M. Morrison, Dartmouth, N. S., *Clerk*

Name	Place	Page.
Aitken, William	Newcastle, N B	170
Allan, James	Cove Head, P E I	170
Archibald, W. P., *M.A*	Cavendish, P E I	171
Baxter, J. J. (*Retired*)	Truro, N S	173
Bayne, E. S	Murray Harbor, P E I	174
Bearisto, J. R	Carleton, N S	174
Bennet, J., *D.D.* (*Retired*)	St. John, N B	175
Blair, D. B	Barney's River, N S	176
Boyd, John	Bass River, N B	177
Boyd, S	Wallace, N S	177
Brown, Archibald	New Dublin, N S	177
Bruce, George, *B.A*	St. John, N B	178
Bruce, W. T., *M.D*	Valley, N S	178
Burgess, J. C., *B.A*	Carleton, N B	178
Burns, R. F., *D.D*	Halifax, N S	178
Burrows, A	Truro, N S	179
Cairns, J. A., *M.A*	U. Musquodoboit, N S	179
Cameron, Alex	Portapique, N S	179
Cameron, John	Bridgwater, N S	180
Cameron, J. G	Souris, P E I	180
Campbell, Malcolm	Strathlorne, C B	181
Carr, A. F., *M.A*	Alberton, P E I	182
Carruthers, J. S	Pictou, N S	182
Chase, J. H., *M.A*	Truro, N S	184
Christie. George	Bedford, N S	184
Clark, Peter,	Cape North, C B	184
Crockett, D. R	Passekeag, N B	187
Cumming, Robert	Westville, N S	187
Cumming, Thomas	Stellarton, N S	187
Currie, J. (*Prof.*)	Halifax, N S	188
Darragh, W. S	Goose River, N S	188
Dickey, A. B	Milford, N S	189
Donald, Andrew (*Retired*)	Hampton, N B	160

Synod of Montreal and Ottawa.

Rev. J. Watson. *M.A.*, Huntingdon, *Clerk.*

Synod of Toronto and Kingston.

Rev. John Gray, *M.A*., Orillia, *Clerk*.

Synod of Hamilton and London.

Rev. W. Cochrane, *D.D.*, Brantford, *Clerk.*

		Page.
Wardrope, D.	Teeswater	248
Wells, John, *M.A*	Ailsa Craig	248
Wilson, T	Seneca	249
Wilson, W. A., *M.A*	St. Mary's	249
Wright, J. K	London East	250
Wright, P	Stratford	250
Yeomans, G. A	Dunnville	250

Presbytery of Manitoba.
Rev. T. Hart, *M.A.*, *B.D*, Winnipeg, *Clerk.*

		Page.
Baird, A. B., *B.D*	Edmonton	172
Bell, Allan	Portage la Prairie	175
Borthwick, H. J., *B.A*	Mountain City	177
Bryce, G., *M.A.*, *LL.B*	Winnipeg	178
Cameron, A. H	Turtle Mountain	179
Campbell, A., *B.A.*	Stonewall	181
Douglas, J	Morris	190
Farquharson, J., *B.A*	Pilot Mound	192
Ferries, J., *B.A*	Brandon	193
Fleet, George	Okanase	194
Gordon, D. M., *B.D*	Winnipeg	197
Hart, Thomas, *M.A.*, *B.D*	Winnipeg	201
Hodnett, W	Birtle	202
Matheson, A	Selkirk	227
Mullins, W	Headingly	230
McConnell, D., *B.A*	Petrel	210
McGregor, D	Big Bend	215
McGuire, T	Emerson	216
McKay, John	Armadale	217
McKellar, H	High Bluff	217
McRae, D	Neepawa	225
Pitblado, C. B	Winnipeg	234
Polson, S	Millbrook	234
Robertson, James	Winnipeg	236
Scott, J	West Lynne	239
Sieveright, J., *B.A*	Prince Albert	240
Smith, A	Cadueis	241
Stalker, D., *B.A*	Gladstone	242
Tunkasuicye, Sol	Fort Ellice	247
Tibb, J. C., *B.D*	Rapid City	246
Wellwood, J., *B.A*	Minnedosa	249

II. Place of Birth, Date of Ordination, &c.

While the name and church of every Minister is given under this head, the editors regret that so comparatively few Ministers responded to their invitation for information required to give biographic sketches. They are much indebted to those Ministers who did supply necessary particulars.

Where Ministers graduated or studied, the places, with universities or colleges merely given, thus "Edinburgh University," "Queen's College," Kingston, "Knox College, Toronto," &c.

Abbreviations alphabetically arranged.

B.—*Born.*
B.A.—*Bachelor of Arts.*
B.D.—*Bachelor of Divinity.*

Ch.—*Church or charge.*
C.B.—*Cape Breton.*

Dau.—*Daughter.*
D.D.—*Doctor of Divinity.*
D.C.L.—*Doctor of Civil law.*

E.—*East.*
Eng.—*England.*

In.—*Inducted.*
Ire.—*Ireland.*

Lic.—*Licensed.*
LL.B.—*Bachelor of Laws.*
LL.D.—*Doctor of Laws.*

N.—*North.*

No. of Com.—*Number of Communicants.*
N.B.—*New Brunswick.*
N.J.—*New Jersey.*
N.S.—*Nova Scotia.*

Ont.—*Ontario.*
Or.—*Ordained.*

Pa.—*Pennsylvania.*
P.E.I—*Prince Edward Island.*
Ph.D.—*Doctor of Philosophy.*
Pres—*Presbytery.*

Que.—*Quebec.*

S—*Son.*
Sc.D.—*Doctor of Science.*
Sth.—*South.*

W.—*West.*

Abraham, John (Whitby, Ont, Pres., Whitby). Or 5. Nov. 1872. No. of com. 197.

Abraham, R. H., M.A. (Knox ch., Burlington. Pres., Hamilton). S. of Joseph Abraham. B. at Toronto. University and Knox College, Toronto. Or. and In. 1 June, 1880. Mar. Annie E. Armstrong, 11 Aug. 1880. Predecessors R. N. Grant and S. U. Fisher. No. of com. 216. Has charge of two stations.

Acheson, Stuart, M A (1st Essa. Burns and Dunn's chs., Clover Hill, Ont. Pres., Barrie). S. of Thomas Acheson, farmer. B. at Mono Mills, Ont. University and Knox College, Toronto. Mar. 13 June, 1877, F. M. Ferguson, dau. of T. R. Eerguson, M.P.

Or. and In. 11 Oct., 1876. Predecessors, Rev. Dr. Fraser, now one of the clerks of the General Assembly and Thomas McGee. No. of com., 186.

Acheson, S. (Wick and Greenbank, Ont, Pres., Lindsay) Or. Aug., 1874. No of com., 166.

Aitken, Wm. (Newcastle, N. B.; Pres. Miramichi) Or. 16 Aug., 1864. No. of com., 250.

Alexander, Jos., M.A. (Norval, &c, Ont; Pres., Toronto). Or. 29 May, 1851. No. of com., 184.

Alexander Thomas, A.M. (Mount Pleasant and Burford, Ont; Pres., Paris). S. of Jas. Alexander, a cloth merchant. B. at Aberdeen, Scotland. Marschal College, Aberdeen. Lic. at Dundee, Scotland, in 1830. Or. at Cobourg, Ont., in March, 1835. Mar. 17 July, 1834, Susan D. Soutar. In. to present ch. 9 Nov. 1874. Predecessors, Patrick Gregg, — Peatie. No. of com., 50 at Mount Pleasant; 25 at Burford. Previous pastorates, Cobourg, for 13 years; two congregations in Scotland, and 14 years minister of Percy and Seymour.

Allan James (Cove Head, P.E.I.; Pres., P.E. Island). Or. Jan., 1846. No. of com. 70.

Allard, Joseph (St. John Street Ch., Quebec; Pres., Quebec) S. of Jos. Allard, farmer. B. at Ste. Anne, Ill. Presbyterian College, Montreal. Mar. 6 Sep., 1882, Minnie Kertson, of Grand Falls, N.B. Or. and In., 15 April, 1882. Predecessors, Mr. Langele, of Switzerland & R. S. Duclos. No. of com., 27. Originally a Roman Catholic, but became a convert to Protestantism, through instrumentality of Father Chiniquy.

Ami, Marc (French Church, Ottawa; Pres., Ottawa). Or. 11 July, 1866.

Amaron, Calvin E., B.A., M.A. (Three Rivers, Que; Pres., Quebec.) S. of Dan. Amaron, of Switzerland, one of the first missionaries of late Free Church Missionary Society. B. at DeRamsay. McGill and Presbyterian Colleges, Montreal. Or. and In. 15 Oct, 1879. Mar. 19 Oct, 1881—Agnes, dau. of Judge McDoughll, of Aylmer. Predecessors, James Thom, Prof. Ferguson, R. J. McLaren, John Bennett, Jas. McCaul. No. of com. 100.

Amos, Walter (Aurora, Ont; Pres. Toronto.) S. of Andrew Amos, blacksmith. B. in Roxburghshire, Scot. University and Knox College, Toronto. Or. and In. 9 Nov, 1876. Mar. 26 Jan, 1881, Margaret Barr. No. of com. 100.

Anderson, Duncan, M.A. (Point Levis, Que; Pres., Quebec). Or. 26 Dec, 1854.

Anderson, James A., B.A., (Whitechurch, Ont, Pres., Maitland) S. of Rev. John Anderson, Minister at Tiverton, Ont, B. in Nepean township, Ont; McGill and Presbyterian Colleges, Montreal. Or. and In. 7 October, 1880. Mar. 27 April, 1882, C. Isabel Masson of Ottawa. No. of com., 187. Predecessor, Robert Leask.

Anderson, John, (Tiverton, Ont, Pres., Bruce) S. of James Anderson, farmer. B. at Strathspey, Scot. Knox College, Toronto. Or. 11 Oct, 1854. Mar. 24 Sep, 1847, Margaret Kennedy, dau. of Alex. Kennedy. Has written Reviews on Articles and published Sermons on Baptism in 1873. In. to present ch. 2 March, 1870. Predecessor, Dr. McKay, now of Puslinch. No. of com., 211. Previous pastorate Lancaster and Dalhousie Mills, 1854–70.

Anderson, Wm., M.A., (Rosemont and Milman, Ont, Pres., Barrie) S. of Wm. Anderson, farmer, &c. B. in Co. of Armagh, Ire. Glasgow University. Or. 29 June, 1860. Mar. 6 June, 1866, E. J. Waters. In. to present ch 5 Nov, 1879. Predecessors, Wm. Lewis, Mal. Colquhoun, Alex. McLennan and others. No. of com., 120. Previous pastorates, Tobermore, Ire., 1860-68; Buckingham and Cumberland, Que., 1869-73; Kincardine, Ont, 1873-1879.

Andrew, Joseph, (Dalhousie and Middleville, Ont, Pres. Lanark and Renfrew) S. of Jos. Andrew, farmer. B at Hull, Eng. Queen's College, Kingston. Or. 28 May, 1874. Mar. 28 March, 1868, Victoria Christner. In. to present ch. 19 July, 1881. Predecessors, W. Clerk, D. J. McLean and W. Cochrene. No. of com., 233. Formerly a minister of Methodist New Connexion Church, and after reception into Presbyterian Church labored as missionary for three years in Muskoka.

Andrews, F., (Keene and Westwood, Ont, Pres. Peterboro) Or. 1851. No. of com., 336.

Archibald, W. P., B. A., M.A., (Cavendish, Pres. P.E. Island). S. of Alex. Archibald, farmer. B. at Mosquodoboit, N.S. Dalhousie College, Halifax. Or. 30 Sep, 1875. Mar. 18 June, 1878, Minnie Ramsay. In. to present ch., 20 March, 1878. Predecessors, D. Geddie and D. J. Murray. No. of com. 190. Previous pastorate, Tryon and Bonshaw, 1875-77.

Armstrong, Wm. C. (St. Andrew's Ch., Hillsburg, Ont; Pres., Guelph.) S. of James Armstrong, carriage builder. B. at Guelph. Knox College, Toronto; Princeton College, New

Jersey. Or. 8 March, 1877. Mar. 27 Dec, 1876, Margaret Ginton. In. to present ch., 26 April, 1881. Predecessors, D. Strachan, R. Fowlie. No. of com., 130. Previous pastorate, Florence and Dawn.

Armstrong, Wm. D., B.A., M.A. Daly St. Ch., Ottawa, Pres.. Ottawa). S. of John D. Armstrong, farmer. B. in Township of Cavan, Ont. Toronto University, and Knox College, Toronto. Won several scholarships and prizes at both, in Natnral Science, Logic, Public Speaking, Reading, and as an essayist; silver medallist of the University in Metaphysics and Ethics; prizeman in Hebrew, Chaldee and Syriac. Before finishing theological course, filled the pulpit of Central Ch., Toronto, and after graduating, took charge of the recently organized church at Point Edward, from which received a call, but declined. Subsequently occupied the pulpit of Charles St. Ch. Toronto, and has been engaged in the service of the Board of Knox College. Or. 14 May, 1874. In. to present ch. 14 May, 1874. Predecessors, Dr. Wardrope, and Prof. McLaren. No. of com., 210. In January, 1883, appointed agent for six months of French Evangelization Board to Great Britain and Ireland.

Atkinson, T. (Enniskillen, &c, Ont, Pres , Whitby). Or. 5 Oct, 1878. No. of com., 133.

Aull, J. M. (Palmerston, Ont, Pres., Saugeen). Or. 20 May, 1868. No of com., 176.

Baikie, John (Harriston, Ont; Pres., Saugeen). S. of Geo. Baikie. B. in Caithnessshire, Scot. Knox College, Toronto. Or. 1 Aug, 1871. In. to present ch. 1 June, 1876. No. of com., 203. Previous pastorate, Brampton and Malton.

Baillie, J. K. (Osnabruck, Ont; Pres., Glengarry). Or. 15 Nov, 1882. No. of com., 300.

Bain, James (Markham, Ont.) Or. 5 April, 1826. A minister on retired list, attached to Presbytery of Toronto.

Bain, William, D.D. (Perth, Ont; Pres. Lanark and Renfrew). Or. 29 Oct, 1845. Is pastor emeritus St. Andrew's Church.

Baird, Andrew B., B.D., M.A., (Edmonton. N. W. T., Pres. Manitoba) S. of Charles Baird, farmer. B. at Fullarton, Ont; University and Knox College, Toronto, Edinburgh and Leipzig Universities. Or. 16 Aug., 1881. In. to present ch. 29 Oct., 1881. No. of com., 15. Edmonton is the latest outpost of the Church in the North-West and is 450 miles from its nearest neighbour. The only Presbyterian ministers, besides its present pastor, who have ever preached there being the late Mr. Nisbet of Prince Albert and Principal Grant who visited it on his trip from "Ocean to Ocean."

Ball, Wm. S., (English Settlement, &c., Ont; Pres. London) Or. 23 Feb. 1849. No. of com., 269.

Ballantine, James, (River St Ch., Paris, Ont. Pres. Paris) S. of Quentin Ballantine, merchant. B. at Irvine, Scot. Glasgow University. Or. as a missionary of United Presbyterian Church of Scotland, 26 April, 1866. Mar. 6 Nov., 1865 Margaret Henry. Author of a volume of poems published in 1865, and of a lecture on the Scottish Covenanters published in 1874. Predecessors, James Robertson, John Anderson. No. of com., 165. Previous pastorates, Stirling, Jamaica, 1866-71, Kingston, Jamaica, 1871-76, Cobourg, Ont. 1876 81.

Ballantyne, Wm. D., B.A., (Pembroke, Ont; Pres. Lanark and Renfrew) S. of James Ballantyne, farmer. B. at Hawick, Scot. University and Knox College, Toronto. Or. Nov., 1867. Mar. Joanna E. Shoolbred. In. to present ch. 17 May, 1876. Predecessors, Andrew Melville, Henry McMeekin, John McEwen. No. of com., 144. Previous pastorates, Brooklyn, Iowa; Whitby, Ont.

Ballantyne, F., B.A., M.A., (N. and S. Westminster chs., Ont; Pres. London) S. of John Ballantyne. University and Knox College, Toronto. Or. and In. 2 Jan., 1879. Predecessors, North W.—Wm. Inglis and Geo. Simpson. South W.—J. McEwen and D. McDonald. 175 com. in former ch., 80 in latter.

Barclay, John, M.A., D.D., (Toronto, Pres. Toronto) B. in Ayrshire, Scot. Glasgow and Edinburgh Universities. Has published various discourses by request. For 28 years was pastor of St. Andrew's Church, Toronto. Has rendered valuable service to the Church as Clerk of the Presbytery, Trustee of Queen's College, Kingston, and as a member of the Temporalities Board. A retired minister attached to Presbytery of Toronto.

Barr, Wm., (Brantford) A minister on retired list attached to Presbytery of Paris.

Barr, Matthew (Seaforth, Ont). Or. 14 Feb, 1854. A minister on retired list, attached to Presbytery of Huron.

Battisby, J. R. (St. Andrew's Ch., Chatham, Ont; Pres., Chatham) Or. 26 Sep. 1877. No. of com., 360.

Baxter, John J. (Truro, N.S; Pres., Truro). Or. May, 1832. Has retired from active service.

Bayne, E. S., M.A. (Murray Harbor, P.E.I.; Pres., P.E. Island). Or. 18 Jan, 1876. No. of com., 180.

Bayne, Geo. D., B.A. (Wakefield, Que; Pres., Ottawa). S. of John Bayne, farmer. B. at Ottawa. McGill University and Presbyterian College, Montreal. Or. and In. 6 Sep, 1881. Predecessors, J. Corbett, Jos. White, Hugh McGuire. No. of com., 236.

Bayne, Geo. T. (Wilberforce, Ont; Pres., Lanark and Renfrew). Or. 21 July, 1881. No. of com., 90.

Beamer, A. (Wardsville, Ont; Pres., London.) S. of Christopher Beamer, farmer. B. at Princeton, Ont. Albert College, Belleville. Or. 25 Apl, 1869. Mar. 15 Apl, 1868, Bertha Choate. In. to present ch., 24 Feb., 1880. Predecessors, Messrs. McKinnon, McKenzie and Donaldson. No. of com., 80. Previous pastorate, Springfield. Was formerly a minister of the Methodist Episcopal Church. Was received into Presbyterian Church 23 June, 1877.

Bearisto, J. K. (Carleton, N.S.; Pres., Halifax) Or. 1869. No. of com., 75

Beattie, David (Rylston and Marmora, Ont; Pres., Kingston). Or. 27 April, 1857. No. of com., 54. Is an ordained missionary.

Beattie, D. M., B.A., (East Oxford and Blenheim, Ont.; Pres., Paris.) S. of Robert Beattie, farmer. B. in Township of Puslinch. University College and Knox College, Toronto. Or. and In. 13 Jan., 1880. Mar. 8 Feb, 1882, Kate McLaren. No. of com., 160. Brother of Rev. F. R. Beattie, Minister of First Presbyterian Ch., Brantford.

Beattie, F. R., B.A., B.D., M.A. (First Presbyterian Ch., Brantford; Pres., Paris.) S. of Robert Beattie, farmer. B. near Guelph. University and Knox College, Toronto. Or. 11 Dec, 1878. In. to present ch. 9 May, 1882. Predecessors, A. A. Drummond, Thos. Lowry. No. of com., 150. Previous pastorate, Baltimore and Coldsprings, 1878-82. Is the first B.D. of Knox College. Was tutor there for two years, and is at present one of the Board of Examiners of that institution. Was Examiner in University College for two years.

Beattie, Robert J. (First Ch. Port Hope; Presbytery, Peterboro'). S. of Robt. Beattie, farmer. B. at Essa, Ont. Knox College, Toronto; Princeton Theological Seminary. Or. 12 April, 1875. Mar. March, 1876, Susan McCoy. In. to present ch., Dec, 1878. Predecessors, John Cassie, David Watters, William Donald. No. of com., 242. Previous pastorate, Fort Edward, New York. 1875-78.

Becket, John (Thamesville, &c., Ont; Pres., Chatham). Or. 27 May. 1868. No. of com., 22.

Bell, Alex. (St. Andrew's Ch., Peterboro'; Pres., Peterboro'). Or. March, 1863. No. of com., 171.

Bell, Allan (Portage-la-Prairie, Man.; Pres., Manitoba.) S. of James Bell, farmer. B. at London, Ont. Toronto University and Princeton College, N.J. Or. 14 July, 1875. Mar. 27 May, 1875, Kate Brown. In. to present ch., Jan., 1876. No. of com., 130.

Bell, George, B.A., LL.D. (Kingston; Pres., Kingston). S. of Rev. Wm. Bell. B. at Perth, Ont. Queen's College, Kingston. Or. 30 May, 1844. Mar. 1st. 18 Nov. 1846, Mary Whiteford; she died, 25 Nov, 1851: 2nd, 22 May, 1855, Ellen Chadwick. First native Canadian student of Queen's College, Kingston. Was minister of Cumberland and Buckingham, 1844-48; Simcoe, 1848-57; Clifton, 1857-73, and Walkerton, 1874-81. Moderator of Synod Presbyterian Church, in connection with Church of Scotland, in 1858. Lecturer in Divinity, Queen's College, 1873, 1877, 1878, and 1882. A Trustee of that College, and is Registrar and Treasurer thereof.

Bell, John W., M A. (Listowel, Ont; Pres., Stratford). Or. 22 Dec., 1868. No. of com., 184.

Bennett, James, D.D. (St. John, N.B.) S. of John Bennett, farmer. B. at Lisban, Ire. Belfast College and Edinburgh University. Or., 30 March, 1843. Mar., 1847, Jane Scott. Author of "The Wisdom of the King," &c. Was minister of Tassagh, Ireland, and St. John's Ch., St. John, N.B. Retired from active service in 1882. Is Clerk of the Presbytery of St. John.

Bennett, John, (Almonte, Ont, Pres. Lanark and Renfrew) S. of John Bennett, gamekeeper on estate of Pitfirran, Scot. B. at Kinross, Scot. Morrin College, Quebec. Or. 29 June, 1869. Mar. 17 Sep., 1869, Mary Chambers. Has published several sermons and also "Letters to "R. F." a Romish Priest on the unscriptural nature of Mariolatry and other Romish Doctrines." In. to present ch. 17 Sep., 1872. Predecessors, John Fairbairn, brother of late Principal Fairbairn of Edinburgh, Dr. McMorine, John Gordon. No. of com., 470. Previous pastorate, Three

Rivers, Que., 1869-72. Was first student to begin and complete course in Morrin College, Que. under Rev. Principal Cook, D.D., LL.D., who was a student of Dr. Chalmers.

Bennett, Thomas, (Carp, Kinburn and Lowny, Ont, Pres. Ottawa). S. of R. R. H. Bennett, farmer. B. at Tayside, Ont. Minnesota State University and Presbyterian College, Montreal. Or. 12 Oct., 1876. Mar. 12 June, 1879, Elsie McClenaghan. In. to present ch. 13 Dec., 1881. Predecessors, – Sinclair, J. Robertson, J. Stewart and J. W. Penman. No. of com , 186. Previous pastorates Beauharnois and Chateauguay 1876-81. Was gold medalist at both seminaries.

Bennett, Wm., (Springville and Bethany, Ont, Pres. Peterboro) S. of John Bennett, farmer. B. in County Down, Ire. Belfast College. Or. Sep., 1855. Mar. in 1859, Amy Knight. In. to present ch. Nov. 1872. Predecessor, Wm. Blaine. No. of com., 135. Previous pastorates, Windsor 1861-64; Winchester 1864-68; Kemptville 1868-72. Sent as a missionary to New Brunswick by Irish Church in 1855. Is Clerk of Presbytery.

Bickett, David (Molesworth, Ont; Pres., Maitland). Or. 17 Oct, 1882. No. of com., 116.

Binnie, Robert (Knox Ch., Cornwall, Ont; Pres., Glengarry.) Or. 20 May, 1861. No. of com., 127.

Black, James (Caledonia, Ont; Presbytery, Hamilton). S. of Wm. Black, farmer. B. at Eskdale, Muir, Scotland. Knox College, Toronto. Or. and In. 9 Nov., 1853. Mar. 15 July, 1856, Christina, eldest dau. of Rev. Wm. Bethune, of Walpole. Published several sermons and lectures. Predecessor, Dr. Ferrier. No. of com., 210.

Black, James S. (Erskine Ch., Montreal; Pres., Montreal) Or. 21 March, 1870. No. of com , 522.

Blain, Wm. (Tara, &c, Ont; Pres., Bruce). Or. 4 July, 1854. No. of com., 222.

Blair, D. B. (Barney's River and Blue Mount, N.S; Pres., Picton). S. of Thos. Blair, shepherd. B. at Strachur, Scot. Edinburgh University. Or. 26 Oct. 1846. Mar. 26 Aug. 1851, Mary Sibella McLean. Author of a Gaelic grammar; "Metrical translation of Psalms in Gaelic;" a volume of Gaelic poems. In. to present ch., Oct, 1848. Predecessors, D. A. Fraser, D. McKichan, Alex. McGillivray. No. of com., 400. Prior to induction a missionary.

Blakely. M. D. M., B.A. (Ross and Cobden; Pres., Lanark and Renfrew). S. of Malcolm Blakely, farmer. B. at Bristol, Que. McGill University and Presbyterian College, Montreal. Or. and In. 5 Oct, 1880. Mar. 5 Jan, 1881, Janet McJanet. Predecessors. Hugh Cameron, Henry Sinclair. No. of com.,100.

Borthwick, Hugh J., M.A. (Mountain City, Man; Pres., Manitoba) S. of John Borthwick, school-teacher. B. in Scotland. Edinburgh University; Queen's College, Kingston; Victoria College, Cobourg. Or. Aug, 1853. Mar. April, 1848, Marion, dau. of John Taylor, W.S., Edinburgh. In. to present ch, Nov., 1881. No. of com., 45. Previous pastorate, Chelsea, Quebec.

Boudreau, Moses F. (New Glasgow, Que; Pres., Montreal). S. of Joseph Boudreau, farmer. B. at St. Anne, Ill. Presbyterian College, Montreal Or. 8 Oct., 1877. Mar. 16 Sep., 1878, Annie Ward, of Montreal. In. to present ch., 31 Jan., 1881. Predecessors, Charles Bronillette and others. No. of com., 75. Previous pastorate, Dunnville, 1877-81. Embraced Protestantism through instrumentality of Father Chiniquy.

Boyd, Jas (Wellesley, Ont; Pres., Stratford) Or. 7 July, 1847. No. of com., 74.

Boyd, Jas. M., B.D. (Beauharnois and Chateauguay, Que; Pres. Montreal)

Boyd, John (Bass River, N. W.; Pres. Miramichi) Or. 9 Sep., 1879. No. of com., 55.

Boyd, Saml. (Knox Ch., Wallace, N. S.; Pres. Wallace) Or. Nov., 1858. No. of com., 152.

Bremner, Geo. (McNab White Lake, Ont; Pres. Lanark and Renfrew) Or. 15 Feb., 1860. No. of com., 225.

Brown, Arch. (New Dublin, N. S; Pres. Lunenburg and Shelburne) Or. 27 Jan., 1864. No. of com., 33.

Brown, B. J. (Luther, Ont; Pres. Saugeen) S. of William Brown, farmer. B. in township of Caradoc. Knox College, Toronto, Or. 11 June, 1873. Mar. 23 Dec., 1874. Margaret Bell McClure. In. to present ch. 30 April, 1879. Predecessor, Donald D. McLennan. No. of com., 114.

Brown, George (Wroxeter, Ont; Pres. Maitland) S. of Robt. Brown, millwright. B. at Stow. Scot University and Free Church College, Edinburgh. Or. Aug., 1856. Mar. 7 Oct., 1856, Anna Maria Whitworth. In. to present ch. April 1866. Predecessor, John Young. No. of com. 192. Labored in Jamaica and Trinidad from June 1852 to January 1861.

Brown, John (Newmarket, Ont) A minister on retired list, attached to Presbytery of Toronto.

Bruce, George, B.A., (St. David's Ch., St. John. N. B.; Pres. St. John) S. of John Bruce. B. in Scotland. University and Knox College, Toronto Or. Sep., 1875. In. to present ch. 28 Jan., 1883. Predecessor, Dr. Waters. No. of com. 300. Previous pastorate, 1st Presbyterian Ch., St. Catharines, Ont. Was four years in mission work in Newmarket and Aurora, Ont.

Bruce, Wm. T., B.A., M.D. (Coldstream Ch. Valley, N. S.; Pres. Truro) S. of Jos. Bruce, farmer. B. at Middle Musquodoboit. Dalhousie College and University, Halifax, also Theological Hall and Halifax School of Medicine. Or. 26 Sep., 1876. In. to present ch. 10 May., 1881. Mar. 8 Nov., 1877, Alice Mary Straton. Predecessors, Jacob Layton, Jas. Carruthers. No. of com., 150. Previous pastorate, Sutherland's River and Vale Colliery, Pictou, N. S., 1876–80.

Bryce, George, B.A., M.A., LL.B. (Manitoba College, Winnipeg; Pres. Manitoba) S. of Geo. Bryce, farmer. B. at Mount Pleasant, Brant Co., Ont. University and Knox College, Toronto. Or. 19 Sep., 1871. Mar. 17 Sep., 1872, Marion Samuel of Broom House, Kirkliston, Scot. Appointed Principal of Manitoba College 1871. Is the author of "Manitoba—Its infancy, growth and present condition" 1882, and a pamphlet, published in 1875 on "The Presbyterian Church in the North-West."

Burgess, J. C., B.A. (Carleton, N. B.; Pres. St. John) Or. 5 May, 1870. No. of com. 81.

Burnett, John R. S. (Alliston, Ont; Pres. Barrie). B. at Montreal. University and Knox College, Toronto. Or. 4 Dec, 1874. Mar. 11 Apl, 1877, Kate B. Melville. In. to present ch., 23 Jan, 1877. Predecessors, John K. Hislop, Robt. Knowles, and Thos. McKee. No. of com., 158. Previous pastorates, Duntroom and Nottawa.

Burnet, John S (Martintown, Ont; Pres., Glengarry). Or. 1 July, 1863. No. of com., 293.

Burnfield, Geo., B D., M.A. (First Ch., Brockville; Pres., Brockville). Or. 3 Jan, 1871.

Burns, Robert F., D.D. (Fort Massey Church, Halifax; Pres., Halifax). S. of Prof. Robt. Burns, of Toronto. B. at Paisley, Scotland. Glasgow University; New College, Edinburgh, and Knox College, Toronto. Or. 1 July, 1847. Mar. Elizabeth Holden, 1 July, 1852. Author of "Life of Dr. Burns," Toronto, published in 1872, and which went through 3 editions.

Has also written pamphlets on Maine Liquor Law; "Life of Abraham Lincoln;" "Our United Church," and other subjects. In. to present charge, 18 Mar , 1875. Predecessor, J. K. Smith, now of Galt. No. of com., 215. Previous pastorates, Kingston, 1847—55; St. Catharines, 1855—67; Chicago, 1867—70; Coté St. Church, Montreal, 1870—75. Fort Massey congregation gives at rate of $100 per family, to church objects, and adopts the free-will offering system on Lord's Day.

Burns, William (Toronto). Or., 18 May, 1869. A minister without charge, attached to Presbytery of Toronto.

Burr, Alex. (Kamoka, Ont). A minister without charge. Presbytery of London.

Burrows, A., B.A. (St. Andrew's Ch., Truro, N.S; Pres., Truro). Or. 29 June, 1864. No. of com , 200.

Burson, George (Knox Ch., St. Catharines, Ont; Pres., Hamilton). Or. 6 June, 1863. No. of com., 250.

Cairns, John (Buxton, Ont; Pres., Chatham). Or. 2 Feb, 1882. No. of com., 48.

Cairns, John A., B.A., M.A. (Upper Musquodoboit, N. S.; Pres. Halifax) S. of Chris. Cairns, farmer. B. at Freetown, P. E. I. Dalhousie College, Halifax; Princeton College, N. J. Or. and In. 9 March, 1882. Mar. 20 June, 1882, Alice Waters. No. of com., 230. Predecessors, Mr. Sprott, Dr. Sedgwicke, James Simpson.

Calder, John A. G. (Lancaster, Ont; Pres. Glengarry) Or. April, 1871. No. of com., 147.

Camelon, David (Vaughan, &c., Ont; Pres. Toronto) Or. 13 Dec., 1859. No. of com., 176.

Cameron, Alex. (Riverside, Portapique, N. S.; Pres. Truro) Or. 16 Sep., 1857. No. of com., 223.

Cameron, A. H. (Nelsonville, Man.; Pres. Manitoba) Or. 12 Nov., 1874. No. of com., 59.

Cameron, Chas. (Kincardine Township, Ont; Pres. Maitland) Or. 1 May, 1861. No. of com., 51.

Cameron, Duncan, (Knox Ch., Lucknow, Ont; Pres., Maitland). Or. 3 March, 1854. No. of com., 141.

Cameron, D. B,, (Acton, Ont; Pres., Guelph). Or. 16 Dec., 1869. No. of com., 175.

Cameron, Hugh, (Kippen, &c, Ont.; Pres., Huron). Or. 8 Oct., 1862. No. of com., 181.

Cameron, Hugh, B.A., (Glencoe, Ont.; Pres., London) S. of Archibald Cameron, farmer. B. at DeWittville, P Q. Queen's College, Kingston. Or. and In. 2 Dec., 1879. Mar. 12 Oct., 1881, M. D. Rose. Predecessors, J. N. Macleod, D. Maceachern. No. of com., 162.

Cameron, James, (Chatsworth, Ont.; Pres., Owen Sound). S. of John Cameron, farmer. B. in Petty, Inverness, Scot. New College and University, Edinburgh; Knox College, Toronto. A silver medallist Edinburgh University. Was editor for six years of "Canada Christian Monthly," seven years of "Presbyterian Year Book," and has written many articles published in various magazines. Or. and In. 16 Feb., 1859. Mar. 4 Jan., 1879, E A. Dunscombe. No. of com., 243. Congregation formed from Mission Station under Mr. Cameron's ministry.

Cameron, John, (Bridgewater, N.S; Pres., Lunenburg and Shelburne). Or. 17 Sep, 1844. No. of com , 115

Cameron, J., M.A., (Millbrook and Centreville, Ont; Pres., Peterboro). Or. Feb, 1876. No. of com., 305.

Cameron, John G , (Souris and Bay Fortune, P.E I; Pres., P. E. Island). Or. 14 March, 1867. No. of com., 225.

Cameron, John J., B.A., M.A., (Pickering, Ont; Pres., Whitby). S. of Robert Cameron, farmer. B. at Georgetown, P.E.I. Dalhousie College, Halifax. Or. 5 March, 1871. Mar. Dec. 1871, Susan Wright. In. to present ch., 1 Oct, 1879. Predecessors, W. R. Ross, Alex. Kennedy. No. of com., 120. Previous pastorates, N. Easthope, N. Hamburg.

Cameron, John M., (East Ch., Toronto; Pres., Toronto.) Or. 23 Nov, 1871. No. of com., 343.

Cameron, John W., B.A., (Laskay, Ont; Pres., Toronto). S. of James Cameron, Lake Captain and Merchant. B at Lansingberg, N.Y. University and Knox College, Toronto. Mar. 20 Dec, 1882, Margaret S. Lockhart. Or. and In. 15 Nov, 1881. Predecessors, Messrs. Adams, Milligan, Hague and Warrender. No. of com., 108.

Cameron, L, (Thamesford, Ont; Pres.. London). S. of Hugh Cameron, farmer. B. in Island of Islay, Scot. Knox College, Toronto. Or. 5 Nov, 1862. Mar. 22 Dec, 1864, Sarah J. Kennedy. In. to present ch., 10 Nov, 1874. Predecessors, Neil Bethune, John Frazer, A. C. McDonald and Kenneth McDonald. No. of com., 200. Previous pastorate, Acton.

Cameron, M. C. Milton, Ont, Pres., Toronto). S of Duncan Cameron, farmer. B. in Elgin County, Ont. Yale College; Princeton College, N.J. Or. and In. 25 March, 1879. Mar. 19 Jan, 1881, Lillie Johnson. Predecessors, Messrs. Coots, Ferguson, Stewart, Mitchel, and John Eadie. No. of com., 262.

Campbell, Alex. B.A (Stonewall, Man.; Pres, Manitoba). S. of Peter Campbell, farmer. B. at Drummond, Ont. Queen's College, Kingston. Or. 9 Oct, 1873. Mar. 27 Dec, 1865, Eleanor Woodside, of Toronto. Appointed missionary to Manitoba (Rockwood Groupe) October, 1876. Without charge at present. Has been also minister of Westmeath, Ont.

Campbell, Isaac (Richmond Hill, Ont; Pres., Toronto). No. of com., 170. Or. 2 Nov, 1874. Is colleague and successor to Rev. Jas. Dick.

Campbell, John, B.A., M.A. (Presbyterian College, Montreal; Pres-, Montreal.) S. of James Campbell, publisher. B. at Edinburgh, Scot. Knox College, Toronto; Toronto and Edinburgh Universities. Or. 3 Nov, 1868. Mar. Sep, 1875, Mary Helen Playfair, of Toronto. Author of numerous reviews, &c. Was minister of Charles Street Ch., Toronto, 1868-73. Appointed a Professor in Presbyterian College, Montreal, June, 1873.

Campbell John, B.A. (Harriston, Ont; Pres., Saugeen). S. of John Campbell, carpenter. B. at Islay, Scot. University and Knox College, Totonto. Or. 2 Sep, 1874. Mar. 13 Jan, 1865, A. J. Langton, who died at Minneapolis. 21 June, 1882. In. to present ch., 29 Aug, 1878. Predecessors, Geo. McLennan; John McIntyre. No. of com., 283. Previous pastorate, Cannington, Sep, 1874 to July, 1878.

Campbell, Malcolm (Strath Lorne, C. B; Pres., Victoria and Richmond). S. of John Campbell, farmer. B. in Cape Breton. Theological Hall and Dalhousie College, Halifax. Or. and In. 30 Aug.' 1881. Mar. 27 Dec, 1879, Annie McAulay. Predecessors, John Gunn and John McLean. No. of com., 106.

Campbell, Robt, B.A., M A. (St. Gabriel Ch., Montreal; Pres., Montreal). S. of Peter Campbell, farmer. B. in Township of Drummond, Ont. Queen's College, Kingston. Or. 10 Apl, 1862. Mar 29 Dec, 1863, Margaret Macdonnell Writer of essays and reviews in various magazines. Was joint editor of *Presbyterian*, from 1867 to 1870. In. to present ch. 13 Dec, 1866. Predecessors, Dr. Inglis, Dr. Kemp, and others No of com., 373. Previous pastorate, St. Andrew's Ch., Galt, 1862-66. Took several scholarships at College, and was first medallist of Queen's. Was Lecturer in Church History in University Sessions, 1880-1, and 1881-2.

Campbell, Robert, M.A. (Renfrew, Ont; Pres. Lanark and Renfrew) S. of Geo. Campbell, carpenter. B. at Montreal. Queen's College, Kingston and Edinburgh University. Or. and In. 26 Oct., 1871. Mar. Mary, eldest dau. of Thomas Drummond, of Kingston. Predecessors, Dr. Alex. Mann and Geo. Thomson. No. of com., 360. Is lecturer on Political Economy, Queen's College, Kingston, and was Bruce of Grange Hill Scholar and Medallist Edinburgh University.

Canning, Wm. T. (Oxford Mills, Ont: Pres. Brockville) S. of Rev. Jas. Canning, Minister of Malin, Ire. B. there. Belfast College and Edinburgh University. Or. 1 May, 1849. Mar. Jemima Rider, 24 July, 1856. In. to present ch. 25 June 1862. Predecessors, Jos. Anderson, Jos. Evans. No. of com., 94. Previous pastorates, Chipman, N. B.; Martin, Michigan; Douglas, Ont.—Licensed by Presbytery of Derry. Sent to Canada by Colonial Committee Irish Pres. Church in 1849.

Carmichael, Jas. (King, Ont; Pres. Toronto) S. of Peter Carmichael, farmer. B. at Beckwith Queen's College and Glasgow University. Or. and In. 2 Oct., 1860. Mar. 28 Aug., 1865, Maria L. Ross. Predecessors, John Tanse, who died in April 1877, on the 48th anniversary of his induction and the 51st year of his ministry; Henry Gordon. No. of com., 160.

Carmichael, James, B.A., M.A. (St. John's Ch., Norwood, Ont; Pres. Peterboro.) S. of W. Carmichael, carbuilder. B. in Scotland. Or. 10 Nov., 1870. Mar. Sarah Barker 25 Oct., 1871. Author of an essay on "Life and character of Jesus Christ" published in 1882. In. to present ch. 19 Oct., 1882. Predecessors, J. M. Fotheringham and others. Previous pastorate, Markham.

Carmichael, J. A. (Columbus and Brooklin, Ont; Pres. Whitby) Or. 25 May, 1875. No. of com., 258.

Carr, A. F., M.A. (Alberton, P. E. I.; Pres. P. E. Island) Or. 4 Oct., 1871. No. of com., 250

Carriere, S. A. (Grand Bend, Ont; Pres. Huron) Or. 31 Oct., 1882. No. of com., 60.

Carruthers, J. S. (Knox Ch., Picton; Pres., Picton). Or. 3 July, 1878. No. of com., 255.

Carruthers, S. (Beverly, Ont; Pres., Hamilton). Or. Oct, 1882. No. of com., 215.

Carswell, James (W. Adelaide and Arkona, Ont; Pres., Sarnia). S. of David Carswell, yeoman. B. in Township of Horton. Knox College, Toronto, and Princeton College, N.J. Or. 17 Oct, 1867. Mar. Christina Junor, 7 Oct, 1869. In. to present ch., 19 Oct, 1880. Predecessors, —Howden, Wm. Deas, Jas. Donaldson, J Lawrence. No. of com., 88. Previous pastorates, Carleton Place and Beckwith, 1867–74; Aylmer, East, from Nov. 1875–79.

Casey, John J., B.D. (Taylor Ch., Montreal; Pres., Montreal). B. in Dublin, Ire. St. Mary's, Montreal; Princetown Seminary, N.J. Or. 12 Dec, 1876. Mar. 22 May, 1878, Margaret L., dau. of Rev. J. Watson, Huntington, Que. In. to present ch., March 16, 1882. Predecessor, J. Jones, an ordained missionary. No. of com., 68. Previous pastorate, Elgin and Athelstan, 1876–82.

Cauboue, Anthony, Minister at Jolliette, Que; Pres., Montreal.

Caven, William, D.D. (Principal Knox College, Toronto; Pres., Toronto). S. of John Caven, school teacher. B. in Parish of Kirkcolm, Scot. Mar. July, 1856, Miss Goldie of Greenfields, Ont. Ancestors on both sides settled in Wigtonshire for centuries, and several of them figured conspicuously in local annals. They were in their day, strenuous supporters of the Solemn League and Covenant, the names of some of them being enshrined on the roll of "Wigton Martyrs." Family emigrated to Canada in 1847. Received his early education at father's school, and choosing the ministry as his profession, subsequently studied under the auspices of the United Presbyterian Church which had been planted in Western Canada through the instrumentality of Rev. William Fraser of Bondhead, and Rev. Alex. Mackenzie of Goderich. The church having then no regular collegiate institution, the training of students was entrusted to the late Rev. Wm. Proudfoot (father of the present Vice-chancellor and Dr. Proudfoot of London) and the above named Mr. Mackenzie. Under the guidance of these learned and godly men, devoted himself to the prescribed literary and theological course, and having studied for two years more, was licensed to preach early in 1852, being shortly afterwards ordained and inducted to St. Mary's and Downie. In 1865 was appointed by the Synod, Professor of Exegetical Theology and Biblical Criticism in Knox College, Toronto, and in 1870, on retirement of Dr. Willis, became Principal. This latter position is held by appointment of the General Assembly. With the aid of his colleague—Professor Gregg—was enabled to procure funds to erect the new college completed in 1875. Was an earnest advocate of union, and when the amalgamation was effected it became his duty, as Moderator of the Canada Presbyterian Church, to sign the articles of union in name of the Church. Takes a deep interest in all questions affecting the public welfare, and specially so in educational matters. Is President of Ontario Teachers' Association as successor to Professor Goldwin Smith.

Caven, Wm. (Buckingham, Ont; Pres., Ottawa). Or. 18 Oct, 1865. No. of com., 90.

Chambers, Thos S. (Storrington, &c. Ont; Pres., Kingston). Or. 23 May, 1855. No. of com., 131. Is Clerk of Presbytery.

Chase, J. H., M.A. Onslow, N.S; Pres., Truro. Or. 5 May, 1869. No. of com., 167. Is Clerk of the Presbytery.

Chiniquy, C. (Ste. Anne, Illinois; Pres., Chatham). An ordained missionary.

Chisholm John, B.A. (Osprey Ch., McIntyre, Ont.; Pres., Saugeen). S. of Hugh Chisholm, farmer. B. at Sutherland's River, Picton Co. Queen's College, Kingston. Or. and In. 3 Aug, 1881. Predecessors, Harkness, R. Knowles, —Greenfield, and —Johnston. No. of com, 150.

Christie, George (Bedford, &c., N.S; Pres., Halifax). Or. 22 July, 1842. No. of com., 70.

Christie, Wm. M, M.A. (Beachburg, Ont; Pres., Lanark and Renfrew). S. of Robt. Christie, farmer. B at Edinburgh. Union College, Schen., N.Y. Or 4 Oct. 1849. Mar. 31 Oct, 1861, Annie C. Flett. In. to present ch, 11 Oct., 1877. Predecessors, Hugh Cameron and Alex. Campbell. No. of com., 133. Previous pastorates, Chippawa, 4 Oct, 1849; Mono Centre, 2 July, 1867.

Chrystal George (West Flamboro, Ont; Pres., Hamilton) Or. 1869. No. of com., 210.

Clark, Geo. M. (New Edinburgh, Ont; Pres., Ottawa). Or. 10 Sep, 1853. No of com., 74.

Clark, Nat. (Lakefield, &c.; Ont; Pres., Peterboro'). Or. May, 1871. No. of com., 140.

Clarke, Peter (Cape North, N.S; Pres., Sydney). Or. 12 Nov., 1873. No. of com., 43.

Clark, Wm. B. (Quebec; Pres., Quebec). S. of Wm. Clark, merchant. B. at Biggar, Scot. Edinburgh University. Or. 1839. Mar. 1st, 1836, Jane Brown; 2nd, 1870. Amelia Torrance, widow of Thos. Gibb. Author of "Book of Family Worship," several editions; "Asleep in Jesus," two editions; "The

Promise of the Spirit." In. to Chalmers' Ch., Quebec, 1853, of which now pastor emeritus. Previous pastorates, Half Morton, Scot., 1839-44; Maxwelltown, Scot, 1844-53.

Cleland, James (Mill St. Ch, Port Hope; Pres., Peterboro). S. of Wm. Cleland, farmer. B. in County Down, Ire. Royal College, Belfast, and Edinburgh University. Or. 9 May 1843. In. to present ch., Feb, 1874. Predecessor, M. W. Maclean, now of Belleville. No. of com., 70. Previous pastorates, Portland, Ire., May, 1843-54; Oswegatchie, N.Y, 1856-73.

Cleland, William (Niagara, Ont; Pres., Hamilton). S. of John Cleland, farmer. B. in Parish of Kilmore, Ire. Royal College, Belfast, Ire. Or. Aug, 1849. Mar. 1 Oct, 1856, Isabella Esther, third dau. of late Rev. Jos. Johnston, and neice of late Rev. Dr. Henry Cooke of Belfast. In. to present ch., March, 1879. Prececessors, Dr. R. McGill, T. Cruickshanks, J. B. Mowat, C. Campbell. No. of com., 122. Previous pastorates, East Brooklyn, New York, 1849-54; Scott and Uxbridge, 1854-69; Mountain and South Gower, 1869-73; W. Gwillimburg, 1873-79.

Cochrane, Wm, B.A., M.A., D.D. (Zion Ch., Brantford, Ont; Pres., Paris). S. of Wm. Cochrane, watch and clockmaker. B. at Paisley, Scot. Glasgow University; Hanover College, Indiana, U.S, and Princeton Theological Seminary, N.J. Or. 7 June, 1859. Mar. 1st, Mary Nelson Hovatover; 2nd, Oct. 2, 1873, Jeanette Elizabeth Balmer. Author of "The Heavenly Vision," 1873; "Christ and Christian Life," 1875; "Warning and Welcome," 1876, &c., &c. In. to present ch., 13 May, 1862. Predecessor, John Alexander. No. of com., 575. Previous pastorate, Scotch Church, Jersey City, New Jersey, 1859-62. Clerk of the Synod of Hamilton, London. Convener Home Mission Committee (Western Section). Moderator of General Assembly, 1882-83.

Cochrane, J. J., M.A. (Townline and Ivy, Ont; Pres., Barrie). Or. 4 Apl, 1876. No. of com., 117.

Cockburn, E., M.A. (Uxbridge, Ont; Pres., Lindsay). Or. March, 1873. No. of com., 129.

Colter, Ashley T., M.A. (Thornbury and Heathcote, Ont; Pres., Owen Sound). Or. 11 Dec, 1878. No. of com., 164.

Cook, John, D.D. (St. Andrew's Ch. and Principal Morrin College, Quebec; Pres., Quebec). Native of Sanquhar, Scot. Or. 24 Dec, 1835. Glasgow and Edinburgh Universities. For three years, prior to ordination, assistant to Minister of Cardross. In April, 1836, preached for first time in Quebec, and has been

Minister of St. Andrew's ever since. Received degree of Doctor of Divinity from Glasgow University, 1838. From commencement of ministry in Canada down to the Union, took an active part in controlling the affairs of the church in connection with the Church of Scotland. Of the Synod thereof, twice unanimously elected Moderator, first in 1838, and again in 1844. One of the original promoters of Queen's College, Kingston, and for many years after its establishment interested himself in its affairs. Was one of the trustees to whom, in 1841, the Royal Charter constituting the corporation of Queen's College at Kingston was granted. Visited Britain twice on business of the College, and was Principal thereof, and also Professor of Divinity during 1857 and 1858. In 1855 chosen as attorney of the Ministers in connection with the Church of Scotland in the matter of creating a fund fromthe proceeds derived through the commutation of the allowances from the Clergy Reserve Fund. By Dr. Cook's instumentality the commutation with the Government was effected, resulting in the formation of the Temporalities Fund, of the Board of Management of which Dr. Cook has since been a member. On the formation of the Presbyterian Church in Canada, by the Union of 1875, was selected the first Moderator of General Assembly, and is the first Principal of Morrin College, incorporated in 1861, and opened in 1862. Was nominated to latter position by the founder of the College, the late Dr. Morrin. In brief, Dr. Cook's services to the church, at large, have been numerous and most valuable.

Cooke, C. H. (Baltimore and Coldsprings, Ont; Pres., Peterboro). Or. Oct, 1882. No. of com., 383.

Coull, Geo., M.A. (Valleyfield, Que; Pres., Montreal). Or. March, 1857. No. of com., 102.

Coulthard, Walter (Picton, Ont; Pres., Kingston). Or. 20 Nov, 1860. No. of com., 75.

Coussirat, Dan'l, B.D., (Montreal.) Or. 8 Dec, 1864. Professor in Presbyterian College, Montreal.

Coutts, David, (Branton.) Or. 1836. A Minister on retired list attached to Presbytery of Toronto.

Craig, Robt. J., M.A. (Deseronto, Ont; Pres., Kingston.) Or. 27 April, 1876. No. of com., 71.

Craw, George, (Hillside, Ont; Pres., Barrie.) S. of James Craw, dyer. B. in Scotland. Free Ch., College Glasgow. Knox College Toronto. Or. and in 27 Dec., 1854. Mer. 6 Oct., 1864. Ann Wilson. No. of com., 169

Crockett, Duncan R. (Hammon River and Saltsprings Passekeag, N.B.; Pres., St. John). S. of John Crockett, farmer. B. at Middle River, N. S. Wanesburg College, Penn., and Theological Seminary, Danville, Kentucky. Or. 29 Oct., 1876. Mar. 10 Mar., 1866. Ellen Robertson. In. present ch. 20 Aug., 1879. Predecessors, Simon Fraser, J. K., Bearisto. No. of com. 81. Previous pastorate, Lawrence, Texas.

Croil, R. M. (St. Paul's ch., Simcoe, Ont; Pres., Hamilton.) Or. May, 1868. No. of com., 83.

Crombie, John, M.A, (Union Ch., Smith's Falls, Ont: Pres. Lanark and Renfrew). S. of John Crombie, nautical instrument maker. B. at City of Aberdeen. Mareshal College and Theological Free Church College, Aberdeen, New College Edinburgh. Or. 8 Aug., 1855. In. to present ch. 4 March, 1869. Predecessor, Wm. Aitken. No. of com. 114. Previous pastorates, La Geurre, 1855-56; Inverness, Que., 1856-69. Is clerk of Presbytery.

Crozier, Hugh, (Port Perry and Prince Albert, Ont; Pres. Whitby). S. of Joshua Crozier, farmer. B. in Township of Mono. Knox College, Toronto, and Princeton College, N.J. Or. 24 March, 1869. Mar. 7 Oct., 1869, Lucinda Turner Gibson. In. to present ch. 2 July, 1879. Predecessors Jas. Douglas, Jas. Thom, G. Jamieson, and R. Monteath. No. of com. 80. Previous pastorate Egremont from 1869 to 1879.

Cruchet, Alfred B., (Canning St. Ch., Montreal, Pres. Montreal). S. of Isaac F. Cruchet, farmer. B. at De Ramsay, Que. Presbyterian College, Montreal. Or. 21 Oct., 1878. Mar. 23 July, 1879, Eugénie Bourgonir. In. to present ch. 30 Oct., 1879. Predecessors Chas. Chiniquy, B. Ourière. No. of com. 55. Previous pastorate, New Glasgow, 1878-79.

Cruikshank, W. R., B.A., (St. Matthew's Ch. Montreal, Pres. Montreal). S of Peter Cruikshank, farmer. B. in Nova Scotia. Dalhousie College, Halifax, Edinburgh and Glasgow Universities. Or. 20 June, 1877. In. to present ch. 15 April, 1879. Predecessors, Wm. Darroch, Joshua Fraser, C A. Doudiet, S. S. Stobbs. No. of com. 438. Was assistant in St. Paul's Ch., Montreal, previous to induction.

Cumberland, Jas., M.A. (Amherst Id., Ont; Pres. Kingston). Or. 3 Feb. 1881. No. of com., 87.

Cumming, Thos. (Stellarton, N.S; Pres. Picton). Or. 23 Sep, 1863. No. of com., 300.

Cummings, R. (Westville, N.S; Pres. Picton). Or. 16 March, 1869. No. of com., 300.

Currie, Arch. (Kilmarnock, Ont; Pres. Chatham). Or. 7 Feb, 1860. No. of com., 60.

Currie, Arch., B.A., M.A. (Brock Sonya, Ont; Pres. Lindsay). S. of Edward Currie, blacksmith in early life, latterly Inspector of Poor. B. at Kintyre, Scot. Edinburgh University and Queen's College, Kingston. Or. 23 Oct, 1861. Mar. 1 Jane Forbes, 10 Sep, 1862. 2 Mary Fergu son, 1 July, 1880. In. to present ch., 11 July, 1867. Predecessor, John Campbell, M.A. No. of com., 145. Previous pastorate, Cote St. George, Lower Canada, 1861-67.

Currie, Donald, (Walla ebuig, Ont; Pres. Chatham). Or. 26 Dec, 1878. No. of com., 77.

Currie, Hugh. (Keady &c., Ont; Pres., Owen Sound). Or. Feb, 1870. No. of com., 205.

Currie, Hector, B. A. (Knox ch., Thedford, Ont; Pres., Sarnia.) S. of Donald Currie, farmer. B. in Argyleshire. Scot. Victoria College, Cobourg, and Knox College, Toronto. Or. and In. 25 Apl., 1876. Mar. Edith Jarvis, 27 Dec., 1877. Predecessors John McAlpine, Peter Goodfellow, and—— Blount. No. of com., 230.

Currie, John (Halifax, Pres., Halifax.) Or. 12 Aug., 1857. A Professor in Presbyterian College, Halifax.

Currie, John (Kintyre, Ont; Pres., London). Or. 8 Aug., 1882. No. of com., 100.

Currie, Peter (Teeswater, Ont; Pres., Bruce). Or. 19 Feb., 1855. No. of com., 117.

Cuthbertson, Geo. (Wyoming, Ont; Pres., Sarnia.) S. of Geo. Cuthbertson, shoemaker. B. at Kilmaurs, Scot. Glasgow University and Knox College, Toronto. Mar. 13 Oct., 1857. Mary Ann Decow. Or. 7 Oct., 1857. In. to present ch. 18 April, 1877. Previous pastorates, Winterbowrie, Woolwich, 1857-63; St. Thomas, 1863-77. Is Clerk of Presbytery.

Danly, Mark (Berne &c., Ont; Pres., Huron). Or. 26 Feb., 1873. No. of com., 232.

Darragh, W. S. (Lindon, N. S. Pres, Wallace.) S. of Andrew Darragh. B. at Ballyboyland, Ire. Theological Seminary, Presbyterian Church, Philadelphia. Or. 12 Nov, 1850. Mar. 29 April, 1851—Rachel Moor. In. to present ch. Nov. 1850. No. of com., 113.

Davidson, Duncan (Langside, Ont; Pres., Maitland.) Or. 8 Oct., 1872. No. of com., 46.

Davidson, John (Alma and Zion, Nichol, Ont; Pres., Guelph). S. of Wm. Davidson, farmer. B. near City of Quebec. Knox College, Toronto. Or. and In. 14 Feb. 1866. Mar. 20 Sept., 1871, Mary McKay. Predecessor John Duff, in part of charge. No. of com., 167.

Dawson, Alex., B.A. (Gravenhurst, Ont; Pres. Barrie). Or. 23 Sep., 1863. No. of com., 81.

Dewar, Robt. (Lake Shore, Ont; Pres. Owen Sound). Or. 7 Oct., 1855. Pastor Emeritus.

Dewey, Finlay M., B.A., M.A. (Richmond; Pres. Quebec). S. of Alex. Dewey, farmer. B. at St. Remi, Que. McGill College, Montreal, Princeton Seminary, N. J. Or. and In. 9 Aug., 1877. Predecessor John McKay. No. of com., 80. Is clerk of Presbytery.

Dey, Wm. J., B.A., M.A. (Presbyterian College, Montreal; Pres. Montreal). S. of Thos. Dey, farmer. B. at East Hawkesbury, Ont. McGill College, Presbyterian College, Montreal. Or. 5 Jan., 1876. Mar. 12 June, 1877, Margaret Imrie. Was minister of Spencerville, 1876-82. Appointed Dean of Presbyterian College, Montreal, 1 Sept., 1882.

Dick, James, (Richmond Hill, Ont; Pres. Toronto). S. of John Dick, farmer. B. in Ayrshire, Scot. Glasgow University and United Secession Hall. Or. 22 Dec, 1842. Mar 16 July, 1844, Mary L. Thansom. In. to present ch. 14 March, 1849. Predecessor, Wm. Jenkins No. of com., 170. Previous pastorate Emily, 1842-49.

Dickie, Alfred B. (Milford & Gays River Chs., Milford, N. S. Pres. Halifax) S. of Adam Dickie, miller. B. at Maitland, N. S. Dalhousie College, Gerrish Street Hall, Halifax and Truro Seminary. Or. 27 Dec., 1869. Mar. 3 July, 1873, Lillian Jane McLeod. In. to present ch. 27 April, 1879. Predecessor. E. Scott. No. of com., 257. Was min. for 9 years at Sheet Harbor.

Dickson, James A. R., B.D. (Central ch., Galt; Pres. Guelph) S. of David Dickson. B. at Tranent, Scot. University, Toronto, Presbyterian College, Montreal, Congregational College. Or. 18 July, 1865. Mar. 20 June, 1867, Isabella E. Fairbairn. Author of "Working for Jesus" published in 1870, "Expository Bible Readings" published in 1882, and various tracts. In. to present ch. 14 Oct., 1879. Predecessors, Dr. John James, W. J. Murdoch, Richard Bentley. No. of com., 410. Was a Congregational Minister prior to admission into Presbyterian Church in June, 1879.

Doak, Wm. (Sarnia) A minister without charge attached to Presbytery of Sarnia.

Dobson, A. B. (Ballinafad, &c., Ont; Pres. Toronto) Or. 29 Nov., 1881. No. of com., 110.

Donald, Andrew (Hampton Village, N. B.; Pres. St. John) S. of Andrew Donald, farmer. B. in Lanarkshire, Scot. Glasgow and Edinburgh Universities. Or. 16 June, 1842. Mar. 1st Sep., 1842, Jane Crozier McGill.—2nd, March 2, 1848, Margaret Scott. Published in 1876 a small volume of poems. Has been minister of Shelburne, Clyde River, and Barrington, N. S.; also of Hammond River, Saltsprings, Norton, Greenfield and Williamstown, N. B. Retired from active service but still preaches more or less frequently as health will permit and opportunity offers.

Donald, W. (Prince Street ch., Picton; Pres., Picton). Or. 31 Oct, 1860. No. of com., 394.

Dondiet, Chas. A. (St. John's ch., Montreal; Pres., Montreal). S. of Rev. Jas. F. Dondiet, Minister of the Reformed Church of France. B. in Geneva. Geneva College, Grande Ligne Bapt. College, and Queen's College, Kingston. Or. 23 Aug, 1869. Mar. 1st 21 March, 1857, Rebecca Robinson of Terrebonne. She died 25 Sep, 1858. 2nd, 9 July, 1861, Eliza Dunbar of Montreal. In. to present ch., 16 Oct. 1877. Predecessors, C. A. Tanner, 1874-76; C. A. Dondiet, 1869-72; G. Goepp, 1866-67; J. E. Tanner, 1862-66. No. of com., 123. Previous pastorates, St. John's ch., Mont., 1869-72; St. Matthew's ch., Point St. Charles, 1872-76; St. Andrew's Unionists, Mont., 1876-77. Family originally from France whence it emigrated when Edict of Nantes revoked and settled in the Canton of Neuchatel, Switzerland.

Doug'as, Jas. (Morris, Man; Pres., Manitoba). Or. 2 Aug, 1865. No. of com., 23.

Douglas, J. M. (Port Hope, Ont; Pres., Peterboro). Or. Oct, 1867. Has been a Missionary in India.

Drummond, A. A. (Newcastle, Ont; Pres., Whitby). Or. 20 Oct, 1847. No. of com., 78. Is Clerk of the Presbytery.

Drummond, D. (Boulardcric, N. S; Pres., Sydney.) Or. 18 June, 1872. No. of com., 118.

Duff, Daniel (North Brant and West Bentinck, Ont; Pres. Bruce). S. of Peter Duff, sanitary superintendent. City of Perth. B. in Perthshire. Knox College and Toronto University, also Free Church College, Edinburgh. Or. 19 April, 1864. Mar. 1869, Mary C. Young. In. to present ch., 19 May, 1868. No. of com., in former place 45, in latter 105. For three years, 1865–67, missionary in British Columbia, and was the first missionary of any denomination that wintered in Cariboo.

Duff, John (Elora, Ont.) Or. 10 Aug, 1836. A Minister on retired list, attached to Presbytery of Guelph.

Duff, Wm. (Lunenburg, N.S). Or. 23 May, 1843. A Minister on retired list, Presbytery of Lunenburg and Shelburne.

Dunbar. John (Dunbarton, Ont.) Or. 10 May, 1853. A, Minister without charge, attached to Presbytery of Whitby.

Duncan, Jas. B. (Forest and Mackay, Ont; Pres., Sarnia.) Or. 1 July, 1848. No. of com., 125.

Duncan, P. (Colborne and Brighton, Ont; Pres., Peterboro). Or. Oct, 1857. No. of com., 128.

Eadie, John (Pinkerton, Ont; Pres., Bruce). S. of Peter Eadie, horticulturist. B in Fifeshire, Scotland. Knox College, Toronto. Or. March, 1862. Mar. Jane McPherson, 27 May, 1863. In. to present ch., 10 July, 1879. Predecessor, D. Duff. No. of com., 215. Previous pastorate, Milton.

Eastman, S. H., B. A. (Oshawa, Ont; Pres., Whitby). S. of W. O. Eastm n, farmer. B. at Smithville, Ont. University and Knox College, Toronto. Or. and In. 25 Nov, 1879. Mar. 30 June, 1881, Belle McColl. Predecessors, R. H. Thornton, D. D., John Hogg. No. of com., 234.

Edmison, Henry, B.A., M.A. (Rothsay, Ont; Pres., Guelph). B. in Peterboro'. Queen's College, Kingston. Or. 20 Oct, 1866. Mar. 31 July, 1867, Mary Lynam. In. to present ch., 2 June, 1880. Predecessor, Daniel Anderson. No. of com., 18?. Previous pastorates, Waterdown, 1866-73, Melbourne, 1873-80.

Edmunds, F. J. (Port Colborne, Ont; Pres., Hamilton). No. of com., 39.

Edmondson. J. B. (St. John's Ch., Almonte, Ont; Pres., Lanark and Renfrew). Or. 21 Oct, 1867. No. of com., 264.

Elliot, Chas.. D.D. (London). A minister without charge. Presbytery of London.

Elliott, Jos. (Cannington, Ont; Pres., Lindsay.) S. of Wm. Elliott, farmer. B. in Roxburghshire, Scot. University and Theological College, London. Or. Oct., 1836. Mar. Ann G. Wylie. In. to present ch. April, 1879. Predecessors, Hugh Campbell; — Currie and J. Campbell. Previous pastorates, Bury St. Edmunds, Eng; Ottawa, Ont, Halifax, N. S. and Montreal. Author of "Walks about Zion," published in 1881.

Ewing John (Omemee &c., Ont; Pres., Peterboro.) Or. Jan., 1846. No. of com., 154.

Fairbairn, Robt, B. A. (Oro, Ont; Pres., Barrie.) B. in Scotland. University and Knox College, Toronto. Or. and In. 11 Dec., 1872. Predecessors W. Johnston, and John Gray. No. of com., 156.

Fairlie, John (L'Orignal and Hawkesbury, Ont; Pres., Ottawa.) Or. 21 Aug., 1873. No. of com., 105.

Farqu'arson, Alex. (St. Andrew's ch. Sydney, C. B.) S. of Rev. A. Farquharson, Minister of Lake Ainslie, N. S. B. at Mid-River, N. S. Free Church College, Halifax. Or. 14 Dec., 1864. Mar. 23 Nov., 1876. Barbara McLeod. In. to present ch. 25 Aug., 1875. Predecessor, Dr. Hugh McLeod. No. of com., 150. Previous pastorates, Leitch's Creek, 1864-67. Glace Bay Mines, 1867-75.

Farquharson, James, B. A. (Pilot Mound, Man; Pres., Manitoba. S. of Chas. Farquharson, farmer. B. at Logie-Coldstone, Scot. University and Knox College, Toronto. Or. and In. 4 Jan., 1882. Mar. Janet E. R. Coutts, 18 Nov.,1882. No. of com., 72.

Farries, Francis W. (Knox Ch., Ottawa; Pres., Ottawa). S. of Robert Farries, farmer. B. in Dumfriesshire, Scot. Knox College, Toronto, and Princeton Theological Seminary. Or. 18 May, 1868. Mar. 21 Jan, 1868, Sophia A. Bugle. In. to present ch., 29 April, 1875. Predecessors, Thos. Wardrope, D.D., Professor McLaren. No. of com., 245. Previous pastorates, Otisville, N.Y., 1868–71; Paris, Ont., 1871–75.

Fenton, Samuel (Vittoria, Ont; Pres.. Hamilton). Or. 1843. No. of com., 66.

Fenwick, Thos. (Metis, Que; Pres., Quebec). S. of John F. Fenwick, doorkeeper to Legislative Council of Old Canada. B. in Jedburgh, Scot. Knox College, Toronto. Or. and In. 31 Oct, 1861. Has written several articles for various magazines. Predecessor, Wm. Macalister. No. of com., 52. Is an amateur artist, and has presented pictures to Knox College, Toronto; Queen's, Kingston, and Presbyterian College, Montreal. Is architect of church built at Metis.

Ferguson, G. D., B.A., (Kingston, Ont; Pres. Kingston). Or. 16 May, 1855. One of the Professors in Queen's College.

Ferguson, J., M.A., B.D. (Chesley, Ont; Pres., Bruce). Or. 30 Dec., 1879. No. of com., 216.

Ferguson, John (Vankleekhill, Ont; Pres., Glengarry). Or. Jan, 1865. No. of com., 165.

Ferguson, Wm. (Kirkhill, Ont; Pres., Glengarry). No. of com., 190.

Ferguson, Wm. (Glenmorris, Ont , Pres., Bruce). Or. 2 Jan, 1873. No. of com., 122.

Ferries, John, B.A. (First Pres., Ch., Brandon, Man ; Pres. Manitoba). S. of the Rev. Peter Ferries. B. at Edinkillie, Scot. Aberdeen and Glasgow Universities. Or. 24 Aug, 1865. Mar. 1866, Annie Broadfoot. In. to present ch., 24 Aug, 1882. No. of com., 115. Previous pastorates, Kingarth, Bute and Edinkillie, Scot. Preached first sermon in Brandon, in a tent. Acted as Missionary until called to occupy pulpit of church when built. Has recently resigned owing to ill health.

Findlay, Allan (Bracebridge, Ont; Pres., Barrie). S. of Rev. Jas. Findlay. B. in New York State. Knox College, Toronto. Or. 30 Jan, 1867. Mar. 1 Jan, 1868, Lucy F. Patullo. In. to present ch. 24 Aug, 1882. No. of com., 100.

Findlay, David, B.A, (Cantley and Portland ; Pres., Ottawa S. of John Findlay, merchant. B. at Coatbridge, Scot. Knox College and University, Toronto. Or. and In. 22 Dec, 1879. Mar. Mary Pritchard, 6 Sep, 1880 No. of com., 45

Fisher, Simeon W. (Knox Ch., Elora; Pres., Guelph). Or 1874. No. of com., 240.

Fleck, James, B.A. (Knox Ch., Montreal; Pres. Montreal) S. of James Fleck, merchant and farmer. B. in County Antrim, Ire. Queen's College and General Assembly College, Belfast. Or. 31 March, 1869. In. to present ch. June, 1876. Predecessors, Dr. Kemp, Dr. Inglis, Dr. Irvine, Mr. Thornton and others. No. of com., 380. Previous pastorate, Second Presbyterian Ch. of Armagh, Ire., 1869–76.

Fleming, P. (Warsaw, &c., Ont ; Pres. Peterboro) Or. Nov., 1876. Is an ordained missionary.

Fletcher, Charles (Goderich, Ont; Pres. Huron) S. of David Fletcher, school teacher. B. at Luthrie, Scot. St. Andrews, Edinburgh, and Glasgow Theological Halls of United Secession Church. Or. 1842. Mar. 13 May, 1843, Helen Martin. Was minister at Chippewawa 1843–47, Goderich 1847–50, which charge he resigned, owing to ill health and is now on the superannuated list.

Fletcher, Colin B.A., M.A. (Thames Road & Kirkton, Ont; Pres. Huron) S. of Hugh Fletcher, farmer. B. in Island of Islay, Scot. Upper Canada College, Toronto University and Knox College, Toronto. Or. and In. 20 Feb., 1879. Mar. Anna M. Agur, 18 Dec., 1879. Predecessors, John Logie and Henry Gracey. No. of com., 310.

Fletcher, D. H. (McNab St. Ch., Hamilton ; Pres. Hamilton) S. of Hugh Fletcher, farmer. B. in Scotland. Knox College, Toronto. Or. 8 Nov., 1860. Mar. Phyllis Eleanor Murray. In. to present ch. 1 May, 1872. Predecessor, Dr. David Inglis. No. of com., 442. Previous pastorate, Scarborough, Ont; 1860–72.

Flett, G. (Okomase, Man; Pres., Manitoba.) Or. 10 Aug., 1865.

Forbes, Jas. A. (Glace Bay, N. S. Pres., Sydney.) Or. 18 Oct., 1881. No. of com., 26.

Forbes, John Franklin (Union Centre & Lochaber, N. S. Pres., Picton.) S. of John Forbes, a soldier. B. in Picton, Co. Toronto University, Knox College. Princeton seminary, N. J. Or. and In. 27 Feb., 1867. Mar. 20 Oct., 1869. Janet C. McMillan. Predecessors, Messrs. Don. McConnachy, Kenneth McKenzie and Alex. Campbell. No. of com., 293.

Forbes, W. G. (Port Hastings. N. S.) Or. 1852. Minister on retired list Presbytery of Victoria and Richmond.

Forlong, Wm. (Henry Ch. Lachute, Que ; Pres., Montreal.) Or. 11 Aug., 1853. No. of com , 197.

Forrest, John (Halifax, Pres., Halifax.) Or. 1866. A Professor in Dalhousie College, Halifax.

Forrest, Wm. (Oungah, Ont.) Or. 18 Feb., 1857. A Minister on retired list attached to Presbytery of Owen Sound.

Fotheringham, John (St. Mary's, Ont ; Pres., Stratford.) S. of Thos. Fotheringham, farmer. B. at Sanday Orkney, Scot. U. P. Theo. Hall, Canada. Or. 27 Feb., 1856. Mar. 29 Feb., 1860. In. to Hibbert at time of ordination, and retired from that charge, on account of ill-health in Oct., 1871. Is Clerk of Presbytery, and was clerk of late Synod of London, Canada Presbyterian Church.

Fotheringham, Thos. F., B.A., M.A. (St. John's Ch, St. John, N. B ; Pres. of St. John). S. of Thos. Fotheringham, accountant. B. in Hamilton, Ont. University and Knox College, Toronto ; United Presbyterian Hall, Edinburgh, and Leipsig University. Or. 21 July, 1875. Mar. 9 Sep, 1875, Annie R. Cruickshank. She died 28 July, 1882. In. to pres nt ch., 9 Jan, 1883. Predecessors, Dr. Robt. Irvine, Dr. Jas. Bennet. No. of com., 90. Previous pastorates, Norwood and Hastings, Ont, Santa Manico, Davisville, Colton and San Bernardino, California.

Fowlie, Robt. (Erin, &c; Pres., Guelph). Or. 25 Oct, 1877. No. of com., 217.

Frame, W. R. (Mount Stewart and St. Peters, P.E I; Pres., P. E. Island). Or. 13 Aug, 1862. No. of com., 149.

Fraser, Alex. (Longwood and Caradoc, Ont; Pres. London). Or. 22 Oct, 1861. No. of com., 111.

Fraser, Alex (Orono, Ont; Pres., Whitby). Or. 15 Oct, 1878. No. of com., 119.

Fraser, Donald, M.A., B.A. (St Andrew's Ch., Mount Forest; Pres., Saugeen). S. of Andrew Fraser, farmer. B at Lochiel, Ont. Queen's College, Kingston. Or. 14 Aug, 1867. Mar 8 June, 1870, Sarah Fraser. In to present ch 27 June, 1877. No. of com., 239. Previous pastorates, Priceville, 1867-75, Saugeen, 1875-77

Fraser D. Stiles, B.A, (Mahone Bay, N. S; Pres., Lunenburg and Yarmouth). S. of Jas. D. Fraser. B. at Durham, N. S. Dalhousie College and Theological Hall, Halifax. Or. and In. 30 Nov, 1877. Mar. 6 Dec, 1877, A. E. Cunningham. Predecessor, E. McNab. No. of com., 85. Is clerk of Presbytery.

Fraser, James, B.A. (Chatham and Grenville, Que; Pres., Montreal). Or. 15 Jan, 1870. No. of com., 125.

Frazer, James, (Georgina, Ont; Pres., Toronto). S. of John S. Frazer, farmer. B. at Equesing, Halton Co., Ont. Knox College, Toronto, Princeton College, N.J. Or. 8 Feb, 1876. Mar. 17 Oct, 1877, Margaret Cooper. In. to present ch., 7 July, 1879. Predecessors, John Gordon and D. V. Niven. No. of com., 98. Previous pastorates, St. Ann's and Wellandport, 1876-79.

Fraser, John, (Indian Lands, St. Elmo, Ont; Pres., Glengarry). S. of John Fraser, farmer. B. in Scot. King's College. Aberdeen. Or. 1845. In. to present ch., 1877. Predecessors, Daniel Gordon, Kenneth McDonald. No. of com., 150. Previous pastorates, St. Thomas, 1850-59; Thamesford, 1859-67; Kincardine, 1867-77.

Fraser, J.B., M.D. (Queensville, Ont; Pres., Toronto). S. of Rev. D. Fraser. B. at Bond Head, Ont. Knox College, Toronto and Victoria College, Cobourg. Or. 15 Sep, 1874. In. to present ch., 27 May, 1878. No. of com., 120. Medical Missionary in Formosa, China, from 1874 to 1877.

Fraser, Mungo, M.A. (Knox Ch., St. Thomas, Ont; Pres., London). S. of Alex. Fraser, carpenter. B. in Scot. Knox College, Toronto. Mar. 27 Oct, 1867, Mary E. Hunter. Or. 10 Oct, 1867. In. to present ch., 22 Nov, 1876. Predecessors, John Fraser, Alex. Young, Geo. Cuthbertson and others. No. of com., 318. Previous pastorate, Barrie, 1867-76.

Fraser, R. Douglas. B.A., M.A. (Claude, Ont; Pres., Toronto). S. of Rev. W. Fraser, D D., Clk. of General Assembly. B. at Bond Head. Presbyterian College, Montreal, and University and Knox College, Toronto. Or. 29 Sep, 1873. Mar. Elizabeth S., youngst dau. of Charles Wilson of Bond Head. In. to present ch., 28 Oct, 1879. Predecessors, R. M. Croll, D. Coutts, S. Porter, D. McMillan. No. of com., 183. Previous pastorates, Cookstown, 1873-75; Charles St. Ch., Toronto, 1875-78. Was gold medallist in natural science, Toronto University, also McMurrich medallist.

Fraser, Simon C., M.A. A Minister without charge, attached to Presbytery of Guelph.

Fraser, Thomas (Montreal). A retired Minister, attached to Presbytery of Montreal.

Fraser, Wm., D.D. (Barrie, Ont; Pres., Barrie). S. of Donald Fraser, miller and farmer. B. in Picton Co., N.S. Studied theology under Thos. MacCulloch, D.D., Principal of Picton Academy. Or. 2 Sept, 1834. Mar. 1st, Jane Geddie, 15 Sept. 1834; 2nd, Nancy McCurdy, 30 Oct, 1844; 3rd Maria Jane Nicholas 8 May, 1866. Was pastor of West Gwillimburg and Cookstown from 9 Aug, 1835, till retirement from active service in the church, 1 June, 1879.

Frizzel, Wm. (Leslieville, Ont; Pres., Toronto). Or. 7 April, 1878. No. of com., 130.

Gallagher, John B. A. (Pittsburgh, Ont; Pres., Kingston. Or. 14 Nov., 1871. No. of com., 44.

Gallagher, John B. A. (Pittsburg, Ont; Pres., Kingston.) Or. 14 Nov., 1871. No. of com., 44.

Galloway, Wm. (Hyndman & S. Mountain, Ont; Pres., Brockville.) Or. 15 Feb., 1879. No of com., 200.

Gandier, Joseph (Coulonge and Upper Litchfield, Ont; Pres., Lanark and Renfrew.) S. of Jos. Gandier, Missionary in Ch. of England. B. in Suffolk, Eng. Queen's College Kingston. Or. and In. Coulonge 31 Dec., 1872. In. to ch. Upper Litchfield, Aug., 1878. Mar. 9 Jan., 1861, Helen Eastwood. No. of com., 77. Predecessor, D. McDonald. Was a Missionary in lumber mission for eight summers, and nine winters.

Gauld, John (Hamilton.) A Minister without charge residing within bounds of Presbytery of Hamilton.

Geddes, John (Minesing, Ont; Pres., Barrie.) S. of John Geddes, bleacher. B. in parish of Mairs, Scot. University, Edinburgh, Knox College Toronto. Or. and In. 11 Oct., 1882. Predecessor,—Millard. No. of com., 110.

George, F. W. (New Carlise &c., Que; Pres., Miramichi.) Or. 15 Mar., 1882. No. of com., 81.

George, John L., B.A., M.A. (Sherbrooke, St. Mary's, N. S; Pres., Pictou) S. of Rev. F. W. George. B. in Halifax, N. S. Dalhousie College, N. S, and Princeton College. N. J. Or. and In. 20 Dec, 1881. Predecessors, Alex. Lewis, John Campbell, Arch. C. Gillies, Jas. Quinn. No. of com., 220.

Gilchrist, J. R., B.A. (Cheltenham, &c., Ont; Pres., Toronto). Or. 10 Oct, 1876. No. of com., 138.

Gillies, E. (Earltown, N. S; Pres., Wallace.) Or. 24 Aug, 1881. No of com., 166.

Gilray, Alex. (College St., Ch, Toronto; Pres., Toronto). S. of Robert Gilray, farmer. B. in Scotland. Knox College, Toronto. Or. and In. 5 Jan, 1875. No. of com., 372

Glassford. T. S., B.A. (Richmond West, Ont; Pres. Ottawa). S. of Thos. Glassford, farmer. B. Beaverton. Queen's College, Kingston. Or. 23 Sep, 1880. Mar. Cassie Shannon, 12 Oct, 1881. In. to present ch. 23 Sep, 1880. Predecessor, A. M. McClelland. No. of com, 80.

Goldie, Peter C. (Knox Ch, Watford, Ont; Pres., Sarnia). S. of James Goldie, farmer. B. at Glasgow, Scot. Knox College, Toronto. Or. 15 Nov, 1877. Mar. Annie E. Sutherland 9 Jan, 1877. In. to present ch., 25 Feb, 1880. No. of com., 130, Previous pastorate, Delaware, Ont, from 15 Nov, 1877, to 25 Feb, 1880.

Goldsmith, Thos. (St. John's Ch., Hamilton; Pres., Hamilton). Or. 5 Jan, 1845. No. of com., 241.

Goodfellow, P. (Antigonish, N.S; Pres., Pictou). S. of John Goodfellow, farmer. B. in Bradford, Ont. University and U.P. Hall, Toronto. Or. 29 Jan, 1862. Mar. 2 Oct, 1879, Susan McNab. In. to present ch, July 1872. Predecessors, T Trotter, D. Honeyman, T. Downie, J. Murray. No. of com., 294. Previous pastorate, Widder and Lake Road, Ont.

Gordon, Daniel M, B. D., M. A. (Knox Ch., Winnipeg. Pres., Manitoba). S. of William Gordon, merchant. B at Pictou, N.S. Glasgow University. Or. 6 Aug, 1866. Mar. Eliza S. youngest dau. of the late Rev. John Maclennan of Kilchrennan, Scot. Author of "Mountain and Prairie," published in 1880. In. to present ch., 9 Aug, 1882. Predecessor, James Robertson, now Superintendent of Missions for the North-West. No. of com., 392. Previous pastorate, St. Andrew's Ch., Ottawa, 1867-82

Gordon Daniel, (Harrington, Ont; Pres., Stratford). Or. Oct, 1849. No. of com., 100.

Gordon, G.L. (Grand River, C.B; Pres., Sydney). S. of James Gordon, carpenter. B. at West Clyne, Scot. Church of Scotland Training College, Edinburgh; Dalhousie College and Theological Hall, Halifax. Or. and In. 6 Oct. 1879. Mar. 29 Oct, 1879, Annie E. Murray, of Economy, N.S. Author of a Gaelic Class Book published in 1876. Predecessor, James Ross. No. of com., 62. Was first Missionary Catechist commissioned by Church of Scotland to Canada. Labored in Cape Breton &c., during vacations in collegiate course. Is Clerk of Presbytery.

Gordon, Jas. M.A. (Niagara Falls; Ont; Pres. Hamilton.) Or. 1854. No. of com., 89.

Gourlay, James, M.A. (Port Elgin, Ont; Pres. Bruce.) B. at Newton Stewart, Scot. University and Free Church College, Edinburgh. Mar. B. A. Shearer. Or. and In. 3 March, 1875. Predecessors, Alex. Fraser, D. G. McKay. No. of com., 150. Is Clerk of the Presbytery.

Gracey, Henry (Gananoque, Ont; Pres. Kingston.) Or. March, 1865. No. of com., 14.

Grant, Alex. (Ashfield, Ont; Pres. Maitland.) Or. Aug., 1858. No. of com., 65.

Grant, Alex., B.A. (Oneida, &c., Ont; Pres. Hamilton.) Or. 27 Jan., 1863. No. of com., 348.

Grant, Alex. (Lake Ainslie, N. S; Pres. Victoria and Richmond.) Or. 1871. No. of com., 60.

Grant, Edward (Stewiacke, N. S.; Pres. Truro.) Or. 26 Oct., 1869. No. of com., 297.

Grant, Geo. M., M.A., D.D. (Principal Queen's College and University; Pres., Kingston). S. of James Grant, school teacher. B. at East River, N.S. Or. 29 Nov, 1860. Mar. Jessie Lawson of Halifax, N.S. Is author of the famous work "Ocean to Ocean," and has published various reviews, lectures, &c. Received early education at Picton Academy and West River Seminary. Having completed studies at latter institution, was selected by committee of Synod of Nova Scotia, one of four bursars to be sent to Glasgow University. Entered University when only 18 years of age, and then began a course of hard study lasting eight years. Career at University distinguished by exceptional brilliancy. Among prizes carried off by Dr. Grant, at this time, were first in Classics, Moral Philosophy and Chemistry, besides the Lord Rector's prize of thirty guineas for best essay on Hindoo Literature and Philosophy. While very studious, was a proficient in all athletic games, thereby being extremely popular with his fellow students, over whom he had great influence. Upon leaving College was ordained by the Church of Scotland, and had flattering inducements held out for him to reside in Scotland. Preferred, however, returning to Canada, and, immediately, on arrival, in 1861, appointed a missionary in County of Pictou. Shortly afterwards translated to a more important sphere in Prince Edward Island. In month of May, 1863, inducted as Minister of St. Matthew's Ch., Halifax, where he labored for 14 years, when appointed to present position. While in Halifax was a director of Dalhousie College, a trustee of the Theological Seminary, a member of various committees of Presbytery and Synod, a zealous advocate of Union, and chairman, secretary or member of many benevolent societies. When Union happily consummated, he, as Moderator of the Kirk Synod, subscribed the articles in its name. In October, 1877, elected Principal of Queen's College, Kingston, succeeding Principal Snodgrass. The unanimity of sentiment displayed in his election by the trustees of the College, his cordial reception by the students, and the warm welcome accorded by the citizens of Kingston, all testified that his labors and abilities had met with recognition. Soon after entering on new duties he perceived that something had to be done to place the College on a more secure footing, and his inauguration of the Building and Endowment Scheme, as well as his successful exertions in raising $150,000, required to carry it out, are too fresh in the public memory to need more than casual mention. Soon after his installation as Principal, his alma mater conferred on him the degree of Doctor of Divinity.

Grant, R. N. (Orillia, Ont; Pres., Barrie.) S. of Alex. Grant. B. in township of Cavan, Ont. Knox College, Toronto. Or. 23 Jan., 1866. Mar. 9 May, 1866, Marianne McMullen. In. to present ch., 1882. No. of com., 233. Previous pastorates Waterdown and Burlington, 1866-71. Ingersoll, 1871-1882.

Grant, Wm. (W. and C. River & Brookfield, P. E. I. Pres., P. E. Island.) Or. 27 Sep., 1869. No. of com., 132.

Gray, Andrew (St. Matthew's Ch., Wallace, N. S. Pres., Wallace.) Or. 19 May, 1880.

Gray, James (Sussex, N. B. Pres., St. John.) Or. 6 Mar., 1857. No. of com., 90.

Gray, James M. (Stirling, Ont; Pres., Kingston.) Or. 4 Aug., 1869. No. of com., 50.

Gray, John B. A., M. A. (Orillia, Ont ; Pres., Barrie). S. of Arthur Gray, an Officer in British Army. B. in Pittenseir, Elgin, Scot. Or. and In. 21 May, 1851. Pastor Emeritus with seat at session, and Presbytery from 1 Jan., 1882. Has published sermons, lectures &c. Mar. 1st in Aug., 1850. Rebecca H. Fraser. 2nd in 7 Nov., 1853, Barbara Ogden. No. of com., when retired from active service, 235.

Gray, John (Windsor, Ont ; Pres., Chatham.) Or. 16 Nov., 1870. No. of com., 150.

Gray, Robert (York Mills, &c., Ont ; Pres. Toronto.) Or. 7 April, 1874. No. of com., 77.

Gregg, Wm., B.A., M.A., D.D. (Knox College, Toronto; Pres. Toronto.) B. at Killycreen, Ire. Glasgow and Edinburgh Universities. Or. 1847. Edited Book of Family Worship, Assisted in preparing Hymnal. Was minister at Belleville 1847–57, Cooke's Ch., Toronto, 1857–72, when appointed Professor of Apologetics in Knox College, Toronto. Has been lecturer in Apologetics, Church History and Theology in Knox College, Toronto, and Presbyterian College, Montreal. Received degree of Doctor of Divinity from Hanover University, United States.

Gunn, Adam, B.A. (Kennetcook & Gore, N. S.; Pres. Halifax.) Or. Feb., 1876. No. of com., 176.

Gunn, Arch. (St. John's Ch., Windsor, N. S.; Pres. Halifax) S. of Wm Gunn, farmer. B. at Six Mile Brook, N. S Dalhousie College and Theological Hall, Halifax. Or. 6 Nov., 1878. Mar. 3 Nov., 1880, Jennie C. third dau. of James Henderson, of Richmond, N B. In. to present ch. 19 Oct., 1880. Predecessors, J. L. Murdoch, E. Amand, A. R Garvie, A. J. Mowatt and others. No. of com , 268. Previous pastorate, Bett's Cove and Little Bay, Newfoundland, 1878–80.

Gunn, S C. (East St. Peter's, P. E. I.; Pres. P. E. Island) Or. 16 Nov., 1870. No. of com., 137.

Haigh, George (Doon, &c., Ont ; Pres. Guelph.) Or. April, 1863. No. of com., 137.

Hally, James (Ste. Therese de Blainville, Que ; Pres., Montreal). Or. 17 Dec, 1872. No. of com., 113.

Hamilton, A. M , M.A. (Winterbourne, Ont ; Pres., Guelph). Or. 22 May, 1877. No. of com., 164.

Hamilton, J. B., B.A., M.A. (St. Andrew's Ch., Kincardine, Ont ; Pres., Maitland). S. of James Hamilton, farmer. B. in Lanarkshire Scot. University and Knox College, Toronto. Or. and In. 27 Apl, 1880. Predecessors, Alex. Dawson, John Ferguson, and Wm. Anderson. No. of com., 72.

Hamilton, Robt. (Fullerton and Avonbank, Ont; Pres., Stratford). Or. 30 June, 1859. No. of com , 231.

Hancock, Wm. (Fonthill, Ont) Or. May 1834. A minister on retired list attached to Presbytery of Hamilton.

Hanran, James (Inverness, Que). A minister on retired list attached to Presbytery of Quebec.

Hart, Thos., B.A., M. A. (Winnipeg; Pres., Manitoba). S. of a bookseller and stationer. B. at Paisley, Scot. Queen's College and Edinburgh University. Or. 30 July, 1872. Mar. 16 Aug, 1872, Isabella Margaret Malloch. Was for several years Principal of Perth High School. Appointed Professor of Classics and French, and Lecturer in Hebrew of Manitoba College, June, 1872. Is Clerk of Presbytery.

Hartley, Alex. Y. (Bluevale and Eadies, Ont; Pres., Maitland). S. of James Hartley, farmer. B. in Wigtonshire, Scot. Knox College, Toronto. Or. June, 1864. Mar. 1st 13 June, 1864, Margaret Fitzgerald; she died, 23 April, 1876. 2nd, 8 Nov, 1877, Emma Sewell. In. to present ch., 25 May, 1882. Predecessors, Messrs. Young, Hastie, Prichard, McKay. No. of com., 187. Previous pastorates, 'Dungannon, 1873-76; Rodgerville, &c., 1876-82.

Harvey Moses, B.A. St. Johns, Nfld). S. of Rev. James Harvey, of Belfast. B. in Armagh, Ire. Queen's College, Belfast. Or. 1843. A retired minister attached to Presbytery of Newfoundland). Mar. 7 July, 1852, Sarah A. Brown. Author of lectures, " Newfoundland, the oldest British Colony," &c, &c.

Hastie, James (Lindsay, Ont; Pres., Lindsay). S. of Wm. Hastie, farmer. B. at Linwood, Scot. Knox College, Toronto. Or. 23 Oct. 1866. Mar 18 Oct. 1866, Eliza A. Hutchinson. Has contributed articles to magazines, papers, &c. In. to present ch., 22 June, 1876. Predecessors, J. A. Murray, E. W. Panton, J. B. Muir, W. Johnston, and J. Dobie. No. of com , 200. Previous pastorates, Bluevale and Wingham, 1866-71, and Prescott, 1871-76.

Heine, Colborne, B.A. (Chalmers' Ch., Montreal; Pres., Montreal). S. of Henry Heine, farmer. B. in Parish of Studholm, New Brunswick. New Brunswick University, and Princeton College, N.J. Or. and In. 17 Nov, 1881. Predecessors, John Jones, Wm. Mitchell, and P. Wright. No of com., 160. Was assistant to Dr. Cook, Quebec, from Nov, 1876, to Mar, 1879.

Henderson, Alex. (Hyde Park Corner, Ont; Pres., London). S. of Alex. Henderson, lawn weaver. B. in Glasgow. Knox

College, Toronto. Or. and In. 10 Oct, 1877. Mar. 16 Nov, 1866, Cecilia G. Brown. No. of com., 90. Prior to being Ordained was a student missionary at Hyde Park and Komoka.

Henderson, John G. (Bruce Mines, Ont; Pres., Bruce). Or. a Missionary, 21 Nov, 1882.

Henry, J. K. (Cookstown, Ont; Pres., Barrie). Or. 19 Apl, 1882.

Henry, Matthew G. (Shubenacadie and Lower Stewiacke, N. S; Pres., Halifax). S. of S.L. Henry, farmer. B. at Musquodoboit. Presbyterian College, Montreal. Or. 4 Feb, 1861. Mar. 6 July, 1865, Mary Parker. In. to present ch., 4 Dec, 1877. Predecessors, James McLean, Geo. Christie and Dr. Honeyman. No. of com., 290. Previous pastorate, Clyde River and Barrington, 1861-67.

Herald, Jas. (Dundas, Ont). Or. 1859. A Minister on retired list, attached to Presbytery of Hamilton.

Herdman, Jas. C., B.A., B. D., M. A. (St. Andrew's Ch., Campbellton, N.B; Pres., Miramichi). S. of Rev. A. W. Herdman. B. in Picton, N.S. Dalhousie College, Halifax N. S. and Edinburgh University. Or. 6 Nov, 1877. Mar. 10 Dec, 1879, Minnie Loudon of Chatham, N.B. In. to present ch., 28 Feb, 1878. Predecessors, James Steven, William Wilson, William Murray. No. of com., 154. Was Ordained Missionary at Chatham, N. B, 1877-78

Hislop, John K. (Avonton & Carlinford, Ont; Pres., Stratford). Or. 19 Nov., 1862. No. of com., 212. Mr. Hislop, died 9th May, 1883.

Hodnett, W. (Birtle, &c. N. W. T. Pres., Manitoba.) Or. 2 June, 1869. No. of com., 88.

Hogg, John (Charles St. Ch., Toronto, Pres., Toronto.) Or. 2 Aug., 1864. No. of com., 306. Has recently resigned owing to ill-health.

Hogg, J. (Moncton, N. B. Pres., St. John). Or. 1 Oct., 1868. No. of com., 212.

Houston, Samuel, B. A., M. A. (Athelstan & Elgin, Que; Pres., Montreal). S. of John Houston, farmer. B. at Killymorris Ire. Queen's College and University Belfast, Ire. Presbyterian College, Belfast and Magee College, Londonderry. Or. 19 Jan., 1869. Mar. Lizzie Campbell 22 Oct., 1868. Author of one of the series of tracts on the Shorter Catechism, edited and published by Rev. W. F. Wylie in 1875. In. to present ch. 23 Aug., 1882. Predecessors, Wm. Cochrane, John S. Lochead, and John J.

Casey. No. of of com., 200 in Athelstan, 150 in Elgin. Previous pastorates Calvin Ch. St., John's N.B., 1869-73. Raisin, Mich. 1874-75. Bathurst, N. B., 1875-82.

Hughes, Robert (Cumberland, Ont; Pres., Ottawa.) Or. 24 Oct., 1876. No. of com., 130.

Hume. Robt., M.A. (St. George, Ont; Pres. Paris.) S. of James Hume, farmer. B. in Township of Esquesing. Theological College, United Presbyterian Divinity Hall, University, Toronto. Or. and In. 22 May, 1860. Mar. 1st, Sep., 1863, Annie Burnside. She died June, 1870. 2nd 25 Oct., 1871, Mary dau. of late John McGregor, of Nelson. No. of com., 140. Predecessor, – Roy.

Hunter, W. A., M.A. (Parkdale, Ont; Pres. Toronto.) S. of Wm. Hunter, farmer. B. at Millbrook, Ont. University and Knox College, Toronto. Mar. 12 Oct., 1881, L. Chambers. Or. and In. 16 Nov., 1880. No. of com., 150.

Hutcheson, Smith (Guthrie Ch., Shanty Bay, Ont; Pres. Barrie.) S. of John Hutcheson, farmer. B. in neighborhood of Paisley, Scot. Glasgow and Edinburgh Universities. Or. 1857. Mar. 1859, Thomasina Bruce. In. to present ch. 1876. Predecessors, Messrs. Frazer and Ferguson. Previous pastorates, Whitehaven, Eng., Mulmur and Sassantia, Ont.

Inglis, Walter (Stanley St. Church, Ayr, Ont; Pres. Paris.) Or. Oct., 1842. No. of com., 267.

Inglis, Wm. (Toronto.) Or. 21 Dec., 1847. A minister without charge attached to Presbytery of Toronto.

Internoscia, Antonio (Montreal.) An ordained missionary attached to Pres. Montreal.

Jack, L. (Springfield, N.B.; Pres., St. John). Or. June, 1845. No. of com., 100.

Jack, T. Chalmers, B.A. (St. David's Ch., Maitland; Pres., Halifax, N.S.) S. of Rev. Lewis Jack. B in Charlotte Co., N. B. New Brunswick University and Halifax Presbyterian College. Or. and In. 14 Oct, 1879. Predecessors, Alex. Dick, Thos. Crowe, Prof. Currie and L. G. Macneill. No. of com., 222. Was Douglas gold medallist of New Brunswick University, 1876, and a prize winner two years in Halifax College.

James, David (Maitland, Ont; Pres., Barrie). S. of Rev. Dr. James. B. at Glasgow, Scot. Knox College, Toronto. Or. and In. 18 May, 1881. Predecessor, Mr. Scott, now of Brookdale. No. of com., 123.

James, John, D.D. (Knox Ch., Hamilton; Pres., Hamilton). S. of Robert James, Calico printer. B. in Milton, Scot. Glasgow University and United Presbyterian Divinity Hall, Edinburgh. Or. 29 Sep, 1857. Mar. 31 Dec, 1845, Agnes Craig. Has published various sermons. In. to present ch., 11 Jan, 1877. Predecessors, Alex. Gale, Ralph Robb. G. P. Young, Dr. R. Irvine, Albert Simpson, W. H. Rennelson. No. of com., 530. Previous pastorates, Galt, 1857–65; Paris, 1865–69; Wolverhampton, Eng., 1869–71; Albany, New York, 1871–77. Had the degree of Doctor of Divinity conferred by Union University Shenectady, New York.

Jamieson, George (Aylmer Que; Pres., Ottawa). S. of Gavin Jamieson, farmer. B. in the parish of St. Mungo, Scot. Glasgow University and Knox College, Toronto. Or. March 1866. In. to present ch., 21 Feb, 1881. Predecessors, Rev. Messrs Gourlay, Dr. Freeland, and—Carswell. Previous pastorates, Port Perry and Prince Albert. Is President of the Branch of the Dominion Alliance for the County of Ottawa, and has always taken a deep interest in temperance work.

Jamieson, John (Maganetawan, &c., Ont; Pres., Barrie). An ordained missionary. No. of com. 85.

Jamieson, W. H. (Garden Hill, &c., Ont; Pres., Peterboro). Or. 1877. No. of com., 88.

Jardine, Robt., B.A., M.A., B.D., D.Sc. (St. John's Ch., Brockville; Pres., Brockville). S. of John Jardine. B. at Brockville. Queen's College and Edinburgh University. Or. 5 Jan, 1870. Mar. 27 Oct, 1873. Author of "Psychology of Cognition," 1874; "Letters to Indian Youth," 1876; "Analysis of Hamilton's Metaphysics," 1877. In. to present ch., 5 May, 1881. Predecessors, John Whyte, Dun. Morrison, D. McGillivray and others. No. of com., 148. Previous pastorate, Chatham, N. B., 1879-81. Has been Professor of Metaphysics in New Brunswick University. In India from Feb, 1870 to 1877, during 6 years of which time had charge of General Assenbly's College at Calcutta.

Jenkins, John, LL.D., D.D. (Montreal; Pres., Montreal). B. at Exeter, Eng. Mount Radford College, Exeter, and Hoxton Theological Institution, London, Eng. Or. 6 Aug, 1837. Mar. 1st Harriette, dau. of Geo. Shepstone, Eng., architect. 2nd Louisa, eldest dau. of the late Rev. John McLennan, Minister of Parish of Kilchrennan, Scot. Author of "Protestant's Appeal to the Douay Bible," "Pauperism in Great Cities" &c., &c. Immediately after ordination proceeded as a missionary to

Mysore, India, under auspices of Wesleyan Missionary Society of London. In 1853, joined Fourth Presbytery (U.S.) of Philadelphia and for 10 years was Minister of Calvary Pres. Ch. in that City. Subsequently, on return to England became a member of Synod, of English Pres. Ch. Afterwards In. to St. Paul's Ch., Montreal, in June 1865 of which now Pastor Emeritus having resigned the pastoral charge thereof in 1881. Has been Moderator of General Assembly.

Johnson, Samuel (Chipman, N.B; Pres., St. John). S. of Adam Johnson, farmer. B. at Stewiacke, N.S. West River Seminary, N. S, Halifax Presbyterian College and Newburgh College, New York. Or. 24 May, 1856. Mar. Eleanor Grant, 29 June, 1857. In. to present ch., 24 May, 1876. Predecessors, —Canning, H. McKay, and Dr. J. Salmon. No. of com., 97. Previous pastorate, Harvey, N.B., from 24 May 1865 to 24 May 1876.

Johnson, Wm., B.A., M.A. (Guelph, Ont; Pres., Guelph). S. of Neil Johnson, Agriculturist. B. in Nelson Township. Queen's College, Kingston. Mar. 17 Jan, 1854, Margaret Kirkpatrick. Or. 15 Nov, 1852. Has been pastor of Saltfleet and Binbroke, L'Original, Arnprior and St. Andrews Ch., Lindsay. Retired from active service in 1864.

Johnston, John (Lobo and North Caradoc, Ont; Pres., London). S. of Joseph Johnston, shoemaker. B. in Scarboro' Township. Knox College, Toronto. Or. and In. 3 Aug, 1880 Mar. 7 Oct, 1880, Isabella M. Wilkie. Predecessors, James Ferguson, Duncan McMillan and John Ferguson. No. of com., 127.

Johnston, J. R. (Alvinston & Napier, Ont; Pres., Sarnia.) Or. April, 1881.

Johnstone, Thos. G. (Blackville & Derby, N. B. Pres., Miramichi.) Or. 21 June, 1855. No. of com., 48.

Johnston, Wm. A. (Rockburn and Gore, Que; Pres., Montreal.) S. of Wm. Johnston, M.D B. at Crowland, Ont. Knox College, Toronto. Or. 25 Sep., 1847. Mar. 12 Sep., 1854. Sarah Ann McKewen. In. to present ch. 8 Feb., 1881. Predecessor, Chauncy Webster. No. of com., 62. Previous pastorate, Oro, Ont., 1867-70.

Jones, John (Montreal.) A Minister without charge attached to Pres., Montreal.

Jones, Samuel (Knox Ch., Brussels, Ont; Pres., Maitland.) Or. Sep., 1853. No. of com., 170.

Jordan, Louis H., B.A., M.A., B.D. (St. Andrew's Ch., Halifax; Pres., Halifax). S. of William Jordan, a retired merchant. B. at Halifax, N. S. Dalhousie College Halifax, N.S.; Edinburgh University; Union Seminary, New York, Princeton Seminary, N. J., University Leipzig, and University Berlin. Or. and In. 7 Dec., 1882. Predecessors, Henry Paterson, Thos. G. McInnes, Dr. Burns, of New Brunswick; John Martin, Geo. Boyd, Geo. M. Grant, John Campbell and Thos. Duncan. No. of com., 80.

Kay, John (Milverton and N. Mornington, Ont; Pres., Stratford). Or. 31 July, 1868. No. of com., 245.

Kellock, David (Spencerville and Ventnor, Ont; Pres., Brockville). S. of David Kellock, land steward. B. at St. Andrew's, Scot. University, St. Andrew's, Scot; Queen's College, Kingston. Or. 26 July, 1881. Mar. 4 July, 1861, Grace McClymont. In. to present ch., 1882. No. of com., 204.

Kelso, Donald (Roslin and Thurlow, Ont; Pres., Kingston). Or. 3 Oct., 1876. No. of com., 92.

Kemp, Alex. F., M.A., LL.D. (Ottawa; Pres., Ottawa.) B. in Greenock, Scot. Edinburgh University; Presbyterian College, London, Eng; McGill University, Montreal, and Queen's College, Kingston. Or. Nov, 1850. Joint editor with Rev. D. Fraser, of the *Presbyter*, for two years. Edited Digest of Minutes of Synod of Presbyterian Church of Canada. Author of numerous scientific papers, and associated with F. W. Farries and J. B. Halkett in editing "Hand-Book of Presbyterian Church in Canada." In 1854 was appointed by the Colonial Committee of the Free Church of Scotland, as Chaplain to the 26th Cameronians, at Bermuda. Called and inducted to St. Gabriel Church, Montreal, Sept, 1855; translated to Windsor, Ont, 1867; accepted the Professorship of Mental Philosophy, Logic and Moral Philosophy, in Olivet College, Michigan, and subsequently in Knox College, Galesburg. Afterwards became Principal of the Brantford Young Ladies' College, and for the past five years has been Principal of the Ottawa Ladies' College.

Kennedy, Alex. (Newcastle, Ont.) Or. 30 Sep, 1835. A Minister without charge, attached to Presbytery of Whitby.

Kippen, A. H. (N. & S. Dorchester, Ont; Pres., London). Or. 25 Feb, 1879. No. of com., 180.

King, J. M., D D. (St. James' Sq. Ch., Toronto; Pres., Toronto). Or. 27 Oct, 1857. No. of com., 513.

King, Wm. (Maidstone, Ont; Pres., Chatham). B. at Newton Co., Derry, Ire. Glasgow and Edinburgh Universities. Mar. 1st, 11 Jan, 1840, Mary M. Phares, who died in 1846; 2nd, 15 Sep. 1853, J. N. Baxter. Or. May, 1851. In. to present ch., Dec, 1880. No. of com., 40. Prior to present pastorate, had charge of Buxton Mission, Beyan.

Kirkpatrick, John (Cooke's Ch., Toronto; Pres., Toronto). S. of John Kirkpatrick, farmer. B. in Parish of Loughguile, Ire. Queen's College and Presbyterian College, Belfast. Or. 28 May, 1868. In. to present ch., 5 Feb, 1880. Predecessors, Dr. R. Irwin, Andrew Marshall, Professor Gregg and Dr. Robb. No. of com., 400. Previous pastorates, Newton, Ire, 1860–74; New York City, 1875–80.

Knowles, Robt. (Ramsay, Ont; Pres., Lanark and Renfrew). Or. 31 Oct, 1866. No. of com., 168.

Lafontaine, C. A Minister attached to the Presbytery of Chatham, Ont.

Laidlaw, R. J. (St. Paul's Ch., Hamilton; Pres., Hamilton). Or. 22 Sep, 1871. No. of com., 410.

Laing, John B.A., M.A. (Knox Ch., Dundas; Pres. Hamilton) S. of Jas. R. Laing, farmer. B. in Ross-shire, Scot. Victoria University, Cobourg, Knox College and University College, Toronto. Or. 6 June, 1854. Author of various tracts. In. to present ch. 5 Nov., 1873. Predecessors, M. Y. Stark, John McColl, R. H. Hoskins. No. of com., 254. Previous pastorates, Knox and Melville Churches, Scarboro, 1854–59; Cobourg, 1859–71. Was tutor in Knox College, Toronto; First Principal of Ottawa Ladies' College; and First Convener Home Mission Committee after Union 1863–71. Is Clerk of Presbytery.

Laing, Robt., M.A. (St. Matthew's Ch., Halifax; Pres. Halifax.) Or. 1873. No. of com., 368.

Laird, R. (Little Harbor, N. S.; Pres. Picton.) Or. 12 Jnne, 1860. No. of com., 182.

Lamont, Hugh, M.A., D D. (Dalhousie Mills, &c., Ont; Pres. Glengarry.) S. of Angus Lamont, schoolmaster and evangelist. B. in Scotland. Edinburgh University, Queen's College, Kingston. Or. 22 Feb., 1865. Mar. 17 April, 1865, Catharine Lamont. In. to present ch. 28 Sep., 1877. Predecessors, Don. Sinclair, Æneas McLean, John Anderson. No. of com., 95. Previous pastorates, Finch 1865–70; Kilmeny, Islay, Scot., 1870–71; Finch, 1871–77. Is Clerk of Presbytery.

Lang, Wm. A., B.A., M.A. (Lunenburg and Avonmore, Ont; Pres. Glengarry.) S. of Wm. Lang, farmer. B in township of Huntley. Queen's College, Kingston. Or. and In. 6 March, 1878. Predecessors, J. Charles Quin, Alex. Matheson and John McIntyre. No. of com., 216.

Lawrence, George (Toronto). Or. 28 Apl, 1837. A minister without charge, attached to Presbytery of Toronto.

Layton, Jacob (Elmsdale, N.S.; Pres., Halifax). S. of Chas. Layton, blacksmith. B. in Londonderry N.S. Dalhousie College, and Theological Hall, Halifax. Lic. 20 Apl, 1869. Or. 22 Nov, 1871. Mar. 10 June, 1873, Margaret, dau. of Rev. Dr. James Smith, Professor Biblical Literature, Theological Hall, Halifax. In. to present ch., 15 Oct, 1879. Predecessors, Robt. Blackwood, John Cameron. No. of com., 160. Previous pastorates, Coldstream, 1871–76. Assistant at Warwick, Bermuda, 1876–78.

Leask, Robert (St. Helen's and E. Ashfield, Ont; Pres., Maitland). S of Peter Leask, yeoman. Knox College. Or. and In. 21 Nov, 1865. Mar. 20 Dec, 1867, Margaret C. McCrae. No. of com., 193. Is Clerk of Presbytery.

Lees, John (N. Williams and N. E. Adelaide, Ont; Pres., Sarnia). Or. 10 July, 1855. No. of com., 72.

Leiper, John (Barrie, Ont; Pres., Barrie). B. in Scotland. Glasgow University, and Free Church College. Or. July, 1864. Mar. 7 Apl, 1874, Margaret H. Jaffrey. In. to present ch., 1 Feb, 1877. Predecessors, Messrs. Whiteman, Mackenzie, Lowry and Fraser. No. of com., 245. Previous pastorate, Chapelton, Scotland.

Leishman, John, (Newburgh and Camden, Ont; Pres., Kingston). S. of John Leishman. B. in Richibucto, N. B. Presbyterian College. Halifax, N. S. Or. 29 Dec, 1874. Mar. Caroline Sophia Glassup, of Kingston, Ont., 6 Apl, 1875. In. to present ch., 15 Nov, 1881, and was the first regularly ordained minister thereof. Was preceded by an ordained missionary. No. of com., 77. Previous pastorate, South Gower and Mountain, 1874-80.

Leitch, R. W. (Point Edward, Ont; Pres., Sarnia). Or, 10 Sep, 1874. No. of com., 65.

Leslie, Alex., M.A. (Newtonville, &c., Ont; Pres., Whitby). Or. 4 March, 1879. No. of com., 204.

Lindsay, Peter, B.A. (St. Andrew's Ch., New Richmond, P. Q; Pres., Miramichi). S. of Peter Lindsay, farmer. B. at Paisley, Scot. Queen's College, Kingston. Or. 12 Oct, 1853. Mar. 20 March, 1862, Amelia W. Grinton. In. to present ch., 20 Aug, 1879. Predecessors, John Wells, John Davidson, Dr. Brooke. No. of com., 225. Previous pastorates, Cumberland, 1855-62; Arnprior, 1862-70; Sherbrooke, Q.; 1872-78.

Little, James, M.A. (Bowmanville, Ont; Pres., Whitby). Or. Nov, 1860. No. of com., 212.

Little, James (Princeton and Drumbo, Ont; Pres., Paris). S. of Robt. Little, farmer. B. in County of Frontenac, Ont. Knox College, Toronto. Or. 31 Oct, 1866. Mar. 23 Jan, 1867, Elizabeth Cowan. In. to present ch., 24 July, 1877. Predecessor, Hector McQuarrie. No of com., 160. Previous pastorates, Nassagawega, 1866-75; St. John's Ch., Hamilton, 1875-77.

Livingstone, M. W. (Simcoe, Ont.) Or. May, 1837. A minister on retired list, attached to Presbytery of Hamilton.

Lochead, John S. B.A., M.A., (Hullet & Londesborough, Ont; Pres., Huron.) S. of Rev. Wm Lochead. B. at Cherry Valley, New York. Princeton Seminary, N.J. Or. Sep., 1866. Mar. 31 Jan., 1867, Margaret Honeyman. In. to present ch. 21 March, 1879. Predecessor, Stephen Young. No. of com., 130. Previous pastorate Elgin, Athelstane and Valleyfield, Que.

Lochead, Wm. (Fenelon Falls, Ont; Pres., Lindsay.) S. of Rev. Wm. Lochead. B. at Albany, N Y. Knox College, Toronto. Or. 20 Sep., 1859. Mar. 14 Sep., 1859, Lucy Shuttleworth. In. to present ch. 2 March, 1869. No. of com., 69.

Logan, John A. (Acadia Mines, N. S. Pres., Truro.) S. of Wm. Logan, farmer. B. at Pembroke, Upper Stewiacke, N. S. Dalhousie College, Theological Hall, Halifax. Or. and In. 7 Aug., 1877. Mar. 6 Oct., 1881, Margaret dau. of Rev. James McLean, minister of Great Villege, N.S. She died 3 July, 1882. No. of com., 159. Predecessor, Rev. Don. Stewart.

Logan, John B. M.A. (St. Paul's Ch., Kentville, N.S. Pres., Halifax.) S. of Robt. Logan, farmer. B. at Duntocher, Scot. Glasgow University, and United Presbyterian Theological Hall Edinburgh. Or. and In. 1 Oct., 1868. Mar. 22 Dec., 1854, May W. eldest dau. of late Rev. Jas. Parsons, York, Eng. Predecessors, Geo. Struthers, Wm. Murray, Wm. Forlong, No. of com., 120. Was licensed in 1852, but owing to ill-health had to relinquish preaching for a time. Was principal of Weston County grammar school for ten years.

Logan, Richmond, B.A., M.A. (Sheet Harbor, N.S; Pres., Halifax). S. of Wm. Logan, farmer. B. at Upper Stewiacke. Dalhousie College and University; Pine Hill Theological College, Halifax. Or. and In. 7 June, 1880. Mar. Henrietta, dau. of late Rev. Dr. Jas. Smith. Author of "Public Roads in Nova Scotia, on what principle can they best be built, &c," published in 1877—a prize essay. Predecessors, John Waddell, A. B. Dickie. No. of com., 255. Has recently resigned this charge.

Logie, John (East Tilbury, Ont; Pres., Chatham). Or. Dec, 1849. No. of com., 144.

Love, Andrew (St. Stephen, N.B; Pres., St. John). Or. 20 May, 1881. No. of com., 69.

Lowry, Thomas (Toronto; Pres., Toronto). S. of Rev. Jos. Lowry. B. in the parish of Kilmore, Ire. Royal Academical Institution, Belfast. Or. 24 Sep, 1833. Mar. 8 Oct, 1833, Florella Reid. Was for a number of years minister of the First Presbyterian Church, Brantford. A retired minister.

Lyle Samuel (Central Ch., Hamilton; Pres., Hamilton). Or. 12 Feb, 1870. No. of com., 738.

McAdam, Thos. (Strathroy, Ont; Pres., London). No. of com., 206.

Macalister, Jno. M., B.A. (Ashton, Ont; Pres., Lanark and Renfrew). Or. 8 Nov, 1872. No. of com., 70.

McAlmon, John (Moore Line, &c., Ont; Pres Sarnia). Or Oct, 1875. No. of com., 175.

McAlpine, John (Widder Street, St. Mary's, Ont; Pres., Stratford). Or. 1863. No of com., 257.

McArthur, Geo., B.A. (Finch, Ont; Pres., Glengarry). Or. 17 Oct, 1882. No. of com., 100.

Macaulay, Evan, B.A. (West Puslinch, Ont; Pres., Guelph). Or. 3 Oct, 1866. No. of com., 122.

McBain, James A. F. (Georgetown, Que; Pres., Montreal). S. of William McBain, farmer. B. in township of Mara, Ont. Knox College, Toronto. Or. 18 March, 1869. Mar, 30 June, 1875, Mary M. Quin. In. to present ch., 5 May, 1882. Predecessors, Alex. McWattie, W. Colquhoun, Dr. J. C. Muir. No. of com., 395. Previous pastorates, Drummondville and Chippawa, 1869–77; Chatham, N.B., 1877–82,

McCannell, D. (Fairview, &c., Man.; Pres., Manitoba). Or. 14 Dec, 1881. No. of com., 60.

McCarter, John McI. (Redbank, N. B.; Pres. Miramichi.) B. in Ayr, Scot. University and New College, Edinburgh. Or. 31 Aug., 1862 Author of "The Dutch Reformed Church in South Africa, an Historical Sketch" which he re-modeled and rendered in Dutch for South African readers. In. to present ch. 19 July, 1880. Predecessor, Wm. McCullagh. For thirteen years minister of Weenen and Ladysmith in Natal.

McCaul, James, B.A. (Stanley St. Church, Montreal; Pres. Montreal.) Or. 24 Aug., 1864. No. of com., 176.

McClelland, Alex. M., B.A. (Russell & Metcalfe, Ont; Pres. Ottawa) S. of A. McClelland. B. at Dumfries, Ont. University & Knox College, Toronto. Or. 1 May, 1877. Mar. 19 June, 1878, Lizzie Baillie. In. to present ch. 23 March, 1880. Predecessors, James Whyte, H. L. McDiarmid, Thos. Muir. No. of com., 180. Previous pastorate, Richmond, Ont., 1877–80.

McClung, John (Shakespeare, &c., Ont; Pres. Stratford.) Or. 4 Aug., 1874. No. of com., 177.

McColl, A. (1st Ch. Chatham, Ont; Pres. Chatham.) Or. 18 Feb., 1848. No. of com., 227.

McConnell, J. A. (North and South Delaware, Ont; Pres., London.) S. of John McConnell, farmer. B. in Co. of Armagh. Ire. Jefferson College, Pa., and Columbia College, La. Or. 10 Dec., 1864. Mar. 31 Dec, 1863, M. M. Fleming. In. to present ch. 1 Dec., 1880. Psedecessors, Messrs. Grant, Hay and Goldie No. of com., 105. Previous pastorates, several in United States, and in Canada Tecumseh and Adjala, 1873-1880.

McConnell, Wm. (Central L. and Craigvale, Ont; Pres., Barrie). S. of John McConnell, farmer. B. in Ireland. Presbyterian College, Belfast. Or. 1854. Mar. 1871, F. S. Porter. In. to present ch., 1871. Predecessors, Messrs. Wightman, Mackenzie and Lowry. No, of com., 220. Previous pastorates, New Orleans, 1854-63; Chicago, 1868; Orangeville, 1869-71

McCoy, Joseph, B.A., M.A. (Egmondville, Ont; Pres., Huron). S. of John McCoy, carpenter. B. in. Hamilton, Ont. University and Knox College, Toronto. Or. and In. 3 Feb, 1879. Mar. 8 April, 1879, Mary H. Huckins. Predecessors, Wm. Graham, pastor for over 25 years; J. B. Scott. No. of com., 180.

McCrae, D. L. (Cobourg; Ont; Pres., Peterboro'). S. of John McCrae, farmer. B. in Scot. McGill College and Presbyterian College, Montreal. Or. 29 July, 1879. Mar. 17 Sep, 1879, Mary W. Little. In. to present ch. 5 July, 1882 Predecessors, Matthew Miller, Thos. Alexander, Don. McLeod, John

Laing, Jas, Douglass, and J. Ballentine. No. of com., 250. Previous pastorate, St. Matthew's, Osnabruck, 1879-82.

McCuaig, Finlay (Chalmer's Ch., Kingston; Pres., Kingston). S. of Malcolm McCuaig, farmer. B. in Parish of Polycarpe, Que. University and Knox College, Toronto. Or. 28 Nov, 1860. Mar. 29 Aug, 1860, Isabella McKinnon. In. to present ch., 26 July. 1877. Predecessors, Robt. F. Burns, D. B, Pierce, Patrick Grey. No. of com., 240. Previous pastorates, Niagara and Port Dalhousie, 1860–64; Ratho and Innerkip, 1864–70; Clinton, 1870–77.

McCulloch, Wm., D.D. (First Ch., Truro, N.S.; Pres., Truro). Or. 14 Feb, 1839. No. of com., 256.

McCulloch, Wm. K. (Leeds. Que; Pres., Quebec). Or. 27 Apl, 1882.

McCurdy, E. A. (James' Ch., New Glasgow, N.S.; Pres., Picton). S. of M. A. Curdy, farmer. B. at Musquodoboit. Presbyterian College, Truro; Theological Hall, Halifax; Free Church College, Edinburgh. Or. 20 June, 1866. Mar. 6 Nov, 1866, Jane W. Waddell. In. to present ch., 2 May. 1871. Predecessors, Dr. James McGregor, Dr. D. Ray. No. of com., 275. Previous pastorates, Musquodoboit, 1866–71. Is Clerk of Presbytery.

McDiarmid, Arch. (Latona, Ont; Pres., Owen Sound). S. of Hugh McDiarmid, farmer. B. in Perthshire, Scot. Knox College, Toronto. Or. 27 Apl, 1859. Mar. 30 Oct, 1862, Mary Ann Grant. In. to present ch., 5 Feb, 1874. Predecessor, Jas. Cameron. No. of com., 250.

McDiarmid, H. J. (East Gloucester, Ont; Pres., Ottawa). S. of Colin McDiarmid, farmer. B. in Township of Moor, Ont. University and Knox College, Toronto. Or. and In. 29 June, 1871. Mar. 27 May, 1873, Mary Heran, of Scarboro', Ont. No. com., 106.

McDiarmid, Neil (Elmira, Illinois; Pres., Chatham). Or. 6 Feb, 1868.

McDonald, Alex., B.A.(West Nottawasaga Ch, Duntroon, Ont; Pres., Barrie). S. of Alex. MacDonald, farmer or tacksman. A native of Inverness-Shire, Scot. Edinburgh University and Queen's College, Kingston. Or. 31 Jan, 1866. Mar. March, 1874, Louise, dau. of Rev. Jas. Campbell, M.A., first minister of Nottawasaga. No. of com., 140. Nottawasaga was divided into East and West Nottawasaga, three years subsequent to Mr. MacDonald's settlement, and he has now charge of three congregations, viz., Duntroon, West Church and St. Andrew's Church.

McDonald, Clinton D. (Thorold. Ont; Pres., Hamilton). S. of Angus McDonald, Shepherd. B. in Dumbartonshire, Scot. University College and Knox College, Toronto, Union and Theological Seminary, New York. Or. 23 Nov, 1875. Mar. 27 Dec, 1875, Janet Cowan. In. to present ch., 4 Oct, 1877. Predecessors, Wm. Dickson, Robt. Wallace, S.C. Fraser. No. of com., 160. Previous pastorates, Point Edward, Ont, 1875-77.

McDonald, D. (Beckwith, Ont; Pres., Lanark and Renfrew). Or. 11 Jan, 1865. No. of com., 188.

McDonald, A.D. (Seaforth, Ont; Pres., Huron). Or. 20 Apl, 1859. No. of com., 485.

McDonald, Donald (Glenarm, Ont; Pres., Lindsay.) S. of Alex. McDonald, farmer. B. at North Uist, Scot. Knox College, Toronto. Or. 20 Nov., 1872. Mar. 7 June, 1875, Catharine M. Ross. In. to present ch. 27 June, 1876. No. of com., 168. Previous pastorate, Arthur Village, Ont.

McDonald, D. B. (Mount Albert, Ont; Pres., Toronto.) Or. 30 Nov., 1882. No. of com., 40.

Mcdonald, John (Scotstown, Que; Pres., Quebec.) Or. 26 Feb., 1864. No. of com., 35.

McDonald, John (Cow Bay, N. S. Pres., Sydney.) Or. 20 May, 1880. No. of com., 90

McDonald, John A. (Bear Creek & Brigden, Ont; Pres., Sarnia.) Or. Dec., 1870. No. of com., 155.

McDonald, Kenneth (Belmont, Ont; Pres., London.) S. of John McDonald, farmer. B. in Glengarry. University and Knox College, Toronto. Or. 25 Oct., 1865. Mar. 12 Apl., 1860, Helen Carruthers. In. to present ch. 24 Apl., 1879. Predecessors, Arch Currie, Neil McKinnon. No. of com., 196. Previous pastorates, East Puslinch, Thamesford, Alexandria, Indian Lands, Williamstown and Martintown. Reared in Roman Catholic Church to which all his relatives still belong. Converted to Methodism when about 25 years of age. Left the Methodist Church to join the Presbyterian; was for two years missionary to the Roman Catholics in Glengarry; had no financial assistance while at college.

Macdonnell, Daniel J., B.A., B.D., M.A. (St. Andrew's Ch., Toronto; Pres. Toronto.) S. of late Rev. Geo. Macdonnell. B. in Bathurst, N. B. Queen's College, Kingston; Glasgow and Edinburgh Universities. Or. 14 June, 1866, by Presbytery of Edinburgh. Mar. 2 July, 1868, Elizabeth Logie Smellie, dau. of

Rev. G. Smellie, of Fergus. In. to present ch. 22 Dec., 1870. No. of com., 608. Previous pastorate, St. Andrew's Ch , Peterborough, Ont., 1866–70.

McDougall, D. (West Bay, C. B.; Pres. Victoria and Richmond.) B. in Whycocomah, C. B. Theological Hall, Halifax. Or. 15 Nov. 1865. Mar. 24 Sep. 1868, Barbara Boak. In. to present ch. 7 Oct. 1879. Predecessors, John Sutherland, Murdoch Stewart, John Stewart. Previous pastorates, New London, P. E. I. Cow Bay, C. B.

MacEachern, Duncan (Dundee, Que.; Pres. Montreal.) S. of Duncan McEachern. B. at Thurso, Que. Queen's College, Kingston. Or. 8 Oct. 1875. Mar. Grace MaCallum. In. to present ch. 20 Sep, 1882. Predecessors, D. Moody, D. Cameron, John Livingstone, D. Ross, J. Cattanach. No. of com., 200. Previous pastorates, Glencoe, 1875–79; Parkhill, 1879–82.

McEwen, Hugh (Erskine, Ch., Ingersoll; Pres. Paris.) S. of Neil McEwen, farmer. B. at Johnstone, Scot. University College and Knox College, Toronto. Or. 8 Sep, 1859. Mar. 5 May 1857, Georgina Clara Playter. Author of Normal Class Teacher published in 1879, and Graded Sabbath School Lessons on Book of Genesis published in 1880. In. to present ch. 22 Dec, 1876. Predecessors, Arch. Cross, Peter Wright. No. of com., 127. Previous pastorates, Cumberland, 1859–63, Pembroke, 1864–76. Prior to removing to the West did much good service for the Bible Society in the Ottawa Valley and elsewhere, leading to the establishment of the present Auxiliary Society and Missionary Enterprise for Shantymen.

McEwen, Jas. (Welland and Crowland, Ont: Pres., Hamilton). Or. 1854. No. of com., 98.

McFarlane, A. H. (Farnham Centre, Que; Pres., Montreal). Or, 2 Nov, 1880. No. of com., 57.

McFarlane, John (Pine River, Ont; Pres., Maitland). Or. 7 Feb, 1872. No. of com., 74.

McFaul, Alex. (Charleston and Alton, Ont; Pres., Toronto). Or. 14 March, 1858. No. of com., 204.

McGillivray, Alex. (Williamstown, Ont; Pres., Glengarry). Or. 21 Sep, 1877. No. of com., 220.

McGillivray, D. (St. James, London; Pres , London). Or. 16 July, 1867. No. of com. 100.

McGillivray, J. D. (Clifton, N. S; Pres., Truro). Or. 7 Feb, 1865. No. of com., 160.

Macgillivray, Malcolm, B.A., M.A. (St. Andrew's Church, Perth; Pres., Lanark and Renfrew). S. of John Macgillivray, farmer. B. in Jura, Scot. Queen's College, Kingston, and Edinburgh University. Or. 21 Oct, 1875. Mar. 20 June, 1877, Clara Robina Dow of Whitby. In. to present ch., 4 Aug, 1881. Predecessors, Thos O. Wilson and Dr. W. Bain. No. of com., 293. Previous pastorate, St. Andrew's Ch., Scarboro.

McGregor, Dugald (Big Bend, Man; Pres., Manitoba.) Or. 1876. No. of com., 38.

McGregor, D. B. A. (Merigomish, N. S; Pres., Pictou). Or. 24 May, 1877. No. of com., 300.

Macgregor, D. (Amherst, N. S.; Pres., Wallace). No. of com., 58.

McGregor, M. (Tilsonburg, &c., Ont; Pres., Paris). Or. 2 May, 1882.

McGregor, P. G., D. D., (Halifax, N.S.; Pres., Halifax). S. of late Rev. Dr. McGregor, Minister of Picton. B. at East River, Picton. Theological Hall, Halifax, under Rev. Dr. Thos. McCulloch. Or. Nov., 1841. Mar. 22 June, 1849, Caroline McColl. Has published lectures &c. Has been pastor of Guysboro and Poplar Grove Churches, and Moderator of Synod of Presbyterian Church of Nova Scotia and of the Lower Provinces. As Moderator of Oldest Synod constituted the First General Assembly of United Church. Was Agent of Synod of the Presbyterian Church of Lower Provinces at time of Union, and was continued in that position which he still holds. At first meeting of Synod of Maritime Provinces, after the Union, Mr. McGregor was nominated for the position of Clerk, which, however, he declined, whereupon the following resolution was unanimously adopted and ordered to be entered on the Minutes:

"The Rev. P. G. McGregor having declined to be elected as Clerk, this Synod would take the opportunity of recording on its minutes its high appreciation of the very efficient manner in which he performed the duties of Clerk in the late Synods of Nova Scotia and of the Lower Provinces, during the long term of 30 years. It would specially notice his kindliness of manner toward all his brethren, his readiness at all times, to give them information on all matters connected with his office, and the deep and active interest which he took in all the schemes of the Church.

It would express heartfelt gratitude to God, that these Synods have been privileged to enjoy for so long a time, the services of one so emenently qualified for that office.

It would acknowledge the valuable services which he has rendered to the Church as Agent and Treasurer of her schemes, during the last eight years, and would express the hope that he may be long spared to serve the Master in this department of his work.

It would also take this opportunity of thanking him for the courteous and efficient manner, in which he performed the duties of the Moderator's Chair, in the Synod of the Lower Provinces, during its last three Sessions."

MacGuire, Thos (Emerson, Man; Pres., Manitoba). S. of John MacGuire, farmer. University and Knox College, Toronto. Or. 8 March, 1864. In. to present ch. 24 March, 1881. No. of com., 70. Previous pastorates, Glenallan and Hollin, 1864-74; Jarvis and Walpole, 1874-81.

McIlroy, James (Matilda, Ont; Pres., Brockville). Or. 1874.

McIntosh, Abraham (St. Anns, N.S; Pres., Sydney). Or. 21 Aug, 1856. No. of com., 125.

McIntosh, Donald (Markham, &c., Ont; Pres.. Toronto). Or. 17 June, 1873. No. of com., 116.

McIntyre, D. C. (Beamsville, Ont; Pres., Hamilton). Or. 3 Sep, 1878. No. of com., 145.

Mackay, Alex. B. (Crescent Street Ch., Montreal; Pres., Montreal). S. of Donald Mackay. B. at Montrose, Scotland. Edinburgh University and English Presbyterian College, London. Or. 16 Aug, 1868. Mar. 10 Aug, 1869. Author of "The Glory of the Cross;" "Your photograph, and other sermons;" "The Strong man and the stronger, &c;" "The Story of Nâaman." In. to present ch. 15 May, 1879. Predecessors, Don. Fraser, D.D; D. McVicar, LL.D., D.D., and R. F. Burns, D.D. No. of com, 546. Previous pastorates, Worcester, Eng; Brighton, Eng.

Mackay, Alex., M.A., D.D. (Duff Ch., East Puslinch, Ont; Pres., Guelph). S. of Robt. McKay, farmer. B. at West Zorra. Knox College and University, Toronto. Or. 25 Apl, 1860. Mar. 28 Dec, 1868, Jessie Watt. In. to present ch., 30 Oct, 1873. Predecessors, William Meldrum, Alex. Mclean and Kenneth McDonald. No. of com., 216. Previous pastorates, Tiverton, 25 Apl, 1860; Elmira, 3 July, 1868.

McKay, Alex. (Ermosa, Ont; Pres., Guelph). Or. 18 Sep, 1882. No. of com., 115.

McKay, Geo. (Osgoode, Ont; Pres., Ottawa). Or. 5 Nov, 1873. No. of com., 220.

McKay, H. B. (River John, N.S.; Pres., Wallace). Or. 22 June, 1855. No. of com., 214.

McKay, John (Armadale Mission, North West Territory; Pres., Manitoba). S. of Jas. McKay, who was employed by Hudson Bay Company on three expeditions in search of Sir John Franklin in the North. B. at Edmonton. Or. 8 May, 1878. Mar. 10 Apl, 1862, Christina McBeath of Kildonan. In. to present ch., 1 July, 1880. No. of com., 12. Has been a missionary, and is Chief Mistawasis reserve.

McKay. Kenneth, B.A. (Richmond, N.B.; Pres., St. John). S. of Geo. McKay, farmer. B. at Harwood Hill, N.S. Or. and In. 22 Feb, 1872. Mar. 9 July, 1873, Margaret A. Grant. Predecessor, Jas. Kidd. No. of com., 190.

McKay, Neil (Summerside, P.E.I; Pres., P.E. Island). Or. 19 Sep, 1855.

McKay, Robt. D. (Shakespeare, Ont.) A minister without charge, attached to Presbytery of Stratford.

Mackay, R. P., M.A. (Scarboro &c., Ont; Pres., Toronto). Or. 9 Oct, 1877. No. of com., 220.

McKay, W. A., B.A. (Chalmer's Ch., Woodstock; Pres., Paris). S. of John McKay, farmer. B. in Co. of Oxford. University and Knox College, Toronto. Or. 1870. Mar. Amelia Jane Youngs, 1863. Author of "Immersion a Romish Invention" and "Baptism Improved, or an Appeal to Parents and Children." In. to present ch., 7 May, 1878. Predecessor, John McTavish, now of Inverness, Scot. No. of com., 310. Previous pastorates, Cheltenham and Baltimore, Ont.

McKay, W. E., B. A. (Orangeville, Ont; Pres., Toronto). Or. 29 Oct, 1856. No. of com., 206.

McKechnie, D. L. (Mattawa, Ont; Pres., Lanark and Renfrew). Or. 28 Sep, 1875. No. of com., 104.

McKee, Thos. Barrie, Ont. A minister on retired list, Presbytery of Barrie. Is Inspector of Schools for County of Simcoe.

McKee, W., B.A. (Clover Hill, Ont). A minister on retired list, Pretbytery of Barrie.

McKeen, Jas. A., B.A. (St. Andrew's, N. S; Pres., Halifax). Or. 26 Aug, 1879. No. of com., 59.

McKellar, H. (High Bluff, Man; Pres., Manitoba). Or. 27 Oct, 1874. No. of com., 62.

McKenzie, Alex. (South Kinloss, Ont; Pres., Maitland). No. of com., 61.

Mackenzie, A. F. (Glammis, Ont; Pres., Bruce). Or. 6 March, 1878. No. of com. 122. Recently In. to present ch.

McKenzie, Donald. Is Pastor Emeritus of Ingersoll Church.

McKenzie, J. A. (Pugwash, N. S; Pres., Wallace). No. of com., 112.

Mackenzie, John (Hampden Ch., Whitton; Pres., Quebec). S. of Murdoch Mackenzie, teacher. B. at Stornoway, Scot. Glasgow University and Montreal Presbyterian College. Or. and In. 13 Feb, 1877. Mar. Ann Murray, 20 Dec, 1877. No. of com., 56.

McKenzie, Kenneth (Baddeck, N. S; Pres., Victoria and Richmond). S. of Alex. McKenzie, farmer. Free Ch. Philosophical and Theological Institution, Halifax. Or. and In. 2 Dec, 1857. Mar. 2 Dec, 1858, Margaret McNab. No. of com., 120.

McKenzie, Malcolm (Richibucto, N. B.; Pres., Miramichi). Or. Feb., 1862.

McKenzie, Robt. M.A. (Dalhousie & North Sherbrooke, Ont.; Pres., Lanark & Renfrew). S. of Wm. McKenzie, farmer. B. at Dundonald. Ire. Royal Academical Institution and College, Belfast. Or. July, 1853. Mar. Aug., 1854, Elizabeth J. Hazel of Dundee Scot. In. to present ch. Oct., 1875. Predecessors Messrs. Scott and Findlay. No. of com. 130. Previous pastorates Barrie, 1854-61; South Gower, 1861-71; Morriston, 1871-75.

Mackeracher, C. M. (English River, Howick; Pres., Montreal. Quebec). S. of Jas. Mackeracher. B. at Aberfeldy, Scot. Edinburgh University. Or. 22 Aug., 1861. Mar. 26 Nov., 1861, Dolina G. McKay. In. to present ch. 21 May, 1867. Predecessors, Jas. Fettes, Wm. Troup, John Milne, Alex. Young. No. of com 160. Previous pastorate W. Gwilliamburg and Bradford.

McKibbin, Robt. V., B.A. (North Gower and Wellington; Pres., Ottawa). S. of Robt. McKibbin, school-teacher. B. at Nepean. McGill University and Pres., College Montreal. Or. and In. 10th Jan., 1882. Predecessors, W. Lochead, A. C. Stewart, and A. C. Morton. No. of com. 115.

McKibbin, W. M., B.A. (Cardinal, Ont.; Pres., Brockville). S. of Robt. McKibbin, school-teacher. B. in County Antrim, Ire. McGill University and Presbyterian College, Montreal. Or. and In. 7th Oct., 1875 Mar. 11 Oct., 1875, Margery E. McDonald No. of Com., 112. Is Clerk of Presbytery.

Mackie, John (First Ch., Lachute, Que; Pres., Montreal). Or. 18 May, 1859. No. of com., 127.

McKillop, Chas., B.A. (Admaston; Pres., Lanark and Renfrew). S. of Donald McKillop, laborer. B. in Campsie. Queen's College, Kingston; Presbyterian College, Montreal. Or. and In. 3 Sep, 1878. Mar. 23 June, 1881, Elizabeth Fisher. No of com., 253. Predecessors, Wm. Lochead, John McMorine, Robt. Stevenson.

McKinlay, W. (Innerkip, &c., Ont; Pres., Paris). Or. 11 July, 1882. No. of com., 109.

McKinnon, Dun. (Little River, N.S.; Pres., Halifax). Or. 4 June, 1862. No. of com., 186.

McKinnon, Neil (Mosa, Ont; Pres., London). S. of Donald McKinnon, farmer. B. at Tyree, Scot. Knox College, Toronto. Or. 21 Feb, 1861. Mar. 24 Feb, 1875, A. C. McGregor. In. to present ch., May, 1877. Predecessors, Arch. Stewart, W. R. Sutherland. No. of com, 206. Previous pastorates, Wardsville, 1861–72; Belmont, 1872–77.

McKnight, Alex., D.D. (Principal of Presbyterian College, Halifax; Pres., Halifax). B. at Dalmellington, Ayrshire, Scotland. Universities of Edinburgh and Glasgow. Showed marked proficiency as a student, carrying off prizes in Logic, Mathematics and Natural Philosophy. Licensed by Free Church Presbytery of Ayr, 18 Feb, 1850, and in Jan, 1855, received from colonial committee of Free Church, the appointment of teacher of Hebrew in Free College, Halifax, N.S. Shortly thereafter called by St. James' Ch. congregation, Dartmouth, of which ordained minister in Jan, 1857, discharging the functions incidental to the Hebrew chair in addition to his pastoral duties. In 1868, resigned the charge of Dartmouth congregation, and undertook Exegetics in addition to Hebrew in connection with the College. On the retirement of Dr. King, in 1871, transferred to chair of Systematic Theology, and by vote of Assembly, in 1878, appointed Principal. His alma mater, Glasgow University, conferred on him the degree of D.D. in 1877. Enjoying the esteem and confidence of the whole church, Dr. McKnight has, by his reputation as a preacher, a lucid expositor of Divine truth, combined with a thorough knowledge of ecclesiastical law, done much to build up and extend the influence of the church.

McKutcheon, Jas. (Corunna and Mooretown, Ont; Pres. Sarnia). Or. 25 Apl, 1882.

McLachlin, A. G., B.A. (Leaskdale, Ont; Pres., Lindsay) Or. Dec, 1882. No. of com., 69.

McLaren, Alex (Almonte, Ont). A minister without charge, attached to Presbytery of Lanark and Renfrew.

McLaren, E. D., B.D. (Brampton, Ont; Pres., Toronto). Or. 23 Sept, 1873. No. of com., 351. Is colleague and successor to Rev. James Pringle.

McLaren, Jas. F., B.D. (Euphrasia and Holland, Ont Pres., Owen Sound). Or. 8 Dec., 1880. No. of com., 124.

MacLaren, Wm., D.D. (Toronto; Pres., Toronto). S. of a merchant; B. in Torbolton, Ont. Knox College, Toronto. Or. 1 June, 1853. Mar. 20 Feb, 1854. Marjory Laing. Is the author of several pamphlets. Elected by the General Assembly, on 6 June, 1873, Professor of Systematic Theology in Knox College, Toronto, into which position inducted 1 Oct, 1873. Predecessors, Dr. Willis and Dr. Inglis. Was minister of Amherstburg, 1853-57; Knox Ch., Boston, Mass., 1857-58; Belleville, Ont, 1859-70; Knox Ch., Ottawa, 1870-73. Lecturer for three months, in 1872, by appointment of the General Assembly, on Apologetics, in Presbyterian College, Montreal. In 1883, Queen's College, Kingston, conferred the honorary degree of Doctor of Divinity.

McLean, Allan (Tryon and Bonshaw, P.E.I; Pres, P.E. Island). Or. 19 June, 1862. No. of com., 45.

McLean, Alex., M.A. (Hopewell, N.S; Pres., Pictou). Or. 14 Dec, 1852. No. of com., 260.

McLean, A. (Burleigh &c, Ont; Pres., Peterborough.) Or. 21 March, 1882.

McLean, Arch. (Blyth, Ont; Pres., Huron.) S. of Donald McLean, farmer. B. in Kintyre, Scot. Or. and In. Nov., 1866. No. of com., 230. Is Clerk of Presbytery.

McLean, Don. J., B.A. (Arnprior, Ont; Pres., Lanark & Renfrew.) Or. 11 Feb., 1863. No. of com., 140.

McLean, James (Great Village, N. S. Pres., Truro.) Or. 13 Nov., 1854. No. of com., 186.

McLean. James A.M., B A. (Clyde, N. N. Pres., Lunenburg & Yarmouth.) S. of Donald McLean, farmer. B. at Vale Colliery. Dalhousie College and Theological Hall, Halifax. Or. and In. 9 Dec., 1879. Mar. 4 Sep,. 1882, Julia G. Kilpatrick. Predecessor, Jas. Byers, Geo. M. Clarke, Hugh McMillan, M. G. Henry and others. No. of com., 90.

Maclean, M. W., B.A., M.A (St. Andrew's Ch., Belleville, Ont; Pres., Kingston.) S. of Malcolm Maclean. B. in Glasgow, Scot. Glasgow University, Queen's College, Kingston, Princeton Seminary, N.J. Or. 15 Aug., 1866. Mar. 29 Sep., 1868, Isabella E. Davidson. In. to present ch. 12 Nov., 1873. Predecessors, Jas. Ketcham, Wm. McEwen, Arch. Walker and J. C. Smith. No. of com., 180. Previous pastorates, Paisley, Ont., 1866-70; Port Hope 1871-73.

McLennan, Alex. (Sydenham, Ont; Pres., of Owen Sound.) Or. 25 May, 1869. No. of com., 82.

McLennan, D.D. (Lion's Head &c., Ont; Pres., Owen Sound.) Or. 18 Dec., 1872.

McLennan, D.H. (Tecumseth & Adjala, Ont; Pres., Barrie.) Or. 6 Mar., 1877

McLennan, Finlay A. (Kenyon, Ont; Pres. Glengarry.) S. of Angus McLennan, farmer. B. in Inverness-shire, Scot. McGill and Presbyterian Colleges, Montreal. Or. and In. 27 Sep, 1877. Mar. 28 Dec, 1881, Anne McKenzie. Predecessor, A. F. McQueen. No. of com., 114.

McLennan, Geo. (Underwood, &c., Ont; Pres. Bruce) Or. 8 Nov, 1864. No. of com., 141.

McLennan, Kenneth, M.A. (St. James Ch., Charlottetown, P. E. I.; Pres. P. E. Island) Or. 1852. No. of com., 175.

McLeod, A. B. (West Cape & Brae, P. E. I.; Pres. P. E. Island) Or. 1882.

Macleod, Alex. W., B.A., M.A. (Durham & West River, N. S.; Pres. Picton) S. of Wm. Macleod, farmer. B. at Onslow, N. S. Dalhousie College, Halifax, Princeton Theological Seminary, N. J. Mar. 18 July, 1877, Annie E. Macdowall. Or. 11 Sep, 1878. In. to present ch., 26 Sep, 1881. Predecessors, D. Ross, Dr, Jas. Ross, Jas. Watson, Geo. Roddick, Jas. Thompson. No. of com., 267. Previous pastorate, Parrsboro, 1878–81.

McLeod, Donald B.A. (Priceville, Ont.; Pres. Saugeen.) S. of John McLeod, farmer. B. in Strathalbyn, P. E. I. Dalhousie College and Presbyterian College, Halifax. Mar. 11 Nov, 1874, Lucy J. K. Cowan. Or. and In. 21 Aug, 1878. Predecessors, Charles Cameron, Donald Fraser. No. of com., 200. This Church was founded by the union of Knox Church of which Mr Cameron was pastor and St. Andrew's Church of which Mr. Fraser was pastor.

McLeod, Duncan D. (Dumfries St. Ch., Paris, Ont; Pres., Paris). S. of Rev. Don. McLeod, Minister of Established Ch. of Scot., and afterwards of Free Ch., Gourock, and ten years min. of Cobourg, Ont. B. at Gourock, Scot. University and Free Ch. College, Glasgow. Mar. in 1867, Annie S. dau. of Rev. Dr. McLean, Min. of Glenorchy Free Ch. Or. July, 1867. In. to present ch., 29 Dec, 1875. Predecessors, F. W. Farries, Dr.

James and Wm. Caw. No. of com., 290. Previous pastorates, Campsie, Scot., 1867-72; Ancaster and Barton, Ont., 1872-76.

McLeod, Hugh, M.A., D.D. (Mira, Sydney; Pres., Sydney). S. of George McLeod, farmer. B. at Retongue, Scot. Or. 1833. Mar. 6 April, 1841, Catherine Ross. In. to present ch., August, 1850. No. of com., 250. Previous pastorates, Erriboll, Sutherland, 1833-37; Gaelic Ch., Edinburgh, 1837-39, and Logie Easter, Ross-shire, 1839-50. Was sent in 1845, and also in 1848, as deputy to visit churches in British Provinces of North America. Sent permanently in 1850. Has been Moderator of the General Assembly.

MacLeod, John (Strathalbyn, P. E. I; Pres., P. E. Island). S. of John MacLeod, farmer. B. at Bernray, Harris, Scot. Glasgow University and Knox College Toronto. Or. and In. 30 Aug, 1881. Predecessors, Don. Morrison and Alex. Campbell. No. of com., 80. Was missionary over 5 years in Partick, Scot., while attending college. Afterwards, owing to ill health, immigrated to Canada for change of climate.

MacLeod, John M. (Zion Ch., Charlottetown, P.E.I; Pres., P.E. Island). S. of Ebenezer MacLeod, farmer. B. at West River, N.S. Presbyterian Seminary, West River; Theological Hall Presbyterian Church of Nova Scotia. Or. 9 Nov, 1854. Mar. 1st 21 Nov, 1856, Amelia Parker; 2nd 21 Dec, 1879, Mrs. L. Taylor. In. to present ch., 19 July, 1871. Predecessor, Alex. Falconer now of Trinidad. No. of com., 210. Previous pastorates, Richmond Bay, P.E.I., 1854-60; Newport, N.S., 1860-70; New Glasgow, 1870-71. Was re-called both to Richmond Bay and to Newport, but declined. Held position Clerk of Presbytery on the Island and in Nova Scotia for twenty-five years.

MacLeod, John R. (Kingsbury and Brampton, Gore, Que; Pres., Quebec). S. of Murdoch MacLeod, farmer. B. in Victoria Co., N.S. McGill University and Presbyterian College, Montreal. Or. 2 July, 1878. Mar. Margaret Currie. In. to present ch., 12 Oct, 1880. No. of com., 80. Previous pastorate, Sault St. Marie, 1878-79.

MacLeod, Malcolm (Longwick, Que; Pres., Quebec). Or. 2 July 1878.

MacLeod, P. McF. (Central Ch., Toronto; Pres., Toronto). S. of Rev Don. MacLeod, Minister of Gourock. Victoria College, Cobourg, London Presbyterian College and Edinburgh New College. Or. 29 June, 1871. Mar. 1st 7 June, 1871, Marion

E. Cochrane. She died in 1873. 2nd 13 May, 1875, Jessie Shannon. In. to present ch., 25 July, 1880. Predecessor, David Mitchell. No. of com., 369. Previous pastorates, Birkenhead, Eng., 1871-74; Liverpool, Eng., 1874-78; Stratford, Ont., 1878-80.

McLintock, J. M. (Maudaumin, Ont; Pres., Sarnia). Or. Aug. 1879.

Maclise, D., D. D., Calvin Ch., St. John, N. B; Pres., St. John). Or. Nov., 1848. No. of com., 150.

McMechan, John (Waterdown, Ont; Pres., Hamilton). S. of Arch. McMechan, Merchant. B. at Seaford, Ire. Royal and General Assembly's College, Belfast. Or. May. 1857. Mar. 1st. in 1861, Mary Jean, eldest dau. of Hon. Arch. McKellar. 2nd in 1873, Amelia, fourth dau. of Philip Clark, Esq. of Bloomfield, Ont. Previous pastorates, Waterdown, 1878-82; Berlin, Ont., 1859-66; Pictou, 1866-78.

McMillan, Angus (Union and Forbes Chs. Malagawacth, C. B; Pres., Victoria and Richmond). S. of M. McMillan, farmer. B. at St. Anns, C. B. Dalhousie College Halifax and Presbyterian College, Halifax. Or. and In. 25 Jan, 1882. Predecessors, W. G. Forbes: A. McKay. No. of com., 86.

McMillan, Duncan (Kamoka, Ont.) A ministea without charge Presbytery of London.

McMillan, D. (Sydney Mines, & N. Sydney, N. S. Pres., Sydney). Or. 4 Dec, 1861. No. of com., 126. Is colleague and successor to Rev. M. Wilson.

McMillan, George, B. A. (Princetown, P. E. I.; Pres., P. E. Island. S. of Duncan McMillan, farmer. B. at Scotch Hill, N. S. Dalhousie University, Halifax. Or. and In. 30th June, 1880. Predecessors, Dr. John Keir and Robert Laird. No. of com., 312.

Macmillan, John, (Knox ch. Mount Forest; Pres., Saugeen, Ont). S. of Neil Macmillan, farmer. B. in Arran, Scot. Toronto University and Knox College. Or. 29 Jan., 1857. Mar. 16 April, 1862, Catharine Walker. In. to present ch. March, 1865. Predecessor Donald McLean. No. of com. 217. Previous pastorate Fingal.

McMillan, John, B. D. (St. Paul's ch. Truro, N. S.; Pres. Truro). Or. 26 March, 1866. No. of com. 118.

McMullen, W. T., (Knox ch., Woodstock; Pres. Paris). S. of Arch. McMullen, farmer. B in County of Monaghan, Ire. Knox College, Toronto. Or. 5th Nov., 1856. Mar. Jan.,

1857, Susanna Gilbert. In. to present ch., 19 April, 1860. Predecessor, W. S. Ball. No. of com. 370. Previous pastorate, Millbank. Convener of General Assembly's Committee for Sabbath observance and Chairman of Joint Committee formed from four churches in Ontario anent introduction of Bible into public schools. Is Clerk of Presbytery.

McNab, Eben (Newport, N.S; Pres., Halifax). Or. 19 May, 1867. No. of com., 313.

Macnabb, James (Lucknow, Ont; Pres., Maitland). S. of Robt. Macnabb, farmer. B. at Mariposa. Knox College, Toronto. Or. 7 Dec, 1867. Mar. 29 Sep, 1869, Jennie Campbell. In. to present ch., 5 Oct, 1882. Predecessor, J. B. Taylor. No. of com., 54. Previous pastorate, S. Kinloss, 1867-69. Was missionary to Red River Territory, 1869-74. Minister of South Mara, 1874-82.

McNaughton, Alex. (Walton, Ont; Pres., Maitland). Or. 24 Aug, 1873. No. of com., 158.

McNeill, Leander G. M.A. (St. John's, Nfld; Pres., Newfoundland). S. of A. M. McNeill, farmer. B. in P.E.Island. Edinburgh University and Princetown Seminary, N.J. Or. 12 Nov, 1872. Mar. 23 Oct, 1880, Annie Putnam, of Maitland, N. S. In. to present ch., 26 Dec, 1878. Predecessors, Moses Harvey, J. D. Patterson, Dr. McRae. No. of com., 315. Previous pastorate, Maitland, N. S., 1872-78.

MacNish, Neil, B.A., B.D., M.A., LL.B., LL.D. (Cornwall, Ont; Pres. Glengarry). S. of Duncan NcNish, factor and farmer. B. in Kintyre, Scot. Toronto, Edinburgh and Glasgow Universities. Or. 29 April, 1868. Mar. 19 Sep, 1876, Anna Harriet Campbell. In. to present ch., 25 Nov, 1868. Predecessors, Harry Leith, Dr. Urquhart. No. of com., 240.

McPherson, H. H., B.A., M. A., (St John's Ch. Halifax, N. S. Pres,, Halifax). S. of Rev. Thos, McPherson, of Stratford, Ont. B. at Ballaghy, Ire. University and Knox College, Toronto. Or. 24 Nov, 1875. In. to present ch. 29 Dec, 1881. Predecessors, Prof. Forrest, Thos. Cumming. Previous pastorate Nassagaweya 1875-81. Was President of Knox College Literary Society and classical tutor in preparatory department of the College.

McPherson, Thos. (Stratford, Ont). Or. 10 Oct, 1838. A minister on retired list, Presbytery of Stratford.

McQuarrie, Hector (Wingham, Ont; Pres. Maitland). S. of Hector McQuarrie, farmer. B. at Pictou, N. S. Knox College and University, Toronto. Or. 22 May, 1866. Mar. 30 Oct, 1867, Miss Ferguson. In. to present ch. 28 Dec, 1876. Predecessors, James Hastie, James Pritchard. No. of com., 255. Previous pastorate Blenheim, Ont; 1866-76.

McQueen, A. F. (Huron, Ont; Pres. Maitland). Or. 15 Dec. 1858. No. of com., 140.

McRae, Alex. (Mid River and Little Narrows, N. S. Pres. Victoria and Richmond). Or. 1877. No. of com., 118.

Macrae, D., D.D., (St. Stephens Ch, St. John, N. B; Pres. St. John). Or. 21 July, 1856. No. of com., 201. Has been Moderator of General Assembly.

Macrae, D. (Meadow Lea, Man., Pres., Manitoba.) B. in Glengarry, Ont. Presbyterian College, Montreal. Or. 29 Jan., 1878. No. of com., 13.

McRae, D. B. (Cranbrook, Ont; Pres., Maitland.) Or June, 1875. No. of com., 142.

McRobbie, Gilbert G. (Mount Zion, Ch., Ridgetown, Pres., Chatham.) S. of Andrew McRobbie, farmer. B. at Puslinch. Knox College, Toronto, and Princeton Seminary, N.J. Or. 17 Nov., 1874. Mar. 30 April, 1873, Kassie Thomson. In. to present ch. 14 Mar., 1881. Predecessors,—Forest and D. Currie. No. of com., 204. Has been pastor of a church in Lambton County, and minister of Tilsonburg and Culloden.

McRobie, John (Petrolia, Ont; Pres., Sarnia.) Or. 21 Oct., 1857.

MacVicar, Donald H., L.L.D, D.D. (Principal of the Presbyterian College, Montreal; Pres. of Montreal) B. in Dunglass, Scot. Parents emigrated to Canada and settled on a farm near Chatham, Ont. In 1853 entered the Academy in Toronto, under the the Rev. Alex. Gale, M.A., subsequently studied in Toronto University College, and in Fall of 1855 entered Knox College. In second and third years of course, taught Classics and English in Brother's Private Academy in Gould Street. First Mission work was at Collingwood in 1858. Conducted public services in the West End of the City. Appointed by Foreign Mission Committee to British Columbia; declined as also calls to Erin, Brantford, Collingwood and from the West Church of Toronto, but accepted a unanimous call to Knox Church, Guelph, where he was most successful as a preacher and pastor. In the Fall of 1860 accepted a call to Coté Street Church, Montreal, as successor to the Rev. D. Fraser, D.D. and was In. 30 Jan, 1861. During a pastorate of eight years, the congregation nearly doubled its membership, increasing to 572, and the Bible Class was one of the largest in the country. In 1868 was appointed by the General Assembly, Professor of Divinity in the Presbyterian College, Montreal, and for several years, with the exception of two occasional lectures, was the only Professor. Then it had only five or six students, now it has sixty on its Roll; five Professors, five Lecturers and a Dean of Residence. Taking a deep interest in the work of French evangelization originated the work of training French speaking Ministers. For many years served on the Board of Protestant School Commissioners, Montreal, and at time of retiring was its Chairman. Has published Primary and an advanced Arithmetic, both of which are standard text Books and extensively used. In 1870 received from the University of McGill College the honorary degree of LL.D, and was elected a Fellow. In 1881 received the Diploma of Membership of the Athénic Oriental of Paris. In 1876 delivered a course of twenty Lectures on Applied Logic, and in 1878 a course on Ethics, before the Ladies Educational Association of Montreal, and during the Session of 1871 was Lecturer on Logic in McGill College. Was appointed by the General Assembly, a delegate to the Pan-Presbyterian Councils which met in Edinburgh, Scotland in 1877 and in Philadelphia, U.S. in 1880, at the last of which he read a paper published in its proceedings on "The Catholicity of Presbyterianism." In 1881 was chosen Moderator of the General Assembly at Kingston the duties of which he discharged with acknowledged firmness, courtesy and judgment. Officiated at the opening of thirty new churches; and as Moderator and Supply of Crescent St. Church during its long vacancy. Was guide and counsel to the congregation in the erection of its magnificient Church. His great work is the founding of the College which commenced in the basement of Erskine Church with no visibility of outward form, but has now a magnificient building with every comfort and convenience for Professors and Students. In 1883 had conferred by Knox College, Toronto, the honorary degree of D. D.

MacWilliam, Wm., B.A., M.A., LL.B. (Streetsville, Ont; Pres., Toronto). S. of Alex. MacWilliam, farmer. B. at Kirkinner, Scot. Glasgow and Toronto Universities. Or. 23 Sept, 1863. Mar. 21 March, 1861. In. to present ch., 18 Nov, 1880. Predecessors, W. Kintoul, R. Ure, – McKay, – Wright, and – Breckenridge. No. of com., 210. Previous pastorates, Harwood, Ont, 1863-80.

Mann, Alex., D.D. (Pakenham, Ont; Pres., Lanark and Renfrew). Or. 14 May, 1840. Has retired from active service.

Mann, David (Rodney, Ont; Pres., London). Or. 26 Dec., 1855. No. of com., 112.

Martin, Wm. M. (Norwich, Ont; Pres., Paris). S. of John Martin, miller. B. at Fergus. Knox College, Toronto, and Theological Seminary, Princeton, N.J. Or. and in. 22 July, 1875. Mar. 27 Aug, 1875, Christina Jamieson. Predecessors, R. Rodgers, Wm. Donald, and James Robertson. No. of com., 220. Has recently accepted a call to Exeter, Pres. of Huron.

Mason, W. A., B.A. (New London, P.E.I; Pres., P. E. Island.) Or. 9 Feb, 1881. No. of com., 111.

Matheson, Alex. (Little Britain and Selkirk, Man; Pres., Manitoba.) S. of John Matheson, farmer. B. in the Parish of Kildonan. University and Knox College, Toronto. Or. 28 Nov. 1860. Mar. 12 Nov, 1862, Victoria Johnstone. In. to present ch. 24 Aug, 1881. Has been a missionary for a number of years, as also pastor of various congregations.

Matheson, John, B.A (Martintown and Williamstown, Ont; Pres., Glengarry). Or. 18 Nov., 1879. No. of com., 267.

Mathieson, Wm. (Winslow, Que; Pres. Quebec) Or. 1 May, 1862. No. of com., 75.

Matthews, Algernon (Trenton, Ont; Pres. Kingston) Or. 2 Aug, 1875. No. of com., 83.

Mathews, Geo. D., D.D. (Chalmers Ch., Quebec; Pres. Quebec) Or. 31 Aug, 1854. No. of com., 222.

Maxwell, Wm. (Annapolis, N. S.; Pres. Halifax) Or. 1854. No. of com., 50.

Meikle William (Oakville, Ont; Pres. Toronto) S. of John Meikle, builder. B. in Ayr, Scot. Glasgow College. Mar. 5 June, 1855, S. V. Hogan. Or. 27 Sep, 1848. In. to present ch. 18 Jan, 1868. Predecessors, Jos. Nisbet, Robert Scott. No. of com., 170. Previous pastorate, Dobbs Ferry Ch., New York.

Meldrum, William. A Minister without charge attached to Presbytery of Guelph.

Middlemiss, Jas. (Chalmers Ch., Elora, Ont; Pres. Guelph) Or. 3 June, 1856. No. of com., 231.

Millan, E. D., B. A., (Lunenburg, N. S; Pres., Lunenburg and Shelburne). Or. 28 Oct, 1873. No. of com., 73.

Millen, W. (Bocabec, N. B; Pres., St John). Or. Jan, 1846. No. of com., 43.

Millican, Wm. (Garafraxa, Ont; Pres., Guelph). Or. 21 Sep, 1859. No. of com., 204.

Milligan, Geo. M., B. A., (Old St. Andrew's Ch., Toronto; Pres., Toronto). S. of Wm. Milligan, fish-curer. B. in Wick, Scot. Queen's College Kingston, Ont; and Princton College, N. J. Or. 4 Feb, 1868. Mar. 19 Nov, 1867. Harriet Ennice Rowse. Has published several sermons. In. present ch., 27 Oct, 1876. No. of com, 370. Commenced present pastorate with 48 members. Was Minister of English Settlement near London, Ont; and also of a church in Detroit.

Milloy, John (Aldboro, Ont; Pres., London). Or. 2 Feb, 1859. No. of com., 100.

Mitchell, David (John St. Ch., Belleville; Pres., Kingston). Or. Oct. 1858. No. of com., 257.

Mitchell, Jas. W., (Mitchell, Ont). A minister without charge attached to Presbytery of Stratford.

Moffat, Robt. C., D.D. (St. John's Ch., Walkerton, Pres., Bruce.) S. of James Moffat, farmer. B. at Langdales, Scot. Glasgow and Toronto Universities. Or. and In. 14 Oct., 1857. Mar. 22 Oct., 1855, Margaret Dickie. Author of "Life Dear and Helpful" published in 1881. No. of com., 175. Had degree of D.D. conferred by Blackburn University, Ill., in 1882.

Monteath, R. (Toronto.) A minister on retired list attached to Presbytery of Toronto. Is clerk of Presbytery.

Moodie, Robert (Stayner and Sunnydale, Ont; Pres., Barrie.) S. of Rev. D. Moodie, incumbent of Clackmannan Parish and Chaplain of the Garrison at Stirling. B. at Clackmannan, Scot. Or. Mar., 1863. Mar. 6 Jan., 1869, Agnes Huggard. In. to present ch. 16 Jan., 1873. Predecessor, Jas. Greenfield. No. of com., 160. Previous pastorates, St. Stephen, N. B., 1863 and Tecumseth, Ont., 1868. Has been clerk of Presbytery of Barrie since the Union and Convener of Presbytery H. M. committee since 1879.

Moore, William, D.D. (Bank St. Ch., Ottawa, Pres., Ottawa.) S. of John Moore, iron founder. B. at Larne Antrim, Ire. Princeton Theological Seminary. Degree of Doctor of Divinity conferred by University of Hanover, Indiana. Or. and In. 28 March, 1866. Mar. Annie Junor, 4 July, 1866. She died 1 Nov, 1879. No. of com., 257.

Mordy, John, M.A. (Walkerton & Balaklava, Ont; Pres., Bruce.) Or. 19 Dec., 1878. Has recently been inducted.

Morison, David W., B.A. (Ormstown, Que; Pres., Montreal). S. of Wm. Morison, contractor. B. at Denny, Scot. McGill University, Montreal; Morrin College, Quebec. Or. 19 Nov.,

1873. Mar. 14 Sep., 1881, Anna Letitia Wales. In. to present ch. 4 March, 1874. Predecessors, Jas. Anderson, Jas. Seiveright, W. C. Clarke. No. of com., 400.

Morrison, Dun., M.A. (Owen Sound; Pres., Owen Sound). Is senior minister of Knox Ch., Owen Sound. Or. 22 Oct, 1851. No. of com., 285.

Morrison, John, M.A. (Waddington, State of New York; Pres., Brockville). S. of James Morrison, manufacturer. B. in Glasgow, Scot., 12 July, 1799. College in connection with United Secession Church, Scotland. Or. 12 May, 1829. Mar. 13 Sep, 1838, Mary Dow. In. to present ch., 1840. Predecessor, Wm. Taylor. No. of com., 206. Previous pastorate, First United Secession Church, Keith, Scotland, of which minister for 10 years. Has been over 42 years minister of the church in Waddington.

Morrison, John (Cedarville, &c., Ont; Pres., Saugeen). Or. 9 Jan. 1866. No. of com., 121.

Morrison, John A. (Sault Ste. Marie, Ont; Pres., Bruce). Or. a missionary, 21 Nov, 1882. No. of com., 46.

Morrison, P. M. (Dartmouth, N. S.; Pres., Halifax). Or. 1865. No. of com., 163.

Mowat, John B., B.A., M.A. (Kingston, Ont; Pres., Kingston). S. of John Mowat, merchant. B. in Kingston. Queen's College, Kingston; Edinburgh University. Or. 2 May, 1850. Mar. in 1861, Emma, dau. of Hon. John McDonald of Gananoque. Became a Professor in Queen's College, Oct, 1857. Was minister of Niagara, 1850–57.

Mowatt, A. J. (Fredericton, N. B.; Pres., St. John). S. of Thos. Mowatt, farmer. B. at Woodstock, N. B. Truro Presbyterian College. Or. 5 June, 1866. Mar. 30 June, 1868, Louisa J. Armand of Gays River, N. S. In. to present ch., 8 Jan., 1880. Predecessors Dr. Birkmyre, Dr. Brooke. No. of com. 240. Previous pastorates, Stellarton, N. S., 1866-73. Windsor, N. S. 1873-80.

Muir, Jas. B., M.A., (St. Andrew's ch., Huntingdon, Que.; Pres., Montreal). Or. 3 April., 1863. No. of com. 260.

Muir, Thomas. (Fordwich and Gorrie, Ont.; Pres., Maitland). S. of Thos. Muir, cotton spinner. B. at Glasgow, Scot. Presbyterian College, Montreal; Toronto University and Queen's College Kingston. Mar. first in April, 1859, Mary-Ann Qua. Second, Annie Fortune in Feb., 1876. Or. 24 Oct., 1876. In. to present ch., 27 Jan, 1880. Predecessor Geo. Brown. No. of com. at Fordwich 106, Forrie 47. Previous pastorate Metcalfe from 1876 to 1879.

Mullan, J. B. (Fergus, Ont; Pres., Guelph). S. of Donald Mullan, farmer. B. in Chatham, Que. Queen's College, Kingston. Or. 23 July, 1862. Mar. 3 Sept., 1863, Sarah Sommerville, deceased. In. to present ch., 13 Sep., 1871. Predecessors, Messrs. Gardiner, Smellie, Drs. Mair and Macdonnell. No. of com. 250. Previous pastorates, Spencerville, 1862-69; East Oxford 1869-71.

Mullin, J. S. (Nashwack, N. B.; Pres., St. John).

Mullins, Wm. (Headingly Hamlet, Man.; Pres. Manatoba). S. of Wm. Mullins, leather merchant. B. at Potsdam, N. Y. Presbyterian College, Montreal. Or. and In. 14 Jan., 1880. Predecessors, J. Black, D. D., J. Nesbitt and Donaldson. No. of com., 25. Has charge of the Headingly group of mission stations.

Munroe, Alex. (Valleyfield, P. E. I.; Pres. P. E. Island). Or. 3 Nov., 1850. No of com. 134.

Munro, Gustavus, B. A., M. A., (Embro, Ont.; Pres. Paris). S. of Geo. Munro, farmer. B. at Dalhousie Mills. McGill College and Presbyterian College, Montreal Or. and In. 19 Aug., 1873. Mar. 27 Aug., 1873, Mary McCuaig. Predecessor, Don. McKenzie. No. of com. 280.

Munro, J. K., B.A. (Manotick, Ont.; Pres. Ottawa). S. of Rev. B. Munro. B. at St. John, N. B. Dalhousie College, Halifax, and Presbyterian College, Montreal. Or. and In. 19 Aug., 1879. Mar. 2 Oct., 1879, M. A. Mackay. Predecessors, W. Lochead, J. White. No of com. 186.

Munroe, John M. (Kintore, Ont.; Pres. London). S. of James Monroe, farmer. B. in Argyleshire. Knox College and University, Toronto. Or. 28 July, 1874. Mar. 5 Nov. 1879, Kate Crawford. In. to present ch. 7 May, 1878. No. of com. 69. Previous pastorate New Glasgow and Rodney, N. S., 28 July, 1874.

Murray, Jas. (Douglastown, N. B; Pres., Miramichi). Or. 3 Nov, 1852. No. of com., 32.

Murray, James A. (St. Andrew's Ch., London, Ont; Pres., London). S. of James Murray, farmer. B. at Roger's Hill, N. S. West River Seminary and Dalhousie College, Halifax. Or. Sep, 1857. Mar. 16 Oct, 1861, Georgiana Smith. In. to present ch., 29 Dec, 1875. Predecessor, John Scott. No. of com., 705. Previous pastorates, Annapolis, N. S., Bathurst, N. B., Mount Forest, Ont., Lindsay, Ont.

Murray, John (Falmouth St. Ch., Sydney, C. B; Pres., Sydney). S. of S. Murray, farmer. B. at Scotsburn, N. S. Dalhousie College and Theological Hall, Halifax, New College, Edinburgh. Or. 3 Jan, 1873. Mar. 27 Oct' 1874, Margaret Fraser, dau. of late John Mackintosh, of Halifax. In. to present ch., 1 Jan, 1876. No. of com., 48. Previous pastorate, New London, P. E. I, 1873-76.

Murray, John D. (St. John's Ch., Buctouche, N. B; Pres St. John). S. of Alex. Murray, farmer. B. at Middle River, Picton Co., N. S. Truro Presbyterian College and Divinity College, Halifax. Mar. in 1855, Margaret Elizabeth Hatfield, of Yarmouth, N. S. Or. 22 Feb, 1865, and In. to present ch, 14 Oct, 1873. No. of com., 60. Previous pastorates, Port Hill, P. E. I. and Moncton, N. B.

Murray, John G. (Grimsby and Muirs Settlement; Pres. of Hamilton). S. of John Murray, farmer. B. in Parish of Rogart, Scot. Knox College, Toronto, and an occasional student at Toronto University. Or. 7 July, 1858. Mar. Isabella Victoria Gurney, 21 May, 1860. In. to present ch., 7 July, 1858. No. of com., 154.

Murray, John L., M.A. (Knox Ch., Kincardine; Pres. Maitland) S. of Alex. Murray, farmer, an elder of Embro Congregation. B. at W. Zorra, Oxford Co., Ont. Knox College, Toronto, Princeton Seminary, N. J., and Hanover College, Indiana. Or. 28 Oct, 1868. Mar. Mary Roberts Keam of Cobourg. In. to present ch. 11 July, 1878. Predecessor, John Fraser. No. of com. about 200. Previous pastorates, Baltimore and Cold Springs 28 Oct, 1868–72. Woodville, 17 Dec, 1872–78.

Murray, Thos. H. (Kempt and Walton, N. S.; Pres. Halifax) Or. 25 May, 1876. No. of com., 95.

Musgrave, Peter (Winthrop, Ont; Pres. Huron) S. of John Musgrave. B. at Milverton, Eng. University and Knox College, Toronto. Or. 20 May, 1868. Mar. Jane Howard. In. to present ch. 25 Sep, 1877. Predecessors, Thos. G. Thomson, Arch. McDiarmid. No. of com., 239. Previous pastorate, Milverton and North Mornington 1868-77.

Mylne, Solomon (St. Andrew's Ch, Smith's Falls, Ont; Pres. Lanark & Renfrew) S. of Robt. Mylne, farmer. B. in County of Derry, Ire. Royal Academical Institution, Belfast. Or. and In. 16 Oct, 1850. Mar. 9 Aug, 1854, Ann Malloch. No. of com., 150. Predecessor, Dr. Geo. Romaney.

Nairn, Robt. (Harvey, N. B.) No. of com., 195.

Neil, John (Nassagaweya, &c., Ont; Pres. Guelph) Or. 5 Dec, 1882. No. of com., 122.

Neill, Robt., D.D. (Burnbrae, Ont; Pres. Kingston). S. of Andrew Neill, pattern drawer. B. at Dunovan, Scot. Glasgow, University. Or. and In. 29 Jan, 1840. Mar. 17 Nov, 1852, Christina Urquhart. No. of com., 175. Had degree of Doctor of Divinity conferred by Queen's College, Kingston.

Nelson, Thos. A. (Dunbar, Ont; Pres., Brockville). S. of John Nelson, farmer. B. at Nepean, Ont. McGill and Presbyterian College, Montreal. Or. and In. 7 Sep, 1880. Mar. 29 Dec, 1880, Jennie M. Baillie. Predecessor, J. M. Chesnut. No. of com., 200.

Nicol, Alex. (N. Luther, &c., Ont; Pres., Saugeen) Or. 27 May, 1879.

Nicol, Peter (Vaughan and Bolton, Ont; Pres., Toronto). S. of Peter Nicol, merchant. B. in Banffshire, Scot. Knox College, Toronto. Or. and In. 27 Oct, 1874. Mar. 4 Oct, 1876, Maggie McKnight. No. of com., 207—113 in Vaughan and 94 in Bolton. Arrived in Canada when 16 years of age with $2.50 to begin life with. Worked as farm laborer for board. Taught school seven years, during which time prepared for college, where he entered in 1868.

Nicholls, John (St. Mark's Ch., Montreal; Pres., Montreal). Or. 1 May, 1869. No., of com., 133.

Nicholson, Thos. (Charlo, &c., N.B.; Pres., Miramichi). Or. 11 March, 1858. No. of com., 126.

Niven, David P., B. A., (Egremont and Normanby, Ont; Pres., Saugeen). S. of Robert Niven, farmer. B. at Niagara. Queen's College, Kingston. Or. Mar, 1870. Mar. Elizabeth McIntyre, 23 Aug, 1871. In. 4 Nov, 1879. Predecessors, Hugh Crozier and Patrick Greig. No. of com., 235. Previous pastorate Georgina, Ont; 1870–77.

Niven, Hugh (Herdman's Corners, Que). A retired Minister, attached to Pres., Montreal.

Oxley, M. S., B. A., (Chelsea and E. Templeton, Que; Pres. Ottawa). Or. 15 Nov, 1881. No. of com., 36.

Panton, E. W, (St. Andrew's Ch., Stratford, Ont; Pres., Stratford). B. at Coupar Fife, Scot. Knox College, Toronto. Or. 19 Dec, 1873. Mar. 22 Sep, 1870. Helen E. White. In. present ch., 2 Jan, 1883. No. of com., 208. Previous, pastorates Lindsay, and Bradford.

Paradis, Jos. H., (Port Stanley, Ont; Pres., London). No. of com., 67.

Park, Wm. (1st Ch., Durham, Ont; Pres., Saugeen). Or. 10 Oct, 1857.

Parsons, Henry M., (Knox Ch, Toronto; Pres., Toronto). Or. 15 Nov, 1854. No. of com., 594.

Paterson, Daniel, M.A. (St. Andrew's, Que; Pres., Montreal). S. of Daniel Paterson, merchant. B. at Greenock, Scot. Glasgow University and United Presbyterian Divinity Hall, Edinburgh. Or. and In. 24 Oct, 1860. Predecessor, Arch. Henderson. No. of com., 105. Mr. Paterson's church was the first Presbyterian Church in County of Argenteuil, and was founded by his predecessor in 1818.

Paterson, J. T. (Hanover, Ont; Pres., Bruce). S. of W. W Paterson, mason. Morrin College, Quebec. Or. and In. 22 July, 1880. Mar. 22 July, 1879, S. J. Woods. Predecessor, R. Gunn. No. of com., 175. Paid own expenses in connection with collegiate course.

Paterson, Nathaniel (Bayfield, Ont; Pres., Huron). S. of Rev. D. N. Paterson, Minister of St. Andrew's Church, Glasgow, one of the Moderators of the Free Church of Scotland. B. at Galashields, Scot. Glasgow University, and Knox College, Toronto. Or. 19 July, 1859 Mar. 8 Oct, 1860, Mary, dau. of Mr. W. Campbell, Architect, Halifax, N. S. Author of several published sermons. In. to present ch., 30 Jan, 1878. Predecessors, Dr. J. M. Gibson, James Greenfield, —Jamieson. No. of com., 80. Previous pastorates, Merrickville, 19 July, 1859–62; York Mills, March, 1862–66; Martintown, Christmas, 1866–78.

Patterson, G. C., M.A. (Summerstown, Ont; Pres., Glengarry). Or. 24 Aug, 1880. No. of com., 93.

Patterson, Jas. (Montreal; Pres., Montreal). Or. 14 Sep, 1857. Has charge of Presbytery's City Mission, Montreal. Is clerk of Presbytery.

Paul, Jas. T. (Bolsover, Ont.; Pres. Lindsay). S. of —— Paul, linen manufacturer. B. at Coupar Fife. Queen's College, Kingston, and in Scotland. Or. 6 June, 1850. Mar. 12 Feb., 1851, Jessie Paton. In. to present ch. 27 March, 1874. Predecessor, E. McAuley. No. of com. 26. Previous pastorates, St. Louis de Gonzague, Que., 1850-69, Drummer, 1869-74.

Peattie, William. Or. 30 June, 1860. A minister without charge, attached to Presbytery of Whitby.

Penman, John W. (N. and S. Mission, Ont.; Pres. Stratford). Or. 5 April. 1880.

Pettigrew, Robt., M.A. (Weston, Ont.; Pres. Toronto). S. of John Pettigrew, farmer. B. at Carmunnock, near Glasgow. University and Knox College, Toronto. Mar. 27 Jan., 1880, Mary Shiell. Or. and In. 3 Jan, 1873. No. of com. 117.

Pitblado, C. B. (St. Andrew's ch. Winnipeg; Pres. Manitoba). S. of John Pitblado, contractor. B. at Dunfermline, Scot. Halifax and Truro Colleges, N. S. Or. 15 Feb., 1865. Mar. Sophia Christie. 13 Jan. 1865. In. to present ch. 14 Dec., 1881. No. of com. 250. Previous pastorates Glenelg, East River and Caledonia, N. S., from 1865-72, Halifax, N. S., from 1872-81.

Pollock, Allan D.D. (Halifax). Or. 1852. A professor in Presbyterian College, Halifax.

Polson, S. (Pointe des Chenes; Pres., Manitoba). Or. 24th Jan., 1880. No. of com. 42.

Porteous, George, (Toledo, Ont.; Pres., Lanark and Renfrew). S. of Nichol Porteous, farmer. B. in Northumberland, Eng. Queen's College, Kingston. Or. 22nd Aug., 1860. Mar. 20 Sep., 1860, Christina Gunn. In. to present ch.. 7 May, 1878. Predecessors, Jos. Anderson, David Evans, Don J. McLean, Wm. White. No. of com. 80. Previous pastorates, Wolfe Island over 10 years, Matilda over 7.

Porteous, John (Port Dalhousie, Ont.; Pres., Hamilton.) Or. Dec. 1842. No. of com. 45.

Porter, Samuel (Barrie). Or. June, 1836. A Minister on retired list, Presbytery of Barrie.

Pringle, James (Brampton, &c., Ont; Pres., Toronto). Or. 19 Jan., 1848. No. of com. 351.

Pritchard, James (Auburn, Ont; Pres., Huron). S. of Jos. Pritchard, farmer. B. in township of Cavan, Ont. Princeton College, N. J., and Knox College, Toronto. Or. 28th Oct, 1868. Mar. Christina McCrostie, 25 Dec., 1879. In to present ch. 17 April, 1878. Predecessors, Stephen Young, Arch. Currie, and John Stuart. No. of com. 190. Previous pastorates, Camden in 1868–70, Parkhill 1870–72, and Wingham 1872–78.

Proudfoot, John J. A., D D. (1st Pres. Ch.. London, Ont; Pres., London). S. of late Professor Wm. Proudfoot. B. in Perthshire, Scot. United Presbyterian Theological Hall. Or 16 July, 1848. Mar. 6 June, 1854, Alathea Mary Coleman. In. to present ch., 28 May, 1851. Predecessor—His father who formed the congregation in 1832, being the first established in Canada of United

Presbyterian Church. Had degree of Doctor of Divinity conferred in 1871 by Monmouth College, United States.

Quinn, James (Tabusintae and Burnt, N. B; Pres., Miramichi). S. of Richard Quinn. B. at Belfast, Ire. Queen's College and General Assembly's College, Belfast. Or. 11 Aug, 1873. Mar. 10 April 1872, Anna Wilson. In. to present ch, 1 May, 1881. Predecessors, William Fogo, James Robertson, James Murray. Simon Fraser was first minister. No. of com., 85. Previous pastorates, St. James, N. B., 1874-77; Sherbrooke, N. S., 1877-81.

Ratcliffe, John H. (Ancaster and Alberton, Ont; Pres., Hamilton). S. of John Ratcliff, farmer. B. in Ontario Co. Knox College. Or. and In. 1 Nov, 1876. Mar. 11 Jan, 1877, Margaret Fletcher. Predecessors in Ancaster, — Shead, M. Y Stark, K. McLennan, John Lees, J. B. Baikie, and D. D. McLeod. No. of com., Ancaster, 80; Alberton, 52. Has accepted call to 1st Presbyterian Church, St. Catherines.

Rees, W. D. (Blackheath, &c., Ont; Pres., Hamilton). No. of com., 77.

Reid, William M. A., D. D., (Western Agent of the Church, Toronto; Pres., Toronto). B. in Aberdeenshire. King's College Aberdeen. Li. May, 1839. Or. and In. to Grafton and Colborne Chs., Ont; 30 Jan. 1840. Translated to Picton, Ont. in Apl, 1849 of which church minister until June, 1853, when appointed to present position. Received degree of Doctor of Divinity from Queen's College, Kingston, in 1876. One of the Clerks of the General Assembly and was Moderator of General Assembly, 1879.

Rennie, John (Ailsa Craig and Carlisle, Ont; Pres. London). S. of Chas. Rennie, farmer. B. at New Pitsligo, Scot. Knox College, Toronto. Mar. 25 Dec, 1857, Annie Taylor. Or. 22 Apl. 1857. In. present ch., 5 May, 1869. Predecessor, Wm. Fletcher. No. of Com., 160. Previous pastorates Beachville, for two years, Dunnville, for eight years.

Renwick, Robt, (Newry Station). Or. Jan, 1863. A minister on retired list, Presbytery of Stratford.

Richards, John J., (Lyn and Caintown; Pres., Brockville). S. of Jos. Richards, farmer. B. at West River, N. S. Dalhousie College, Halifax, and Princeton Seminary, N. J. Or. 10 Aug, 1874. Mar. 16 Nov, 1876. Anna Paul. In. to present ch., 8 Jan, 1880. Predecessors, Arch. Brown, John Burton, R. McKenzie. No. of com., 72. Previous partorate, Westport 1874-80.

Roberts, Edward (Malou, N. S; Pres., Victoria and Richmond). Or. 1853. No of com., 112.

Robertson, James (Winnipeg, Pres., Manitoba.) Or. 18 Nov., 1869. Is superintendent of missions in the North-West.

Robertson, Jas. (Litchfield, Ont; Pres., Lanark & Renfrew.) Or. 4 July, 1882. No. of com., 100.

Robertson, John, M.A. (Black River, N.B. Pres., Miramichi.) Or. July, 1868. No. of com., 66.

Robertson, John L., M.A. (Strabane, Ont; Pres., Hamilton.) S. of of John Robertson, mason and farmer. B. at Queenston Heights, Ont. Westminister College, New Wilmington, and Theological Seminary, Xenia, Ohio Was reared and educated in the United Presbyterian Church of North America, thus receiving preparatory training at her seminaries. Or. 11 Sep., 1867. Mar. 3 Sep., 1860, Mary Jane, adopted dau. of late Rev. John Russell, D.D. of Stamford, Ont. In. to present ch. 11 Sep., 1877. Predecessor, Alex. McLean. No. of com., 120. Previous pastorates, Walton, Ont. Plumer. Pa

Robertson, W., M.A. (Chesterfield, Ont; Pres., Paris.) Or. 26 Jan., 1859. No. of com., 195.

Rogers, Robt. (Collingwood, Ont; Pres., Barrie.) S. of Alex. Rogers, farmer. B. in Perthshire, Scot. University St. Andrew's, Scot. Union College, New York State. Or. 26 Dec., 1851. Mar. 31 Oct., 1856, Anna, youngest dau. of Donald McLean of Toronto. In. to present ch. 20 Aug., 1861. Predecessor, —Young. No. of com., 154. Previous pastorates, Chestertield, Norwich and Tilsonbury, Culloden.

Roger, Walter M., B.A., M.A. (Ashburn, Ont; Pres., Whitby). S. of Rev. J. M. Roger, M.A. B. at Kincardine O'Neil. University and Knox College, Toronto. Or. Nov, 1866. In. to present ch., 1 Oct, 1874. Predecessors, Messrs. Dawson and Sharpe. No. of com., 119. Previous pastorates, Perth and Petrolia.

Rogers, Anderson (Yarmouth, N S.; Pres., Halifax). Or. 1882. No. of com., 122.

Rosborough, J., B.A. (Musquodoboit, N.S.; Pres.. Halifax). Or. 23 July, 1873. No. of com., 135.

Ross, Alex. (Harbor Grace, Nfl'd; Pres., Newfoundland). S. of Don. Ross, farmer. B. at Earlton, N.S. Halifax Free Ch. College. Or. and In. 21 Nov, 1855. No. of com., 42. Mar. 30 July, 1868, Euphemia Thomson of Halifax. Is Clerk of Presbytery.

Ross, Alex., M.A. (Woodville, Ont; Pres., Lindsay). S. of D. Ross, farmer. B. in Ross-shire, Scot. Aberdeen and Edinburgh Universities. Or. 19 Sep, 1860. Mar. 7 Jan, 1862, Isabella, dau. of late Rev. Jas. Campbell of Kildonan, Scot. Has written articles for periodicals. In. to present ch., 2 July, 1879. Predecessors, J. M. Farish and J. L. Murray. No. of com., 224. Previous pastorate, Pictou, N.S, 1860–79, and was a missionary in Hebrides three summers, 1857–59.

Ross, David Y., B.A., M.A. (Westport, Ont, Pres., Brockville). S. of Jas. Ross, carpenter. B. in Kingston, Ont. Knox College and University, Toronto. Or. and In. 29 Dec, 1880. Predecessors, Arch. Crawford, Andrew Melville and J.J. Richards. No. of com., 73.

Ross, Donald—A Minister without charge in the Presbytery of Glengarry.

Ross, Donald, B.D. (Lachine, Que; Pres. Montreal) Or. 3 Oct, 1865.

Ross, Ebenezer (Truro, N. S.; Pres. Truro) Or. 31 Oct, 1849. Has retired from active service.

Ross, J., B.A. (Bethesda and Alnwick, Ont; Pres. Peterboro) Or. March, 1881. No. of com., 200.

Ross, James, B.A., B.D., M.A. (Knox Ch., Perth, Ont; Pres. Lanark & Renfrew) S. of Jas. Ross, surfaceman on G. T. R. B. at Countess Wells, Scot. Queen's College, Kingston. Or. and In. 8 Sep, 1881. Predecessors, Andrew Melville, 1846–47; Jas. B. Duncan, 1848–66; Walter M. Roger, 1866–68, and Wm. Burns, 1869–80. No. of com., 190. Declined call to St. Andrew's Ch., Ottawa, 1883.

Ross, John, B.A. (Melville Ch., Brussels, Ont; Pres. Maitland) S. of Arthur Ross, farmer. B. in township of Nichol, Wellington Co., Ont. University and Knox College, Toronto. Or. and In. 28 Oct, 1879. Mar. Dec, 1879, Elsie, dau. of Alex. Watt, Elora, Ont. Predecessor and first minister of church John Ferguson, now of Vankleek Hill. No. of com., 154. Was silver medallist in metaphysics and ethics at University in 1876.

Ross, Peter R. (Knox Ch., Ingersoll; Pres. Paris) S. of John Ross, farmer. B. in West Zorra. McGill and Presbyterian Colleges Montreal. Or. 24 Feb, 1881. Mar. 24 Dec, 1876, Bessie Craig. In. to present ch. 30 Jan, 1883. Predecessors, – Straith and R. N. Grant. Previous pastorate, Coté-des-Neiges 1881–83.

Ross Robt. (Brucefield, Ont.; Pres. Huron). Or. Oct., 1851. No. of com., 144.

Ross, William, (Megantic, Que.; Pres. Quebec). S. of Alex. Ross, builder. B. in Ross-shire, Scot. University and Free ch. College, Edinburgh. Or. 5 Sep., 1860. Mar. 25 Dec. 1862, Jane Sutherland, who died 31 July, 1881. No. of com., 40. Previous pastorates, West River and Brookfield, P. E. I., 1860-69; Lochiel, Ont., 1869-80.

Ross, W., B. A. (Prince William, N. B.; Pres. St. John.) Or. 14 Nov., 1876.

Rowat, Andrew, (West Winchester, Ont.; Pres. Brockville). S. of John Rowat, farmer. B. in township of Flos. Upper Canada College, Knox College and University Toronto; also Free Ch., College, Glasgow. Or. and In. 2 March, 1871. Mar. 6 May, 1866, Margaret, eldest daughter of Rev. D. McKenzie. Predecessor, Wm. Bennet. No. of com., 250.

Russel, Alex. (Dalhousie, N. B.; Pres. Miramichi). Or. 22 Feb., 1876. No. of com., 105.

Russell, Alex. (Hawkesville, Ont.; Pres. Guelph). Or. 2 June, 1880. No. of com., 40.

Scott, Alex. A., B.A., M.A. (Carleton Pl ce, Ont.; Pres. Lanark & Renfrew). S. of M. Scott, farmer. B. in East Zorra. University College, Knox College and University Toronto. Or. and In. 21 Feb., 1878. Mar. 21 Nov., 1878, Bella C. Mills of Toronto. Predecessor, James Carswell. No. of com., 132.

Scott, Alex. H., M.A. (Knox Ch., Owen Sound, Ont; Pres. Owen Sound). Or. 22 Aug, 1878. No. of com., 285. Is colleague and successor to Rev. D. Morrison.

Scott, E. (New Glasgow, N.S; Pres., Pictou). Or. 20 Sep, 1875. No. of com., 329.

Scott, James Russell (Cambray, Ont; Pres., Lindsay). S. of Alex. Scott, merchant, Edinburgh. B. in Fifeshire, Scot. Edinburgh University and Secession Hall. Or. June, 1849. Mar. J. C. Halliday. In. to Cambray in 1878. Retired 1875. Was Minister of Creetown, Scot; Perrytown, Ont. and Whitby, Ont. Is Clerk of the Presbytery.

Scott, John, D.D. (North Bruce and Saugeen; Pres., Bruce). S. of John Scott, game keeper, and subsequently keeper of Melrose Abbey. B. at Bowhill, Scot. Knox College, Toronto. Or. 10 Oct, 1850. Mar. 17 Feb, 1857, Elizabeth Lunn. She died 25 July, 1852. In. to present ch.; 28 Apl, 1875. Predecessor William Matheson. No. of com., 189. Previous pastorate, St. Andrew's Ch., London, Ont, 1850 75. In April 1883,

Knox College, Toronto, conferred on him and Principal McVicar the degree of D.D., the first time it had exercised the power recently accorded by Statute.

Scott, John (West Lynne &c; Pres., Manitaba). Or. 29 June, 1853. No. of com., 36.

Scott, John Bain (Knox Ch., Leamington, Ont; Pres., Chatham). S. of Wm. Scott, engineer. B. at Redgorton, Scot. Glasgow University, and St. Andrew's College, Scot. Or. 24 Nov. 1874. Mar 17 Mar, 1875, Margaret Elliot Moscrip. Author of a Brief Outline of Presbyterian Faith and Practice published in 1881. In. to present ch., 1 Sep, 1880. No. of com., 79. Previous pastorate Egmondville, 1874-80. Is member of the University Council of the United Colleges of St. Leonard and St. Salvador, St. Andrews, Scot. and was an associate member of the Pan Presbyterian Council held in Edinburgh July 1877.

Scott, Mathew H., B. A., (Bristol, Que; Pres., Lanark and Renfrew). S. of Henry Scott, farmer, elder in 1st congregation Ermosa. B. there. McGill College of which is gold medallist: Presbyterian College Montreal, where obtained McKay Scholarship. Or. and In. 2 Oct, 1879. Mar. 20th Dec. 1882, Jessie Gray Thomson, of Arnprior. No. of com., 280. Predecessors, Andrew Melville, David Wardrope, Andrew M. Tait and Alex. Maclaren.

Scott, Peter (Hibbert, Ont; Pres., Stratford). Or. 5 March 1872. No. of com., 199.

Scott, Robert (Brooksdale, Ont; Pres., Stratford). S. of Walter Scott, farmer. B. at Hawick, Scot. Knox College, Toronto. Or. 3 Aug. 1875. Mar. M. A. Campbell, 7 Mar, 1868. In to present ch., 2 Feb, 1881. No. of com., 76. Previous pastorate Penetanguishene from Apl, 1875 to Jan, 1881. Was a blacksmith for 16 years prior to entering the ministry.

Scott, Wm. (Bedeque, P. E. Island) Or. 1853. No. of com. 84.

Scouler, Thomas. (Erskine ch., Hamilton, Ont.; Pres., Hamilton). S. of Gavin Scouler. merchant. B. in Avondale, Scot. Knox College, Toronto. Or. and In. 7 December, 1880. Mar. 11 Nov. 1880, Lillian W. Hardie. No. of com. 157.

Scrimger, John M.A. (Presbyterian College, Montreal; Pres. Montreal). S. of John Scrimger, farmer. B. at Galt. Knox College and University, Toronto. Or. 28 Aug. 1873. Mar. 23 April, 1874, Charlotte C. Gairdner. In. Professor of Hebrew, &c., Montreal College, 4 Oct., 1882. Was pastor of St. Joseph st. ch.

Montreal, 1873-82, and in conjunction therewith, lecturer on Hebrew and Greek Exegesis in Presbyterian College, Montreal.

Sedgwick. Robt. D.D. (Middle Musquodoboit, N. S.; Pres., Halifax). Or. Sep. 1836. No. of com. 175.

Sedgwick, Thomas. (Tatamagouche, N. S., Pres., Wallace). S. of Rev. Dr. Sedgwick. B. at Aberdeen, Scot. U. P. Theol. Hall, Edinburgh and Presbyterian College of Nova Scotia. Or. and In. 19 Sep., 1860. Mar. 23 Jan., 1868, Christina P. Macgregor. Predecessors. Hugh Ross, R. Blackwood and Jas. Byers. No. of com. 293. Is Clerk of Presbytery.

Shearer, Wm. (Aylwin, Que.; Pres., Ottawa.) S. of John Shearer, contractor. B. in Kingston, Ont. Presbyterian College, Montreal. Or. 10 Jan., 1881. Mar. 28 Dec., 1880, Isabella Reid Russell. In. to present ch., 31 Aug., 1882. Predecessor, D. McNaughton. No. of com. 94. Ordained missionary at Bearbrook during 1881 and part of 1882.

Shore, Godfrey (Mill Haven, Ont; Pres., Kingston.) No. of com., 55.

Sieveright, Jas., B.A. (Missionary Prince Albert, N.W.T; Pres., Man). S. of Wm. Sieveright, merchant. B. in Aberdeen, Scot. Marschal College and Free Church College, Aberdeen; Queen's College, Kingston. Or. July, 1857. Mar. Aug, 1859, Frances Anne Petrie. Appointed a Missionary for three years in 1880. No. of com., 30. Previous pastorates, Melbourne; Ormstown, and Chelsea, Que; Goderich, Ont The first missionaries were in connection with the Foreign Mission. Rev. Jas. Duncan was the first Home Missionary.

Simpson, Allan (Poplar Grove Ch., Halifax, N.S; Pres., Halifax). S. of Alex. Simpson, farmer and miller. B. at Cavendish, P. E. I. Truro Seminary and Halifax Theological School. Or. 7 Aug, 1866. Mar. 11 July, 1872, J. M. Stuart. In. to present ch., 21 May, 1868. Predecessor, Dr. P. G. McGregor. No. of com., 205. Had a pastorate in Hants Co., 1866–68. No. of com., 382. Is Clerk of the Presbytery.

Simpson, J. A., B. A. (La Have, N.S; Pres., Lunenburg and Shelburne). Or. 16 July, 1873. No. of com., 80.

Sinclair, A. McLean (East River, N. S; Pres., Pictou.) Or. 25 July, 1866. No. of com. 382.

Sinclair, Gavin (Loch Lomond, N. S.; Pres., Sydney). Or. 25 April, 1877. No. of com , 52.

Sinclair, Henry (Uptergrove, Ont; Pres., Lindsay). Or. Nov, 1872. No. of com., 92.

Sinclair, Jas. (Huntley, Ont.) A retired minister attached to the Presbytery of Ottawa.

Sinclair, James (Upper Londonderry; Pres., Truro). Or. 11 Sep, 1867. No. of com., 250.

Smellie, Geo. (Melville Ch., Fergus, Ont; Pres., Guelph). S. of Rev. Jas. Smellie. B. at the Manse of St. Andrews, Orkney. Edinburgh University. Or. 30 March, 1836. Mar. 19 June, 1843, Margt. L. Logie. Author of Memoir of Dr. Bayne, published in 1871. In. to present ch., 13 Dec, 1843. Predecessor, Alex. Gardner. No. of com., 359. Was assistant and successor Lady Parish, North Isles, from 1835 to 1836.

Smith, Alex. (Rapid City, N.W.T.; Pres., Manitoba). Or. 27 Sep, 1866. No. of com., 61.

Smith, Edwin, B.A. (Middle Stewiacke, N.S.; Pres., Truro). Or. 3 Oct, 1871. No. of com., 249.

Smith, Frederick (Amherstburgh, Ont; Pres., Chatham). S. of Geo. Smith, carpenter. B. at Tufton, Eng. Grammar School, Whitechurch, Hants. Or. April, 1867. Mar. 8 July, 1881, Mary Batt. In. to present ch., 4 Aug. 1874. Names of predecessors, Geo. Cheyne, Robt. Peden, Wm. McLaren, Arch. McDermid No. of com., 94. For eight years a minister of the Methodist Episcopal Church.

Smith. J. C., M.A., B.D. (St. Andrew's Ch., Guelph, Pres., Guelph.) Or. July, 1864. No. of com., 335.

Smith, Jas. K., M.A. (Knox Ch.. Galt, Pres., Guelph). S. of Alex. Smith, merchant. B. at Aberdeen, Scot. Marschal and Free Church Colleges, Aberdeen; studied also at Edinburgh under Dr. Chalmers. Or. 13 Jan., 1853. Mar. 20 Oct., 1857, Christina Cumming. In. to present ch. 17 Dec., 1874. Predecessors, J. Stewart, 1832-35, Dr. John Bayne, 1836-59, Dr. John Thomson (now in Scotland), 1861-64. No. of com., 870. Previous pastorates, Ramsay, Ont., 1853-56, Brockville, 1856-65, Galt, 1865-72, Fort Massey, Halifax, N. S., 1872-74. Had charge of First Presbyterian Church in San Francisco for 6 months during winter of 1870-71. Has been twice called to Knox Church, Galt, and settled there.

Smith, John (Erskine Ch., Toronto, Pres., Toronto). S. of Robt. Smith, farmer. B. in the County of Armagh, Ire. Toronto Academy, Knox College and University. Or. 2 Feb., 1851. Mar. 22 Oct., 1851, Elizabeth McArthur. In. to present ch. 20 July, 1875. Predecessor, Dr. John Jennings. No. of com., 350. Previous pastorate, Bowmanville, 1851-75.

Smith, John, W. (Grafton & Vernonville, Ont; Pres., Peterboro.) S. of Arch. Smith, farmer. B. at Garvagh, Ire. Belfast College, Ire. Or. Mar, 1849. In. to present ch. Nov, 1849. Mar. May, 1849, Jessie Sunham. Predecessor, Rev. Dr. Reid. No. of com., 190.

Smith, T. G., D. D. (St. Andrew's Ch., Kingston, Ont; Pres., Kingston). Or 3 Aug, 1856. No. of com., 330. Has recently been In. to St. Andrew's Ch., St. John, N. B.

Smythe, Wm. J., B.A., Ph.D. (Scot & Uxbridge, Ont; Pres. Lindsay) S. Thos. C. Smythe, teacher. B. in Belfast, Ire. Knox College, Toronto, Queen's College, Kingston, Toronto and Illinois Wesleyan Universities. Or. and In. 20 Oct, 1878. Mar. 10 Feb, 1870, Sarah Bagshaw. No. of com., 120. Predecessors, Wm. Cleland, Alex. McClennan. Recently called to First Presbyterian Church, New Carlisle, Ohio.

Somerville, John, B.A., M.A. (Division St. Church, Owen Sound; Pres. Owen Sound) S. of James Somerville, farmer, long an elder in Knox Ch., Vaughan. B. in township of Vaughan. Knox College and University, Toronto. Or. and In. 25 Aug, 1875. Mar. 27 July, 1870, Martha R. Ershaw. Predecessors, *Jas. Gibson, Thos. Stevenson and C. C. Stewart. No. of com., 262. Is Clerk of Presbytery.

Spenser, Adam (Darlington, Ont; Pres., Whitby). Or. 4 Aug, 1868 No. of com., 70.

Stalker, D., B.A., (Gladstone, Man; Pres., Manitoba). Or. 24 July, 1881. No. of com., 57

Stevenson, Archibald (St. Vincent and Sydenham, Ont; Pres., Owen Sound). S. of Wm. Stevenson. B. at Stirling, Scot. Glasgow University; New College, Edinburgh. Or. and In. 20 Jan, 1874. Mar. 10 Feb, 1875, Sebina, dau. of Robert Hall, C.M., Meaford. Predecessors, Robt. McDowall, Arch. Brown. No. of com., 160.

Stevenson, R. (Waubaushene, &c., Ont; Pres., Barrie). An ordained missionary. No. of com., 75.

---

* Rev. Jas. Gibson came to this country in June, 1856, having been Minister of the United Presbyterian Church in Brechin, Scotland. He was minister of the Division Street Ch., Owen Sound, for three years from Sep, 1856, when he accepted a call to New York in the Autumn of 1859 and died there in April, 1860, at the early age of 48. Father of Rev. Dr. J. M. Gibson, of London, Eng.

Stewart, Archibald (North Easthope, Ont; Pres., Stratford). S. of James Stewart, farmer. B. in Argyleshire, Scot. Glasgow and Toronto Universities, and of Knox College, Toronto. Or. 26 Nov, 1862. Mar. Annie Forbes, 1 March, 1864. In. to present ch., 10 Jan, 1877. Predecessor, Daniel Allen, who was minister of the church 37 years. No. of com., 130. Previous pastorate, Mosa, Ont.

Stewart. Alex., B.A. (Clinton, Ont; Pres., Huron). Or. 22 Sep, 1875. No. of com., 270.

Stewart, A. C. (Belmore, &c., Ont; Pres., Saugeen). Or. 13 Oct, 1875. No. of com., 181.

Stewart, Alex. S. (Belfast, P.E.I.; Pres., P.E. Island). Or. 26 March, 1879. No of com., 275.

Stewart, Donald (Wallacetown, Ont; Pres., London). S. of Robert Stewart, farmer. B. in Nova Scotia. Free Church College, Halifax and New College Edinburgh. Or. 31 Oct, 1866. In. to present ch., 7 Oct, 1880. Predecessors, Arch. McDiarmid, N. McDermid and J. A. McDonald. No. of com., 160.

Stewart, James (Arundel and DeSalibury, Que; Pres., Montreal). Or. 10 May, 1859. No. of com., 44.

Stewart, Jas. B. (Castleford, Ont; Pres., Lanark and Renfrew). Or. 5 Jan, 1853. No. of com., 80.

Stewart, Wm. (Hornby, Ont; Pres., Toronto). Or. 22 March, 1848. No. of com., 33.

Stirling, Alex. (Clifton and Granville, P.E.I; Pres., P.E. Island). Or. June, 1857.

Strachan, Donald (Rockwood, Ont; Pres., Guelph). S. of John Strachan, weaver. B. at Kintyre, Scot. Queen's College, Kingston. Or. 8 Sep, 1868. Mar. 1st 21 Sep, 1851, Margaret Reanè; 2nd 17 Jan, 1877, Elizabeth N. Farries. In. to present ch., 28 March, 1876. Predecessors, James Thom, Edward Reeve. No. of com, 100. Previous pastorate, Hillsburgh and Princes' Corner, 1868-76. Rockwood and Eden Mills were formerly united. Separated at induction of Mr. Strachan. Then there were only 17 families at Rockwood, now there are 60.

Straith, John (Shelburne and Primrose, Ont; Pres., Toronto). S. of Wm. Straith, farmer. B. in Scotland. Knox College, Toronto. Or. 31 Jan, 1857. Mar. 15 July, 1857, Mary Bruce. Author of "Fidelity of the Bible," published in 1864. In. to present ch., 1882. No. of com., 178. Previous pastorates, Tilbury, 1857-60; Ingersoll, 1860-71; Paisley, 1871-82.

Straith, Peter, B.A., M.A. (Holstein and Fairbairn, Ont; Pres., Saugeen). S. of Peter Straith. B. in Aberdeen, Scot. Toronto University and Knox College. Or. 26 Sep, 1877. Mar. 28 Dec, 1880, Janet Jackson Martin. In. to present ch.. 9 March, 1880. Predecessor, Hugh Crozier. No. of com., 173. Prior to settlement an ordained missionary at Battleford, Manitoba, 1877-79.

Stuart, James (Toronto). Or. 22 Aug, 1849. A Minister without charge, attached to Presbytery of Toronto.

Stuart, James (Prescott, Ont; Pres., Brockville). Or. 27 Sep, 1872. No. of com., 150.

Stuart, Jas. G., B.A. (Balderson and Drummond, Ont; Pres., Lanark and Renfrew). S. of Rev. Jas. Stuart, a retired minister. B. at Markham, Ont. Queen's College, Kingston. Or. and In. 21 Oct, 1880. No. of com., 108.

Stuart, William (Salem Ch, Greenhill, N.S; Pres., Pictou). S. of Rev. Alex. Stuart, Minister of Lawrencetown, N. S. B. in Aberdeen, Scot. Free Church College and Hall, Halifax· Or. 17 May, 1865. Mar. 30 Oct, 1866, Eliz. Ramsay. In. to present ch., 17 Sep, 1877. Predecessor, Rev. Dr. Patterson. No. of com., 181. Previous pastorates, West Point, P.E.I., 1865-70: Fredericton, N.B., 1870-75.

Sutherland, Alex. (Ripley, Ont; Pres. Maitland.) Or. 14 Mar, 1846. No. of com.. 110.

Sutherland, Donald (Gabarus, N. S; Pres. Sydney.) S. of Nicholas Sutherland, blacksmith and farmer. B. at Earltown, N. S. Halifax Presbyterian College. Or. 6 June, 1860. Mar. July, 1870, Christina McLean, of Pleasant Bay, C. B. In. to present ch., 1875. Predecessors, Isaac McKay, David Drummond. No. of com., 40. Previous pastorates, Cape North, 1860–64; Hays City, United States, 1873–74. Has been extensively engaged in mission work throughout all the Provinces and the Labrador Coast.

Sutherland, Donald, M.A. (Percy and Campbellford; Pres. of Peterboro'.) S. of Alex. Sutherland, farmer. B. in Caithness, Scot. University, and Free Church Theological College, Edinburgh. Or. and In. 11 Nov, 1873. Mar. 17 June, 1875, Mary M. Watson. No. of com., 275. Predecessors, Thos. Alexander, David Beattie.

Sutherland, Geo. (Fingal, Ont; Pres., of London). Or. 14 Nov, 1866. No. of com., 175. Is Clerk of Presbytery.

Sutherland, J. A. F. (Topique, &c., N.B; Pres. of St. John). Or. 4 May, 1864. No. of com., 217.

Sutherland, John M., B.A. (St. James, N. B; Pres. St. John). S. of Wm. Sutherland, farmer. B. at Brook, West River, N. S. Dalhousie College, Halifax, and Edinburgh University. Or. 5 Dec, 1872, by Presbytery of Kintyre, Scot. Mar. 17 June, 1875, Maggie Fraser. In. to present ch. 30 Mar, 1880. Predecessors, Jas. C. Quinn, John Turnbull, Lewis Jack, *et al.* No. of com., 121. Previous pastorate, St. Matthew's ch., Pugwash, 1873–78.

Sutherland, W. R. (Knox Ch., Ekfrid, Ont; Pres., London). S. of Hugh Sutherland, farmer. B. in Scotland. Picton Academy, Edinburgh University and Knox College, Toronto. Or. and In. 28 Feb, 1848. Mar. 1st in 1849, Elizabeth McBean, 2nd in 1859, Miriam Ross. No. of com., 104.

Sym, Fredrick P. (Melbourne and Windsor Mills, Que; Pres., Quebec). S. of William Sym, farmer. B. in Lansingburgh, New York. Glasgow University, Queen's College, Kingston. Or. 29 Sep, 1852. Mar. 1st 8 June, 1854, Isabella Crawford, 2nd 8 Sep, 1875, Margaret N. McMorine. In. to present ch., 17 May, 1881. Predecessors, Dr. McMorine, Robt. McFarlane, Dr. T. G Smith and others. No. of com., 95. Previous pastorates, Woodstock, 1852–55, Russelltown, 1855–60, Beauharnois, 1860–73, Clifton, 1873–81.

Tait, Alexander (Mono Mills, Ont; Pres., Toronto). S. of Donald Tait, farmer, B in Scotland. University and New College, Edinburgh. Or. and In. 28 May, 1878. Mar. 7 Oct, 1882, Margaret H. Wright. No. of com., 179.

Tait, Donald B. A. (Berlin, Ont; Pres., Guelph). S. of Donald Tait, former. B. in Caithness, Scot. University College and Knox College, Toronto. Or. and In. 6 Oct, 1879. Mar. 30 Dec, 1879, Mary B. Wallace, who died 27 Sep, 1881. No. of com., 95. Predecessors, A. C. Geikie, John MacMechan, A. J. Fraser, J. F. Dickie.

Tait, James (Fitzroy, &c., Ont; Pres., Ottawa). Or. 3 Oct, 1866. No. of com., 142.

Tallach, Thos. M. A., (Dresden, &c., Ont; Pres.. Chatham). Or. 24 June, 1857- No. of com., 82

Tanner, Chas, A. (Scarboro, Ont; Pres., Toronto.) S. of Rev. John E. Tanner. B. at Aveze, France. Queen's College, Kingston; Morrin College, Quebec. Or. 27 Oct, 1869. Mar. 27 Dec, 1864, Jane Shaw. In. to present ch. 23 March, 1882. Predecessors, Dr. Jas. George, James Bain, M. McGillivray. No. of com., 313. Previous pastorates, Sherbrooke, Que., 1869, Eglise St. Jean, Montreal. Has been engaged in French mission work from Ottawa to Chicoutimi.

Taylor, Hugh (Pakenham, Ont; Pres., Lanark & Renfrew.) Or. 3 Sep, 1878. No. of com., 105.

Thompson, John (Sarnia, Ont; Pres., Sarnia.) Or. 25 Apl, 1866. No. of com., 290.

Thomson, A. F. (Economy, N.S. Pres., Truro.) S. of Wm. Thomson, farmer. B. at Antigonish, N.S. Dalhousie College and Theological Hall, Halifax. Or. 8 Sep, 1874. Mar. 20 July, 1876, Agnes R. Y. youngest dau. of Hon. W. McKeen of Mabou, N. S. In. to present ch. 18 March, 1879. Predecessors, Andrew Kerr, James Watson, James Thomson, James M. G. McKay. No. of com., 270. Previous pastorate, Mabou, C.B. 1874-70.

Thomson, John, M A. (Knox Ch., Ayr, Ont; Pres., Paris.) Or. 20 Nov, 1871. No. of com., 232.

Thomson, Robert, M.A., D.C.L. (Chippawa and Drummondville, Ont; Pres., Hamilton.) S. of late Rev. Robt. Thomson, minister of Carnock, Scot. B. in Edinburgh, Scot. University & New College, Edinburgh, and Aberdeen New College. Or. 2 Nov, 1863. In. to present ch. 4 Feb, 1879. Predecessors, Robt. Wallace and J. A. F. Macbain. No. of com., 250. Previous pastoral work chiefly on Continent of Europe.

Thomson, Thos. G. (Union Ch., Brucefield, Ont; Pres., Huron). S. of Jas. Thomson, copper-engraver. B. in Parish of Campsie, Scot. University and Free Church College, Glasgow, also Knox College, Toronto. Or. 26 Nov, 1874. Mar. 22 Dec, 1874, Mary Spence. In. to present ch, 21 Feb, 1877. No. of com., 150. Previous pastorate, Duff's Church, McKillop, Winthrop, 1874–77.

Thynne; R. (Knox Ch., Port Dover; Pres., Hamilton). S. of John Thynne, schoolmaster. B. at Morebattle, Scot. Upper Canada College, and Knox College, Toronto. Mar. Isabella Currie, 9 Nov, 1860; she died 3 Nov, 1867. Or. 17 Feb, 18,5. In. to present ch., 5 Oct, 1882. Predecessors, Andrew Wilson and Wm. Craigie. No. of com., 154. Previous pastorates, English Settlement and Proof Line Congregations; Presbytery of London, Feb. 15 to May, 1877; Beverly, 1877–82.

Tibb, J. Campbell, B.D., M.A. (Rapid City, Man.; Pres., Manitoba). S. of Rich'd Tibb, farmer. B. in Peel Co., Ont. University and Knox College, Toronto; Edinburgh University. Or. and In. 15 Dec, 1881. Mar. 12 April, 1882, Mary Craig James. Predecessor, A. Smith. No. of com., 35.

Tolmie, Andrew (Southampton, &c., Ont; Pres., Bruce). Or. 2 June, 1853. No. of com., 325.

Torrance, E. F., M.A. (St. Paul's Ch., Peterboro; Pres., Peterboro). Or. July, 1876. No. of com., 610.

Torrance, Robt. (Guelph, Ont.) Or. 11 Nov, 1846. A minister on retired list, attached to Presbytery of Guelph, of which he is Clerk.

Tully, A. F., (Mitchell, Ont; Pres, Stratford). Or. 10 Feb, 1876.

Tunkansuicuye, Sol. (Sioux Reserve; Pres. Manitoba.) No. of com., 44.

Turnbull, J. A., M.A. (Knox Ch., Goderich, Ont; Pres., Huron) Or. 13 Sept, 1881. No. of com., 365,

Turnbull, Mark (Alice, Ont; Pres. Lanark and Renfrew). Or. 2 Sept, 1873. No. of com., 104.

Ure, Robert, D.D. (Knox Ch., Goderich, Ont; Pres., Huron). S. of John Ure, iron manufacturer. B. in Parish of Shotts, Scot. Knox College, Toronto. Or. 2 Oct, 1850. Mar. 1st, Margaret Gale; 2nd, Mary Fraser, widow of late Sheriff McDonald, of Goderich. In. to present ch. 1862. Predecessors, Charles Fletcher and J. Fraser. No. of com. 300. Previous pastorate, Streetsville, Ont. Had degree of Doctor of Divinity conferred by Queen's College, Kingston.

Urquhart, Alex (Dunwich, Ont; Pres., London). Or. 5 Jan, 1871. No. of com., 117.

Waddell, A. W. (Harwich, Ont; Pres., Chatham). Or. 30 Nov, 1847. No. of com., 207.

Waits, Wallace, B.A. (Chatham, N.B; Pres., Miramichi). Or 13 June, 1872. No. of com., 300.

Walker, George (New Glasgow, N. S.; Pres., Pictou.) Or. 1838. Pastor Emeritus Union Church, New Glasgow.

Walker, William (Chatham, Ont.; Pres., Chatham.) S. of David Walker, merchant. B. in Glasgow, Scot. Glasgow University. Or. Oct, 1853. Mar. 30 Oct, 1857, Janet Smith. In. to present ch., 30 June, 1857. Predecessors, – McFaddyen and John Fraser. No. of com. 230. Previous pastorates, Ramsay, Isle of man, 1853-57. Is Clerk of Presbytery.

Walker, Wm. P. (Binbrook and Saltfleet, Ont; Pres., Hamilton.) S. of James Walker, merchant. B. at Lochwinnoch, Scot. University and Free Church, Theological College, Glasgow. Or. 31 Jan, 1872. Mar. 11 June, 1873, Margaret A. Fortune. In. to present ch., 5 Sep, 1875. Predecessor, Geo. Cheyne. No. of com. 140. Previous pastorate, from Jan, 1872, to Sep, 1875, Ancoster, East and West. Was licensed by the Presbytery of Irvine, Scot. First appointment assistant to Dr. Patterson, Sunderland. Then Strathblane in Sterlingshire. Previous to coming to Canada, missionary in the Broad Close Mission, Greenock.

Wallace, John B.A., Warwick, Bermuda, N. S.; Pres., Halifax.) Or. 17 Feb, 1875.

Wallace, Robt. (West Ch., Toronto; Pres., Toronto). S. of Samuel Wallace, farmer. B. in the County of Monaghan, Ire. Queen's College, Kingston. Knox College, Toronto. Or. 15 July, 1846. Mar. 3 Sep, 1850, Marianne Barker, of Ingersoll. Has published several pamphlets and sermons on temperance. In. to present ch.. 6 Nov, 1867. Predecessor, James Baikie. No. of com., 450. Previous pastorates, Clanabel, 1846-47; Ingersoll, 1849-60; Dunnville, 1862-67.

Warden, R. H. (Montreal). Or. 15 Nov, 1866. Is agent for the church.

Wardrope, David, (Teeswater, Ont; Pres., Bruce.) S. of Rev. Thos Wardrope. B. in Scotland. Knox College, Toronto. Or. June, 1855. Mar. Jane G. Gray, 15 Aug, 1855. In. to present ch. 31 Jan, 1871. No. of com., 160. Previous pastorate, Bristol, P.Q., from June, 1855 to Nov, 1868.

Wardrope, Thos., D.D. (Chalmers Ch., Guelph; Pres., Guelph). S. of Thos. Wardrope, school-teacher. B. at Ladykirk, Scot. Or. 13 Aug, 1845. Mar. 6 Feb, 1844, Sarah Masson. In. to present ch., 30 Sep. 1869. No. of com., 353. Previous pastorate, Knox Ch., Ottawa, 1845-69.

Watson, Jas., M.A. (2nd Presbyterian Ch., Huntingdon Que; Pres., Montreal). S. of John Watson, farmer. B. at Middlemuir, Scot. King's College and University, Aberdeen. Or. 29 Aug, 1849. Mar. 11 May, 1854, Margaret F., second dau. of Rev. Adam Lind, Minister of Whitehill, Scot. In. to present ch., 8 Nov. 1854. Predecessor, Peter D. Muir. No. of com., 80. Previous pastorate, Walker, Eng. Was for eight years Clerk of Presbytery of Montreal Can. Pres. Ch., and is Clerk of Synod of Montreal and Ottawa.

Weir, George, M A., LL.D. (Morrin College, Quebec; Pres. Quebec.) S. of Patrick Weir, farmer. B. in parish of Aberdour, Scot. King's College, Aberdeen. Is a licentiate of the Church. Mar. in 1856, Williamina Lowe. Appointed in 1864 Professor of Classical Literature, Logic and Hebrew, Morrin College, and previous thereto was, for 11 years, Professor of Classical Literature in Queen's College.

Wells, John, M A. (East Williams, Ailsa Craig, Ont; Pres. Sarnia) S. of Robt. Wells, farmer. B. in parish of Johnstone, Scot. Glasgow University. Or. Aug, 1861. Mar. 4 Feb, 1868, Annabella, dau. of Rev. Jas. Steven, first Presbyterian Minister in Restigouche, N. B. In. to present ch. 24 July, 1877. Predecessors, Robt. Chambers, – McLeod, Robt. Stevenson. No. of com., 79. Previous pastorate, New Richmond, Que., 1861–76.

Wellwood, Jas. M., B.A. (Minnedosa, Man.; Pres. Manitoba) S. of Wm. Wellwood, merchant. B. in Co. Leeds, Ont. McGill University, Montreal Presbyterian College. Or. 16 Sep, 1873. Mar. 2 June, 1874, Sarah J. Mitchell. In. to present ch. 1 June, 1881. No. of com., 33. Previous pastorate, Cote des Neiges, Montreal, 1873–81.

Whillans, Robt., B.A. (Nepean & Bells Corners, Ont; Pres. Ottawa.) Or. 26 Sep, 1872. No. of com., 135.

White, Jos., B.A. (Rochesterville, Ont; Pres. Ottawa.) Or. 7 Aug, 1862. No. of com., 100. Is Clerk of Presbytery.

Whittier, J. S. (Little Bay, Nfld.; Pres., Newfoundland). Or. 10 May, 1880.

Whittier, W. S. (Chalmer's Ch., Halifax; Pres., Halifax). Or. Apl, 1880. No. of com., 180.

Wilkie, John (Pres., Guelph). Or. 9 Sep, 1879. A missionary to India.

Williamson, Jas. LL.D., (Kingston Ont; Pres., Kingston). Or. 25 Feb, 1845. One of the Professors in Queen's College.

Wilson, Andrew (Brock St. Ch., Kingston ; Pres., Kingston). S. of Andrew Wilson. B. in County Down, Ireland. Victoria College, Cobourg, and Knox College, Toronto. Or. Jan, 1851. In. to present ch., 10 Nov, 1853. Previous thereto was pastor for three years of the united congregations of Port Down, Simcoe and Victoria. Mar. 1st in June, 1851, to Sophia Jane Wright, of Toronto; who died in April, 1871. 2nd in Aug, 1877, to Elizabeth Knight, of Halifax. No. of com., 220. Predecessor, Robert Reed. Has recently been inducted to Carlton Street Church, Toronto.

Wilson, Andrew (Markdale, Ont; Pres., Sangeen). Or. 16 Aug, 1881. No. of com., 104.

Wilson, James., M.A. (Lanark. Ont; Pres. of Lanark and Renfrew). Or. 14 July 1856. No. of com. 112.

Wilson, Matthew, M.A. (Sydney Mines and N. Sydney, N.S; Pres. Sydney). Or. June, 1842. No. of com., 126.

Wilson, Thos. (Caledonia, Ont; Pres. of Hamilton.) Or. 28 Apl, 1863. No. of com., 77.

Wilson, W. A., B.A., M.A. (Knox ch., St Mary's Ont; Pres. Stratford.) S. of Andrew Wilson, farmer. B. at Nelson, Ont. University and Knox College, Toronto. Or. and In. 19 Nov, 1878. Mar. 25 Dec, 1879, Margaret E. Caven. No of com., 138.

Congregation organized in May, 1878, with 63 members. Church costing $10,000 opened Oct, 1880; debt removed April, 1881.

Wishart, David (Madoc, Ont; Pres. Kingston.) Or. 6 April, 1857. No. of com., 112.

Wright, John Knox (King st. ch., London; Pres of London.) S. of Rev. Walter Wright. B. in London, Eng. Knox College, Toronto. Or. and In. 18 Oct; 1880. Mar. 18 Oct, 1880, Florence Corlett. No. of com., 116.

Wright, Peter (Knox ch., Stratford, Ont, Pres. Stratford.) Or. 23 Aug, 1870. No. of com., 490.

Windell, W. O. (Lotus, Ont.) A minister on retired list, attached to Presbytery of Peterboro.

Wyllie, A. L. (Richmond Ch., Halifax, N. S.; Pres., Halifax). Or. 12 Aug, 1852. No. of com., 39.

Yeomans, Geo. A., B A. (Knox Ch., Dunnville, Ont; Pres., Hamilton). S. of David P. Yeomans, A.M., M.D., Professor of Chemistry in Lafayette College, Easton, Penn., afterwards a physician in Ontario. Queen's College, Kingston, and Princeton Theological Seminary, N. J. Or. 22 Sep, 1869. Mar. 14 Nov, 1872, Sophronia Hendry of, Conestogo. In. to present ch., 25 April, 1876. Predecessors, W. Porterfield, Robt. Jameison, John Rennie, Robt. Fleming. No. of com., 95. Previous pastorate, Winterbourne. About 1874 and 1875, the congregation of Dunnville was almost extinct.

Young, Alex. (Napanee, Ont; Pres., Kingston). Or. 8 Jan, 1857. No. of com., 97.

Young, Stephen (Clifford, Ont; Pres., Saugeen). Or. 19 Sep, 1866. No. of com., 143. Is Clerk of Presbytery.

Young, W. C. (Toronto). Or. 6 Sep, 1854. A minister without charge, attached to Presbytery of Toronto.

III. RETIREMENT OF MINISTERS &c.

1. *Legislation*, 1877.

Halifax, p. 46. The Assembly resolved—That the whole question of the status of retired ministers be remitted to Presbyteries for consideration, and that the names which are already on the Roll be retained in the meantime.

1878.—Hamilton, p. 35. The Assembly resolved—That the names of ministers who have received leave from the Assembly to retire, shall be retained on the Rolls of their respective Presbyteries with the understanding that they have liberty to take part in the deliberations of the Court, but not to vote.

Page 53. Presbyteries were also reminded that all applications for retirement, should give a statement of the reasons on which such applications are based. and their judgment thereon.

Page 36. The Assembly resolved—That the names of ordained Missionaries employed for one year or a longer period, by Presbyteries on particular Mission Districts with the sanction of the Assembly's Home Mission Committee be placed on the Roll of the presbytery within whose bounds they labor.

1879.—Ottawa, p. 27. The Assembly resolved—That the question of retaining on the Roll of their respective Presbyteries the names of Ministers who have been permitted by the General Assembly to retire on account of age or infirmity from the actual duties of the Ministry, and who continue to reside within the bounds of the Presbytery to which they had belonged, be remitted to the Presbyteries of the Church for consideration.

2. *Permanent Act,* 1880.

Montreal, p. 51. The Assembly resolved—That with the approval of the majority of the Presbyteries of the Church as shown by the returns to the remit of 1879 the names of Ministers who have retired from the active duties of the Ministry with the leave of the Assembly, be retained on their respective Presbytery Rolls, such Ministers retaining all their judicial functions as long as they reside within the bounds of the several Presbyteries in which they resided at the time of their retirement.

3. *Title of Pastor Emeritus not Sanctioned*

St. John N.B., 1882, p. 51. Resolved—The Presbytery decline at present to sanction the title of *Pastor Emeritus* but instruct the Committee of the Aged and Infirm Ministers' Fund to consider by what, if any, special designation Ministers should be known who have received leave to retire by the General Assembly.

4. *Foreign Missionaries on Presbytery Rolls.*

Page 30. The Assembly resolved—That the names of the Ministers of the Church who are engaged in Foreign Mission work, be placed on the Rolls of the Presbyteries of the Church within the bounds of which they resided at the time of their several appointments.

5. *Ministers permitted to retire.*

1876.—Revds. D. Allan, John Cook, D.D.; Andrew Donald, S. C. Fraser, M.A.; M. W. Livingstone, J. Paterson, J. M. Roger, M.A.

1877.—Revds. Wm. Barrie, D.D.; R. Dewar, Thos. Macpherson.

1878.—Revds. Wm. Graham, Alex. Kennedy, H. McLeod, D.D.; Geo. Walker.

1879.—Revds. James Dick, Wm. Forrest, Wm. Fraser, D.D.; Wm. Hancock.

1880.—Revds. Wm. Barr, Wm. Duff, J. Hanran, Geo. Lawrence, W. C. Young, Wm. Wright.

1881.—Revds. Wm. Bain, D.D.; R. Hall, Thos. Lowry, J. D. McGregor.

1882.—Revds. J. Bennett, D.D.; S. Bernard, G. W. Forbes, J. Gray, M.A.; C. G. Glass; Fredk. Home, Dr. Mann, A. P. Millar, Wm. McCullogh, John Porteous, R. Renwick, John Scott, D.D.; R. Sedgwick, D.D.; M. Stewart, M.A.; W. C. Windell, W. D. Whinster, R. Torrance, J. Jenkins, D.D.; Dr. Elliott, D. Ross.

6. *Ministers, Professors and Officers in Colleges.*

Revds. Geo. Bell, M.A., LL.D.; Geo. Bryce, M.A., LL.B; J. Campbell, M.A.; Wm. Caven, D.D.; J. Currie, D. Coussirat, B.D., B.A.; W. J. Dey, M.A.; John Forrest, Alex. Fowler, Geo. D. Ferguson, B.A.; Geo. Monro Grant, M.A., D.D.; Wm. Gregg, M.A., LL.D.; Thos. Hart, M.A.; Alex. F. Kemp, M.A., LL.D.; J. B. Mowat, M.A.; Alex. McKnight, D.D.; Wm. McLaren, D.D.; D. H. MacVicar, D.D., LL.D.; Allan Pollok, D.D.; J. Scrimger, M.A.; Geo. Weir, M.A., LL.D.; James Williamson, M.A., LL.D.

7. *Ministers—Agents of the Church.*

Revds. Wm. Reid, D.D.; P. G. McGregor, D.D.; R. H. Warden, James Robertson.

8. *Ministers, Otherwise Without Charges.*

Revds. James Bain, J. Barclay, D.D., J. Baxter, D. Blue, J. Brown, Wm. Burns, A. Burr, W.B. Clark, Wm. Coutts, H. Crawford, A. Cross, Wm. Doak, J. Duff, P. Fleming, C. Fletcher, Wm. Fotheringham, Thos. Fraser, J. Gould, Moses Harvey, M. A., A. Hudson, Wm. Inglis, W.H. Jamieson, J. Jones, Wm. Maxwell, Wm. Meldrum, J. Wm. Mitchell, R Monteath, Thos. McAdam, R. D. McKay, D. McKenzie, Wm. McKee, B A., Thos. McKee, G. A. McLachlin, Alex. McLaren, C. D. McLaren, R. G. McLaren, D. McMillan, J. H. Nelson, H. Niven, S. Porter, Ebenezer Ross, Godfrey Shore, J. Sinclair, J. Stuart, and James Thompson.

9. *Missionaries and Probationers,* 1881-2.

Revds. J. Anderson, A.B. Baird, D. Beattie, T. Bouchard, J.M. Boyd, A.H. Cameron, Alex. Campbell, J.H. Cameron, Dr. Collins, D Currie, J.R. Cragie, W. Callagher, J. Coomacto, B.D., J. Douglas, R. P. Duclos, J. Dunbar, E. J. Edmunds, A. Findlay, J. Ferguson, D. Farquharson, J. Ferries, J. R. Fitzpatrick, S. W. Fisher, T. Fenwick, D. Findlay, W. Galloway, J. Geddes, A. Glendinning, R. F. Gurnay, J. Herald, J.G. Henderson, J. Howie, And. Henderson, Wm. Hodnett, J. A. Hay, R. Jamieson, D.C. Johnson, J.R. Kean, P.S. Livingstone, E.B.M. Millard, A. Matthews, James McKenzie, Alex. Mackenzie, D. L. McKechnie, D.H. McLennan, W. R. McCulloch, Farquhar McRae, A. McLean, Hugh McPhadyan, H. McKay, J. McKay, H. McKellar, D. McNaughton, D. McRae, A. McFarlane, R. Nairn, W.S. Oxley, S. Polson,. J W. Penman, Wm. Peattie, W.R. Ross, A. Rogers, Wm. Reeve, W. D. Rees, J. M. Reikie, J. S. Stewart, John Stewart, G. A. Smith, A. Smith, J. Scott, D. Stalker, A.Sillars, J. Sieveright, R. G. Sinclair, James Stewart, W. Shearer, R. Stevenson, J. C. Tibb, Ed. Thoope, J. A. Townsend, Wm. Turnbull, E. Vincent, Wm. White, Robt. Watt, J. Wellwood.

Summary.

Retired by permission of the Assembly, 47. In Colleges, 22, Agents of the Church, 4. Without Charges otherwise, 49. Missionaries and Probationers in the Home field, East and West, 85. Total, 207.

THE CHURCH—ITS MISSIONS.

UNION RESOLUTION.

Minutes, 1875, p 6. The United Church shall heartily take up and prosecute the Home and Foreign Missionary and benevolent operations of the several churches, according to their respective claims; and with regard to the practical work of the Church and the promotion of the schemes, whilst the General Assembly shall have the supervision and control of all the work of the Church, yet the United Church shall have due regard to such arrangements, through Synods and Local Committees, as shall tend most effectually to unite in Christian love and sympathy the different sections of the Church, and at the same time to draw forth the resources and energies of the people in behalf of the work of Christ in the Dominion, and throughout the world.

REGULATIONS OF THE GENERAL ASSEMBLY.

I HOME MISSIONS.

1. Regulations.

Minutes, 1876, pages 47, 48, 49, 50. 1. There shall be a Central Committee for Home Missions, dividing itself into two sections, the one embracing the Maritime Provinces and the other the rest of the Church.

2. The Assembly shall appoint annually a Home Mission Committee. consisting of forty-five members, of whom one-third shall be from the Maritime Provinces and two-thirds from the rest of the Church. Each of these divisions shall constitute a sub-Committee for the carrying on of Mission work within its own territory.

Each section shall be empowered to act separately in conducting operations within its own territory.

3. The operations of the Committee shall have respect to—

(1) Mission Stations, which, having been recommended by Presbyteries and approved by the Committee, shall be placed on the list of aid-receiving Stations and Mission Stations, directly under the care of the H. M. Committee; provided always that no application for aid shall be entertained by the Committee on behalf of any station, unless the Presbytery of the bounds shall

have made arrangements with the people for contributing according to their ability to the salary of the Missionary; and the Presbytery shall see to the implementing of such engagements. The Committee shall make like arrangements in the case of stations directly under its care.

(2) Mission Stations reported by Presbyteries, but not receiving aid.

(3) Congregations not self-sustaining, but prepared to contribute at least four hundred dollars ($400) per annum, at the rate of at least four dollars fifty cents ($4.50) per communicant, and seven dollars ($7.00) per family, and in which, in the judgment of the Presbytery, a pastor is desirable. Such congregations, having made application to the Presbytery of the bounds, and furnished satisfactory information in regard to their statistics, financial position and prospects, and having received the approval of the Presbytery, (which application and information shall also be laid before the sub-Committee), may be placed on the list of congregations receiving supplement. Cases in which the application of this rule appears to affect injuriously the congregations now upon the list or seeking to be placed on it, shall be reported to the General Assembly, and supplements granted to them only when its sanction has been given.

4. The system adopted hitherto in differennt sections of the Church—in the Maritime Provinces, of two funds, one for Home Missions proper and another for suplimenting the stipends of Ministers in weak congregations, administered by two Committees; and in the Western section of the Church, of one fund for both objects administered by one Committee—be continued for the present year, and that it be sent down to Presbyteries to consider the subject and report to the next General Assembly.

5. The list of Missionaries shall consist of Licentiates and ordained Ministers of this Church, also Students of Divinity and Catechists, duly approved as the Assembly may direct. Each of these Missionaries shall be recommended to the Committee by some Presbytery.

6. The Committee shall prepare and send down to Presbyteries and through Presbyteries to Missionaries blank forms for their reports, so as to ascertain the peculiar circumstances, necessities and general state of the mission stations and supplemented congregations throughout the Church.

7. The sub-Committees shall consider the reports thus rendered by Presbyteries and distribute the Missionaries among the Presbyteries, as, in view of the detailed information before them, may be deemed advisable.

8. The sub-Committees shall give to mission stations and supplemented congregations, in paying their Missionaries or Ministers, such aid as, in view of the detailed information before them, may be deemed advisable.

9. The General Committee shall prepare a full annual report of all the Home Mission and Supplemental operations of the Church, to be submitted to the Assembly, and shall publish from time to time such information as may serve to call forth the interests and liberality of the Church.

10. The sub-committees shall be empowered to establish mission stations and conduct missionary operations directly in those parts of the Dominion which are not within the bounds of any Presbytery.

11. In mission fields placed directly under the Home Mission Committee, and in new and destitute fields of wide extent within the bounds of Presbyteries, the sub-Committees shall be empowered—in the latter case acting in concert with the Presbytery of the bounds—to secure the services of suitable Missionaries, who may be willing to occupy them for a term of years, and to pay them in excess of the ordinary salaries paid to Missionaries.

12. The Committee shall not be responsible for the salary of Missionaries beyond the amount of aid promised by it to the stations or congregations, and for the time during which they may have laboured in said stations or congregations.

13. The amount of salary to be paid by each congregation, station, or group of stations, shall be determined by the Presbytery of the bounds, and specified to the sub-Committee, and there shall be paid by the Presbytery and sub-Committee conjointly for a Licentiate or Ordained Minister a minimum of eight dollars ($8) per Sabbath with board; for a Student of divinity, during the summer, at the rate of six dollars ($6) per sabbath, with board and travelling expenses to the field of labour; and for a Catechist, of five dollars ($5) per Sabbath, with board.

14. The amount of aid granted to any congregation receiving supplement shall in no case exceed the amount necessary to make the salary of the Minister from all sources seven hundred dollars ($700.) But the sub-Committees are empowered to supplement, beyond that amount, the salaries of ordained Ministers engaged in mission work in towns and cities.

15. The supplement of all aid-receiving congregations shall be calculated from the first day of the ecclesiastical year, and Presbyteries are instructed to make their reports accordingly—supplements being payable half-yearly.

Minutes 1876, p. 55, 56 16. Presbyteries are instructed, at an ordinary meeting previous to the first of October in each year, to revise the list of Mission-stations and Supplemented Congregations, and make such changes as they may deem necessary, reporting the amended list to the sub-Committees. The list, thus amended, shall form the basis of the operations of the Committee for the then current year.

17. Presbyteries are enjoined to furnish information to the sub-Committees in accordance with the requirements of the above scheme, and to co-operate with the Committee.

18. All congregations and mission stations are enjoined to make an annual contribution in the Western sections of the Church to the Home Mission Fund; and in the Maritime Provinces to the Home Mission Fund and Supplemental Fund.

19. The travelling expenses of members of Committee shall be borne equally by the two funds, and the cost of all exploring and aggressive missionary work, undertaken and sanctioned by Presbyteries, shall be defrayed out of the Home Mission Fund.

20. In regard to arrears due by supplemented congregations to their Ministers, these congregations shall be required to report to the Committee, through the Presbytery, in the form provided, before the beginning of each ecclesiastical year, the amount paid by them as stipends during the previous twelve months; and in cases, where the amount falls short of the stipend promised by them, power shall be given to suspend the payment of the supplements until the arrearages are liquidated.

Page 57. The Assembly appreciate the important services rendered to the Church by the Students' Missionary Associations connected with our Colleges; and, in order to secure the best results from their operations, desire Presbyteries to point out to the Associations such fields within their bounds as may be taken up by the Students with advantage.

Page 58. At least one joint meeting of the two sub-Committees of the Home Mission Committee shall be held each year, in order to secure the co-operation of the Eastern section of the Church in Mission work in Manitoba, as well as to promote the General interests of the Church's Missions.

British Columbia.

Page 57. The General Assembly, while preferring that all mission work in British Columbia, as it is a part of the Dominion, were conducted nominally in connection with this Church, and hoping that matters may soon shape themselves in that direction, meanwhile express their satisfaction at the liberal provision made for sustaining ordinances in that Province by the Church of Scotland. Mr. Jamieson, our Missionary in that Province, and his congregation are hereby allowed, if they see fit, to connect themselves with the Presbytery of British Columbia, in connection with the Church of Scotland—the grant proposed by the Committee to be sanctioned and continued, and his relation to the Ministers' Widows' and Orphans' Fund to remain unchanged by such action, on condition of his still paying the Ministerial rate and procuring an annual contribution to that fund from his congregation.

Minutes, 1877, p. 33. As the Trustees of New Westminster Church in British Columbia, have complied with the conditions imposed by a former assembly, the sum of twelve hundred dollars ($1,200), for the past year is hereby granted to Mr Jamieson, and the Assembly request him, in order to the continuance of the grant, to send the necessary statistics either directly through the Session or through the Presbytery with which he is connected.

Minutes, 1878, p. 30. The congregation in New Westminster is hereby instructed to furnish regularly to the Home Mission Committee a statement of its affairs, either directly through its Pastor or the Presbytery of which he is a member.

Manitoba.

1. Require each station, or group of stations, hereafter to guarantee a certain sum per annum, or for each Sabbath's supply according to the ability of the people.

2. Instruct the Presbytery of Manitoba to forward before the 1st October in each year, to the Home Mission Committee, a statement of the amount which each station has agreed to pay, and which, in the opinion of the Presbytery is an equitable sum to be contributed by each station.

Page 34. 3. Recommend the Presbytery to take steps when a minimum contribution of three hundred dollars ($300) per annum from any field is reached, to have the congregation call a Pastor in regular form.

4. Instruct the Home Mission Committee to take steps to obtain such additional Missionaries as in their judgment may be necessary for that field ; and further, empower those members of the Home Mission Committee, who may be present at this meeting to take the requisite action with a view to this end.

2. Instructions to Presbyteries, 1877.

Minutes, p. 34. 1. The Assembly enjoin Presbyteries to deal with those congregations, which have not contributed to the Home Mission Fund.

2. A congregation, which does not return full statistics and contribute to the Schemes of the Church shall not receive aid.

3. In regard to the continuous supply of Mission stations the Assembly instruct Presbyteries to aim at so grouping stations as to afford full employment for an active Minister—a considerable portion of the salary being derived from the field in which he labours.

4. Recommend that the salaries of suitable missionaries, accepting an engagement for more than one year, shall be on such a scale of remuneration as may be deemed appropriate by the Home Mission Committee.

5. Suggest that an effort be made to secure the services of our young men, so soon as they have been licensed, for engagements in the mission-fields for a term of not less than two years.

6. Permit Presbyteries to ordain such Missionaries, when it is deemed necessary, with a view to labouring for such term in a particular field, and confer on them the full privilege of Ministers of the Church.

7. Instruct Presbyteries to see that Missionary Associations be established in all the congregations within their bounds.

3. INSTRUCTIONS TO H. M. COMMITTEE, 1877.

8. Commend to the consideration of the Home Mission Committee the suggestion regarding the employment of lay agency, brought before the House in the Overture from the Presbytery of Barrie.

9. Appoint a Committee to develope a more detailed scheme on the basis of the above recommendations, and to report through the Home Mission Committee to the next General Assembly, Dr. Cochrane, *Convener.*

10. The Assembly consider it inexpedient to entertain this year the proposal, made by the Presbytery of Toronto, to divide the Home Mission fund of the Western section.

11. The Assembly adopt the recommendation of the Home Mission Committee regarding the congregations of St. Sylvester, Mille Isles, Farnham Centre, Proton, Camden and Sheffield. That they be placed on the Supplemental List and receive—the three first $200, the fourth $100 and the fifth $150 per annum.

12. In view of the want of funds, which at certain seasons occasions difficulty, the Assembly recommend the Treasurers of congregations to send to the General Treasurers all moneys for any of the Schemes so soon as they have been collected; such congregations being expected to forward to these Treasurers a report, so soon as they have decided upon the allocation of the money to the several Schemes of the Church.

Page 35. 13. The Assembly hereby empower the Western sub-Committee to grant to weak congregations in distant or destitute fields such aid as may in their judgment be necessary, although this aid may be in excess of the amount permitted by the rules which are laid down for the guidance of the Committee, with instruction to report their action in all such cases to the General Assembly.

14. The Assembly deem it inexpedient to adopt so radical a change in the mode of conducting the Home Mission work as is proposed in the Overture from the Presbytery of London, anent an assignment of the management thereof to the several Synods of the Church.

15. The Assmbly rejoice to learn that the effort made last year by the Western sub-Committee to liquidate the debt has been so successful as to realize the sum of eight thousand seven hundred and ninety-one dollars ($8,791)—almost the entire amount required; and at the same time regret to observe that several Presbyteries have failed to contribute that portion of the assessment assigned to them.

4. Resolution of Assembly, 1878.

Minutes, p. 30. 1. The existing arrangements regarding the payment of Missionaries in Manitoba are continued, viz.:—That a salary of nine hundred ($900) and seven hundred dollars ($700) be paid to married and unmarried Missionaries respectively, irrespective of other sources of income.

2. Presbyteries are earnestly recommended to see that Missionary Associations are formed in each congregation under their care.

3. In regard to localities, where assistance may be needed from the Board of French Evangelization and the Home Mission Committee, arrangements shall be made for a joint meeting of sub-Committees, in order to secure the necessary co-operation.

4. Presbyteries are recommended to use due diligence in making a thorough investigation of every new application, which may be presented to the Home Mission Committee, for support.

Page 31. 5. The Assembly express approval generally of the scheme for the continuous supply of Mission Stations for the Western Section, sanction action in accordance with its provisions as far as practicable, under the approval of the Home Mission Committee, and re-appoint the Committee of last General Assembly, with instructions to perfect the same, and report to next Assembly—Mr. Bruce, Convener.

6. Congregations, collecting their contributions to the Mission Schemes by monthly or quarterly subscriptions, are recommended to send forward their contributions to the Treasurers of the Church without unnecessary delay.

7. All congregations and Mission Stations are hereby enjoined to contribute to the Home Mission funds of the Church.

8. The Assembly, in recognizing the important services rendered by the Students' Missionary Associations, renew the advice tendered to such Associations by the General Assembly of 1876. (See page .)

9. The Assembly refer to the Committee on Statistics for consideration the recommendation of the Committee on Supplements anent the opening of a new column in the Statistical Tables for contributions to the Supplementing Scheme of the Synod of the Maritime Provinces.

10. The Assembly continue the Committee on Supplements in the Maritime Provinces, and earnestly commend the scheme to the increased liberality of the Church in that Section.

5. Resolutions of Assembly, 1879.

Minutes, pp. 48-49. That the Assembly approve of the changes suggested by the Committee on Continuous Supply; and Grant leave to the Committee of the Western Section to supplement the congregations of Balsover and Vittoria, as asked by the Presbyteries of Lindsay and Hamilton respectively.

2. That the Assembly approve of the resolution of the Superintending Committee of the Maritime Provinces respecting the payment of the half-yearly supplements due on the first day of July next, with this modification, that one-half to be obtained by loan shall be paid on the first of July, and the other half so soon as the funds are supplied by the congregations, which result it is confidently hoped will be realized before the first of October.

3. That the proposal of the Committee of the Western Section as to the reduction of the salaries of the Missionaries in Manitoba be not acceded to; but that these salaries be paid as heretofore, and that the attention of the Presbytery of Manitoba be specially directed to the eleventh recommendation.

4. That the request of the Committee of the Eastern Section as to Manitoba College, be not acceded to; but that the Committee be required to contribute five hundred dollars ($500), and the Committee of the Western Section two thousand dollars ($2,000), as hitherto, for the support of the College in Manitoba.

5. That the Assembly shall approve of the estimate of the amount required for the coming year, based on the payment in full of grants for the current six months: *Western Section*: Debt, ($11,000) eleven thousand dollars. For the current year, ($35,000) thirty-five thousand dollars. Total estimate, ($46,000) forty-six thousand dollars. *Eastern Section:* Debt, ($2,400) two thousand four hundred dollars. For the current year, ($11,000) eleven thousand dollars. Total estimate, ($13,400) thirteen thousand four hundred dollars.

6. That, instead of making a special appeal for the removal of the present deficits, there be but one appeal for the deficits and the current year's expenditure combined, and that congregations be instructed to forward contributions to the respective Treasurers as early as possible, as there is due on the first of October (including the present debt) about thirty-two thousand dollars ($32,000), so as to warrant the Committee's paying in full all grants, and to render unnecessary the reduction of twenty-five per cent. as contemplated by the Committee of the Western Section.

7. That a Committee be appointed, the Moderator, Convener, to prepare a short appeal, to be signed by the Moderator, to the members and adherents of the Church, setting forth the conditions and requirements of the Fund, and enjoin every Minister to read this appeal from the pulpit on some Lord's Day on or before the last Sabbath of September next, and to afford opportunity to every individual to contribute by subscription or in any other way that the Session or the Deacons' Court may have previously resolved upon. The Assembly further enjoin Presbyteries to take order at their first meeting thereafter that this injunction has been complied with, and report to next Assembly. The Assembly further require that a copy of the appeal be addressed to each Presbytery, together with a statement of the amount which may reasonably be expected as the fair proportion of the Presbytery's share of the total sum required.

8. The Assembly instruct the Committees, in their future administration of the Fund, to equalize the expenditure and income of each year, and to entertain no applicants for new grants or for the continuance of old grants, for either Supplemented Congregations or Mission Stations, until there be laid on the table of the Committee an Extract Minute of the Presbytery making the application, showing that the grants have been

revised since the meeting of Assembly, and that deputies have visited the Supplemented Congregations and Mission Stations within the bounds, with a view to the reduction of the grants.

9. The Assembly instruct the Committees to entertain no new applications for grants until the state of the Fund shall warrant them in so doing.

10. The Assembly instruct the Western Section of the Home Committee to take such action as may secure the payment in full of the twenty-five per cent. which the Committee were reluctantly constrained, from lack of funds, to withold from the several Presbyteries of the Church in April last for services rendered during the preceding half-year.

From this decision Messrs. John Laing and Straith dissented.

The Assembly agreed to print the foregoing resolutions, with instructions to forward a copy thereof to each Presbytery without delay.

Changes referred to in first Resolution.

Minutes, 1879, app. p. 22. I. That in clause (3) in (II) instead of the words "who are willing to engage in this work" the following be inserted :—"who may in exceptional cases be engaged in this work.

II. That in the case of Students the term of appointment be for eighteen months, in place of two years.

III. That the following blank form be prepared and distributed to Presbyteries, and that it be required that a copy of this, duly filled, accompany every application to the Home Mission Committee, for supply under the provisions of this scheme.

Blank Form for Continuous Supply.

A copy of this form duly filled must accompany each application to the Home Mission Committee for supply under the provisions of this scheme.

1st. Name or destination of field and its location.

2nd. Distances apart from Presbyterian Churches nearest to the field.

3rd. Number and denomination of other Churches in or near the field.

4th. Estimated total number of families of all denominations within the range of the field.

5th. Number of families professedly Presbyterian.
" Communicants " "

6th. Number of families not attached to any Church.

7th. General character of the field and prospects as to its growth and development

8th. Amount per annum to be raised by the field or provided some other way in connection with it?

9th. Is the field taken up by the Church now for the first time?

10. If not, how long has it been supplied, and in what way?

11. Remarks.

IV. That a period of three months be allowed, in which the Missionary elect may be in the field on probation before the engagement be considered as completed: such time however being counted as part of the two years if the engagement is finally confirmed.

6. Resolutions of Assembly, 1880.

Minutes, p. 24. 1. That the report of the Home Mission Committee of the Western Section be received and adopted, and the thanks of the Assembly tendered to the Committee, and especially to the Convenor, for the attention given to this important part of the Church's work.

2. That the General Assembly acknowledge, with deep thankfulness to God, the success which has attended the effort to raise the amount of money sufficent to meet the requirements of the work throughout the year, and also to remove the large debt resting on the Fund at the date of last meeting of Assembly.

3. That the Assembly regards with much satisfaction the the great extension which the Church is receiving, through the Committee's efforts, in Manitoba and the North-West, and the consolidation of the Church in Ontario and Quebec. That it views, also, with much satisfaction, the work of Students' Missionary Societies in Montreal, Kingston and Toronto as contributing to this result.

4. That the thanks of the Assembly be given to the Church of Scotland, the Free Church of Scotland, and the Presbyterian Church of Ireland, for their continued interest in our Home Mission work, and for their liberal donations on its behalf.

5. That the approval of the Assembly be given to placing on the roll of supplemented congregations, those numbered on page xxii of the Report, notwithstanding that they do not reach the minimum contribution per member required by the Assembly, viz: New Glasgow, Dalhousie, North Sherbrooke, Melrose, Lonsdale, Balsover, Ayton, East Normanby, Vittoria, Kinloss and Bervie.

6. That the sanction of the Assembly be given to the reduction of the amount to be paid by the Home Mission Fund of the Western Section to Manitoba College, to the extent of the two hundred and fifty pounds (£250) granted to the College by the Free Church of Scotland and the Presbyterian Church of Ireland.

7. That the Assembly express its regret at the inability of the Rev. Donald Ross to proceed to the important field in the North-West to which he had been appointed, and its sympathy with him in the illness which disqualified him for work there.

8. That in the obligations which it contracts for the current year, the Home Mission Committee, to be appointed, be instructed to keep its expenditure within the amount which the fund may reasonably be expected to reach.

Page 41. 9. That it be an instruction to the Home Mission Committee, Western Section, to pay the twenty-five per cent. deducted from the payments to supplemented ministers, where this has not been done.

7. *Resolutions of Assembly*, 1881.

Minutes 20, 21, 22. Adopt the reports, from the Maritime Provinces, on the subject of Home Missions and Supplementing; rejoice in the work accomplished under both Committees; grant the request of the Supplementing Committee for temporary delay in the payment of debt unavoidably incurred; but instruct both Committees to adopt measures for removing the debt at the earliest day practicable, and for drawing out the liberality of our congregations in the Maritime Provinces, so as to become entirely self-sustaining; and further, direct the Statistical Committee to open a column for contributions to the Supplementing Fund from congregations in the Maritime Provinces.

Resolutions Anent Manitoba.

1. That congregations in Manitoba, having settled pastors, and not self-sustaining, be placed on a list, distinct from stations supplied by missionaries, to be called the list of Supplemented Congregations; that a minimum contribution of $450 towards the salary of the Minister be necessary in order to entitle any congregation to be placed on this list, and that, in view of the greater cost of living in Manitoba compared with Ontario and Quebec, the Committee have power, if it sees fit, to supplement the salaries of ministers laboring in these congregations up to $850 per annum.

2. That the committee hereafter simply make grants to the fields, and that the list of laborers to be employed by the Presbytery in supplying these fields, be revised at the semi-annual meetings of the Home Mission committee; with the understanding that the committee are only liable for the amount of the grant to the field, except in the case of those missionaries directly appointed by this Committee, whose term of service has not expired.

3. That the distinction hitherto made in the remuneration of married and unmarried missionaries be done away, and that $800 be the salary of missionaries to be hereafter sent to Manitoba, during the period of their direct appointment by the Committee, unless in cases in which the great distance from Winnipeg would render a larger salary necessary; with the understanding that the amount promised by the field to which the missionary is appointed to be regarded as a part of the salary named.

4. That a semi-annual grant be made to the Presbytery of Manitoba for exploring and giving temporary supply in new districts, the details of the expenditure to be submitted to this Committee.

Appointment of Superintendent of Missions.

The General Assembly further agreed to grant the prayer of the Overture from the Home Mission Committee of the Presbytery of Manitoba, and to appoint a Superintendent of the Missions within the bounds of said Presbytery, in the extensive and growing fields in Manitoba and the North-West.

1. That the salary of the Superintendent shall be at the rate of two thousand dollars ($2,000) per annum, and that this amount

shall cover all expenses while the Superintendent may be labouring within the Province of Manitoba, or its immediate neighbourhood, but that when he is engaged in visiting distant mission fields, such as Edmonton, the travelling expenses shall be a matter of special arrangement with the General Assembly's Home Mission Board.

2. That the Rev James Robertson, of Knox Church, Winnipeg, be appointed Superintendent of Missions for the North-West.

Minutes page 35, 36. Dr. Cochrane, appointed last Saturday to communicate with Mr. James Robertson as to his acceptance of the appointment of Superintendent of Missions in Manitoba and the North-West, reported that he had communication with Mr. Robertson, as instructed, and that Mr. Robertson had accepted the appointment with the condition that his salary, instead of being $2,000 without expenses, should be the same as that of the Professors in Manitoba College, and travelling expenses. On motion the General Assembly reconsidered and rescinded the resolution come to on Saturday last in regard to the salary offered to Mr. Robertson, and adopted the following resolutions in regard to this appointment, namely :—

1. That the Rev. James Robertson be appointed Superintendent of Missions in Manitoba and the North-West Territory, at a salary of one thousand eight hundred dollars ($1,800) and travelling expenses.

2. That the Presbytery of Manitoba are hereby instructed to take the regular steps for loosing Mr. Robertson from the Pastoral charge of Knox Church, Winnipeg, in order to his entering on said office.

3. That the Home Mission Committee of the Western Section, in conjunction with the Presbytery of Manitoba, are instructed to prepare a code of rules for the guidance of the Superintendent of Missions in the prosecution of his work; said rules to be reported for approval to next General Assembly.

4. That the Convener of the Western Section of the Home Mission Committee, along with any other ministers of the Home Mission Committee, who may be in Manitoba, be requested to meet with the Presbytery of Manitoba, on occasion of Mr. Robertson's entering upon the office of Superintendent of Missions, and also confer with the Presbytery in regard to other matters affecting our mission work in the North-West Territories.

8. RESOLUTION OF ASSEMBLY, 1882.

Rules for the Guidance of the Superintendent of Missions in Manitoba and the North-West.

Minutes, p. 19–22. 1. His duties shall include the oversight and visitation of all the mission stations and supplemented congregations within the aforesaid territory; the organization of new stations and the adjusting of the amounts to be paid by the different stations and congregations for the support of ordinances, and the amounts to be asked from the Home Mission Committee; and in general the supervision and furtherance of the entire mission work of our Church in Manitoba and the North-West.

2. In the prosecution of his work he shall consult with and report to the Presbytery of Manitoba, or such other Presbyteries as may hereafter be erected. He shall also submit to the meetings of the Home Mission Committee, in March and October, a detailed statement of the progress of the work, including the adaptability of the Missionaries to the fields assigned to them, and the fulfilment on the part of stations and supplemented congregations of the engagements entered into for the support of the Missionaries.

3. He shall transmit to the Home Mission Committee an annual report for presentation to the Assembly, containing complete statistics of the membership, families and adherents in each mission station and supplemented congregation; also, the additions made during the year, and the extent of the new territory occupied during the same period, with any other information and recommendations that may be deemed important for the Committee and the General Assembly to know.

4. All Home Mission grants shall be paid by the Superintendent of Missions to the stations and supplemented congregations; and he shall be empowered, should he see cause, to withhold payments of said grants in cases where the stations and supplemented congregations have not fulfilled their monetary engagements, or where statistics have not been regularly furnished.

5. Payments shall be made to the stations and congregations quarterly.

6. No draft shall in any case be drawn by the Superintendent of Missions until he has sent to the Convener of the Home Mission Committee a detailed quarterly statement of the amounts due to each station and congregation, and until he has received his sanction to draw for such amounts on the Treasurer of the Church.

7. In the meantime the Missionary of Prince Albert shall receive his payments directly through the Convener of the Home Mission Committee.

8. The Superintendent of Missions shall spend a portion of his time, as directed by the Home Mission Committee, in the other Provinces, with a view to enlist the sympathies and evoke the liberality of the Church in the mission work in Manitoba and the North-West.

9. The Superintendent shall report his travelling expenses every six months to the Presbytery, to be passed by it before being paid by the Home Mission Committee.

Regulations for Church and Manse Building Fund.

1. The Fund shall be called the Church and Manse Building Fund of the Presbyterian Church in Canada for Manitoba and the North-West.

2. The amount to be aimed at in the first place shall be one hundred thousand dollars ($100,000); the Fund shall be raised by subscriptions and bequests, and the canvass outside the limits of Manitoba and the North-West for subscriptions should not extend beyond two years, and the amounts should be payable within three years, at most, from the date of subscription.

3. The money constituting the Fund shall be, at the discretion of the Board, either invested, and the revenue accruing therefrom be given in the form of grants to congregations engaged in the erection of churches and manses, or shall be lent to such congregations for a limited number of years, either with or without interest.

4. The management of the Fund shall be intrusted to a Board of nine members, six of these to be appointed annually by the Assembly; the other members of the Board to be the Superintendent of Missions for Manitoba and the North-West,

the Convener of the Home Mission Committee, Western Section, and one member appointed by the Home Mission Committee. The ordinary place of meeting of the Board shall be Winnipeg. The Board shall have power to fill any vacancies made by death or resignation, until the next General Assembly thereafter.

5. All applications for aid shall be made to this Board through the Presbytery of the bounds, and before being considered by the Board must be recommended by the Presbytery, but the Board is to be sole judge as to the merits of the application, and the amount of aid to be granted.

6. The assistance where made in the form of a grant, shall not, except in special circumstances, exceed one-fifth of the total cost of the building; and when made in the form of a loan shall not exceed fifty per cent. of the cost. The money shall be payable only when the building can be used for service, in the case of grants. In the case of loans, it may be advanced from time to time. No grant to be made or loan effected until the Board is satisfied that a valid title to the property, or a bond to that effect, has been secured by the congregation, and that the deed be in the form approved by the General Assembly.

Board Appointed.

Minutes p. 42. That Messrs. C. B. Pitblado, A. Bell (Portage la Prairie), Duncan McArthur, John F. Bain, G. D. McVicar, and D. M. Gorden, together with Dr. Cochrane, James Robertson, and the person that may be appointed by the General Assembly's Home Mission Committee, be and are hereby appointed a Board to administer the Church and Manse Building Fund for Manitoba and the North-West; and further, that the Board thus constituted be, and hereby is empowered to petition the Dominion Parliament for incorporation.

Home Mission Fund—Relieved.

Page 46. The Assembly adopted the following resolution:—That the Home Mission Committee of the Western Section, and that also of the Eastern Section, be relieved of the grants of $1,000 and $250 respectively hitherto paid from their funds for the support of Manitoba College.

7. It shall be competent for the Board, with the approval of the General Assembly, to make changes in these regulations, but such shall not extend to the alienation of the capital intrusted to the Board.

8. The Board shall report its transactions annually through the Home Mission Committee to the General Assembly.

Rev. J. Robertson was requested to act as interim Treasurer of the Fund till the Board is duly constituted.

Bequest of the late Joseph Mackay, Esq.

On the recommendation of the Committee in reference to the bequest of the late Joseph Mackay, Esq., of Montreal, the Assembly adopted the following resolution:—That with regard to the liberal bequest of the late Mr. Joseph Mackay for the Home Mission work of the Presbyterian Church in Canada, amounting to ten thousand dollars ($10,000), it is ordered that the interest of the money, and so much of the capital as may be necessary together with the interest to make two thousand dollars ($2.000) may be spent annually until the amount is exhausted, in assisting to carry on the Home Mission work of the Church.

British Columbia.

The Committee submitted the following Minute in regard to the relations of the Rev. Mr. Jamieson to this Church, and as to the changes in these which it may be expedient to make, as well as in regard to the whole subject of the arrangements which it may be desirable and dutiful to make respecting the work of the Church in British Columbia.

" At the last meeting of the Committee, the Convener having laid on the table and read communications from Rev. R. Jamieson, of New Westminster, and the Rev. Dr. Gray, Convener of the Colonial Committee of the Church of Scotland, in regard to the British Columbia field, a sub-committee was appointed to take the correspondence into consideration, and report. The following is their Report and recommendations, which were adopted:—

The letters submitted to your sub-committee from Mr. Jamieson and Dr. Gray set forth the following facts:—

1. Mr. Jamieson intimates his desire to be disjoined from the Presbytery in connection with the Church of Scotland in British Columbia, and to be connected with Presbyterian Church in Canada; and further expresses his willingness to have a r duction of two hundred or three hundred dollars ($200 or $300) made in the grant.

2. The congregation of Nanaimo has expressed its desire to have a minister sent from the Presbyterian Church in Canada, and correspondence has taken place with the Colonial Committee of the Church of Scotland regarding the giving of aid in the event of a minister being appointed.

3. The Colonial Committee makes no objection to this Church responding to the application from Nanaimo; but the state of the Committee's funds is such that no guarantee of pecuniary aid can be given.

4. Mr. Jamieson represents that the First Congregation in Victoria would readily connect itself with the Presbyterian Church in Canada in the event of a Presbytery being formed.

Resolutions of the Assembly on B. C.

1. That a Deputy be appointed to visit British Columbia to confer with the Presbytery there, and make inquiry in order to ascertain the condition and prospects of the Church in the whole field.

2. That in regard to the application of Mr. Jamieson to be connected with a Presbytery in this Church, and in regard to the proposed reduction of the grant made for his support, action be deferred in the meantime.

3. That in view of what the Church of Scotland has done and is doing for British Columbia, and in the hope of securing the hearty support of that Church in any action that may hereafter be taken in the interests of Presbyterianism, the Colonial Committee be informed without delay of the proposed action of this Church.

Report of Home Missions for 1882 Adopted.

The General Assembly adopt the Report as a whole; express their gratitude to the Great Head of the Church for the continued increase of prosperity which He has been pleased to grant in our Home Mission field, Western Section, during the past year, as appears from the Report which has just been submitted; that the thanks of the Assembly be given to the Committee, and especialy to the Convener, for the time and care they have expended on the field of duty which has been under their special care; that the recommendations of the Report with regard to British Columbia, and the Rules for the guidance of the Superintendent of Missions in Manitoba and the North-West, and the Regulations for Church and Manse Building Fund, be adopted; That the suggestion as to the disposition of the money bequeathed by the late Joseph Mackay be approved; and that the Moderator, Dr Cochrane, be appointed a Deputy to visit British Columbia, confer with the Presbytery there, and make inquiry in order to ascertain the condition and prospects of the Church in that District; and further, that the Assembly thank Mr Robertson for his energetic efforts in connection with the Church and Manse Building Fund, and those subscribers whose prompt and generous contributions have made these efforts so largely successful.

Note.—The amount of Subscriptions to said Fund reported was $63,726.

Disposal of Report—Eastern Section.

The General Assembly adopted unanimously the following resolution, moved by Dr. McGregor, seconded by Mr. A. J. Mowatt, for the disposal of the Report on Home Mission in the Eastern Section of the Church:—The General Assembly approves the reports and recommendations of the Committees on Home Missions and Supplementing in the Maritime Provinces, and while expressing satisfaction at the work done during the past year, and at the improved financial condition of both Committees, trusts that every effort will be made to remove the debt on the Supplementing Fund within the current year. The General Assembly desires to record grateful acknowledgement of the valuable services of the Rev. Dr. Waters, now of Newark, and of the Rev. C.

B. Pitblado, now of Winnipeg, the joint Conveners of the Committe for several years.

Note.—The Eastern Home Mission field, comprises the Maritime Provinces including Newfoundland, and its affairs are administered under similar regulations to those of the Western, only that its Supplementary Fund is managed by a separate Committee.

9. CONVENERS.

Western section Rev. W. Cochrane, D. D., Brantford, Ont., Eastern Section, Rev. John McMillan, B. D., Truro, N. S., Supplement Committee Rev. T. Sedgwick, Tatamagouche, N. S.

10 HOME MISSION AND SUPPLEMENTAL FUNDS
1875 to 1882.

Receipts.

WESTERN SECTION.			EASTERN SECTION.
1875-76	Totals,	$24,518.40	$6,841.81
1876-77	"	36,783.17	12,416.26
1877-78	"	29,637.15	9,571.38
1878-79	"	29,688.34	9,551.11
1879-80	"	46,869.77	10,485.74
1880-81	"	37,233.58	7,001.75
1881-82	"	39,649.23	8,849.38
		$244.381.59	$64,718.43

Total for the whole Church for seven years $309,100.02 or an annual average of $44,242.86, to which the average expenditure about approximates.

MISSION TO LUMBERMEN.

1. HISTORICAL STATEMENT.

Minutes, 1876, App. p. 184. For seven years immediately prior to union, the Synod of the Presbyterian Church of Canada in connection with the Church of Scotland prosecuted a Mission to the lumbermen in the Valley of the Ottawa. In presenting this, their first Report, to the united Churches, the Committee entrusted with the management of the Mission record their deep gratitude to God for the consummation of union, and for the beneficial effects it has had, and is likely to have, upon the Mission to the lumbermen.

The object of the Mission is to bring the power of the Gospel to bear upon the large number of men engaged in the shanties during the winter, when they are cut off from Church ordinances. It is the endeavor of the Mission to accomplish this object by a twofold agency: (1.) By the preaching of the Word by the ministers who may devote a certain portion of the winter to the work of visiting the shanties for this purpose; and (2.) By the distribution of large quantities of English and French tracts, illustrated papers in both languages, such as *British Workman*, *Cottager and Artisan*, *L'ouvrier Francais*, and other appropriate literature, these papers and periodicals being distributed not merely by the ministers who may visit the shanties, but also by the employers and others, who kindly co-operate in the circulation of such literature.

2. Resolutions of Assembly.

Minutes, 1876, p. 50. Thatthe support of this Mission be specially commended to the members of the Church in the Synod of Montreal and Ottawa.

Minutes, 1877, p. 27. That further Presbyteries of the Church in those parts of the Dominion where lumbering operations are largely carried on be instructed to consider, and as far as possible promote the spiritual welfare of the lumbermen.

Minutes, 1878. p. 29; 1879, p. 49. The Assembly commend the Mission to the confidence and liberality of the Churches.

3. Mission transferred to the Synod.

Minutes, 1880, p. 42. 1. That the Mission be placed under the supervision of the Synod of Montreal and Ottawa, commending it to the special sympathy and support of the congregations within the Synod, with instructions that any report of the Mission approved by that Synod, shall be embodied, for the information of the General Assembly, in the report of the Assembly's Home Mission Committee.

2. That the Committee to be appointed for the current year shall hold office until the next meeting of the Synod of Montreal and Ottawa, when their successors will be appointed by the Synod.

4. Report 1882.

Minutes, App. pp. 8-9. From which it appears that over 200 shanties were visited containing several thousand men with whom religious exercises were held on Sabbath and week days, and among whom large numbers of Bibles and religious books were distributed.

As in former seasons, the committee have, during the past winter, distributed large quantities of English and French publications among the shantymen through the colporteurs of the Ottawa Bible Society. The colporteurs invariably find that these publications are gladly welcomed and highly prized by the men. One of them, Mr. Robert Stewart, reports that he distributed them among 35 shanties on the Magnasippi and Kippewa, containing 1,241 men. Another colporteur, Mr. Alexander Stewart, distributed his supply among 13 shanties and 4 depots, containing about 320 men, chiefly on the Madawaska and its tributaries. Mr. Stewart bears testimony to very excellent work wrought by two students from Queen's University in the township of Carlow during the summer of 1881, illustrating the way in which the work of this Mission aids in developing the general work of Home Missions in some of the outlying districts.

This Mission has been specially entrusted by the General Assembly to the supervision and support of the Synod of Montreal and Ottawa, and although an increasing number of congregations contribute to the funds of the Mission, yet the great majority of the congregations within the bounds of the Synod still fail to render any assistance. The committee are of opinion that the work of the Mission should, at least during the winter, receive the undivided efforts of several missionaries, and they would endeavor to secure the services of such men if the funds at their disposal were sufficient to warrant the engagement of them. In the meantime they recommend that, as heretofore, there be secured for the Mission, during part of the winter, the services of some of those ordained ministers or missionaries whose fields of labor are adjacent to the lumbering districts.

They also recommend that, in future, increased supplies of French publications be procured for distribution.

Receipts, $579.19. Expenditure, $492.07. Balance on hand, $87.12.

Rev. W. Moore, D. D., Convener. Mr. A. Drummond, Treasurer.

II. FRENCH EVANGELIZATION.

1. Assembly Regulations.

Minutes, 1875. p. 14. 1. That the work of French evangelization hitherto carried on by the churches, be united under a General Assembly Board of French Canadian Evangelization, whose office shall be in Montreal.

2. That the members of the said Board resident in Montreal, constitute an Executive Board for the conduct of the Board's operations in the Provinces of Quebec and Ontario; and that the members resident in the Maritime Provinces constitute a similar Executive Board, having its seat at St. John, N. B., for the conduct of the same in the said Provinces.

3. That for the successful prosecution of the work, a General Secretary be appointed, who can speak and preach in French and English, and whose duties in addition to raising funds shall

4. That the training of French Ministers and Missionaries in the Presbyterian College, Montreal, be made, as heretofore, in the Canada Presbyterian Church, a first charge upon the Fund for French Evangelization.

5. That Schools and Mission Stations be planted, wherever openings can be made for them, throughout the wide extent of the French Canadian and Acadian fields.

Appointment of Secretary and Agent.

Page 15. It was further resolved to appoint the Rev. C. A. Tanner General Secretary of the Board, with a salary of $1,600 and travelling expenses, and the Committee was instructed to define his duties for the present year and report thereon.

Minutes 1876, pages 81, 82. The General Assembly resolved: -- to agree to the appointment of an additional Agent; and that the Rev. R. H. Warden be appointed Agent in terms of the above resolution, with a salary of $1,600.

Miscellaneous Legislation.

Minutes 1877, p. 39. The General Assembly resolved :—

1. To recommend that, in order to avoid confusion, all moneys contributed to the support of French Evangelization be sent direct to the Treasurer, the Rev. R. H. Warden, 210 St. James Street, Montreal.

2. To place the entire control of the work of French Evangelization under one Board of management, which shall carry on its operations as far as possible through the Presbyteries within whose bounds the special fields may be found.

Minutes 1878, p. 30. The General Assembly resolved that :— In regard to localities where assistance may be needed from the Board of French Evangelization and the Home Mission Committee, arrangements shall be made for a joint meeting of sub-Committees of the Board of French Evangelization and the Home Mission Committee, in order to secure the necessary co-operation.

Minutes 1878, p. 49. The General Assembly resolved :—To enjoin anew that all moneys contributed to the support of French Evangelization (including the Rev. C. Chiniquy's work) be sent direct to the Treasurer, the Rev. R. H. Warden, 210 St. James Street, Montreal.

Minutes 1879, pp. 53, 54. The General Assembly resolved :— That the Report be adopted, with the exception of the recommendation regarding Mr. Ami, leaving it to the discretion of the Board of French Evangelization to take what steps they may think best in order to provide him with a suitable place of worship; and that the matter of the employment of an Agent in Britain be left to the judgment of the Board.

Transfer of Pointe-aux-Trembles to the Board.

Minutes 1880, p. 31. The General Assembly agreed :

1. To sanction the agreement between the Board of French Evangelization and the French Canadian Missionary Society as to the transfer of the mission schools at Pointe-aux-Trembles, and the whole work of that Society.

2 To empower the Board to secure the services of the Rev. C. A. Tanner, to canvass for a time in America and Great Britain, with a view to convey information as to the work of the Board, and especially as to the new arrangements, and to raise contributions for the purchase and maintenance of the schools at Pointe-aux-Trembles.

Agreement with F. C. M. Society.

(1) The value of the property to be determined by two competent persons. This has been done and the price fixed at $5,500.

(2) The terms of payment and other details to be arranged by the Board and a Committee of the Society appointed for the purpose.

(3) The proceeds of the sale of the property and effects at Pointe-aux-Trembles to be expended, after meeting all existing liabilities and engagements of the Society, in the support of Colporteurs, circulation of the Holy Sriptures and of French religious literature, as hitherto.

(4) On the completion of the sale to the Board of French Evangelization, and the consequent withdrawal of the French Canadian Missionary Society from its Mission School work at Pointe-aux-Trembles, the Society has decided to withdraw from all Missionary work, and to bring its existence to a close so soon as the funds derived from the sale of the property at Pointe-aux-Trembles, together with any other unsolicited contributions meanwhile received, will have been expended; it being further understood that the Society will not solicit contributions as heretofore, and will at once issue a circular explanatory of the decision come to, and the providential indications of its duty now to withdraw from the field of missionary work among the French Canadians, which it has been honoured of God to occupy for the past forty years with such important results.

(5) That the balance of a legacy from the late B. Gibb, Esq., as received by the Society from the Craig Street Church, Montreal, be handed over to the Board of French Evangelization, subject to the interest being appropriated for educational work at the Mission Schools.

Appointment of Board.

Minutes, 1881, p. 30.—The Board recommend that the General Assembly, instead of appointing, as heretofore, a Board consisting of between fifty and sixty members, and an Executive Committee of those members residing in Montreal, appoint a Board numbering thirty members, to hold at least two regular meetings annually, the travelling expenses of the members to be paid from the fund, and the Executive to be appointed by said Board at its first meeting each year. This was done, with Rev. Principal MacVicar, D.D,, LL.D., Chairman, and Rev. R. H. Warden, Secretary-Treasurer.

2. Report—Progress of French Canadian Evangelization.

Though Canada ceased to be a French colony and was ceded to Britain in 1763, yet the Protestant churches of the parent country neglected for fifty long years the spititual interests of the French Canadians,—the Church of Rome, during these years, gained many proselytes from English-speaking nominal Protestants who had settled in the colony.

The first French Protestant missionary was a Wesleyan, from Guernsey, who laboured among the French in several parts of the Province of Quebec from 1815 to 1821. During the next thirteen years nothing seems to have been done. The Grande Ligne Mission was established in 1834 and the French Canadian Missionary Society in 1839. This latter Society, while supported largely by Presbyterians, was non-denominational. After an honourable record of over forty years it recently withdrew from the field because of the prosecution of the work of French Canadian Evangelization by the several branches of the Protestant Church in Canada. During the period of its existence it circulated upwards of 57,000 copies of God's Word and some 650,000 French tracts and religious publications. It established mission schools at Pointe-aux-Trembles as well as at other points in the Province. It formed, and for a time fostered, a number of mission congregations, and prosecuted the work of colportage with much vigour and success. To the efforts of this Society, under God, are largely owing the great changes that have taken place in the religious sentiments of the French-speaking people of the

Province of Quebec during the last forty years. It may not be out of place here to mention the names of the Rev. Dr. Wilkes, Mr. James Court, and the late Mr. James R. Orr and the Rev. Dr. Taylor, of Montreal, to whom more than any other, under God, the Society owed its existence and its long career of usefulness. It is encouraging to state that, though the Society has now ceased operations, many of its life-long friends continue to take a deep interest in the work of French Canadian Evangelization, and are among the warmest supporters of the work of the Board. Not only are the Pointe-aux-Trembles schools, but also nearly all the congregations and most of the missionaries and colporteurs of the Society now in connection with the Presbyterian Board.

Prior to 1875 the several branches of the Presbyterian Church carried on separate French Canadian Missions. Since the union of the Churches in 1875 the work has made rapid strides, each succeeding year showing marked progress.

French-Speaking Population of the Dominion.

According to the recently published census of 1881, the French-speaking popultaion of the Dominion is 1,300,000, of whom 10,000 are in Prince Edward Island, 41,000 in Nova Scotia, 57,000 in New Brunswick, 13,000 in Manitoba and the North-West Territories, 100,000 in Ontario, and upwards of 1,000,000 in the Province of Quebec.

The great aim of the Board is to give the Gospel of Jesus Christ to this class of our fellow-subjects, comprising as they do nearly one-third of the entire population of the country.

The Means Employed by the Board.

In seeking to accomplish this aim the following three agencies are employed by the Board:—

1. Colportage.—In many of the French settlements there is not a single Protestant to be found, and to attempt opening a Preaching Station or even a Mission School in such places would not only be a dangerous but futile step. The only method of reaching the people in these spiritually destitute districts is by means of the Colporteur going from house to house, scattering

broadcast the seed of the Kingdom, conversing on Divine things with those willing to listen, reading with them the Word of Life, and, when permitted, leaving in their homes a tract or copy of the Bible.

2. Mission Schools.—As soon as a group of families in any settlement has been brought to a knowledge of the truth, and has abjured Romanism, one of the first steps is to open a Mission School for the education of the young, and especially for their instruction in the principles of the Bible. The Teachers employed have been in some instances earnest Christian ladies, but more generally French Students for the Ministry. Many of these teachers occupy part of their time in the work of Colportage and also in conducting Mission Servicee on the Lord's Day.

3. Preaching Stations.—The main branch of the Board's work is the planting of Mission Stations and the formation of congregations, wherever, in the providence of God, there is an opening for such.

Mission Schools.

Minutes, 1882, App. p. CXX. When a family severs its connection with the Church of Rome, the Colporteurs of the Board have instructions to endeavour to get the parents to send one or two of the older children to the Central Mission Schools at Pointe-aux-Trembles, these schools being open to them as well as to the children of Roman Catholics.

Where, however, there are two or three French Protestant families residing near each other, the Board appoint a teacher a d open a Mission School, meeting in whole or in part the expenses connected therewith. Into these schools are gathered the children of converts, as also such of the Roman Catholics as can be induced to attend. In all the schools connected with the Board both French and English are taught, and special prominence is given to the religious training of the pupils. The teachers, in addition to their school duties, give a portion of their time to colporting in the district, more especially with a view of getting the Roman Catholic families to send their children to school.

During the year, schools were maintained as follows in the fields under the care of the Board :—

Pointe-aux-Trembles, number of pupils attending, 86 : Port-au-Persil, 17 ; Pointe-au-Bouleaux, 13 ; St. Jude, 19 ; St. Hyacinthe, 23 ; St. Antoine Abbe, 10 ; Russell Hall, Montreal, 45 ; Canning Street, Montreal, 21 ; Joliette, 16 ; Grenville, 30 ; Namur, 35 ; Masham Mills, 20 ; Ste. Anne, Illinois, 145 ; total teachers, 19 ; pupils, 480.

Point-aux-Trembles Schools.

These Mission Schools, situated on the north shore of the St. Lawrence River, nine miles east of Montreal, were founded in 1846 by the French Canadian Missionary Society, and were purchased by last General Assembly and immediately thereafter transferred to the Board. On the Mission property there are two buildings, one for boys, which can accommodate about 150, and the other for girls, with accommodation for between 40 and 50. Upwards of 2,000 French Canadians have already been educated here. Many of these now occupy positions of trust and influence as ministers, teachers, physicians, lawyers, merchants, etc. Pupils are admitted between the ages of thirteen and twenty-five, the average age being about seventeen. A preference is given to the sons and daughters of French Roman Catholic parents and to the children of recent converts living in parishes where there is no Protestant school. The session begins in October each year, and continues for seven months. The pupils all reside in the buildings, and thus enjoy the advantages of a Christian home, under the watchful nurture of earnest, devoted teachers. They all take their share of house-work. The day's duties are thus laid out: Rise at 5.30 a.m. All are in the class rooms studying privately from 6 to 7. Breakfast at 7. House and out-door work from 7.30 to 8.45. Family worship, when all assemble together, boys and girls, at 8.45. School begins at 9, with united Bible class for all, and continues till 12. Dinner at 12, followed by recreation to 1.30. Then, classes till 4, recreation from 4 to 5, classes from 5 to 6, tea at 6, recreation to 7. Studying privately in the class room till 9, then family worship (boys and girls in their separate buildings) at 9, and all in bed, and lights out by 9.30 p.m. There are five teachers, two of whom are married, and all of whom reside in the buildings. They are all earnest Christians, of devoted missionary spirit, thoroughly consecrated, it is believed, to their work. The principal, Mr. J. Bourgoin, has been eleven years connected with the Institution, and is admirably adapted for his position. Special prominence is given to religious instruction and to the teaching of the Bible on the points of difference between Protestants and Roman Catholics. In these every pupil is thoroughly indoctrinated, and it is no exageration to state that comparatively few of our English-speaking young men and women are better acquainted with their Bibles, or better able to give a reason for the hope that is in them, than can the pupils of Pointe-aux-Trembles when they leave the Mission Schools there. The Board have no hesitation in warmly commending these Institutions as worthy of public confidence, assured that no means are more likely, by the blessing of God, to be efficacious in the work of French Canadian Evangelization, and in advancing the cause of Christ in the Province of Quebec, than these central Mission Schools, now providentially connected with our Presbyterian Church.

After deducting the fees paid by the pupils, and expense of repairs, etc., the average cost to the Church of each pupil is about $50 per session. The Board are most anxious that the Institutions should be supported by means of scholarships of $50 each, guaranteed by private individuals or by Sabbath Schools. A particular pupil is assigned to the donor of a scholarship, to whom reports as to the progress made are forwarded from time to time. In this way a Sabbath School, contributing a scholarship, is put directly in correspondence with the Mission School, and the letters, if read publicly to the Sabbath School, tend to keep up their interest in the work. Moreover, the School can, every Sabbath, remember, by name, in its prayers, the pupil it supports, and can scarcely fail itself to receive the benefit by being thus directly brought into contact with the pupil educated by means of its missionary contributions.

The session just closed, has by God's blessing, been one of the most successful in the history of the schools. The attendance was somewhat less than in the previous session, chiefly owing to the opening of a similar institution in the city of Montreal and to careful discrimination on the part of the Committee in the admission of pupils. The number in attendance was eighty-six. The schools were regularly visited and examined each month by a Committee of the Board. A superior class was instituted for the training of pupils as teachers and colporteurs, and to fit those who desire to do so to enter upon a course of study for the ministry or other of the learned professions.

Fields.	Stations.	Church's	Members.	Families	Attendance.	Sabbath School.	Bibles & Testa'ts.	Contributions.
Grand Falls, N.B........	2	1	....	31	105	33	19	$112 07
Vanburen, Maine........	1	..	....	13	30	29	37	47 77
Caraquet, etc., N.B......	4	1	....	18	120	18	24	43 50
Stellarton, N.S.	1	..	....	12	20	10	43	....
Pointe-au-Bouleau.......	1	..	9	5	16	13	18	....
Port-au-Persil, Que......	1	..	11	6	21	17	22	....
Murray Bay, Que........	1	1	....	....	50	....	57	32 06
Quebec City............	1	1	27	12	40	18	33	97 78
St. Valerien, Que...... ..	2	..	13	11	45	....	41	36 00
Theodore d'Acton, Que..	1	..	....	8	20	....	16	....
St. Hyacinthe...........	1	1	17	22	35	30	20	450 00
St. Jude................	2	..	....	10	25	21	81	....
Sorel....................	1	..	17	12	35	....	52	60 00
West Farnham..........	1	..	18	15	35	20	93	40 00
St. Antoine Abbe........	1	1	8	9	20	12	56	60 00
Laprairie...............	2	1	21	19	50	20	31	46 00
St. John's, Montreal.....	1	1	141	170	140	54	210	399 54
Canning Street, Mont....	1	1	45	55	75	58		160 00
Italian Mission, Mont....	1	1	....	24	30	14	14	....
Cote St. Louis, etc.......	2	..	....	19	30	25	33	....
Pointe-aux-Trembles.....	1	1	39	7	100	90	116	11 77
St. Martin's etc., Que.....	2	..	11	15	50	....	29	....
Shawbridge and Morin, Q	2	..	13	21	120	U.S.	134	....
Joliette, Que............	1	1	11	11	30	30	18	50 00
Rawdon, Que	1	1	....	14	75	U.S.	22	100 00
New Glasgow, Que......	1	1	60	50	90	35	14	375 00
Grenville, etc., Que......	4	1	27	36	100	26	20	76 00
Namur, Que.............	2	1	34	38	60	30	68	22 00
Angers, etc., Que........	2	1	28	32	50	44	105	240 00
Montebello, etc., Que....	2	..	6	16	30	....	30	....
Masham Mills, Que......	1	1	12	16	50	32	41	65 00
Ottawa..................	1	..	26	13	35	10	94	65 00
Leslie and Thorne, Que..	4	..	27	15	40	24	37	42 50
Drysdale, etc., Ont......	2	1	21	22	45	....	24	28 78
Ste. Anne, Illinois.......	3	1	425	150	300	250	212	600 00
Headingly, etc., Man.....	4	1	25	60	110	45	50	260 00
Districts other than the above	11	..	....	160	300	....	1150	....
Totals......	72	22	1092	1147	2527	1006	3064	$3520 77

French Canadian Missions of all the Churches.

App. p. 129. Though our Presbyterian Church has been greatly honoured of God, and stands in the forefront in this work of French Canadian Evangelization, yet the work is not altogether confined to it, but is participated in by other three Protestant denominations. In December last representatives of the several denominations met and resolved to hold a Union Public Meeting, in the interest of French Missions, during the week of the Anniversary Meetings in Montreal. The meeting was held in January, and was one of the most successful of the series, in point of numbers and interest. About 2,000 persons were present. The venerable Dr. Wilkes presided. The singing was conducted by a choir of two hundred French Canadian pupils from the Mission Schools, and addresses were delivered by four of the Missionaries engaged in the work. The following carefully prepared statistics of the work in Canada, in connection with the several Protestant Churches, were presented to the meeting. The first column gives the statistics of *all* the Churches, and the second those of our own Church :—

	All the Canadian Churches.	Presbyterian Church in Canada.
Ordained Missionaries	40	21
Unordained Missionaries	14	10
Mission Day School Teachers....	41	19
Colporteurs	11	11
Bible Women	4	3
Total number of labourers employed	110	64
Preaching Stations	94	47
Church Members	3,276	1,345
Adherents	10,461	5,200
Sabbath Schools	48	34
Sabbath School Scholars	2,000	1,350
Institutes and Mission Day Sch'ls	23	13
Pupils in " "	827	490
Theological Students	30	16
Copies of Scripture distributed in 1881	3,440	3,140

In addition to the above, the Montreal, Ottawa and Quebec Bible Societies employed during the year 1881 seven French Colporteurs, and issued 3,595 French copies of the Scriptures in whole or in part.

3. Finances.

Comparative Statement.

	Received.	Expended.	Balance on hand.
1876.	$19,504.04	$16,067.68	$3,436.36
1877.	34,683.48	37,167.47	1,747.67
1878.	24,460.90	23,657.42	803.48
1879.	24,467.55	21,354.64	112.91
1880.	21,456.96	20,741.05	715.91
1881.	23,203.09	22,154.55	1,048.54
1882.	38,552.13	31,486.32	7,065.81

Debt on Mission Building, $13,325.00.

4. Ladies' French Evangelization Society, Montreal.

The object of the Society is to co-operate with the General Assembly's Board of French Evangelization in extending the Gospel to our French-speaking fellow-citizens. The membership of the Society is composed of all ladies of the Presbyterian Church in Canada who are willing to aid in the work, and who contribute the sum of at least one dollar annually towards its funds. The officers of the Society consist of a President, two Vice-Presidents, a Corresponding Secretary, a Recording Secretary, and a Treasurer; who, together with representatives from the several Presbyterian congregations of the city, form an Executive Committee. The regular meetings of this Society are held in the afternoon of the first Tuesday of each month.

Report, 1880, *App. pp.* 127, 128.

The Society employs two Bible women, who labor respectively in the eastern and western districts of the city, visiting the homes of the poorer converts and also of many Roman Catholics. They have thus been the means of circulating many copies of the Scriptures and religious works, of alleviating distress, and of leading many persons to attend the services of the French Presbyterian congregations in this city.

Last fall it was deemed advisable to extend the work still more by opening a Mission Home in a central part of the city. This has been done and so far has been attended with success. To this Home all can come for advice and help, and women escaping from persecution in Roman Catholic families in the city or elsewhere may here find a temporary home. Here the Bible women reside, and one is always present to meet with those requiring aid. Meetings of a social and religious character have been held ever since the opening, and have been most encouragingly attended. It has been the aim of this Society to endeavor to make the women help themselves as much as possible, and thus guard against pauperism. Situations are found in connection with the Home for those requiring work, and a Registry Office for servants is here kept.

At a recent meeting of the Society it was decided to try and procure part of the funds necessary for carrying on the work by members' fees. Any lady belonging to the Presbyterian Church in Canada may become a member by the payment of an annual subscription of one dollar. It is thus hoped that the necessity for unduly burdening the friends in Montreal with special collections may be done away with, and an opportunity given to those in other parts of the Dominion of taking a more lively interest in the work.

Minutes, 1882, App., p. 130. The Annual Report for the year ending 18th October, 1881, of the Ladies' French Evangelization Society—an auxiliary of the Board—is appended to this Report. This Society has recently been merged in the newly organized Montreal Woman's Presbyterian Missionary Association.

Report 1882, *App. pp.* 132-4.

In conducting the active missionary work of the Society, a change has been made since last annual meeting. It having been thought best to employ the services of a missionary and his wife, your Committee were fortunate enough to procure those of Monsieur Lockert, who was for some time in connection with the French Canadian Missionary Society, and who was very highly recommended to us, together with those of Madame Lockert. Since they have entered upon their duties your Commiitee have been much satisfied with the efficient manner in which they have conducted their work, having labored with untiring energy. The number of visits made since the 1st of December is two thousand eight hundred and twenty, of which eight hundred and sixty-two were to Protestants, and one thousand nine hundred and fifty-eight to Roman Catholics. The number of Bibles and Testaments sold since the same date is four Bibles and one hundred Testaments, while only two Bibles and fifteen Testaments were distributed gratuitously. The colporting may appear at first sight small, but it must be borne in mind that the difficulties become greater as Monsier Lockert is better known. At times he has very nearly met with serious injury, while he can hardly enter certain streets without receiving all kinds of slights. But already he seems to have made some good and lasting impressions.

In the early part of the summer the Society met with a great loss in the death of their matron, Mrs. Oliver, who was taken away after a few days' illness. Herself a convert from Romanism, she was devotedly attached to the work of the Society, and discharged the humble duties devolving on her with great fidelity. Since Mrs. Oliver's death the house work of the Home has been under the management of Mrs. Lockert. Every Thursday morning during the winter the House Committee met for the purpose of seeing anyone who might wish work or assistance. In no case was help given until the Committee were fully satisfied that it was deserved. Very few indeed of those aided have given cause to regret having rendered the necessary assistance. During the cold weather hot soup and bread were provided for the women on Thursday morning, and this in some instances constituted their whole breakfast. Your Committee would take this opportunity of thanking the friends who so kindly supplied the means for affording this enjoyment.

Finances.

Receipts $1,074.42. Expenditures $1,494.62.

OFFICERS,

Mrs. M. H. Campbell, *President.* Miss H. M. Gordon, *Treasurer.*

III. FOREIGN MISSIONS.

1. Resolution of Assembly, 1876.

Minutes page 46. That the reports, now read, be received and remitted to a Committee, Mr. D. M. Gorden, *Convener*, with instructions to consider these and report; that the thanks of the Assembly be given to the Committees and especially to their Conveners; that the Assembly rejoice at the success of Mission work on the Saskatchewan, in China, India, the New Hebrides and Trinidad, and in the prospects of extended usefulness opening up to the Church, as also at the engagement of additional Missionaries, who are soon to proceed to their fields of labor; that the Assembly approve of the formation of the "Woman's Foreign Missionary Society," and anticipate valuable aid from such an Association; and commend the cause of Foreign Missions to the prayers and increasing liberality of the Church at large.

2. Proposed Regulations Anent Foreign Missions.

Minutes 1876, pp. 65, 66. 1. There shall be a central Fund, to be designated the Foreign Mission Fund, from which the operations of the Church in the Foreign Mission department of her work shall be sustained; and all the Congregations and Home Mission Stations throughout the Church shall be required to make an annual contribution to this Fund.

2. There shall be one Board appointed annually by the General Assembly for the direction of the Foreign Mission work of the Church, and it shall be the duty of said Board—1. To administer the funds provided for Foreign Mission purposes, and render an account of the same to the General Assembly at its annual meeting. 2. To take the oversight of the Missionaries now engaged, or who may hereafter be engaged, in the service of the Church, and to issue, from time to time, to said Missionaries such orders and instructions as may be deemed necessary. 3. To seek out such Ministers or others that may be willing to undertake Foreign Mission work, to judge of their qualifications, (where necessary to conduct their preparatory training), and to appoint them to their particular fields of labour.

3. The Foreign Mission Board shall, in the meantime, be divided into two sections, one comprising the members in Ontario, Quebec and the North-West, and the other the members in the Maritime Provinces, each of these sections to have special charge of the Missions now existing in connection with the Western and Eastern portions of the Church respectively, and such other Missions as may hereafter, by the General Assembly, be assigned to any or either of them. The two sections of the Board shall, during the year, hold at least one joint meeting, and shall combine the reports of their operations in their respective sections, to be submitted, year by year, to the General Assembly.

4. The travelling expenses of members of the Foreign Mission Board, in attending meetings of the Board, with all other incidental charges connected with the transaction of the business entrusted to it, shall be defrayed from the Foreign Mission Fund.

3. Report of Committee on Reports of Foreign Missions.

In accordance with its recommendations, it was resolved as follows, viz.:—

1. The Assembly authorize the Presbytery of Manitoba to ordain Mr. John McKay as a Missionary to labor among the Indians, when, after consultation with the Foreign Mission Committee, it may be thought desirable in the interests of the Mission to do so.

2. The Rev. J. Fraser Campbell, in accordance with his previous appointment, is directed to proceed to Madras, but empowered to visit Central India and, if he should consider that to be a more promising field of labor, to report the fact to the Eastern section of the Foreign Mission Committee.

3. In view of the recent resignation of the Rev. J. D. Murray, Missionary to Aneiteum, the Assembly express sympathy with him in the circumstances which have rendered necessary his withdrawal from that field of labor and direct the Foreign Mission Committee to take such action as they may deem expedient in the circumstances.

4. The Assembly direct the Committee to accept the offer which the Rev. Jas. Douglas, of Cobourg, has made of himself for Foreign Mission work, and authorize them to send him out to labor in Central India, as soon as circumstances will permit. Further, the Assembly instruct the Presbytery of Peterborough to take the necessary steps for his release from his present charge.

5. The Assembly—finding that the sum of twenty-six thousand dollars ($26,000) annually, is required to carry on the work already undertaken; that a large additional expenditure of not less than five thousand eight hundred dollars ($5,800) will be required to cover the outfit, passage money and salaries of the Missionaries now about to be sent to India; that the income of the Fund must reach nearly thirty-two thousand dollars ($32,000) to enable the Committee to meet the annual expenditure to which the Church has now committed itself; and that the Treasury is at present virtually empty—commend these facts to the prayerful liberality of all their congregations.

4. Resolution of Assembly, 1877.

Minutes, p. 36. 1. The Assembly authorize a separation between the mission work among the Indians and the maintenance of Gospel ordinances among the settlers at the Prince Albert Mission in the North-West—the school to be maintained in the meantime in connection with and under the supervision of the Foreign Mission, but the supply of Gospel ordinances to the English-speaking people to devolve on the Home Mission Committee.

2. Empower the Foreign Mission Committee to send another Missionary to the Island of Formosa, if the state of the fund should warrant the necessarily increased expenditure. Further, the Assembly agree, in the event of the Rev. J. Fraser Campbell signifying his desire to be at Indore in connection with Mr. Douglas, to accede to his wish; his support from January 1st, 1878, to devolve on the funds of the Western section of the Foreign Mission Committee.

3. Authorize the Foreign Mission Committee to send deputations to visit the congregations of the Church or to employ other suitable means to evoke increasing liberality in support of this scheme.

4. Leave the appointment of a fourth Missionary to Trindad with the sub-Committee for the Maritime Provinces, to be dealt with as they may find it to be expedient and practicable.

5. With a view to awaken deeper interest in the Mission work of the Church by affording more full and accurate information, the Assembly authorize the Western sub-Committee to procure suitable wall-maps of the different Mission-fields, and instruct both sections of the Committee to furnish interesting information respecting the origin and history of our several Missions.

6. Refer for consideration to the Foreign Mission Committee the subject-matter of the following recommendation, viz:—" The " Committee suggest to the General Assembly that it would be " desirable to recommend the formation of Woman's Foreign " Mission Societies in each Presbytery of the Church, with branch " societies in the several congregations of the Presbytery; and " that the Presbyterial Societies should, if they see fit, send their " reports to the Conveners of the sub-Committees on Foreign " Missions and their contributions to the Treasurers of the Foreign " Mission funds."

Page 49. The Assembly agreed to pospone consideration of the "proposed Regulations anent Foreign Missions" (*vide* Minutes 1876, p. 65), until the next meeting of Assembly, and to continue during the present year the system now in operation.

5. Resolutions of Assembly, 1878.

Minutes, p. 50. 1. Authorize the Sub-Committee of the Western Section to proceed with the erection of buildings for residence of Missionaries at Indore: enjoin Ministers to lay the urgent need of such buildings before their congregations, as part of the ordinary requirements of the Fund; and at the same time empower the Committee to lay this work before such well-known friends of Missions as they may think proper to address, and in such manner as in their judgment may seem wise.

2. Appoint a Committee to consider in what manner the Foreign Mission Committee and the Juvenile Mission Committee may most harmoniously and efficiently prosecute their work, Dr. Wardrope, Convener; with instructions to report to next General Assembly.

3. The Assembly thankfully recognize the important service rendered by the various Woman's Foreign Missionary Societies in raising funds for the support of work among the women and children of heathen lands, and in stimulating the Missionary zeal of the Church at home; and, having had submitted the Constitution of "The Woman's Foreign Missionary Society of the Presbyterian Church in Canada (Western Section)" record their general approval of the same, and cordially recommend the formation of Branch Societies in Presbyteries and congregations in the manner provided for in its Constitution, with the consent and authority of Ministers and Sessions.

4. Authorize the Eastern Section of the Foreign Mission Committee to take such steps as they may deem necessary to send a fourth Missionary to Trinidad.

5. Refer the subject of granting aid to Missionaries, who may find it necessary to send their children home for education, to the sub-Committees to mature a scheme to be submitted to next General Assembly; and authorize the Eastern Section to make such provision in the meantime to meet such cases as have emerged or may emerge during the year, as they see to be just to all parties.

6. Express gratification at the continued energy and usefulness of the Juvenile Mission, and recommend it to the hearty support of the Sabbath-Schools of the Church.

6. Resolutions of Assembly, 1879.

Minutes, pp. 30–31. That the report for the Western Section be adopted, and that the Committee be authorized to take steps, as soon as practicable, to send Mr. John Wilkie as a Missionary to India or China.

Unanimously adopted the following motion. The General Assembly hereby instruct the Convener of the Foreign Mission Committee to apply to the Dominion Government for the issue of the patent or patents, for the various Foreign Mission premises belonging to or that may in future be granted to the Church in Manitoba and the North-West Territory, and hereby appoint John Black, D.D., of Kildonan, Professor George Bryce, of Winnipeg, in the Province of Manitoba, Professor William McLaren of Toronto, in the Province of Ontario, the Rev. Donald Ross and James Jamieson Campbell, both of Prince Albert, North-West Territory, as the Trustees to whom the said patent or patents may be issued, to hold the lands and premises to be thereby granted, for the benefit of the Presbyterian Church in Canada, for the use of the Indian Missions of the said Church or upon such trusts and to such use and for such other purposes as the General Assembly of the said Church may, by any resolution or resolutions duly passed at any meeting thereof, declare and appoint. And in the event of any of the said Trustees, or of the Trustees for the time being, dying, resigning, becoming incapable of acting or ceasing to be a member in full communion with the said Church, the said General Assembly may at any meeting thereof elect a new Trustee or Trustees in the place and stead of the Trustee or Trustees for the time being, so dying, resigning, becoming incapable of acting, or ceasing to be member in full communion with the said Church.

It was moved and carried unanimously, that the action of the Eastern Section of the Foreign Mission Committee in raising the salaries of the Missionaries in Trinidad for the past year by an increase of fifty pounds (£50) sterling, be sanctioned and the Committee authorized to continue the same rate o. payment for the future; that the reports be published in the "Presbyterian Record;" and that the report as a whole be adopted.

Extracts from Reports 1879.

Minutes, App. pp. 88-89. Your Committee have drawn up a series of Regulations for the conducting of the Mission in Central India which they trust will aid in the harmonious and orderly prosecution of the work. In preparing them they have been guided largely by the experience of other bodies, which are prosecuting Missionary work in the same field. Time may show the necessity of minor modifications in these rules; but your Committee do not anticipate that any very radical change is likely to be required. A copy of these regulations which have been adopted *ad interim* will be found appended to this report.

7. Regulations for Missions in Central India, (Western Section.)

1. Until such time as the Presbytery can be established, the male Missionaries shall be instructed to meet as a Council, quarterly at least, and consult in reference to the work of the Mission; and they shall also assume the general oversight and direction of the work, subject to the directions of the General Assembly's Committee.

2. Until there are three or more Missionaries in the field, the ordained Missionaries shall preside alternately, each for a period of one year. The Rev. J. M. Douglas shall be the first President. After three or more Missionaries are in the field, they shall elect their own President annually, in such manner as they may see fit.

3. The Committee will regard the Council as charged with special responsibility for the expenditure of the funds remitted by the Treasurer or Agent of the Church, or received in the field for the use of Missionaries,—it being understood that the salaries of Missionaries shall be paid at the par rate of sterling exchange, and also that the salaries of Canadian Missionaries shall be subject to the current rate of exchange in India; and the Committee will require the Council's recommendation of all estimates and expenses before giving its approval to them.

4. The Committee shall designate Missionaries to particular fields of labour; and if, in the progress of the work, a change is deemed desirable, it may be determined by the Council, subject to the approval of the Home Committee.

5. All itinerancies or district work shall be determined by the Mission Council, all expenses thereby entailed, over and above the Missionary's average home expenditure, shall be borne by the Mission.

6. No individual Missionary shall incur, in schemes of work, an expenditure exceeding $50 per annum.

7. The Mission Council shall nominate a Treasurer for appointment by the Assembly's Committee, who shall carefully preserve all deeds of Mission property and other legal papers not transmitted to the Committee; receive moneys from the Treasurer or Agent of the Church and from other sources, for Missionary purposes; pay the salaries of the Missionaries at the end of each month or at such other stated period as the Council shall determine; and defray the regular expenses of the Committee, and in no case exceeding them without its approval. He is expected to keep, in books procured at Mission expense, clear and correct account of all receipts and payments and to have vouchers of the latter; his books must be open to the inspection of the other members, or to any one of them, at any time; his accounts must be audited by a Committee of two members of the

Mission appointed each year for this purpose; and a report of all receipts and payments must be made to the Treasurer or Agent of the Church yearly, or more frequently if desired, with a balance sheet, clearly exhibiting the condition of the Mission Treasury. Neither the Treasurer nor any member of a Mission may draw on the Treasurer or Agent of the Church for funds, without first receiving permission, formally expressed.

8. All agents employed in the Mission shall be paid from the Treasury of the Foreign Mission Committee, and the names of native agents who may be supported by Congregations or Sabbath Schools, shall be furnished to said Committee from time to time by the Mission Council.

9. The Mission Council shall prepare, at the end of the year, a general report of missionary work, to be sent to the Committee in the first week in January. Each Missionary is requested to prepare also a personal narrative of his labours during the year, with any statement of his own views of the missionary work, or of the Lord's dealings with him, which he may think proper to give; this narrative, in the form of a letter, should be sent to the Convener of the Assembly's Foreign Missson Committee, early in January. All communications of the nature of complaints, or proposals requiring immediate action on the part of the Assembly's Committee, shall be transmitted through the Mission Council.

10. At the end of one year after the arrival of a missionary in the field, the Mission Council is requested to make a report to the Committee in regard to his knowledge of the native language and his skill in the practical use of it. The ability to write and speak the native language well, is an indispensable qualification for missionary work, without which no one can expect to coninue in the service of the Committee.

11. The Mission Council shall prepare, at the end of each year, a careful estimate of the probable necessary expenses of its work for the year ensuing, specifying the different objects in detail, to be forwarded to the Committee the first week in January. When there is more than one station in a mission, each station shall prepare its estimates, to be submitted for examination and approval by the Mission Council at its annual meeting. It is the desire of the Committee that the estimates should be so complete as to preclude special application to Churches, Sabbath

Schools, or Associations, for objects not specified in them. No missionary should apply to the Committee for funds for mission work without first conferring with the Mission Council. When these Mission estimates have been approved by the Committee, they govern the expenditure of the year, and must not be exceeded. If special cases arise, calling for new expenditure, they should be made matters of correspondence with the Committee, except when funds are provided from other sources than the treasury of the Church, such as the donations of Christian friends at the station or from other sources, as those referred to in the next paragraph.

12. The object of missionary life must ever be held sacred, that of " preaching Christ and Him crucified ;" but if, without turning aside from this object, missionaries should be temporarily led, by Providential circumstances, with the consent of their brethren in the Mission and the approval of the Commitee, to engage in work which brings to them pecuniary remuneration, the money so received shall be turned over to the treasury of the Mission, to be used as local funds under its direction, and to be reported to the Committee. In such cases the missionaries will continue to draw their usual salaries from the Committee.

13. The salary of a missionary, although varying in different countries, according to the expense of living, is fixed on the principle of giving only a comfortable support to the missionaries while they continue in the service of the Committee, in the mission field and work. Usually a house is provided or house rent paid ; a salary to a married man, and an allowance to each child under eighteen years of age ; two-thirds of the salary of a married man to one unmarried ; and to single women, such salary as may be agreed upon after conference with the Mission Council. The salary in every case begins on the missionary's arrival at his station, and ends when he leaves it on his return to the country from which he was designated, or on connection with the Committee being terminated. Provision for missionaries on visits to Canada, or for a missionary remaining at his post while his wife returns to Canada, will be made from time to time as the Committee may consider equitable.

14. All female missionaries employed in zenana work shall be subject to the above regulations; and the Council shall consult them in all matters pertaining to their work.

15. The Council shall prepare and submit to the Assembly's Committee for approval, a fixed scale of payment for all Native Agency, uniform with other missionary societies in the field, which shall be framed with a reference to individual attainments and adaptation for the work.

16. The Mission Council is authorized to submit to the Assembly's Committee any alterations or additions to the above regulations which experience or the progress of the work may demand.

8. Resolution of Assembly, 1880.

Eastern Section.

Minutes, pp. 32-33. 1. The General Assembly records, with profound gratitude to God, the progress of the missions in the New Hebrides and in Trinidad during the year past—noticing, more especially in the New Hebrides, the publication of the entire Bible in the language of the Aneiteumese, at their own expense; and of the Acts of the Apostles in the language of the Erromangans and of the Fateans; and in Trinidad, the increase of schools, the opening up of a new field for a fourth missionary, the praiseworthy liberality of the proprietors, and the gratifying development of self-support among the coolie converts.

2. Approve of the training of a native ministry in Trinidad. Sanction the Syllabus prepared by the Presbytery of Trinidad, and authorize the Presbytery to proceed to license and to ordain, if they are satisfied with the qualifications of the candidates.

3. Authorize the sending of a fourth missionary to Trinidad so soon as the finances of the Eastern Section will, in the judgment of the Eastern Committee, warrant that step, and express the hope that our people in the Lower Provinces will remove the existing hindrances without delay.

4. Approve of the raising of the salaries of our missionaries in the New Hebrides from £150 stg., to £175 stg., with an allowance of £10 for each child, as formerly, and Widows' rate paid.

Western Section.

On motion the recommendation of the Committee's report was adopted, as follows:—The General Assembly call upon congregations to make a special effort to double their contributions to Foreign Missions for the present year, and enjoin upon Presbyteries to use all diligence to secure this end.

9. Rev. Dr. McKay's Address—Resolution of Assembly, 1881.

Minutes, p. 33. Dr. G. L. McKay, the first Missionary of this Church in the Island of Formosa, now on furlough in this country, being present, on the request of the Assembly addressed the house at length, giving large details of his labours in that island, during the period of eight years, and of the success with which these labours were crowned.

It was moved and carried by a standing vote—That the members of the General Assembly rejoice to welcome amongst them the presence of their honoured and beloved brother from Formosa, the Rev. Dr. McKay, They record with gratitude to God the eminent success which has attended his self-denying Missionary labours in that island. They acknowledge the great honour which has been conferred by the Giver of all good upon the Church in Canada in the gifts with which their beloved brother has been endowed. They pledge themselves to follow Dr. McKay on his return to Formosa with their prayers to God for the safety on their journey of himself and family, as well also that yet greater success may yet be vouchsafed to him and his fellow-labourers in their future. The General Assembly would also recognize the obligation which Dr. McKay's presence among them enforces upon its members and upon the Church generally of sustaining with larger liberality the great work of Foreign Missions.

Eastern Section.

Minutes, p. 47. The General Assembly, in receiving the report of the work conducted under the Eastern Section of the Committee, would record their gratification that the Aneiteumese possess, and are now reading, the whole Bible in their own tongue, and that the missionaries on the other islands are making progress in translating and printing portions of the Holy Scriptures, and teaching the natives to meet the needful expense. The General Assembly rejoices in the progress of the Gospel in Erromanga, sympathizes with Mr. McKenzie, of Efate, in his illness, welcomes him home to rest for a season, and prays that he may soon recover his strength and re-occupy his field. The Assembly learns with satisfaction of the extinction of the debt, by the liberal contributions of the people of the Maritime Provinces, and of the entrance of the fourth missionary to Trinidad on his work, and commends that expanding mission, as well as the older missions to the New Hebrides, to the protection and blessing of the great Master.

10. Resolutions of Assembly, 1882.

Trustees for property at Prince Albert.

Minutes p. 30. Whereas no patents for the lands—the property of the Foreign Mission Committee—have been issued to the Trustees mentioned in the resolution of the Assembly adopted at Ottawa in 1879, as set out on page 30 of the Minutes of said Assembly; and whereas it is desirable to substitute the names of other Trustees instead of some thereof; the Assembly do hereby appoint Professor George Bryce, of Winnipeg, Manitoba, Professor William McLaren, of Toronto, Rev. James Robertson, of Winnipeg, Rev. Hugh McKellar, of High Bluff, Manitoba, and the Hon. Alexander Morris, of Toronto, to be Trustees in lieu of the Trustees named in said resolution, to whom and their successors in office the lands referred to may be conveyed, and with the same powers and under the same trusts as defined by the same.

Western Section.

Minutes p. 30. That the Report of the Committee be adopted and the Assembly express satisfaction with the measure of success that has attended the labors of the Missionaries of the Church in their various fields of operation and with the state of the funds and the increased liberality on the part of the Church, on behalf of Foreign Missions.

Eastern Section.

1. The Assembly recognizes with gratitude to God the evidences of vitality and progress in the New Hebrides and Trinidad Missions, as set forth in the Report received, and now adopted, and would commend the Missionaries to the affectionate sympathy and prayers of the whole Church.

2. The Assembly would express satisfaction at the intelligence that the Rev. Mr. McKenzie, with his family, has sailed for Great Britain on his long way to the mission field, so restored in health as to afford the prospect of being able in a few months to resume his work in Efate.

3. The Assembly has heard with approval of the measures and success of Mr. Morton in the field into which he has recently entered, and trusts that the requests made for donations to pay for the new mission buildings at Tunapuna—The Central Station—may be generously responded to at an early day by the friends of missions throughout the whole Church.

Missionaries to be on Presbytery Rolls.

Resolved that the names of the ministers of this Church who are engaged in Foreign Mission work, and whose names are not now on the rolls of the Presbyteries of the Church, be placed on the rolls of the Presbyteries within which they resided at the time of their several appointments.

II. COMMITTEES, 1882.

(1) *Western Section.*

Minutes, p. 40. Prof. McLaren, D.D., *Convener*; Principal Grant, D.D., Dr. Moore, Dr. Smith, Dr. Jardine, Dr. J. B. Fraser, Messrs. T. Lowry, R. Campbell, (Montreal), W. A. McKay, John Smith, J. S. Burnet, D. J. McLean, M. W. McLean, R. J. Beattie, D. D. McLeod, A. H. Scott, J. S. Black, J. R. Battisby, A. D. McDonald, J. Ferguson, (Chesley), J. Robertson and Dr. McDonald, Messrs. W. B. McMurrich, C. Davidson, J. Y. Reid, Thos. Gordon, and F. B. Stewart.

(2) *Eastern Section.*

Mr. Alexander McLean, *Convener*; Dr. McGregor, Dr. Mc Culloch, Dr. Burns, Messrs. A. McL. Sinclair, E. A. McCurdy, E. Scott, H. B. McKay, D.B. Blair, W. Donald, Peter Goodfellow, P. M. Mor-rison, K. McLennan, Dr. George Murray, Messrs. John Millar and D. C. Fraser.

12. FOREIGN MISSION FIELDS.

The Foreign Mission Fields of the Church are five in number. The *New Hebrides Mission* and the *Trinidad Mission* are under the supervision of the Assembly's Committee for the Eastern Section of the Church; the other three, the *Mission to the Indians in the North-West*, the *Mission to China*, and the *Mission to Central India*, are controlled by the Assembly's Committee for the Western Section. The history of these Missions now extends over a period of many years, and is full of events of deepest interest. The progress made in all the Fields has been encouraging—in some of them remarkable—and the outlook for the future is full of hope. The limits of the *Handbook* will admit only of a brief statement respecting each of them.

1. Eastern Section.

I. New Hebrides.

This group of Islands lies about 1,000 miles due North of New Zealand, about midway between New Caledonia and the Solomon Islands. There are about forty islands in the group, of which thirty are inhabited. The total population is about 30,000, but decreasing rapidly. Anietyum is supposed at one time to have had a population of ten or twelve thousand; in 1858 it had only 3,500; twenty years later the population was reduced to 1,279, In greater or less degree, a like decrease, a like process of decay is depopulating the whole of the South Sea Islands. The reasons assigned for this melancholy state of matters are war, infanticide, epidemics, drink and the infamous "Liquor Traffic."

These Islands were first discovered by the Spaniards in the year 1606, but more extensively explored by Captain Cook in 1774; when they received the names they now bear. As a field for missionary enterprise they were first brought into notice by John Williams, of the London Missionary Society, who went out as their missionary in the year 1816 to the Society's islands. In 1834 he visited England, where he published a narrative of missionary enterprise in the South Seas, and also printed the New Testament in the language of Raretonga. In 1838 he again sailed from England, with nine additional missionaries and, after visiting other groups, he made for the New Hebrides. After planting three missionaries on Tanna, he proceeded to Erromanga, where he landed with Mr Harris. They were immediately attacked by the natives and cruelly murdered on the 20th November, 1839.

Aneityum.—In 1846, the late Dr John Geddie, minister of Cavendish, in Prince Edward Island, decided to give himself to the work in the South Seas. Having been duly appointed by the Presbyterian Church of the Lower Provinces, and after a long and circuitous route he reached Aneityum in the middle of 1848. In 1852, having, in the meantime, with his family suffered many trials and hardships, he formed his first church in the New Hebrides. A few years later, through his efforts and those of his fellow-laborer, Mr Inglis, the whole of the population, numbering 3,500 was professedly Christian. In 1863, by their united efforts the Aneityumese were supplied with the complete New Testament in their own language. In 1872, Dr. Geddie was smitten with a stroke of paralysis, and retired to Geelong, near Melbourne, to join Mrs. Geddie, and to assist in having the Bible printed in the language of the New Hebrides, and there he died on the 14th December, 1872. Not long after his death a marble tablet to his memory was placed in the wall of the chapel where he had so often preached in Aneityum, and on it these words worthy of being printed in letters of gold :—*When he came there were no Christians, and when he went away there were no heathen.*

In 1872 the Presbyterian Church of the Lower Provinces appointed the Rev. Joseph Annand, as missionary to Aneityum, and he is still faithfully occupying the field.

Erromanga, another island of the group, has a population of about 3000, and is about 80 miles in circumference. On this island the Rev. G. N. Gordon and his wife, after five years' labors, were murdered by natives on the 20th May, 1861. The Rev. James D. Gordon, a brother of the martyred missionary, went out from Prince Edward Island to take his place upon Erromanga, in 1864, and in March, 1872, he too fell by the tomahawk of a native. In the same year, the Rev. H. A. Robertson, who began his life in the New Hebrides with Dr. Geddie, on Aneityum, as agent for a London Cotton Company, and who had thus become familiar with the character and the languages of the natives, was appointed his successor, and under his faithful ministry, the seed that had been watered by martyr's blood has sprung up and yielded fruit. Mr. Robertson still occupies the island, assisted by a band of native teachers.

Tanna is an island of about the same size as Erremanga, and separated from it by a strait 18 miles wide. It is one of the most beautiful and fertile islands of the group. The population is estimated at from ten to twelve thousand. On this island, the Rev. S. F. Johnston, a native of Middle Stewiacke, N. S., accompanied by his wife, took up his abode in 1860. They found the natives naked and living in a condition of social degradation past description. Mr. Johnston's labors there were brief. He died on January, 21st 1861. The Rev. John W. Matheson, of Roger's Hill, N. S., sailed with his wife for these islands in 1858. They spent most of their time on Tanna, but were driven from it by sickness and native hostility. Both died in 1862.

Efate is the central island of the group, and is rich and fertile. It is about 100 miles in circumference. On this island Mr. and Mrs. Morrison, from Nova Scotia, labored successfully for some years, and here also the Rev. Joseph Annand, now of Aneityum, was stationed for a time. Our mission on Efate is now under the charge of the Rev. J. W. McKenzie, who has been associated in the work by the Rev. D. McDonald, a son-in-law of Dr. Geddie, connected with the Presbyterian Church of Victoria. His principal stations are Pango and Eraker, at both of which there is a church.

Espiritu Santo is an island 80 miles long and 40 wide. It is covered with lofty mountains and fertile valleys which give it a magnificent appearance. The climate, however, is unhealthy. Dr. Geddie visited this island several times, and on one occasion, in 1861, left some Raretongan teachers on it, but they took sick and died a few months afterwards. No missionary seems to have been stationed here until the year 1869, when the Rev. John Goodwill, formerly of Roger's Hill, Nova Scotia, was sent out by the Church of Scotland, in the Maritime Provinces. Mr. Goodwill returned to Nova Scotia in 1875.

Altogether *twelve* ordained missionaries have gone from the Maritime Provinces to the New Hebrides; nine of them took their wives with them; making in reality *twenty-one* missionaries. From "The New Hebrides and Christian Missions" by Rev. Dr. Steel, the following statistics are taken:—European Missionaries, 11; native teachers, 89; stations and out-stations, 50; Church attendants, 2,644; communicants, 814; schools, 86; scholars, 2,433. In thirty years, 4,500 converts have been won from heathenism. Since its commencement, 24 ordained missionaries have been connected with the mission. Eight are dead and four are retired. The 12 now in the field have formed themselves into a Synod which meets annually. The statistics of the mission of our Church as given in Committee's report to the General Assembly in 1881—(See Minutes, 1881, App. p. 68) are as follows:—

Rev. Joseph Annand, Anelcauhat, Aneiteum.—Teachers, 22; Schools, 22; Mr. and Mrs. Annand's school, 54; Communicants, 215.

Rev. J. W. McKenzie, Erakor, Efate.—Elders, 9; Teachers, number not given; Scholars, 50; Mr. and Mrs. McKenzie's School, 80; Communicants, 81.

Rev. H. A. Robertson, Dillon's Bay, Erromanga.—Stations, 2; Teachers and Schools, 25; Communicants, 50.

Presbyterian Missions in the New Hebrides, 1882.

MISSIONARY.	Appointed.	Location.	Church Supporting.
Rev. J. W. Mackenzie	1872	Efate.	Presbyterian Church in Canada.
Rev. J. Annand, M.A.	1873	Aneiteum.	
Rev. H. A. Robertson	1872	Erromanga.	
Rev. Thos. Neilson..	1866	Tanna.	Free Ch. of Scotland.
Mr. James H. Lawrie	1879	Aneiteum.	
Rev. John G. Paton.	1858	Aniwa.	Presbyterian Church of Victoria.
Rev. D. Macdonald..	1871	Efate.	
Rev. William Watt..	1869	Tanna.	Pres. Ch. of N. Zealand.
Rev. Peter Milne....	1869	Nguna.	Presbyterian Church of Otago and Southland.
Rev. Oscar Michelson	1878	Tongoa.	
Rev. Mr. Gray	1881	Not located.	Pres. Ch. of South Australia and Tasmania.
Rev. Mr. Fraser....	1881	Not located.	

The Mission is of a composite character. The missionaries are sent out and supported by the different Churches named; and to them are severally responsible. They, however, meet annually in Synod, and deliberate and decide on measures to be carried out for the common good, and for the evangelization of the group. Rather more than one-fourth of the located missionaries are from the Presbyterian Church in Canada.

2. *Trinidad Mission.*

Minutes, 1876, App. pages 161, 162. The Trinidad mission has for its object the evangelization of natives of India who are living either temporarily or permanently in the West Indies, and more especially in the Island of Trinidad. The mission originated in a visit to that island by Mr. Morton for health some ten years ago. He there saw a large body of Asiatics, chiefly Hindoos, from India, indentured to labour for five years, with the privilege of return at the expiration of that time. The British Government took care that they should be treated as men, not as slaves, and that wholesome food and medical attendance should be provided. While the body was thus cared for, no provision appeared to be made by either Church or State for their souls. The spirit of the young traveller was stirred within him, and on returning home he laid the facts before his Synod, and asked them to send the Gospel to the coolies of Trinidad.

After the delay of a year for full enquiry, the information gathered, and the providential indications all pointing in the same direction, the Synod unanimously determined to send a missionary, and Mr. Morton went forth, and commenced at once to lay the foundations on which he and others should build. After three years of devoted and successful labour, the mission was strengthened by the arrival of Rev. K. J. Grant, and two years ago Rev. Thomas Christie went forth as the third missionary.

The island, or rather so much of it as our mission covers, is, therefore, divided as it were into three districts, the Mission Village District, superintended by Mr. Morton; the San Fernando District, by Mr. Grant; and the Couva District, by Mr. Christie. These districts contain about 5000 coolies each, so that of the whole coolie population, say 30,000, one-half are on estates to which our missionaries have access.

Report, 1878.

Minutes, App., page 67. This mission has entered the second decade, and a brief review may not be out of place. In the fall of 1867, Rev. J. Morton sailed for Trinidad, opened a school for children, and began to study the language of the Hindoos. In 1870 he was followed by Rev. K. J. Grant, and in 1873 by Rev. T. M. Christie.

For a time the prospect was disheartening, partly from the persistent opposition of the Orientals and partly from the apathy, and doubt of residents generally, and years passed before one convert was baptized. Our Missionaries were prepared to meet difficulties; they went to labor for those whom they knew to be hostile to Christianity, and they sowed the good seed in faith and hope and waited for fruit. Nor have they waited in vain, for during the past year seventy adults and twenty-five children have been baptized. Five converts devote their whole time to make known the Saviour to their fellow-countrymen, and others are employed as instructors of the young.

Report, 1881.

Minutes, App., page 81. The most noteworthy fact in connection with this mission is the selection and sending out of the fourth missionary under the sanction of the General Assembly, conditioned on the removal of the debt by the people of the Maritime Provinces. This they did in the course of the summer, but before it was fully accomplished the Committee advertised in advance for a suitable missionary. Various offers were received from various quarters, but it was not till November 23rd that a decision was arrived at, and Mr. John Wilson McLeod, a graduate of Presbyterian College, Halifax, appointed. Mr. McLeod, being a licentiate, was immediately taken on trial by the Presbytery of Halifax, and on December 20th was ordained and designated, the charge being delivered by the Chairman of this Committee. In less than a month he, with his young wife, was in Trinidad, ready to enter on the study of the Hindustani.

Prior to his arrival the Mission Council, after examining the question of locality on all sides, had decided, and in the opinion of this Committee, wisely, that Mr. Morton should take charge of the new field, and that Mr. McLeod should occupy Mr. Morton's house, and enter into his labors, in due time, it is hoped, to gather in much fruit from the seed sown by his predecessor.

In reference to Mr. McLeod's work it is sufficient to say that he has addressed himself to the acquisition of the language with good prospect of success.

Report, 1882.

Minutes, 1882, App. pp. 75, 76. Rev. John Morton.—Caroni District, residence, Tunapuna. Teacher, Bakhan at Arouca; at Tunapuna, Allah Du'a.

Rev. K. J. Grant.—San Fernando District. Assistants, Lal Behari, George Sadaphal; teacher in main school, Joseph Corsbie.

Rev. T. M. Christie.—Couva District. Teachers, besides monitors, three—Narayan, Ramjas and Madhu.

Rev. J. W. McLeod.—Savanna Grande District, residence, Princetown. Assistants, Joseph Annagee and Juramin; teacher of main school, Miss Annie L. Blackadder.

The Committee have to report for the first time that four Missionaries have laboured in this Mission during the year, in the districts above mentioned, and with the assistance specified. They have all had the disadvantage of an unusually sickly season, during which, through the prevalence of yellow fever or a malarial fever, closely resembling the deadly malady just named, many Asiatics and a good number of Europeans died. We have much reason for gratitude that the Lord protected the Missionaries and their families so that they were preserved in safety. Mr. Christie and Miss Blackadder were both for a time disabled from work, but have been mercifully restored.

The Committee will present only a few particulars respecting the different districts.

The new District.

Mr. Morton having introduced Mr. McLeod to his people and work at Savanna Grande, removed his family to his new district, and having selected Tunapuna, a village, in population ranking the highest after San Fernando, rented a temporary dwelling and addressed himself to his work. As soon as possible he opened four out-stations, and carries on his work at five centres, Tunapuna, the Caroni, Arouca, Orange Grove, and Curepe. Four of these have a Sabbath service, and the last named a weekly Tuesday evening meeting. Here the people raise the rent of the school room, $5 monthly. In Orange Grove, the Estate school room is occupied. In Arouca, where difficulties have been greatest, Rev. Mr. Dickson has given valuable aid by furnishing a free school room. In Tunapuna, meetings and school are held in the Mission premises, and in Caroni, a contribution of £37 9*s.* from James R. Craig, Esq., Glasgow, will commence a fund for building a school room, offers of help from the people having been already received. Ten hospitals have been visited and service respeatedly held with the patients.

Building of Mission House.

Mr. Morton's rented dwelling being uncomfortable and unhealthy, a proper house was indispensable, and it was decided the house should combine dwelling and school-room. This has been carried out at a cost of £584 sterling, to which something like £50 will have to be added yet for painting. No special appeal for funds having been made, the debt on the building at the end of 1881 was £448. At the suggestion of Mr. Morton the Committee decided that payment should be spread over a few years, that for the present year one hundred pounds be paid from the funds to cover interest, insurance and leave a balance to reduce the debt, and that both in Trinidad and Canada special donations from funds might be obtained during the year. It was also agreed that £50 be granted for other buildings in this new field, to enable Mr. Morton to deal with the Caroni for a teachers' room at Arouca, and perhaps also a school-room there, as no Government aid can be obtained in the present room.

The half of these sums have been remitted and a good begining made in special contributions, a lady of the United Church, New Glasgow, has sent $100, and has been followed by another of like mind, Mrs. Thomas Davison, of Portapique mountain, who has given an equal sum. A few more such liberal givers, with smaller donations than these, for all cannot give in hundreds, would soon reduce the debt, and greatly cheer the missionary grappling with the difficulties of the new field.

It will thus be seen that a great deal has been done in a single year, and that the new field is being really occupied. School attendance and baptisms given elsewhere.

Statistics.

Preaching stations, 21. Schools, 29. Children on roll, 1,139. Daily average, 749. Communicants, 135.

STATE OF ACCOUNTS.

First Account—Foreign Missions.

Receipts, $13,000.26. Expendit's, $12,172.62. On hand, $927.64.

Second Account--Dayspring and Mission Schools.

Receipts, 3,447.46. Expenditures, $3,781. Balance due, $334.23.

2. WESTERN SECTION.

Mission to the Indians in the North-West.

In the summer of 1866, the Rev. James Nisbet was sent to establish a mission to the Cree Indians. This tribe inhabited the region along the Saskatchewan. They numbered about 4000.

Mr. Nisbet made his headquarters at Prince Albert, where he established a school. During recent years the character of the mission has been greatly changed by the large influx of immigrants, who have settled in Prince Albert and along the Saskatchewan. In their report to the Assembly, in 1876, the Committee said: "But while Prince Albert is yearly growing less suitable, as a centre of Indian work, it is becoming rapidly more important as a Home Mission Field. A large English-speaking settlement has sprung up around the Mission. It has now a population of at least four hundred, and it is constantly increasing. The rich soil, excellent climate, and entire freedom from the ravages of the grasshoppers, have drawn many settlers from Red River to this locality." In 1876 a mission was commenced at Okanase, a reserve set apart for the Indians, about 160 miles north-west of Winnipeg, and about 20 miles from Fort Pelly, by the Rev. Geo. Flett. There are about 400 Indians in that region, among whom he has laboured with encouraging success. In 1877 a school was erected upon the Roseau Indian Reserve, near Pembina. Concerning this school, the Committee report, in 1878: from a variety of causes, the attendance did not average more than twelve-and a-half during the year. Should the attendance not increase, or some more economical method of conducting the school not be discovered, it may become a question whether it should not be discontinued. The attendance continued to decrease, until it became too small to warrant the expenditure necessary to sustain a teacher, and in 1881 it was decided to close it and dispose of the building. In 1871 a very encouraging commencement was made near Fort Ellice, of a mission to the Sioux or Dakota Indians, who, some years before, fled from the United States to British territory. They are among the most intelligent, as well as the most warlike and vigorous of the Indian races. Rev. Solomon Tuncansuicye, an ordained missionary of the Presbyterian Church of the United States, himself a Sioux, was secured to labour among this branch of his tribe. He arrived in November of 1877, and was well received by the Indians at the Sioux Reserve. He still labours among them, and the whole tribe appears to be making satisfactory progress in religious knowledge and material comfort. The missionaries, with their respective fields in the North-West, are,—Rev. John Mackay Prince Albert; Rev. John Flett, Okanase; Rev. Solomon Tuncansuicive, Fort Ellice; Miss Baker, teacher, Prince Albert; Mr. C Mackay, teacher, Crow Stand.

2. *Mission to China.*

On the 1st of November, 1871, the Rev. George Leslie McKay sailed from San Francisco as the Church's first Missionary to China. After a prosperous voyage he landed at Hong Kong about the end of the month. After spending some time on the mainland, he resolved to visit the Island of Formosa before selecting a field of labor. This large Island lies between what the Chinese call Nan-hai and Tong-hai, or the Southern and Eastern Sea, and is separated from the mainland by the strait of Fokien, which is about 91 miles wide in its narrowest part. Formosa is nearly 250 miles long and 80 broad, and has a population ot about 3,000,000. The inhabitants are divided into three classes: 1. The Chinese, many of whom have emigrated from the neighborhood of Amoy, and speak the dialect of that district, while others are Hakkas from the vicinity of Swatow. (2). The subjugated Aborigines, now largely intermingled with the Chinese. (3). The uncivilized Aborigines of the Eastern region, who refuse to recognize the Chinese authority and carry on raids as opportunity occurs. These Aborigines, of both classes, are broken up into almost countless tribes and clans, many of which number only a few hundred individuals, and their language consequently presents a variety of dialects, of which no classification has yet been effected in the district of Posia alone, says Dr. Dickson, of the Presbyterian Mission, there are "eight different mutually unintelligible dialects." (For character and customs of the people, and products of the Island, see *Ency.* Brit., Ninth Edition, Art. *Formosa*). After spending some time with the brethern of the English Presbyterian Church on the Island, Mr. McKay selected Northern Formosa as the scene of his future labors. In this part of the Island there were no missionaries and unbroken heathenism reigned everywhere. Early in 1872, he landed at Tamsui, and at once devoted himself to the mastery of the language. In five months from the time of his arrival in China, he began to proclaim the Gospel in their own tongue and ten months later, he baptized five converts. From that time to the present, the work has prospered to an extent seldom seen so early in a mission. In 1874, the Rev. Dr. G. B. Fraser was sent to Tamsui as a medical missionary, and took charge of the hospital there. He retired owing to severe domestic affliction; in less than three years, and until 1878, Mr. McKay occupied the field again, alone. In that year, Rev. K. F. Junor was sent to

Formosa to aid him. The labor and the climate have very seriously affected his health, and he has been constrained to withdraw from the field for a time.

3. *Mission to Central India.*

In 1873, two young ladies, Misses Rodger and Fairweather, having prepared themselves for service in the Foreign mission Field, were sent out to India, and as the Canada Presbyterian Church had no missionaries then, in India, under whose protection and guidance they could labor; they were placed under the control and care of Foreign Missions of the Presbyterian Church in the United States. They sailed from New York in the latter part of October, 1873, and in due time reached their destination in safety. For some time they labored at Mynpoorie, near the Ganges, and about 750 miles north-west of Calcutta. But having suffered from bilious and jungle fever, in the beginning of 1874, they were appointed to a station at Rakha, near Futtehgurh. This station is situated on the Ganges, almost 720 miles north-west of Calcutta.

Report 1876.

In the opinion of your Committee, the time has arrived when the Presbyterian Church in Canada should seek to do more for the perishing millions of India than has yet been attempted. They can scarcely conceive a more appropriate way to signalize the approaching Union of the various Presbyterian Churches of the Dominion than by devising and accomplishing more liberal things on behalf of the heathen. The young ladies whom we have already sent to India plead earnestly that the Canadian Church shall enter at once on this work. The brethren of the American Presbyterian Mission urge us to send missionaries to this destitute field. They are exceedingly anxious that the Presbyterians of Canada should organize a mission without delay in the Province of Indore, in Central India. This field is entirely unoccupied. None of the Churches or Missionary Societies has entered upon this extensive region. The district is under British rule, and is considered in every way suitable as a field for a promising mission. It is accessible both from Bombay and from Calcutta, by way of Allahabad. Your Committee trust, however, that such decided action will be taken that another year will not elapse until Canadian Presbyterianism shall be represented by one or two ordained missionaries in India.

Report 1877.

It can now be said that there is a Canadian Mission in India. Since 1874 Misses Rodger and Fairweather have laboured in India under the care of the American Presbyterian Missionaries. But while they were sustained by the Canadian Church, Canada had no regularly organized Mission of its own, with which they could be connected. Now, after having done excellent service for the brethren of the American Presbyterian Mission, they form part of the regular staff of the Canadian Mission, established in Central India by Rev. J. M. Douglas.

Mr. Douglas having been accepted by the last General Assembly as a Missionary to India was designated to his work at Cobourg, on the 26th September last, and early in October he left for India, with instructions to establish, should the way appear open, a Mission in Indore.

After a prosperous voyage he reached Bombay on the 22nd December, where he received a cordial welcome from Rev. R. Stothert, and other Missionary brethren. He then proceeded to Allahabad, where he met a considerable number of the Missionaries of the American Presbyterian Church, who could not have shown him any greater kindness had he been one of their own Mission staff. And when, on the 19th January, he set out for Central India, Rev. J. F. Holcomb accompanied him all the way to Indore, and gave him the benefit of his experience and counsel in selecting the Mission field to be permanently occupied. They also supplied Mr. Douglas with a trained native Catechist, through whose agency the work of preaching the Gospel to the heathen could be commenced at once. On the 25th of January they reached the capital of the Holkar's territory, and Mr. Douglas found himself the sole Protestant Missionary in a heathen city of 70,000 inhabitants. As Indore is in a native state, under British protection, but not directly under British rule, some uncertainty was felt in regard to the reception which Missionaries might receive. After surveying the field and gaining such information as he could collect on the spot, Mr. Douglas judged that a favorable opening presented itself and he decided to establish himself there. A suitable house was secured for himself, and another for Misses Fairweather and Rodger, who removed immediately to Indore and entered on their work. They have already obtained access to a number of high-caste Zenanas, and a school for Mahommedan girls has been begun. Educated native gentlemen have expressed their cordial interest in female education, and there seems to be a good prospect that the young ladies sent out from Canada will find in this growing city an ample field for successful work. Mr. Douglas has been appointed officiating Chaplain to Her Majesty's troops at Mhow, which is thirteen miles from Indore. This position he values highly for the influence it gives him. By the officers of the British Government he has been shown much kindness, and from one of them, he has received the donation of a valuable case of Bibles, books and tracts. These are sold by the Catechist to the people, who seem ready to secure them.

Your Committee have learned with pleasure that the Rev. J. F. Campbell has, as authorized by last Assembly, decided to visit Indore, and they would greatly rejoice should his visit result in his permanent removal to that field. It seems desirable that all missionaries sustained by the Church in India should in the meantime be united in one vigorous mission.

Report of 1878.

This Mission has been greatly strengthened during the year. When the last Foreign Mission Report was presented to the General Assembly, Rev. J. M. Douglas and Misses Rodger and Fairweather constituted its entire staff. There are now two ordained Missionaries and four ladies, besides native agents, regularly employed in this field. In the month of July last, Rev. J. F. Campbell who had been sent to Madras under the auspices of the Eastern Committee removed to Central India, and joined Mr. Douglas in his work. This step taken, as it was, with the full sanction of the last Assembly, will, it is hoped, secure greater unity and vigour in the prosecution of the work in India. In the month of December, Rev. J. M. Douglas was cheered by the arrival of his wife and three of his children from Canada; and the Mission received a valuable accession to its strength in the persons of Misses Forrester and McGregor, who reached India by the same steamer as Mrs. Douglas.

When Rev. J. F. Campbell removed to Central India, Mr. Douglas, guided by the advice of those in whose judgment he had confidence, deemed it inexpedient for both Missionaries to remain at Indore. It was supposed that too great display of force at first would stir up opposition. It was therefore considered better for Mr. Campbell to occupy Mhow, a city thirteen miles distant, where there are a large body of British troops, and a native population of 20,000, and where he will be within easy reach of the other Missionary.

As Indore is now said to have a population not of 70,000, as at first reported, but of nearly 200,000, it seemed a pity that the entire Mission staff could not remain in such an important centre. In matters of this kind, your Committee feel that much respect must always be paid to the views of the Missionaries upon the ground. Yet they have felt it necessary to ask more specific information respecting the grounds for those apprehensions which have led to this course, and they are not without hopes that with due regard to the interests of the work, it may soon be found possible to concentrate the Mission staff at Indore.

After the arrival of Misses Forrester and McGregor, it was decided, largely owing to the difficulty of securing suitable accommodation for all the ladies at Indore, to send Misses Rodger and Forrester to Mhow, while Misses Fairweather and McGregor remained in the Holkar's capital. By this distribution of labourers, one lady fully acquainted with the languages of the natives was secured to each station.

Report, 1879.

The Mission, for the time that it has been in operation, has been attended by an encouraging measure of success. It is still only in the initial stage of its progress. It employs, however, a great variety of agencies to make known the Gospel to the people of Central India. There has been no addition made to the Canadian labourers. Messrs. Douglas and Campbell and four young ladies have constituted the mission staff for the year at Indore and Mhow. They have, however, been aided by a goodly band of native assistants in the various departments of their work.

On the 9th September, 1879, Rev. John Wilkie, M.A., was designated as a missionary to Central India by the Presbytery of Guelph, and shortly after he and his wife sailed from Quebec. They arrived at Bombay in December 22nd, and reached Mhow on the 25th, and next day went on to Indore where they took up their abode. Mr. Wilkie was appointed Treasurer of the Mission, and Miss Fairweather returned to Canada during this year. In 1882 Rev. James Douglas returned to Canada.

Chart of our Foreign Missions, 1883.

1. *The New Hebrides Mission.*

Missionaries.—Rev. H. A. Robertson, Martyr's Church, Eromanga, appointed, 1871. Rev. Joseph Annand, at Aneityum, appointed, 1872. Rev. J. W. Mackenzie, at Efate, appointed, 1872.

Total population, 2040; Worshippers, 540; Communicants, 55; Teachers, 25. Population in Mr. A's district, 565; Sabbath attendance, 300; Prayer meeting, 150; 22 schools taught by Natives; Communicants, 233. Five Mission Stations; 81 Communicants; 280 Worshippers; 2 Bible Classes.

The "*Day Spring*" *Mission Ship*, last year sailed 10,000 miles, paid many visits, to Mission Stations, Harbours, and heathen islands, carrying Missionaries, their wives, families, and native Teachers and natives, besides making her two regular voyages to Sydney in N. S. Wales.

2. *Trinidad Mission.*

Missionaries.—Rev. John Morton, Tunapuna, in Caroni District; first appointed 1867; Bhukard, Cathechist; Miss Agnes M. Semple, Teacher.

Rev. Kenneth J. Grant, San Fernando District; appointed 1870; Rev. Lal Behari, Assistant Missionary; Jacob Corsbie, teacher; Jai-Par-Gas-Lal; George Sadaphal; Ramjas and Madhee, Catechists.

Rev. T. M. Christie, Couva District, appointed 1873; Rev. J. W. McLeod, Princestown, Savannah Grande Dis., appointed 1881; Miss Annie L. Blackadder, Teacher; Joseph Annajee, Native Evangelist.

Coolie population above 30,000. Total number of schools, 29; scholars, 1,139. Salaries of Native Evangelist from $200 to $335 each. The Woman's F. M. S., Halifax, provides Miss Blackadder's salary, $406; Communicants, 135.

Mission to the Indians in the North-West.

Missionaries.—Rev. John Mackay, Prince Albert, Saskatchewan, appointed 1878; Rev. George Flett, Okanase, appointed

1873; Rev. Solomon Tunkansuiciye, Fort Ellice, appointed 1877; Mr. C. Mackay, Teacher at Fort Pelly; Miss Baker, Teacher at Prince Albert, 1879.

Mission to Formosa.

Missionaries.—Rev. G. L. Mackay, D.D., Tamsui, appointed; 1871; Rev. K. F. Junor, 1877.

In a little more than nine years, 20 Chapels have been opened and 2 Mission Houses built, and 20 native helpers trained; 5 Schools are sustained; 300 Communicants are enrolled, and nearly 3,000 persons have renounced idolatry and attend Christian worship. There is also an Hospital in Tamsui, doing excellent work. An Hospital has also being established at Kelung, under the care of Dr. Mann. A training college for native missionaries has been instituted under the presidency of Rev. Dr. Mackay*

5. *Mission to CentralIndia.*

Missionaries.—Rev. John Wilkie, at Indore, appointed 1879 Rev. James Fraser Campbell, Mhow, appointed 1876; Miss Rodger, on furlough in Canada, appointed 1873; Miss McGregor, at Indore, appointed 1877; Miss Ross, appointed 1882; Rev. S. J. Taylor, under appointment, 1883.

The *Indian Orphanage and Juvenile Mission,* besides supporting four high-caste Zenana Day-Schools, and providing for the support and education of seven or eight orphans at Calcutta and Poona, supports about fifteen orphans and two Bible-women at Indore, and contributes to the *Day Spring* and the Trinidad Mission.

Contributions from 1861 *to* 1882,

Minutes 1882, App. p. 8, 85. It is both interesting and encouraging to note the steady growth of liberality in the Church in connection with the support of the Foreign Mission cause. The

---

*Note during the present month, April, 1883, a telegram has been received from Dr. Mackay, stating that a community of the Aborigines on the Eastern side of the Island, have cast away their idols and accepted Christianity.

following table exhibits the givings of the Canada Presbyterian Church during the period from the first to the second Union, and of the whole Church from the second Union in 1875 down to the present time:

1861–62	—Contributions	from all sources	....	$2,067 06
1862–63	"	"	....	2,798 23
1863–64	"	"	....	3,475 59
1864–65	"	"	....	3,486 53
1865–66	"	"	....	3,997 39
1866–67	"	"	(in. £100 from Free Ch.)	4,809 50
1867–68	"	"	....	4,341 18
1868–69	"	"	....	5,179 58
1869–70	"	"	....	5,526 26
1870–71	"	"	....	6,312 62
1871–72	"	"	(including $1,168, legacy and outfit)..........	11,212 32
1872–73	"	"	....	10,522 38
1873–74	"	"	....	11,084 41
1874–75	"	"	(Year of second Union)	12,588 40
1875–76	"	"	....	14,811 85
1876–77	"	"	....	15,039 18
1877–78	"	"	....	21,170 74
1878–79	"	"	....	21,815 39
1879–80	"	"	....	22,471 59
1880–81	"	"	....	35,434 58
1881–82	"	"	....	47,116 89

13. Woman's Foreign Missionary Societies.

In January, 1871, "The Canadian Woman's Board" of Foreign Missions was organized. This Society represents various evangelical churches. It has now four auxiliaries, the total receipts since its formation, to January, 1882, being $10,166,50. It is pledged to support a girl's school in Madura, India, and a scholarship in the Seminary for girls at Beirut, Syria, also a girls' high caste school in Calcutta. In addition to these pledges it contributes various amounts to several other missions each year, in accordance with the undenominational character of the Society.

In connection with the Presbyterian Church in Canada we have at present three Societies, viz., "The Woman's Foreign Missionary Society of the Presbyterian Church in Canada" (Western Section) "The Woman's Foreign Missionary Society of the Presbyterian Church in Canada" (Eastern Section) and "The Woman's Foreign Missionary Society of the Presbytery of Kingston"; also, previous to August, 1879, "The Woman's Foreign Missionary Society of the Presbytery of Hamilton," was an independent organization, but since that period has been affiliated with the Society of the Western Section. The first named of these societies was established in April 1876, headquarters in Toronto; number of auxiliaries, 57; Mission Bands, 12; amount raised last year $5,629 86. Total raised since its establishment, $20,478.99. Last year this Society supported two lady missionaries in Central India, one Bible reader and 3 day schools; with other incidental expenses connected with the work of the Canadian Mission, Indore. The second was formed in October, 1876, headquarters at Halifax; total amount raised since that period, $3,051.93; number of auxilaries, 7. This Society is engaged in Evangelistic work among the women and children of the Island of Trinidad.

"The Woman's Foreign Missionary Society in the Presbytery of Kingston," was organized in April, 1876; number of auxiliaries, 8; amount raised last year $371.97; total amount raised since organization, $1,126.58. This Society has no special laborer in the field, but divides its contributions between the Formosa Mission, and Mrs J. F. Campbell's work at Mhow, India. There are other societies connected with the Presbyterian Church, of whose work we regret that we cannot present statistics, viz., "The Indore Society," Quebec, and "The Woman's Missionary Society," Winnipeg, also the "Woman's Missionary Society," Montreal There are also two Societies in Newfoundland, viz., the "Woman's Foreign Missionary Society," St John's, and the "Woman's Foreign Missionary Society," Harbor Grace. These are included in the auxiliaries reported in connection with the Eastern Section.

Report of Western Section, 1876.

Minutes, App. p. 160. Your Committee, guided by the instructions of the General Assembly of the late Canada Presbyterian Church, with the view of securing the more full co-operation of the female membership of the Church in support of the women who are employed as missionaries among the heathen, took steps to have organized a Woman's Foreign Missionary Society, as an auxiliary of your Committee. A meeting of ladies interested in the work was called by public notice, and after the necessary steps were taken, a Constitution was adopted, a copy of which is appended to this Report, and thereafter a Society was duly organized. This Society proposes to aid your Committee in its work among the women and children of heathen countries. This Society desires to organize branches as generally as possible over the Church so as to enlist the entire mass of the earnest Christian women of the Church on behalf of their heathen sisterhood a :d their children. The Society, as its Constitution shows, in no way interferes with the regular ecclesiastical supervision and control of the labourers employed. It is constructed in thorough loyalty to the recognized principles of Presbyterianism.

Woman's Foreign Missionary Society of the Presbyterian Church in Canada, Toronto.

1 *Constitution.*

1. This Society shall be called "The Woman's Foreign Missionary Society of the Presbyterian Church in Canada," and its central point of operations shall be in the city of Toronto.

2. Its object shall be to aid the Foreign Missionary Committee or Board of Missions, by promoting its work among the women and children of heathen lands, and for this purpose it shall receive and disburse all money which shall be contributed to the Society, subject to the action of that Committee or Board, in the appointment of Missionaries supported by the Society, and fixing their salaries and location. For the furtherance of this end it shall endeavour to organize similar associations throughout the Church, and these associations shall bear the name of Auxiliary Societies to the Woman's Foreign Missionary Society of the Presbyterian Church in Canada, and shall report their work to this Society at such times as the By-Laws may direct.

3. Each person paying one dollar annually, through an auxiliary, or direct to the treasury, shall become a member of this Society. The payment of twenty-five dollars, by one person at one time shall constitute a life membership.

4. The business of the Society shall be conducted by a Board of thirty-two managers, including the President, four Vice-Presidents, a Recording Secretary, two Corresponding Secretaries, and a Treasurer. They shall be elected from the members of the Society, annually, by the members who are present at the Annual Meeting. They shall have power to elect not more than ten non-resident Vice-Presidents, and of appointing corresponding members, when the objects of the Society shall be promoted thereby; they shall also have authority to fill vacancies occurring in their body during the year.

5. There shall be an Executive Committee composed of the officers, and four other managers, to be elected annually. This Committee shall have power to transact such business as may require attention in the intervals between the stated meetings of the Board. Five members shall constitute a quorum.

6. The Annual Meeting of the Society shall be held on the second Tuesday in April, in the City of Toronto, (unless postponed for special reasons by the Board), at which time the Board of Managers shall report to the Society the operations, condition and prospects thereof, and an election shall be made of Officers and Managers for the ensuing year.

7. A Special Meeting of the Society may be called at any time by the President, upon the request of three Managers.

8. This Constitution may be altered at any regular meeting of the Society, by a vote of two-thirds of the members present, notice in writing of the intended alteration having been given at a previous meeting.

2. *By-Laws.*

1. The Board of Managers shall hold its stated meetings on the first Tuesday of each month, at 3 o'clock p.m. at such place as it shall appoint. Five members shall constitute a quorum.

2. The President shall preside at all meetings of the Board, and perform such other duties as are incident to the office. She shall call special meetings upon the request of three members, and shall be *ex officio* a member of all standing committees. She shall sign all drafts upon the treasury before they are paid.

3. The Senior Vice-President present shall, in the absence of the President, perform all the duties of her office.

4. The Treasurer shall receive, and hold, and keep an account of all money given to this Society, and shall disburse it as the Board of Managers shall direct. She shall report the state of the treasury at each regular meeting. Her annual report shall be examined by an auditor appointed by the Board.

5. The Recording Secretary shall keep a fair record of the proceedings of the Board, and give proper notice of special and stated meetings.

6. It shall be the duty of the Corresponding Secretary for the Foreign Field to conduct the official correspondence with the Foreign Mission Committee or Board, and also with the missionaries, teachers and bible-readers supported by this Society. She shall, in conjunction with the other Secretaries, prepare the annual Report of the Board of Managers. Missionaries supported by this Society shall be required to make regular reports to her.

7. The Corresponding Secretary for the Home Field shall correspond with Churches and individuals, in localities where it is possible to awaken an interest in the branch of Missionary work for which this Society was formed. It shall be her duty to extend information on the subject in all proper directions. She shall organize Auxiliary Societies wherever it is practicable.

8. Auxiliary Societies shall be required to make an annual Report to the Board on or before the first Tuesday in March.

9. Any Manager who shall be absent from three successive meetings of the Board, without notifying the same of the reason of her absence, shall forfeit her position, and her place may be filled.

10. The Society shall meet with the Board of Managers on the first Tuesday of each month, for three-quarters of an hour, for devotional exercises and the reception of Missionary intelligence, after which the board shall, by itself, proceed to the transaction of its business.

11. These by-laws may be amended at any meeting of the Society, by a vote of two-thirds of the members present, but notice of any proposed amendment must be given in writing at the meeting preceeding such vote.

Constitution of an Auxiliary Society.

1. This Society shall be called the———of the Woman's Foreign Missionary Society of the Presbyterian Church in Canada.

2. Its object shall be to aid the General Society in sending to Foreign Fields and sustaining female missionaries, Bible-readers, and teachers, who shall labour among heathen women and children.

3. Any person may become a member of this Society by the payment of $———annually.

4. The officers of this Society shall be a President, Secretary and Treasurer.

5. The President shall preside at all meetings, and have a general oversight of the work.

6. It shall be the duty of the secretary to record the proceedings of the Society, give notice of meetings, and prepare the Annual Report. She must also keep the General Society informed of the condition of the Auxiliary, and forward a list of officers, with the Report and the Treasurer's statement.

7. The Treasurer's duty shall be to report the state of the treasury at every meeting, and remit the funds yearly to the Treasurer of the General Society, on or before the first Tuesday in March.

8. This Society shall hold regular stated meetings, when all suitable measures shall be adopted to promote interest in this branch of missionary work, also an annual meeting to elect officers and hear the Annual Report.

9. An auxiliary Society, raising sufficient means, may have the privilege of designating a missionary whom they might wish to support

4. *Memorandum.*

Any rules relating to the local affairs of the Society may be adopted, provided they do not conflict with the Constitution and By-Laws of the General Society.

NOTE.—Do not interfere with other organizations. Make no appeal that shall conflict with duties church members owe to any other benevolent work.

5. *Directions for forming Mission Bands.*

1. An association of young ladies banded together to aid the Woman's Foreign Missionary Society of the Presbyterian Church, shall be called a Mission Band, auxiliary to the Missionary Society of the church in which it is formed, or the Parent Society in Toronto.

2. Each band shall be responsible for not less than $20 a year.

3. Any one may become a member of a Mission Band by the annual payment of twenty-five cents.

4. The officers of a Band shall be a President, Secretary, and Treasurer, who shall be elected annually.

5. The duty of the President shall be to preside at all stated meetings, and have general oversight of the work of the Band.

6. The duty of the Secretary shall be to keep a record of the proceedings of the Band, and make an Annual Report to the Missionary Society to which it is auxiliary, or to the Woman's Foreign Missionary Society in Toronto.

7. The Treasurer shall receive and hold all funds, paying the same annually to the Treasurer of the Auxiliary of the church in which the Band is formed, or to the Treasurer of the Woman's Foreign Missionary Society of Toronto.

8. Each Mission Band must select an appropriate name not already in use, and report the same to the Society to which its money is sent.

6. *Report of the Seventh Annual Meeting*, 1883.

The following facts indicate the rapid growth of the Society, and its far-reaching influence for good. The branches of this Society now extend throughout the whole Church in Ontario and Quebec. At the Annual Meeting there were nearly 200 delegates present, including representatives from Ashburn, Cobourg, Almonte, Hamilton, Peterboro', Fergus, King's Road, Newcastle, Lindsay, Ottawa, Newtonville, Uxbridge, North Georgetown, Port Perry, Seaforth, Bowmanville, Port Hope, Agincourt, Toronto, Beaverton, Harriston, Sarnia, Oshawa, Brooklyn, Whitby, Galt, and Ypsilanti, Michigan. The Society has 66 Auxilaries, 11 Mission Bands, and 4 Presbyterial Societies, numbering in all about 2,000 members, including 25 life members. During the seven years that the Society has been in existence its progress has been rapid and distinctly marked, as the following amounts contributed during the different years very clearly show: 1st year, $2,107 ; 2nd year, $2,166 ; 3rd year, $3,225 ; 4th year, $3,682 ; 5th year, $4,666 ; 6th year, $5,629 ; 7th year, $7,125.

7. *Officers of the Society.*

President, Mrs Ewart ; vice-presidents, Mrs McLaren, Mrs Macdonnell, Mrs W. Reid, Mrs McMurrich, and the presidents of all the auxilaries and Presbyterial societies ; recording secretary, Mrs MacMurchy ; home secretary, Miss Topp, foreign secretary, Mrs Harvie ; treasurer, Mrs King. General Committee, Mrs Morrison, Ormstown ; Mrs Beattie, Port Hope; Miss Gordon, Whitby ; Miss James, Hamilton ; Mrs Cooper, Chatham ; Miss Harman, Ottawa ; and the following from Toronto : Mesdames Alexander, Blaikie, Bryce, M. Clark, Crombie, Ewart, Harvie, King, Kerr, Kirkland, Macdonnell, McLaughlin, H. H. McLachlan, MacMurchy, Milligan, Maclennan, Miller, Morris, McCracken, Paterson, Richardson, W. Reid, J. Y. Reid, Smith, Thorn, and the Misses Top, Haight, and Jeffrey.

8. *Juvenile Indian Mission.*

This is the oldest Foreign Missionary scheme connected with our Church, having been originated more than twenty years ago, by John Paton, Esq., now of New York, who succeeded in interesting in the subject of Indian female education first the

Sabbath School of St. Andrew's Church, Kingston, of which h was a member, and then a number of other schools connected with that branch of the Church; and who continued, during the whole of his residence in Canada, the efficient secretary-treasurer of the scheme. The work gradually extended itself, till the contributions amounted to over $1000 per annum; some fifty orphans being supported simultaneously at the four Scottish Orphanages of Calcutta, Madras, Poona, and Sealkote, under the auspices of the Scottish Ladies' Association for promoting Female Education in India. In this way, it is not too much to calculate, that since the inception of the scheme upwards of two hundred low-caste children have thus received in the orphanages, by its means, the blessings of a Christian education. A separate school for high-caste children, called the Canadian School, has also been for a good many years supported, or nearly so, by Canadian contributions. During the last two or three years, also, the operations of the scheme have been further enlarged, by the employment of a Zenana teacher, to carry the glad tidings of the gospel within the dreary wall of the Zenanas, or female households of the high-caste Hindoos, where the secluded inmates grow up in blank and total ignorance, intellectual and spiritual. Three Zenana schools have also been established, in connection with our Zenana Mission, at which a large number, probably considerably more than a hundred children, out of the Zenanas, are receiving a Christian education, the teachers being former pupils at the orphanages. Of these schools, from which we receive good accounts through Miss Pigot, of Calcutta, one at Dhoba-Parah, near Calcutta, is supported by a Montreal Juvenile Association. Another division of the same school of Dhoba-Parah is maintained by St. Gabriel Street Sabbath School, Montreal; and another at Badoor-Bagan, also a suburb of Calcutta, is partially maintained by the South Georgetown Sabbath School. We may thus count, in all, about 250 Hindoo children at present receiving Christian instruction, through the agency of this mission besides the diligent work of the Zenana teacher, who visits the Zenanas themselves, and instructs their secluded inmates. The cost of maintaining an orphan at the orphanages is about $20, and some of our schools maintain two, and even in one instance *three*. The maintenance of a Zenana school costs $70, and may be divided between two or three contributing schools. The Assemblies of 1876 and 1877 commended this mission to the hearty sympathy and assistance of the Sabbath Schools of our Church.

9. *Resolutions of Assembly* 1878-79.

Minutes, p. 50. The Assembly appoint a committee to consider in what manner the Foreign Mission Committee and the Juvenile Mission Committee may most harmoniously and efficiently prosecute their work, Dr. Wardrope, Convener, with instructions to report to next General Assembly.

Minutes, p. 31. This Committee made the following report to the Assembly in 1879, which was unanimously received and adopted :—

That feeling the great importance of enlisting the youth of our Church in her mission scheme, and the necessity of cultivating a Missionary spirit among them by every available means at present employed or that may be employed under the directions of the Assembly, and yet feeling the necessity of unity of action in all our great Missionary schemes, the Committee would recommend :

1. That the Foreign Mission and Juvenile Mission Committees be amalgamated—the said Committee so amalgamated to take charge of and be responsible for the work, duties and obligations heretofore done by or imposed upon the said Committees respectively.

2. That a standing Committee of five members shall, at the first meeting of the Foreign Mission Committee after its appointment by the General Assembly, be appointed from the members of the same, to whom shall be relegated the work heretofore done by the Juvenile Mission Committee and such other work as may be ordered by the said Foreign Mission Committee, and for which they shall be directly responsible to the said Foreign Mission Committee.

3. That the standing Committee, so appointed, be recommended to continue the present Secretary of the Juvenile Mission Committee as their Secretary.

10. *Treasurers Report to Assembly.* 1882.

By whom Contributed.	Place.	Object or Orphan.	Orphanage or Place.	Am't.
St. Andrew's S. S.	Kingston	Aladie	Calcutta	$20 00
" "	"	Canadian School	"	10 00
" "	"	Day School	Indore	20 00
" "	Martintown	Ruth	Calcutta	20 00
" "	Seymour	Canadian School	"	10 00
Juvenile Workers for Christ	Montreal	Dhoba-párâh S. sen. div.	"	70 00
St. Gabriel Street S. School	"	Dhoba-párâh S. S, jun. div.	"	20 00
St. Paul's S. S.	"	Dhoba-párâh S. S., jun div.	"	40 00
" "	"	Day schools	Indore.	10 00
St. Andrew's S. S.	Arnprior	"	"	15 00
" "	Toronto	"	"	50 00
" "	"	Dayspring	New Hebrides.	50 00
" "	Belleville	Day schools	Indore	25 00
Sabbath School	St. John, N.B.	"	"	20 00
"	Annan	"	"	5 00
"	Kippen (2 years)	"	"	40 00
"	Westport	"	"	5 00
"	S. Georgetown	Badoor Bagan S.	Calcutta	20 00
"	Lanark	"	"	13 50
"	Toledo	"	"	10 15
"	Mimosa	"	"	2 00
"	Smith's Falls	"	"	5 00
"	Williamstown	Dayspring	New Hebrides.	20 00
Chalmers Ch. S. S.	Guelph	Day schools	Indore	10 00
St, Andrew's S. S.	King	"	"	8 00
St. Paul's	Hawkesb'y (2 yrs.)	"	"	1 50
"	Hamilton	"	"	36 36
Sabbath School	Picton	"	"	5 00
"	Ormstown	"	"	25 00
Indore Miss'n Soc'y	Quebec	Zenana Teachers	"	90 00
Ladies' Miss'y Ass'n	Scarboro'			35 00
Chil'n W. J Passmore	Conestoga			3 00
Portsmouth S. S.	Kingston			5 00
				$719 51

14. General Facts respecting Protestant Missions.

(Gospel in all Lands, April 12th, 1883.)

1. *Great Britain.*

Missionary Societies, 23; Annual income, $4,415,310; number of missionaries, 1615; communicants connected with their stations, 353,266; adherents connected with stations, 1,189,764.

2. *North America.*

Missionary Societies in Canada and the United States, 22; their incomes, $2,305,750; missionaries supported by them, 701; communicants connected with their stations, 109,617; adherents, 312,530.

3. *Europe.*

Missionary Societies in Europe, 27; income, $745,250; missionaries supported by them, 634; communicants connected with stations, 111,062; adherents connected with stations, 369,783.

4. *Totals.*

Societies in Great Britain, Europe and N. America, 72; Incomes, $8,566,310; missionaries, 2,950: communicants, 573,945; adherents, 1,872,077; number of adherents belonging to all the Protestant missions among the heathen, 2,283,700.

In America.

Greenland and Labrador	10,300
North American Indians	130,000
West Indies	407,800
Central and South America	140,000
	688,100

In Africa.

North Africa	1,500
West Africa	100,000
South Africa	190,000
East Africa	1,100
African Islands	285,000
	577,600

Carried forward....................$1,265,700

Brought forward	$1,265,700

In Asia.

Indian Archipelago	150,000
India	500,000
China	60,000
Japan	9,000
Further India	35,000
	754,000

In the South Sea Islands.

Polynesia	220,000
Micronesia	8,000
Melanesia	15,000
New Zealand	20,000
Australia	1,000
	264,000
Grand Total	2,283,700

5. *List of Foreign Missionary Societies.*

In "The Gospel in all Lands Missionary Almanac," for 1883, published by Eugene R. Smith, Bible House, New York, there is given a list of the principal missionary societies of the world, the date of organization, so far as could be ascertained, and the names and addresses of the Secretaries.

Note.—In the *Presbyterian Record* for *May*, 1882, a list of Foreign Missionary Societies is also given, and in the *Record* of *March*, 1881, the Missionary Roll of the Presbyterian Church in Canada may be found.

6. *The World and Christ.*

Inhabitants.—There are 1,433,887,500 inhabitants on the earth. Of these about 850,000,000 are idolators, 170,000,000 Mohammedans and Jews, making two-thirds of the population of the earth who either know nothing of Jesus or are opposed to Him. Of those who are called Christians only 100,000,000 are nominally Protestants, and only 20,000,000 are members of Protestant Churches.

Missions.—There were seven Protestant Missionary Societies at the commencement of this century: now there are over one hundred. There were 70 Protestant Missionaries in the year 1800. Now there are over 2,600 ordained European and American Missionaries engaged in Foreign Mission work, assisted by over 600 lay missionaries and 1,600 female missionaries, with over 24,000 native preachers, teachers and helpers, and about 575,000 native communicants. Of these communicants over 24,000 were received during 1881. For the year closing April, 1882, about $8,500,000 were given by Protestants for Foreign Mission work.

The Gospal in all lands Missionary Almanac, p. 62.

THE CHURCH—ITS BENEVOLENT FUNDS.

Union Resolution.

Minutes, 1875, page 5. Steps shall be taken at the first meeting of the General Assembly of the Union Church, for the equitable establishment and administration of an efficient Fund for the benefit of the Widows and Orphans of Ministers.

MINISTERS' WIDOWS & ORPHANS' FUND—WESTERN SECTION.

1. Regulations.

1878, p. 33. 1. That one Fund be created for the whole Church.

2. That the terms of the Act of the Province of Quebec, 38 Victoria, chapter lxi , relating to the Ministers', Widows and Orphans' Fund of the late Presbyterian Church of Canada in connection with the Church of Scotland, providing that, in the event of the amalgamation of that Fund with the Funds of the other Churches that were parties to the recent Union, "no widow or orphan of a minister, who had formerly belonged to the Presbyterian Church of Canada in connection with the Church of Scotland, shall receive less annuities from the Fund of the United Church, than would have pertained to them in terms of the scale in force by this Board at the date of Union, if the said Churches had not united," be accepted, and an amalgamation of the four Funds effected.

3. That in addition to the revenue derived from the capital sum formed by the uniting of the four Funds presently existing, the Fund shall be maintained by an annual contribution from each minister and congregation, and the interest of such donations and bequests as shall from time to time accrue.

4. That the rate of ministerial contributions shall be as follows: Ministers at present connected with the Funds in Ontario and Quebec shall continue to pay the same rates as hither-

to, and those connected with the Funds in the Maritime Provinces a uniform rate of eight dollars per annum. Ministers of this Church at present not connected with any Fund, and any ministers, who after this date shall be admitted to participate in the benefits of this Fund, under thirty-five years of age, shall pay into the Fund annually eight dollars ($8); such as are between thirty-five and forty years of age, ten dollars ($10); those who are between forty and fifty years of age, shall pay twelve dollars ($12) per annum. The application of any minister, over fifty years of age, to be admitted to the benefits of the Fund, shall be made the subject of special consideration.

5. That the allowances to widows, from the common Fund, be equal; the case of the widows of the ministers formerly belonging to the Presbyterian Church of Canada in connection with the Church of Scotland, as already provided for, only excepted; provided also that no widow, at present receiving an annuity from any of the Funds, nor the widow of any minister of the United Church, who had formerly belonged to the Presbyterian Church of Canada in connection with the Church of Scotland, shall receive a less allowance than one hundred and fifty dollars ($150) a year.

6. That the following be the scale of annuities payable to widows and orphans:—Each widow shall receive one hundred and fifty dollars ($150) per annum. If a widow have children, she shall receive in addition to her own annuity, for one child, twenty dollars ($20) per annum; for two children thirty six dollars ($36) per annum; for three children fifty dollars ($50) per annum; and ten dollars ($10) per annum for each additional child; but she shall not receive anything from the Fund for children over eighteen years of age. The claim of the widow shall date from the beginning of the half-year in which the death of her husband occurred, and the annuity shall cease at the end of the half-year following her death or re-marriage. In the event of her re-marriage the children's claims shall continue.

7. In the event of the decease of both parents, if there be only one orphan the Board shall pay for the benefit of such orphan one hundred and fifty dollars ($150); if there are two orphans twenty dollars ($20) shall be added to the allowance made for

one; If there are three orphans, sixteen dollars ($16) more shall be paid on their behalf; and if there are four orphans, fourteen dollars ($14) shall be added to the allowance; and ten dollars ($10) shall be given for each additional orphan; but no allowance shall be made for children over eighteen years of age.

8. That on behalf of Professors, Foreign Missionaries, Missionaries under the French Evangelization Committee, Ministers on the Aged and Infirm Ministers' Fund, and the Agents of the Church, the sum of eight dollars shall, in addition to the personal rate, after the amalgamation of the Funds, be paid to this Fund by the Boards or Committees with which they are respectively connected. Ministers, who have retired from active duty with permission of the Church, and for whom no aid is sought from the Fund for Aged and Infirm Ministers, shall pay the sum of eight dollars annually, in addition to the rates previously paid by them.

9. Any minister withdrawing from the Church shall continue to enjoy his rights in this Fund, on condition of his paying annually into the Fund twelve dollars, in addition to the rate previously paid by him.

10. That it be an instruction to Presbyteries to use their utmost endeavours to secure that every minister, when he is inducted into a charge, shall become connected with the Fund.

11. That any minister, who may, at the time of his induction, decline to join the Fund, may be allowed to do so within four years from the date of his induction, on condition of his contributing a sum equivalent to the total payments he should have made, provided he had connected himself with the Fund at his induction, together with an addition of one dollar for each year he has declined to contribute to the Fund after his induction.

12. The rates of payments may be revised once in every five years.

13. That an actuary be employed to examine the Funds presently existing, and report as to the most equitable way in which the amalgamation can be effected, and that the Treasurers of the several Funds be instructed to furnish the data which such actuary may require.

2. Finances.

Receipts, 1882.

Balance including Suspense account	$4,866.13
Congregational Contributions &c	4,696.18
Ministers' rates	2.172.37
Interest	6,229.57
Principal repaid	650.00
	$18,614.25

Expenditures

Annuities paid	$8,153.00
Harstone Mortgage	1,436.37
Sundry payments	38.75
Invested	8.033.18
Proportion of Salary	525.00
General expenses	344.16
Balance	83.79

State of Fund.

Debentures	$70,200.00
Mortgages	28,010.00
Balance Cash	83.79
	98,293.79
Last year	96,226.13
Increase	$2,067.66

Annuitants 49.

II. MINISTERS' WIDOWS, AND ORPHANS' FUND—MARITIME PROVINCES.

1. Amalgamation Act, 1883.

The Preamble recites the facts concerning the union of the Churches and the agreement of all the parties concerned to amalgamate the funds with consent of the General Assembly, asked and obtained. The 1st clause incorporates certain persons therein named by the name of "The Trustees of the Ministers'

Widows and Orphans' Fund of the Synod of the Maritime Provinces of the Presbyterian Church in Canada," investing them with general corporate powers. The 2nd clause directs that their successors shall be elected by the General Assembly, and states their qualifications. The 3rd clause transfers all properties rights and obligations of the separate funds to the new Trustees. The 4th clause gives directions as to officers, their elections and qualifications; and the 5th gives power to make by-laws, rules and orders for the administration of the said Trust which shall only have force when approved of by the General Assembly.

2. Specific Provisions.

Clause 6. All by-laws, rules or orders which may hereafter be made by the said Corporation in relation to persons already interested either as contributors or as annuitants in either of the two funds by this Act amalgamated, shall be subject to the following provisions, that is to say:—

1. Those ministers now contributing to the fund of the Ministers' Widows' and Orphans' Fund of the late Presbyterian Church of the Lower Provinces shall continue to pay the same amounts per annum as heretofore, that is to say: those in the first class, eight dollars, those in the second class, twelve dollars, and those in the third class, sixteen dollars.

2. Those ministers now contributing to the said other fund who have been paying the ministerial rate of twelve dollars per annum, with a rate from their congregations, may continue to pay in the same manner, or if they prefer they may pay at the rate of sixteen dol ars in lieu of both, and those who have been paying only the ministerial rate of twelve dollars may continue to pay at the same rate and shall be in the same position as those in the second class of the Presbyterian Ministers' Widows' and Orphans' Fund, but it shall be open to them up to the first day of July next to join the higher class, paying thenceforward at the rate of sixteen dollars per annum.

3. Widows and orphans now annuitants upon the Presbyterian Ministers' Widows' and Orphans' Fund shall (subject to such diminution as the Corporation hereby created may find it necessary hereafter to make) receive the following amounts per annum: widows in the first-class, seventy-five dollars; widows

in the second class, one hundred and twelve dollars and fifty cents; widows in the third class, one hundred and fifty dollars; if a widow be in the highest class she shall receive, in addition, for one child twenty dollars, for two children thirty-six dollars, for three children fifty dollars, and ten dollars for each additional child, and if she be in either of the other classes, in the same proportion. In the event of the decease of both parents, if there be one orphan the said Corporation shall pay for the benefit of such orphan two-thirds of the amount payable to widows in each class, and for the highest class, if there be two orphans, twenty-five dollars shall be added to the amount; if there be three, twenty dollars more, if there be four, seventeen dollars and fifty cents more, and twelve dollars and fifty cents for each additional orphan, and the other classes in proportion; to be continued in each case till they reach the age of eighteen years.

4. Widows and orphans now annuitants upon the said other fund, receiving on account of both ministerial rates and congregational contributions, and those who may hereafter be annuitants upon the amalgamated fund entitled to receive on account of both, shall receive at the highest rate received by the widows and orphans of the other fund; and those only entitled to receive the rate allowed for ministerial contributions alone, shall hereafter receive at the same rate as widows and orphans in the second class of the said other fund.

5. In all other respects all connected with either fund shall be subject to the rules that may hereafter be adopted for the management of the amalgamated fund.

6. It shall be the duty of the officers and members of the said Corporation, for the time being, to prepare annually, and to cause to be laid before the said Synod and General Assembly at their annual meetings, a full account of the receipts and disbursements of the said Corporation during the year next preceding such meetings, and also a general statement of its funds and property.

7. Until by-laws for the management thereof are framed and passed by the said Corporation and approved of by the said General Assembly and Synod, the proposed rules for the management of the said amalgamated fund agreed upon by the Joint Committee appointed to arrange the terms of such amalgamation, shall, so far as the same are not inconsistent with this Act, be the by-laws of such Corporation.

8. All provisions contained in any Act of the Legislature of Nova Scotia inconsistent with the provisions of this Act, relating to the said Presbyterian Ministers' Widows' and Orphans' Fund, are hereby repealed.

3. Proposed Rules for the Management of the Fund.

Rule 1 is contained in the Act and pertains to the appointment of Trustees.

2. The Trustees shall meet by notice from the chairman to each member, or by regular adjournment from one meeting to a specified date.

3. It shall be the duty of the Secretary to keep a regular minute book of all the proceedings of the Trustees, and also a record book in which shall be inscribed a correct record from the schedules forwarded to him, of the names and dates of birth of of all ministers contributing, the names and dates of birth of their wives and children, the names of widows and orphans in receipt of aid, and such other statistics as may be required, and he shall also prepare an annual statement to be submitted to the Synod and General Assembly of such changes as may have taken place during the year preceeding in the statistics of the ministers contributing, and their families, through admissions, marriages, births, deaths, or the like.

4. The Treasurer shall every year prepare an account to be laid before the Synod and General Assembly, of the sums of money received and expended since the previous statement, and also a general statement of the funds and effects in the hands of the Trustees.

5. Ministers ordained by any Presbytery of the Synod of the Maritime Provinces or ordained over congregations which did not enter the union, may be admitted to the benefits of the scheme by entering on or previous to the second 1st July following ordination and paying the regular rates from that date. Bnt should any one neglect doing so at that time he may join any time within three years after, by paying arrears from that date with interest.

6. Each applicant shall be required to furnish the committee, in writing, with a statement of the date of his birth, and if married of the date of his wife's birth, and also a statement of the name and date of the birth of each of his children under 18 years of age.

7. There shall be two classes of beneficiaries, and every person on becoming a member shall signify which class he chooses; and the choice being once made, he shall not afterwards have the power of rising to the higher class; but he shall at any time have the liberty of taking the lower class, it being understood that no part of the sum already paid or due by him can be returned or abated to him, and that his widow or orphan children will henceforth be entitled only to the annuity of class then chosen by him.

8. Every person coming on the scheme shall pay annually, on or before the 1st July in each year, at the following rates:

	Class 1.	Class 2.
Ministers under 35 years of age,	$8.00	$16.00
" between 35 and 45,	10.00	20.00
" " 45 " 50,	12.00	24.00

11. The application of any minister over fifty years of age shall be made the subject of special consideration. In all future cases there shall also be chargeable a marriage equalizing tax for every year exceeding five, that the ministers age exceeds that of his wife.

	Class 1.	Class 2.
Under 45, - - - -	$2.00	$4.00
Under 60, - - - - -	4.00	8.00
Over 60, - - - - -	6.00	12.00

With the understanding that the committee shall have power in special cases to remit or reduce the amount. The same to be paid on every subsequent marriage, except when he marries a widow already on the fund. In all cases he shall be bound to furnish a statement of the date of his own birth and of that of his wife.

9. Members not making payment of their annual rates on or before the 1st July in each year, shall be subject to the following fines:

Class 1.	Class 2.
10 cts.	20 cts.

For each month thereafter until payment be made; and those who neglect payment for four full years, shall from that period cease to be members, and shall forfeit all privileges connected with the fund, and shall have no claim to the money they have paid into it. Intimation shall in all cases be sent to ministers in arrears before they shall be cut off from the benefits of the fund.

10. As soon as correct tables for the purpose can be prepared, members shall be entitled at any time to redeem their annual rates, payable for life by the payment of a single sum at once, or to commute them into an increased annual payment to cease on their completing the 60th or 65th year of their age.

11. The annuities for widows shall be as follows:—

Class 1.	Class 2.
$75.	$150.

That in order to enable the widow to recover an annuity, six payments of annual rates shall be made, such payments so far as they have not been made, to be deducted yearly from the annuity.

12. Annuities to widows shall be payable half-yearly on the 1st January and 1st July of each year, commencing at the date of their husbands death and ending at their own death, or subsequent marriage.

13. There shall also be payable to each orphan child of any member the following sums yearly, until such child shall reach the age of 18:

If a widow be on the highest class she shall receive in addition, for one child $20, for two, $36, for three, $50, and $10 for each additional child, and if she be on the other class in the same proportion. In the event of the decease of both parents, if there be one orphan, the Board shall pay for the benefit of such orphan two thirds of the amount payable to widows in each class, and for the highest class if there be two orphans $25 shall be added to the amount, if there be three, $20, if there be four, $17, and $12.50 for each additional orphan, and the other class in proportion, to be continued in each case till they reach the age of 18.

14. The funds, so far as they are not required for immediate application or expenditure, shall be invested in security upon real estate or in Savings banks or Government or city securities, or in any of the chartered banks of the Dominion, in the name of the trustees.

15. There shall be an investigation of the funds of the Institution every fifth year, and a revision of the rates, when the amount of annuities to widows and orphans may be increased or diminished as the state of the funds will warrant, or the amount of the annual rates may be altered. But no alteration in these shall take place at other times.

16. No alteration in these rules shall be made, until considered by the Committee and the proposed alterations be submitted to a meeting of those in full standing as contributors, and adopted by a majority of those present, and afterwards submitted to Synod and Assembly and approved by them.

17. All differences or disputes that may arise in regard to sums due shall be referred to arbitrators, of whom the Trustees shall name and elect one, the other party one, and if necessary a third to be chosen by these two, being persons not beneficially interested directly or indirectly in the funds of the Institution.

18. In the case of any minister, a widower or unmarried, having made 40 payments and having reached the age of 70 years, on his agreeing to relinquish all claims upon the fund, he shall be entitled to receive the sum of $300 when on highest class, and $150 when on the lowest.

19. In the event of any minister or professor ceasing to be a minister or professor of the church by resignation, deprivation, or in any other way, it shall nevertheless be in his power to uphold and continue the right and interest of his widow and children to participate in the benefits of the fund, by making regular payment of all sums payable under these regulations.

20. Every minister on the fund shall be required to furnish annually to the Secratary a notice of the changes in his family, by birth, death, or marriage, which shall be duly entered on the Record book.

21. The annuities payable to widows and orphans, being intended as alimentary provisions, form no part of the estate of the contributor, and shall not be assignable or subject to arrestment or other legal proceedings at the instance of creditors, but shall be paid only to the widows, and the tutors and guardians of the children, and in case the widow shall be under any legal or natural disability, or in case the children shall have no tutors or guardians, it shall be competent for the Trustees of the Widow's Fund to name two or more persons as trustees to manage and apply the annuities in such a manner as shall appear tc them to be most for the benefit of such widows or children.

22. Ministers ordained elsewhere and being inducted in congregations of the Synod of the Maritime Provinces, or in congregations of the late Synod of the Maritime Provinces which did not enter the union, shall have the privilege of joining the scheme on the terms laid down for ministers at present inducted but not now upon the fund. See No. 7 and 8 of terms of amalgamation.

4. FINANCES.

Total receipts, $1,574.18 Expenditures, $1,298.56. Balance in Bank, $275.62. Total assets, investments, &c., $12,343.62.
Annuitants, 3, receiving $290 per annum.

III. WIDOWS' AND ORPHANS' FUND OF THE SYNOD OF THE PRESBYTERIAN CHURCH IN CONNECTION WITH THE CHURCH OF SCOTLAND.

This Fund was created by an Act of the Parliament of Upper and Lower Canada in 1847, 10 & 11 Vict., Cap. 103, in which the usual corporate powers were granted to certain individuals named, and provisions made for the continuance of the Trust, the holding of meetings, the election of officers, the framing of statutes, by-laws, rules and orders, touching the good government and administration of the Fund, for fixing the scale and rate of contributions and annuities; and specially providing that the Professors of Queen's College, at Kingston, for the time being, whether ministers or laymen, shall at all times be entitled to the benefit of the said fund, on the same terms and conditions as any minister of the Church, and requiring that an annual report of the affairs of the Corporation be presented to the Synod.

This Act was amended by the Legislature of Quebec, which however, is understood to have no legal effect. And as no Act of Incorporation has yet been obtained for the Widows' and Orphan's Fund of the Presbyterian Church in Canada, further Legislation seems to be deferred till an agreement to amalgamate the two funds has been reached. The Regulations consequently in use under the original Act of Incorporation, are still retained, and the Trust is still administered under them.

Abstract of the By-Laws.

1. *Rates and Collections.*

The rate is $12 per annum, paid half-yearly by a written order on the Temporalites Board, and a collection from each congregation of not less than $12.

2. *Annuities and Conditions.*

The corporation to determine the equal annuity to be paid to widows and orphans from the first Fund and the proportionate scale from the second Fund. In the meantime the sum shall be from the Ministers Fund $50 per annum, and from the congregational collections if under $12 a discretionary annuity of $60, but where the average collection is between $12 and $18 the grant will be $80 rising by a gradual scale till the collection reaches $108 when the grant is $240, which no annuity shall exceed.

For boys under 18 and girls under 21 the annuities will be for one $16, for two $28, for three $36, for four $40; and for each additional, $4, paid to the mother.

In case of orphans, till the daughters are 21 and the sons 18, or if studying for the Ministry 21, the widows' rate will be payable for the minors. When the youngest daughter shall have attained 21 years, the managers may allow to each unmarried daughter for her natural life as long as unmarried an annuity of $50. In the case of boys older than 18 years incapable of supporting themselves, an annuity for a longer time may be granted, but in no case to exceed the half allowed to a widow.

In the case of congregations not contributing or ministers leaving, the province their widows and orphans shall only have a claim on the Ministers' Fund provided the Ministers' contributions be regularly paid.

Any minister refusing to pay his annual contribution or to take up a collection from his congregation, his widows and orphans shall have no benefit from the Funds. Any minister ceasing to contribute, may resume his status by paying arrears with interest. Any minister leaving the province shall only have a right to the annuity from collections, provided he continues his own contributions, and an amount agreed upon in lieu of congregational collections.

Any minister at 40 years of age and over at his admission, who shall marry, can obtain the benefit of the Funds by paying three annual subscriptions, but coming into the Church after this age must make special application to the Board for terms.

The full text of the by-laws may be seen in "Taylor's Statutes &c."

Temporalities Fund.

An Act was passed, 22 Vict., cap. 66, July, 1858, by the Legislative Council and Assembly of Canada incorporating the "Board for the Management of the Temporalities' Fund of the Presbyterian Church of Canada in connection with the Church of Scotland," for the administration of certain Trust Funds, the revenues of which were to be appropriated for the encouragement and support of Ministers and Missionaries of the said Church, and for other purposes. The usual powers for the maintenance of the Corporation and the distribution of its funds were accordingly granted. They had power to appoint their own officers and to frame statutes, by-laws, rules, and orders for good government, for the collection, investment, appropriation and management of the Trust Funds; such regulations to be only operative *ad interim* until confirmed or rejected by the Supreme Court of the said Church, to which also an annual statement was to be submitted of its receipts and disbursements.

This Act was amended by 32 Vict., cap. 76, April, 1869, by the Legislature of Quebec for the purpose of defining the classes of securities in which the said Board may invest their funds, giving them power to invest in stocks or bonds of Quebec, Ontario, or the Dominion, or of any city, municipality, or corporation of the same, or in real estate in the Province of Quebec; providing also for the protection of real estate hypothecated to the Board in the same Province.

It was further amended by the Legislature of Quebec, 38 Vict., cap. 64, in 1874, and in the same year by the Legislative Assembly of Ontario, section 8th of the Union Act, but as both Acts were found to be *ultra vires* of these Provinces and so declared by the Privy Council, a new Act was obtained from the Dominion Parliament, 45 Vict., cap. 124, 1882.

This Act confirmed all the acts and doings of the Board under the Union Acts and authorized the present acting members of the Board to hold office and administer the fund under this Act, and provided for the continuance of the Trust, until the vested rights of all Ministers and Probationers shall have lapsed, which rights are specified as follows :—

1. The annual receipt by beneficiaries of $450, $400 or $250 as formerly during life and good standing. 2. The annual receipt of $2000 by Queen's College, 3. Of $200 by all ministers, probationers and licentiaties of the Church at the time of the Union in active service during life and good standing; and that all salaries of $200 be increased to $400 when their receipients in the Province of Quebec shall retire, or have retired, with the consent of the Church, and that the Board shall have power to draw upon the capital to meet said requirements. Further, so soon as any part of the Fund shall no longer be required for these purposes it shall, with the exception of the $2000 to Queen's College (which may be capitalised and paid to the College), be appropriated to a Home Mission Fund for aiding weak charges in the United Church. Provision is also made to preserve intact the rights of parties who did not enter into the Union, and of Ministers who may be professors in Queeen's College. It further gives the beneficiaries the right to nominate members of the United Church to fill vacancies in the Board; the remanent members of the Board to elect from such nominees new members, and in the event of no nominations being made to supply the vacancies themselves. Within twelve months after the passing the Act the Board shall also call a meeting of the beneficiaries, who shall have power to make by-laws to regulate the filling of vacancies in the Board. It is also provided that after the extinction of the 1st and 3rd classes of payments named in section one of the Act, and provision made in perpetuity of the same for Queen's College, each congregation that did not enter the Union and has not at the time united, shall be entitled to the proportional share of one to the whole number of congregations at the date of the Union. Printed reports are to be

sent annually to beneficiaries, the books and affairs are to be audited by auditors appointed by the beneficiaries; and the 3rd section of the Act relating to filling of vacancies in the Board shall be in force until the number of beneficiaries fall below fifteen, when the Board shall be continued by the remanent members electing ministers or members of the United Church to fill vacancies; they shall also appoint auditors.

The by-laws to regulate the provisions of the Dominion Act of 1882, have not yet been published, but will probably be similar to those contained in "Taylors Statutes &c.," page 202.

Church and Manse Building Fund Manitoba.

Act of Incorporation, June, 1883.

Corporate powers were by the Dominion Parliament granted to certain persons with succession under the name of "the Board of Management of the Church and Manse Building Fund of the Presbyterian Church in Canada for Manitoba and the North West"; also to hold and possess Funds for the purchase of real estate, and erection of Churches, Manses and buildings, and their maintenance; of loaning moneys on the security of real estate or otherwise and of acquiring property for particular Churches or Mission Stations.

Section 3rd gives the General Assembly full power of control over the Corporation, and to appoint successors and fill vacances in the Board.

Section 4th gives power to hold all kinds of legal securities and real estate for the purposes of the Presbyterian Church in Canada in Manitoba and the North West; provided that after acquisition of any real estate they shall dispose of the same within ten years except in so far as it may be required for use and occupation or other like purposes of the Corporation. Subject to the limitations specified power is also granted to frame by-laws for the transaction of business; the ordinary place of meeting to be in the City of Winnipeg, Manitoba.

The Regulations for the administration of this Fund will be found under Home Missions page 270.

Regulations anent Probationers and Vacancies.

1. The distribution of Probationers within the Provinces of Ontario and Quebec shall be made by a small Committee appointed by the Assembly. Within the Maritime Provinces it shall be left in the hands of the sub-Committee for that territory. The roll of Probationers, etc., shall consist of preachers who have been licensed less than five years, and Ministers who have been loosed from their charges, or who have been receiving appointments from the Committee less than four years (reckoning, in both cases, from the date of their admission to the roll).

2. Preachers who have been on the roll for five years, and Ministers for four years, without settlement shall have their names removed from the list; allowance being made in all cases of sickness, leave of absence or time occupied in the public business of the Church, or Mission work, apart from fulfilling regular appointments. Provided, also, that the Assembly alone may order the retention of a Probationers name on the list beyond the above specified times.

3. Ministers or Probationers, who have retired from the ministry and entered in some other calling for a time, shall not have their names put on the distribution list without the permission of the General Assembly to that effect.

4. Probationers concerning whom complaints of inefficiency have been received from their Presbyteries by the Committee, may have their appointments withdrawn till a decision of the Assembly shall be given in the case.

5. As soon as a preacher is licensed, the Presbytery shall report the fact to the Committee on Distribution.

6. When a congregation desires a hearing of a particular Probationer, or a further hearing of one formerly heard, they shall communicate their desire to the Presbytery; and, if the Presbytery see it expedient to concur in it, the application shall be transmitted to the Convener of the Distributing Committee, and as soon as practicable, effect shall be given to the request; it being understood that in case any extra expense is incurred by the Probationer, it is to be defrayed by the congregation in addition to the ordinary allowance.

7. When a preacher accepts a call he shall give notice to the Convener of the Distributing Committee, and no further appointments shall be given to him ; but he shall be required to fulfil the appointments already made, unless relieved by the Presbytery to whose bounds he has been designated.

8. Missionaries and Probationers shall be required to labor in the localities, and discharge the duties assigned to them by the Presbyteries, at whose disposal they may have been placed by the Committee on Distribution. These duties comprise, generally, conducting public worship on Sabbath, and prayer meetings in the course of the week, teaching Bible classes, organizing and fostering Sabbath Schools, visitation of families—and especially of the sick—so far as circumstances render advisable.

9. Missionaries and Probationers are required to submit to Presbyteries written reports of their labors.

Distribution of Probationers.

The Assembly of 1878 adopted the following regulations with reference to the distribution of Probationers :

I. *Probationers and Ministers now on the Roll.*

(1) The names of Probationers and Ministers on the Roll for the past four years shall be continued on said Roll for three months longer—thereafter, if not settled, to be removed from the Roll.

(2) Those on the Roll for the past three years shall be continued six months longer—thereafter, if not settled, to be removed from the Roll.

(3) Those on the Roll for two years shall be continued for another year and then removed.

II. *Probationers and Ministers to be Placed on the Roll.*

(1) Probationers shall be allowed three years on the Roll.

(2) Ministers, who resign their charges, shall be allowed two years on the Roll after each resignation.

(3) The above regulations, so far as they can be applied, shall refer to Ministers and Licentiates, who come from the Presbyterian Churches in Great Britain and Ireland.

(4) Ordained Ministers, who have been received from other Churches, with leave of the Assembly, shall be placed on the Roll for one year.

III. *Salary of Probationers.*

Presbyteries are recommended to induce congregations to pay Probationers as liberally as possible—it being understood that the minimum be eight dollars ($8.00) per week, with board.

IV. *Supply of Vacancies.*

(1) Presbyteries are hereby instructed to regard Probationers as having a prior claim to be heard in vacancies, and to secure such hearing for them :—

(2) Also to consider the propriety of appointing Probationers to vacancies for not less than two weeks, in order that the duties of the pastoral office may be attended to by them, as laid down in Minutes of Assembly, 1876, p. 59, clause 8.

(3) Students shall not be appointed to vacancies, save in exceptional cases.

(4) Presbyteries are enjoined not to report as a vacancy any congregation not prepared to call.

(5) Presbyteries are instructed to place all their vacant congregations prepared to call on the list of vacancies, and congregations are allowed to procure their own supply through the Presbytery for half the time, when they so desire.

(6) Employment shall hereafter be given by the Committee to none but those whose names are transmitted to this Committee through some Presbytery of the Church.

Minutes, 1882, p. 47—Resolved: that sub-section 5 of Section IV. of the regulations adopted by last Assembly be amended so as to read as follows, viz :—Presbyteries may place their vacant congregations prepared to call on the list of vacancies, and congregations are allowed to procure their own supply through the Presbytery, when they so desire.

Proposed New Plan of Distribution.

A Committee was appointed by the Assembly of 1882 to prepare an amended plan for the Distribution of probationers, the present plan not meeting with universal acceptance.

The plan proposed has been published and will be submitted to the Assembly of 1883. Its leading features are that it assigns the distribution to the Synod of the Church and gives Presbyteries the power of permitting vacant congregations to find their own supply, otherwise the regulations are similar to those now in use.

THE CHURCH—ITS STATISTICS.

Compiled from Reports furnished the General Assembly.

I.—RESPECTING CONGREGATIONS.

YEAR.	No. of Churches & Stations.	No. of Congregations.	No. of Ministers.	No. of Families.	No. of Communicants.	No. of Elders.	No. of other Office-bearers.	No. of Baptisms.	No. in S. S. & Bible Classes.	No. of Teachers.
1875-76	1,265	745	589	54,132	88,228	3.412	4,970	9,550	79,204	7,139
1876-77	1,406	805	590	56,163	93,788	3,596	5,278	9,244	72.867	7,405
1877-78	1,399	911	618	60,746	98,830	3,704	Not rep'd	9,321	Not re	port'd
1878-79	1,613	857	637	64,162	107,715	4,077	"	9,851	"	"
1879-80	1,350	813	659	63,843	107,871	4,125	"	9,837	83.265	8,574
1880-81	1,506	916	685	65,103	112,970	4.340	6,540	9,724	85,856	10.306
1881-82	1,524	903	697	65,623	116,883	4,410	6,720	10,385	91,257	9,934
1882-83	1,714	...	693	69,507	119,608	4,611	6,984	10,093	94,177	10.517
Increase since Union.	449	158	104	15,375	31,380	1,199	2,014	543	14,973	3,378

* The total number of Baptisms since the Union has been 78,005 of which about three-fourths were children.

II.—CONTRIBUTIONS TO SCHEMES.

Year.	College Fund.	Home Mission Fund.	French Evangelization Fund.	Foreign Mission Fund.	Aged & Infirm Ministers' & Widows' & Orphans' Fund.	Contributions to Missions by S. S. & Bible Classes.	Stipend paid by Congregations.
	$	$	$	$	$	$	$
1875-76	15,963	25,948	11,811	17,833	6,460	10,067	442,321
1876-77	15,789	31,804	15,235	18,819	6,935	20,801	451,550
1877-78	18,009	28,324	13,095	19,114	6,516	11,586	484,178
1878-79	29,249	26,574	12,855	21,254	7,182	12,600	475,573
1879-80	35,682	44,806	13,274	22,972	7,665	11,939	486,242
1880-81	37,561	35,519	16,818	32,732	8,305	12,903	498,475
1881-82	94,258	41,408	17,589	32,891	10,070	14,464	509,873
1882-83	42,883	45,079	17,598	33,006	6,551	14,751	Not known when going to press.
Increase since Union.	26,920	19,131	5,787	15,173	91	4,684	67,552
Totals since Union.	289,394	279,462	118,275	198,621	59,684	109,111	3,348,212

N. B.—As it was not deemed of sufficient interest to give the revenue received for Manses and Contributions for strictly Congregational purposes, these figures have been omitted, but the following show the total income of the Church and the increase since the Union :—

	Total Income.	Increase.		Total Income.	Increase.
1875-76..........	$ 982,672		1879-80...........	$1,162,154	$51,773
1876-77..........	986,115	$3,443	1880-81	1,245 495	83,341
1877-78..........	1,030,386	44,271	1881-82	1,409,748	164,253
1878-79..........	1,110,381	79,995	1882-83	1,436,811	27,063

Total income for eight years, including Manitoba, $9,363,762 ;_ total increase including Manitoba, $454,139.

IN MEMORIAM.

The Obituaries of the several years will be found in the Assembly's Minutes in full.

1876.

Rev. Alexander Buchan, of Stirling, Presbytery of Kingston, died 1876.

Rev. John F. A. S. Fayette, of Watford, died at London, Feb. 27.

Rev. John Jennings, D.D., of Bay St. Church, died at Toronto, Feb. 24.

Rev. John McColl, of Central Church, died at Hamilton, June 7.

Rev. James McIntosh, died this year at Amherst Island.

Rev. Adam McKay, died at Ripley in March of this year.

Rev. William McKenzie, died at Almonte, May 7.

Rev. William H. Rennelson, M.A., of Knox Church, Hamilton, died this year.

Rev. James Salmon, died at Chipman, N. B., June 8, 1875.

Rev A. J. Traver, M.A., of the First Church, Brockville, died this year.

Rev. James Thomson, of Erin, Ont., died May 7.

Rev. Andrew Halkett, formerly of St. Andrew's Ch., St. John, N. B., and subsequently parish Minister of Brechin, Scotland, died at St. Andrew's, Fifeshire, 1 Sep., 1874.*

1877.

Rev. James Bayne, D.D., of Pictou, N. S., died December 9, 1876, aged 62.

Rev. Arch. Henderson, M.A., of St. Andrew's, Que., died January 19, aged 93.

Rev. John Hogg, D.D., of St. Andrew's Church, Guelph, Ont., died March 3.

Rev. Patrick Gray, of Chalmers Church, Kingston, Ont., died Oct. 29, 1876, aged 57.

Rev. John McLean, of Knox Church, Oro, died at Stayner, Ont., March 24.

---

* Father of J. B. Halkett, associate editor of "The Hand Book."

Rev. Alexander McLean, M.A., of Nairn Church, Flamboro, Ont., died April 3.

Rev. John Munro, of Wallace, N.S., died on May 25, aged 68.

Rev. William Smart, of Gananoque, Ont., died September 9, at an advanced age.

Rev. William Taylor, D.D., Erskine Church, Montreal, P. Q., died at Portland, Maine, U. S., Sep. 4, 1876.

Rev. John Tawse, M.A., of King, Ont., died April 8.

1878.

Rev. George Cheyne, M.A., Saltfleet and Binbrook, Ont., died April 1, aged 75.

Rev. Andrew Dryburgh of Hawksville and Elmira, Ont., died May 6, aged 47.

Rev. J. M. Roger, M.A., of St. Paul Church, Peterboro, Ont., died January 8, aged 71.

Rev. James Ross of Grand River, C.B., died July 12, 1877.

Rev. David Taylor of Bass River, N.B., died April 28, aged 50.

1879.

Rev. James Adams of the Toweship of King, Ont., died June 5.

Rev. James Baikie of St. Thomas, Ont., died July 30, aged 38.

Rev. James Byers of Clifton, N.S., died in May, aged 63.

Rev. Charles James Cameron of New Edinburgh, Ont., died March 3, aged 42.

Rev. William Cochrane of Middleville, Ont., died May 29.

Rev. Alexander Lewis of Mono Mills, Ont., died December 4, aged 58.

Rev. James McConochey of Leeds, P.Q., died at London, Ont., April 12, aged 64.

Rev. Donald McDonald of Napier, Ont., died October 16, 1878, aged 46.

Rev. Hugh McGregor of Adboro, Ont., died in May, aged 41.

Rev. A C. Morton of North Gower, Ont., died March 22, aged 29.

Rev. John Paterson of Bobcaygeon, Ont., died at Chatham, July 30, aged 77.

Rev. Wm. Richardson of St. Andrews, N.B., died at New York, N.S., July 18, 1878, aged 44.

Rev. Alex. Spence, D.D., of St. Andrews' Church, Ottawa, died at Elgin, Scotland, September 14, 1878, aged 74.

Rev. James Whyte of Manotick, Ont., died at Ottawa, Ont., July 17, 1878, aged 48.

1880.

Rev. Daniel Anderson of Rothesay, Ont , died October 11, 1879, aged 58.

Rev. William Barrie, D.C., of Eramosa, Ont., died at Guelph, Ont., July 28, aged 79.

Rev. James Breckenridge of Streetsville, Ont., died December 10, 1879, aged 48.

Rev. Hugh Mackerras, M.A., of Queen's College Kingston, Ont., died at Peterboro, January 9, aged 48.

Rev. Alex. MacLennan, B.A., of Amherst Island, died May 18, aged 54.

Rev. John Stewart of New Glasgow, N.S., died May 4.

Rev. Alexander Topp, D.D., of Knox Church, Toronto, died Oct. 6, 1879, aged 64.

Rev. Michael Willis, D.D., LL.D., Principal Knox College, died at Aberdour, Scotland, August 19, 1879, aged 81.

Rev. Henry Gordon of Gananoque, Ont., died December 1. 1880, aged 90.

Rev. James Hume of Kennebec Road, P. Q., died January 28.

Rev. Dugald McGregor of North Mara, Ont., died Sep. 19, 1880, aged 71.

Rev. John McLean of Kempt, N. S., died November 20, aged 33.

Rev. Alexander Stewart of Lawrencetown, N. S., died January 26, aged 74.

Rev. John L. Stewart of Trenton, Ont., died at Florida, May 6.

1882.

Rev. John Black, D.D., of Kildonan, Man., died February 12.

Rev. John M. Brooke, D.D,, of Fredericton, N. B., died Jan. 16, aged 81.

Rev. Wm. Craigie of Port Dover, Ont., died October 23, aged 59.

Rev. Alexander Forbes of Inverness, P. Q., died at Waterdown, Ont., October 30.

Rev. Robt. Hall of East Missouri. Ont., died July 26, aged 50.

Rev. Peter McDermid of Point Edward, Ont., died October 15.

Rev. John G. McGregor of Elora, died this year, aged 82.

Rev. Donald McKerracher, of Wallaceburg, died July 13.

Rev. James C. Muir, D.D., of North Georgetown, P. Q., died July 9. aged 83.

Rev. Walter Ross, of Beckwith, Ont., died at Carleton Place, Ont., July 7, aged 48.

Rev. Thomas Scott, of Plantagenet, P. Q., died in June, 1881.

Rev. James Watson of New Annan, N.S., died December 12, aged 78.

Rev. Walter Wright, of Muskoka, died at Liverpool, England, April 26.

Resolution of Assembly.

Kingston, p. 40. The Committee appointed to prepare Obituary notices of Ministers reported also, as instructed by the Assembly to consider the expediency of continuing in future the practice of inserting Obituary Notices in the Minutes, that in the opinion of the Committee the practice should not be continued, only in so far as not to include the discontinuance of a brief record of the names and dates of the death of Ministers. On motion the Assembly ordered the notices submitted to be engrossed in the minutes, and adopted the recommendation of the Committee, in regard to the discontinuance of Obituary Notes in future.

MISCELLANEOUS DECISIONS.

STATE OF RELIGION 1876.

Minutes, p. 23. The Assembly received and adopted the Report of the Committee, on the state of religion, and as recommended :—

1. Enjoin on Sessions, Presbyteries and Synods that they give even greater prominence to this subject in their conferences and in their prayers.

2. Appoint a day on which the subject of the revival of religion and of the need, in order thereto, of a copious outpouring of the Holy Spirit, shall be presented from the pulpits of all our congregations.

1877.

Minutes, p. 31. The General Assembly receive the report, and, in doing so, would express their thanks to Almighty God for the many encouraging facts which it reveals, especially for the signal blessings vouchsafed to many congregations during the year ; and in reference to the evils complained of—such as the neglect of family worship by many of our people, the small share of labour taken in the work of the Church on the part of many Elders, the prevalence of intemperance and other sins, and the great number that have reached mature years living unpledged to a Christian life—the General Assembly deplore the same and appoint that, in their devotions to-morrow morning, humble confession of these sins be made at the throne of the Heavenly Grace, and that supplication for a time of refreshing from the presence of the Lord be offered up.

1878.

Minutes, p. 43. It was agreed :—That the Assembly receive the report; adopt its recommendations; express their gratitude to Almighty God for the many encouraging facts which the report reveals, especially for the increasing interest shown by the Presbyterians in the great schemes of the Church, for the times of refreshing vouchsafed to many congregations, and the signs of spiritual life observed aronnd us; and in reference to the complaints, such as neglect of family worship—the small share of labour rendered to the Church by many from whom good service might be expected—the prevalence of sin in various forms—the large number living without God, the General Assembly deplore the same, and urge that supplication be made for a larger measure of the Holy Spirit—and Resolve,

1. That a pastoral letter bearing upon the evils referred to in this report be issued by the Moderator, in name of this Assembly, to the members of the Church, to be read by all the ministers and missionaries to their congregations on the first Sabbath of January next, or at such other times as the Moderator may deem suitable.

2. That with the view of enabling the Committee to prepare the report with greater ease and efficiency, the reports of Presbyteries be transmitted by the Conveners of the Synodical Committees, along with their own reports, to the Convener of the General Assembly on or before the first day of May next.

1879.

Minutes, p. 55. It was agreed that the Assembly receive the report; thank the Committee, and especially the Convener, for their services; and express their gratitude to Almighty God for the blessing of His grace vouchsafed to the Church during the past year, and the many signs of spiritual progress, especially those seasons of spiritual refreshing enjoyed in several localities. In reference to the evils complained of in the returns, as intemperance, the influence of sceptical and frivolous literature, and especially the worldliness reported as widely prevalent and injurious, the General Assembly deplore the same, and urge that supplication be made for a season of refreshing from the presence of the Lord.

1880.

Minutes, p. 11. It was agreed that the Assembly receive the report, adopt its recommendations, thank the Committee, and especially the Convener, for their services, and express gratitude to Almighty God for the many marks of His favor which the Church has enjoyed during the past year. The Assembly would again urge upon Presbyteries the necessity of procuring full returns from the congregations under their care. In reference to the evils complained of, as intemperance, engrossing worldliness, especially the neglect, by not a few, of family training, the Assembly enjoins upon Sessions the duty of using all the means within their power in order that "pure and undefiled religion" may flourish in the families under their care, and especially :—

1. That the attention of parents and Sessions be again earnestly and affectionately called to the important subject of religious training in the family.

2. That Sessions send full and prompt replies to the Clerks of the various Presbyteries, and that the schedules be sent to the Clerks of the separate Presbyteries, to be distributed by them to Sessions.

3. That each Presbytery holds a conference during the year on the state of religion within its bounds.

1881.

Minutes, p. 25. It was agreed—That the report be received and adopted, and the General Assembly express satisfaction at the evidence given in the report of steady progress in different departments of Christian life and work, especially as regards attendance on and interest in public ordinances, family worship, missionary zeal and the grace of Christian liberality. Still, in the wide prevalence of lukewarmness and worldly conformity, in the tendency to substitute the form for the power of godliness; in the continuance, though happily in not a few cases in diminishing degree, of certain practical evils which have ever proved formidable obstacles to the rise and progress of religion in the soul and in society, the General Assembly finds abundant ground for humiliation before God. In adopting the recommendations of the Committee, the General Assembly remits it to Synods, Presbyteries and Sessions to take order that these be faithfully carried out, to the end that our beloved Zion may be blessed yet more than heretofore with times of refreshing from the presence of the Lord—

1. That the ministers should make the questions sent down on the State of Religion and the answers given thereon by their respective sessions, the subject matter of a discourse to the people at some diet of worship on the Lord's day.

2. That the Christian young men, and young women also, of our respective congregations should be encouraged to form themselves into bands, to go out two by two and invite the young

who do not go to church to go with them to Sabbath school and to the Lord's house; and that office-bearers be urged to countenance and assist them in the work.

3. That elders in visiting their districts, and ministers in their ordinary visitation, be urged to talk in a familiar and friendly manner with heads of families in regard to family religion, and especially Bible reading and instruction in the family circle.

4. That brethern be enjoined to assist each other in special services on all opportune occasions, so as to promote a healthy and lively spiritual interest in all the congregations of the Church, and if possible to make inroads on the careless and ungodly around.

5. That all the Presbyteries be recommended to hold conferences on the State of Religion, and to see that Sessions within their bounds send in returns in due time.

6. That all the office-bearers and members of the Church be earnestly exhorted to abstain from and, as opportunity offers, to discountenance the evils complained of, so that those things which are pure and lovely and of good report may prevail.

1882.

Minutes, pp., 14, 15. The General Assembly resolved:—That the Report be received and adopted, and in doing so record its thanksgiving to Almighty God for the tokens of His presence vouchsafed to the Church during the past year, more especially in such seasons of refreshing as have been granted to so many of the congregations; for the very marked increase in the grace of liberality towards both the support of the ministry at home, and the propagation of the Gospel in foreign and heathen lands, and for the continued, and in many cases, the increasing interest shown by the people in the ordinances of His house. While, at the same time, in the prevalence of lukewarmness and worldly conformity, in the hesitancy with which the Report speaks of family training, the want of proper zeal among young people, and especially young men, and in the existence of practical evils which hinder the growth of true piety, notwithstanding the efforts made to meet and overcome them, the General Assembly finds great cause for humiliation before God. The General Assembly adopts the recommendations of the Committee, and remits it to the Synods, Presbyteries, and Sessions to take order that these be faithfully carried out, so that a more abundant blessing may be granted us in times of refreshing from the presence of the Lord. (Recommendations same as 1881).

Rev. John James, D.D., Hamilton, Convener of Ass'bly Com.

SABBATH SCHOOLS.

1876.

Minutes, p. 50. The Assembly called for the report of the Committee on Sabbath Schools, which was given in and read. It was moved and unanimously agreed to, that the report be received; that its recommendations be adopted, namely:

1. With a view to the early training of the young in practical benevolence, and especially to the cultivation of a missionary spirit, your Committee recommend that the Assembly encourage the formation of *Missionary Associations* in connection with our schools wherever practicable: convinced that by this means the contributions to our Mission Scheme would be largely increased, and that the young themselves would reap great profit in having their interests in the Church and her work deepened, and a missionary spirit developed.

2. Convinced that our Sabbath Schools are the great nurseries of the Church, from which our members are to be drawn, and also of the importance of Sabbath School instruction, we recommend the Assembly to enjoin Presbyteries to see that Sabbath Schools be established at every preaching station if at all possible. In this way many of the young, at present not under any religious training, would be gathered in.

3. Your Committee are fully persuaded that the Sabbath School enterprise demands far more attention from our Church Courts than is given to it at present, and they ask the Assembly to urge Presbyteries and Synods to give at least one *Sederunt* to the consideration of a subject so vital, and also to collect statistics and send tabulated returns to the Assembly's Convener.

4. They also recommend the preparing and sending forth of a *pastoral letter* by the Moderater in the name of the Church, especially addressed to the young; they are convinced this would be productive of great good.

1877.

Minutes, p. 48. The report of the Committee on Sabbath Schools, was presented and read. It was moved, duly seconded. and passed unanimously that the report be adopted. The General Assembly further express their deepening interest in the godly upbringing of the young, and recommend :—

1. That more importance be attached to *Doctrinal* teaching in our schools, and especially to those *great doctrines of grace* that distinguish our *Presbyterianism.* And with such an admirable compend of Gospel truth as our *Shorter Catechism,* our schools might be made more efficient than those of any other Church that does not use this synopsis of doctrine.

2. That the Church give more attention to the training of *Teachers* for our schools, by the establishing of *Institutes* or *Normal Schools* in all our cities and towns, and wherever they could be conducted with efficiency.

1878.

Minutes, p. 28. The following motion was proposed, seconded and passed unanimously : Receive the report : empower the Committee to issue schedules for the purpose of eliciting information, and urge on all Ministers and Sessions diligence in replying thereto ; appoint the Moderator, in his pastoral letter on the state of religion, to press the recommendations of the report on the attention of the Church ; instruct Presbyteries to give diligent attention to the oversight of Sabbath school work within their bounds ; and, where practicable, to hold Presbyterial Sabbath-school Conferences, and to encourage the formation of classes for training Sabbath-school Teachers ; and authorize the Conveners of the Committees of the several Synods to act as a Committee, if they see fit, to inquire into and report on the subject of Sabbath-school literature. The Assembly recommends :—

1. That the Committee on the State of Religion omit this department from their schedule, and that the Assembly's Sabbath School Committee be empowered to issue a blank form on the whole subject, say for two years, embracing questions on Sabbath School Instruction, Sabbath School Organization, Sabbath School Equipment, Sabbath School Benevolence and Work.

2. That the schedules be forwarded to every congregation and mission station. Each Presbytery appoint one of its members fo tabulate the results within their bounds and report to the Presbytery, which report be forwarded to the Conveners of Synod's Sabbath School Committee, who in turn deal with the subject, and forward to the Convener of the Assembly's Committee. Two years of such returns would tend to mould the whole church into some uniform line of effect, and enable the Assembly to arrive at some definite idea of the tendencies of this work.

3. That Presbyteries hold, anually, conferences with the parents and teachers on their work.

4. That the Moderator issue an address to Parents, Teachers and Children to be read from the pulpit and in the schools; and that this address make special mention of the following points:— That the Sabbath School is under the authority of the session; that the financial needs of the school be a congregational responsibility; that the Bible, and not the lesson helps, be used in instruction while the school is in session; recommend Parents to study the lesson with their children, and that they be enjoined to give special attention to the Shorter Catechism; recommend teachers' weekly meetings for the study of the Scripture lesson

5. That the Conveners of the Assembly's and Synod's Sabbath School Committees be a sub-Committee to give special attention during the year to Sabbath School literature, such as, Libraries, Teachers, Magazines, Lesson Leaves, Hymns etc., and report to next Assembly.

6. That the Church, in this department of work, as in others, be devided into East and West with their respective Committees.

1880.

Minutes, pp. 28,29. The Assembly resolved that the report be received, and that this Assembly, while regretting that so many congregations have failed to make returns, yet rejoice in the growing interest and increased efficiency, indicated by the report, in the work of the Sabbath Schools, commend its recommendations to the careful considerations of Sunday School workers, and enjoin congregations to furnish the information asked, and use every legitimate means to promote the religious nurture of the young: Further, appoint a Standing Committee in accordance with recommendation number twelve, in the report, and for the objects named therein; thank the Committee, and especially the Convener, for their valuable services in this important department of the Church's work, and re-appoint them with authority to carry out as far as practicable the recommendations and suggestions contained in the report.

Recommendations Commended.

Minutes, App. pp. 131–132.

That the International Series of Lessons be supplemented by:—

(1)The addition of a portion of the Shorter Catechism to be committed with each day's lesson.

(2) By adding a portion of Scripture, more especially the Pslams, to be committed for each Sabbath.

(3) That proofs from Scripture be required for the leading doctrines held and taught by the Presbyterian Church, embracing also our Church polity, and the Scriptural significance of the Sacraments of Baptism and the Lord's Supper.

2. That in the meantime the Westminster Series of Lesson Helps be supplied in each congregation for the use of the teachers and scholars.

3. That there be a Teacher's Meeting for the Study of the Lesson, or, should that be found impracticable, that the pastor take up the Lesson at the Weekly Prayer Meeting, or on some other suitable occasion.

4. That the teacher in every case, as far as possible should be a member of the Church in full communion.

5. That where schools are already organized, new teachers or other officers, when needed, be proposed by the teachers and officers now acting, subject to the approval and ratification of the Session, and when new schools are organized the appointing of teachers and officers be made under the supervision of the Session.

6. That, when practicable, a Normal or Training Class be formed at a suitable time during the year, in connection with

each pastorate, either by the minister or by some one under his care and with his approval, and that the course of lessons used for the present be the Westminster course.

7. That a scheme of Normal Class Lessons, suitable for different circumstances either in towns or cities, or in rural districts, be recommended by a committee chosen for that purpose, under the auspices of the General Assembly.

8. That this Synod repsectfully overtures the General Assembly to appoint a committee for the purpose of carrying out such recommendations in this Report as would require the action of the Assembly.

9. That at an early day, say the last Sabbath of June, special supplications be offered for the baptized youth of the Church, and the subject of their Christian nurture, their early acceptance of Christ, and open confession of Him, as great vital concerns of the parents in the home, and the elders and pastors in the church, be distinctly and earnestly brought before each congregation.

10. That it be an instruction to Presbyteries to hold conventions with the people, and to encourage the for mation of classes for the training of teachers.

11. The Assembly call the attention of Sessions to the importance of their exercising a living and intelligent control of the Sabbath school work in their congregations.

12. That every school, large or small, be expected to raise money for strictly missionary purposes, and that the necessary and current expenses of the school be a charge on the ordinary revenue of the congregation.

13. That a full record of attendance of teachers, scholars, and of moneys collected, be kept in every school and reported to the congregation as the Session and Deacons' Court may direct.

14. That feeling convinced that much of the literature used in our Sabbath schools is of an unhealthy character, and recognizing the difficulty of securing proper books, the General Assembly appoint a standing committee whose duty it shall be to examine books and periodicals prspared by societies and publishers for the use of Schools, and to issue, from time to time, a

list of such books as they may deem suitable for Sabbath schools, and thus aid Sessions and teachers in securing proper materials for this department of Church work.

1881.

Minutes, pp. 24-25. The Assembly receive the report, and tender thanks to the Committee, and especially to the Convener; express satisfaction with the fuller returns made by all the Synods, and with the increased interest and progress which the returns shew; adopt the recommendation as to the line of study proposed for next year, and recommend it to the favourable consideration of the Church; but resolve that hereafter no provision be made by the Assembly's Committee for competitive examinations, or for awarding prizes in money or books, or for reporting the names of successful candidates to be engrossed in the records of the Church; also, express satisfaction with the provision made for supplying literature for Sabbath school libraries, as reported, and commend it to the favourable consideration of all Sabbath schools; and further recommend that, on the last Sabbath of September, special prayer be offered for the youth of our Church, in accordance with the recommendation of the report.

Dissent.—Mr. Neil McKay craved leave to enter his dissent from this decision.

For the line of study and other matters referred to in this deliverance, see Report of the Committee on Sabbath Schools, *Minutes* 1881, App. pp. 126–132.

1882.

Minutes, p. 30. The Assembly agreed to refer the Report of the Committee on Sabbath Schools to a Committee, consisting of the members of the S. S. Committee who are members of this Assembly to bring in a deliverance. This Committee presented this report which was adopted, and is as follows; *Minutes* p. 54: That the report on Sabbath Schools as now presented be received and adopted, and printed in the Appendix of the Assembly's Minutes.

The recommendations annexed to the Report are :—

1. That the Paper of Mr Hoosie—which contains a Constitution for Sabbath Schools, suggests the formation of a Board of Sabbath Schools, and outlines the duties of such a Board—be printed in the Appendix to the Minutes, and referred to the Committee, to be reported on next year. (See App. pp. 139–141.)

2 That the Sabbath School be fully recognized as a part of the Church, under the control of the Session in all its appointments.

3. That greater attention be given to the study of the Shorter Catechism, both in the Sabbath School and in the family.

4. That each Presbytery devote at least one Sederunt in the year to the consideration of Sabbath School work within its bounds, and that Superintendents and others interested in such work be invited to be present.

5. That the day to be appointed by the Moderator as a day of prayer for Colleges, be also a day of prayer for the youth of the Church generally.

STATISTICS.

	1882.		1881.		1880		1879.
S. S. Scholars........	91,247	..	85,856	..	83,856	..	78,628
Teachers and Officers.	10,934	..	10,240	..	8,574	..	8,208
Communicants added.	1,428	..	1,812	..	428	..	——
Expended on Schools.	$21,861	..	$15,273	..	$8,907	..	——
Contributed to Miss'ns.	$11,931	..	$10,878	..	$3,603	..	——
Vols. in S.S. Libraries.	173,285	..	162,164	..	——	..	——

REV. A. SIMPSON, Halifax, N. S.,
Convener of Assembly's Committee.

SABBATH OBSERVANCE.

1875.

Minutes, p. 21. There was produced and read a reference from the late Synod of the Presbyterian Church of the Lower Provinces, bearing on the matter of a desecration of the Sabbath by the Railway Companies of Nova Scotia and New Brunswick. It was unanimously agreed: that the documents connected with this reference be committed for consideration to the Assembly's Standing Committee on Sabbath Observance, hereafter to be named. Further, it was agreed to petition the Dominion Parliament to abolish unnecessary Sabbath labor on public works, and traffic on Railways under Government control, and recommend Presbyteries to petition to the like effect.

1878.

Minutes, p. 33. The General Assembly resolved as follows: Receive the report; express gratification at the success attending their efforts to secure a better observance of the Lord's Day throughout the Dominion; adopt the recommendations contained in the report and refer them to the Standing Committee on Sabbath Observance, with instructions to take such measures as they may judge best to have these recommendations carried into effect, namely—

1. That Synods, Presbyteries, and Sessions, and the Members of the Church in general, be exhorted to ererciseexercise increased vigilance in regard to all incipient forms of Sabbath profanation of a public kind, and adopt prompt measures for the suppression of the same.

2. That the Assembly petition the Dominion Government to close the Post Offices throughout the Province of Quebec during the whole of the Lord's D y.

1879.

Minutes, p. 57. The Assembly heard read the report of the Committea on Sabbath Observance. It was agreed to receive the same and adopt its recommendations, and appoint the Moderator and the Hon. Alex. Morris a Committee to wait on the Government with reference to the desecration of the Sabbath referred to in the report: The recommendations are:—

1. That a deputation be appointed to wait on the Members of Government in Ottawa, with the view of securing that all persons employed in the Parliament Buildings be relieved from duty on Sabbath, and an opportunity afforded them of enjoying the privileges of the public worship of God and the means of grace.

2. That the Committee be authorized to print and circulate as widely as possible, in fly sheet form, the civil law of the Sabbath, for the information of the public.

1880.

Minutes, p. 58. The Assembly resolved as follows: Receive the Report, and direct the Assembly's Committee on this subject to co-oporate in all well-directed efforts with the Committees on this subject appointed by the Synods and Presbyteries of our Church, and with other local Committees in various parts of the country, whose aim is the promotion of the due observance of the Lord's day.

Joint Conveners.—Rev. Dr. McCullock ; Rev. N. T. McMullen.

The Assembly called for the report of the Deputation appointed last year to wait upon the members of the Government at Ottawa, with the view of securing that all persons employed in the Parliament Buildings be relieved from duty on the Sabbath, and be afforded the opportunity of enjoying the privileges of the public worship of God and the means of grace. Dr. Reid reported verbally that the Deputation had carried out the purpose of their appointment, and had such conference as instructed, but were told merely, in effect, that the employés in the Parliament Buildings were under the direction of the two Houses of Parliament, and that the Government proper had no control in the matter.

1881.

Minutes, p. 47. The Assembly agreed that the Committee be authorized to remonstrate with corporations, or other public companies, who may be found violating the Lord's day by unnecessary labour thereon.

1882.

Minutes, p. 50. The General Assembly having heard the Report of the Committee on Sabbath Observance, desires to express gratitude to God for the successes which have attended the efforts to preserve the sacredness of the Sabbath ; enjoins ministers and office-bearers of the Church to be diligent in their respective localities in resisting unlawful inroads upon the Sabbath rest ; and recommends the formation of local associations, composed of all Christian Churches, for the purpose of co-operating in the endeavour to guard the sanctity and secure the proper observance of the weekly day of rest.

TEMPERANCE.

1876.

Minutes, p. 82. Then was read a memorial from the Dominion Alliance for the total suppression of liquor traffic, and the following motion was agreed to. The Assembly receive the communication and express their sympathy with those who are engaged in seeking to remove or mitigate the evils of intemperance, as well as their desire to co-operate in all well directed efforts to gain this important end.

1877.

Minutes, p. 50. The Clerk read a Memorial from the Dominion Alliance for the total suppression of the Liquor Traffic.

The following motion was proposed and passed unanimously, The Assembly reiterates its testimony as to the enormous evils entailed by intemperance on the Church and the world. The Assembly expresses satisfaction at the progress of legislation for the repression of these evils, and at the growth of a healthful Temperance sentiment throughout the community. Further, the Assembly instructs Sessions to have continued regard to the causes and cure of intemperance within their respective bounds, and recommends to the office-bearers and members of our Church generally to cultivate and exemplify the principles of Bible temperance.

1878.

Minutes, p. 52. 1. The General Assembly is devoutly thankful to God for the advance made in the direction of Temperance reform in this and other countries, and commends the practice of total abstinence to the prayerful consideration of all connected with its congregations, especially the office-bearers thereof.

2. The Assembly expresses its desire to co-operate in all well-directed efforts to mitigate or remove, if possible, the evils of intemperance and prays the Great Head of the Church to bless and prosper all such efforts.

Overture, 1880.

Minutes, pp. 56 57. There was presented and read an Overture from the Synod of Toronto and Kingston, setting forth the great evils of intemperance, and praying the General Assembly to take the whole subject into consideration, and devise there anent such measures as may tend to the glory of God, and the good of the Church, especially by the appointment of a standing committee on temperance. There was read, also, a memorial on the same subject, praying for an expression of the Assembly's estimate of the Canada Temperance Act, so that our people may be encousaged to avail themselves, in their several localities, of the facilities for the restriction and regulation of the traffic in intoxicating liquors.

On motion the Assembly resolved as follows:—That the Overture from the Synod of Toronto and Kingston be received; that the Assembly appoint a standing committee on temperance, with authority to make inquiries of the various Presbyteries within their bounds regarding the prevalence of intemperance, and the best means of promoting a healthy scriptural temperance sentiment and practice; that Presbyteries be enjoined to hold conferences on this subject, and frame and forward to the Convener of the Temperance Committee such answers as they may be able to give, together with such views and suggestions on the whole question as they may deem proper; that the Assembly recommend the appointment of Synodical Committees on Temperance, where such do not exist; and that the Standing Committee now to be appointed consist of a member from each Presbytery of the Church.

RESOLTTIONS, 1881.

Minutes, pp., 45, 52, 53. 1. That this Assembly renew the testimony repeatedly borne by this Church, in all its branches, against the evil of intemperance, as a great sin against God, and a bitter curse to man, obstructing the progress of ths Gospel of our Lord Jesus Christ in the world, and weakening its power over the hearts of men; and while we rejoice in the healthy advancement made in recent years in temperance sentiments, practice and legislation, we yet express our deep regret that the evil is still largely prevalent and deeply rooted, and express our solemn conviction that it is the duty of the Church to make every endeavour to do away with intemperance, and the customs and practice which lead to it, and thus purge ourselves from all fellowship with this "unfruitful work of darkness."

2 That we recommend to our people the practice of entire abstinence from the use of intoxicating liquors as a beverage, as the best safeguard for the individual, as an example to others, especially to the young, and as, in the light of experience, the best working principle upon which people can unite in dealing with this question; and we further recommend ministers and elders to take the lead in this matter.

3. That we recommend our sessions, by means of congregational associations or committees, the use of pledge books, the

circulation of temperance literature, by co-operation with existing temperance societies, or by any other means that may be deemed suitable in the circumstances, actively to prosecute temperance work within their bounds, paying special attention to the Sabbath School children, and the young generally.

4. In view of the great evils necessarily connected with the manufacture and sale of intoxicating liquors for use as beverages, we earnestly counsel the members of the church engaged in the traffic to abandon it, and entreat others not to engage in it.

5. That the Assembly approve of the Legislative prohibition of the liquor traffic as correct in principle, and specially that the Assembly approve of the principle of the Canada Temperance Act of 1878, and trust that any amendments made to it will be in the direction of increased stringency and efficiency, and that all retrogressive legislation will be avoided.

6. That recognizing the importance of the principle of "overcoming evil with good," the Assembly recommend to the members of the Church to aid and encourage the establishment of coffee houses, as a substitute for public houses in which intoxicating liquors are sold.

7. That the Committee on Temperance be instructed to send circulars down to sessions, to report through Presbyteries and Synods to the General Assembly, and that Presbyteries and Synods be instructed to hold conferences on the subject.

Dissents and Reasons.

Dr. Proudfoot craved to have his dissent from the action of the Assembly on the fifth resolution marked in the minutes, for reasons to be given in at next Sederunt.

Dr. Proudfoot handed in and read the reasons of dissent of which he gave notice at last Sederunt, in terms following:—

1. Because such resolution expresses approval af Acts of Parliament and amendments thereto, which are not before the house, and which many of us have not read.

2. because its tendency is to bring a direct and *quasi* political pressure to bear on the Legislature of the country, whereas it is our duty as ministers of the Gospel rather to enlighten the people, and through them to influence legislation.

3. Because as ministers of the Gospel we are bound to use the moral means which God has provided for reclaiming a sinful world, and which I believe to be suitable and adequate; reserving, however, to ourselves as citizens, and to the members of the Church, the liberty of seeking prohibitory or any other legislation that we consider best.

Mr. J. Laing dissented from the action of the Assembly adopting the fifth resolution, for the reason following:—Because I believe that the resolution will be by many construed as regarding not only the principle of prohibition, bnt also particular Acts of Parliament and amendments thereto.

Resolutions—1882.

Minutes, p. 53. 1. That the Assembly draw attention to the deliverance of last year, on the Temperance question, with the request that it be made known to our people where this has not been done.

2. That Presbyteries and Sessions be recommended to consider the best methods of advancing the cause of temperance within their bounds, especially to consider what form of temperance organization would be most suitable as recognizing the authority of the Session, and affording scope for the energies of the members of the Church.

3. That the attention of tbe Governments of the various Provinces in the Dominion be called to the desirability of instructing the children in our Public Schools regarding the effects of alcohol on the human system, and the influence of the drinking usages on society, either by the use of Temperance Manuals or by the introduction into the Reading Books of some lessons setting forth the results of scientific investigation, and the teachings of history and experience, on the subject, and that the Clerk be instructed to send copies of this resolution to the Ministers or Superintendents of Education in the various Provinces.

4. That we recommend the members of our Church to unite with other temperance workers, organizing in our counties and townships branches of the Dominion Alliance, or any other well-conducted association having for its object the Legislative Prohibition of the Liquor Traffic.

There was taken up, in connection with the Report, and read, an Overture from the Synod of Toronto and Kingston, requesting the Assembly to instruct its Committee on Temperance to correspond with other Churches, with a view of united action in the suppression of the evils of intemperance. The Overture was received, and referred to the Committee on Temperance.

There was, further, submited to the Assembly a Memorial from the Women's Temperance Union. The Memorial was received, and referred to the Committee on Temperance.

Rev. J. McCaul, Montreal, Convener of Assembly's Committee.

The Bible as a Text Book in Public Schools.

Minutes, 1870, p. 58. It was resolved that the Assembly being deeply impressed with the importance of having the youth of this country imbued with the principles of Christian morality, earnestly urge all the members of this Church in their several stations and relations to endeavor as far as practicable to have the Word of God read by the children in the public schools and appoint a Committe to watch legislation on the subject of Education.

Hymnology.

Minutes, 1882, p. 55. The Assembly called for the Report of the Committee on a "Hymnal." The Report stated that the Committee had issued during the year a Sabbath School edition, and a larger sized edition with music; that they contemblated publishan edition intermediate between the Sabbath School and the the larger sized copy, and also a Sabbath School edition with music; that about 40,000 of all the editions had been sold; that the royalty last year amounted to $1,192.03; that the sums advanced from the Assembly Fund had been returned, and that there remained in hand a balance of $300. The Report closed by recommending that the amount now at the credit of Committee, and the amount which may be received next year, be devoted to the Aged and Infirm Ministers' Fund, in proportion to the number of ministers connected with or having an interest in each of the Funds for Aged and Infirm Ministers; and that the Hymnal Committee be re-appointed.

The Report was received, its recommendations were adopted, and the Assembly decerned and ordered in accordance therewith. An overture on Music for the Psalms was remitted to the same Committee.

PRESBYTERIAN RECORD. 1882.

Page 54. The report on the *Presbyterian Record* was submitted, and gave the circulation at 34,500, and said that a much larger number would require to be issued to reach every family on the Church, and stated that somewhat less money had been received and disbursed than in the year before—receipts, $9,388.-65; payments, $8,514.95; leaving a balance of $873 70. The Report was received; thanks were tendered to the Editors; and the *Record* was commended to the support of the congregations of the Church.

DELEGATES TO THE SECOND PAN-PRESBYTERIAN COUNCIL.

Minutes 1879, p. 28. The Assembly resolved to appoint the delegates by ballot. Against this decision a dissent was entered for the following reasons:—

1. Because the decision of the General Assembly to take the vote by ballot is a method of procedure unknown to the Supreme Court of the Church.

2. Because the method of taking the vote by ballot is not contemplated by the rules which the Assembly has adopted for taking the vote.

3. Because it seems, at least, very doubtful whether such a method of taking the vote is consistent with the responsibility of the Assembly as a representative body.

RE-ORDINATION OF ROMAN CATHOLIC PRIESTS.

Minutes, 1881, p. 23. The General Assembly does not find it necessary to come to any deliverance on the general question of the re-ordination of ex-priests of the Church of Rome, who shall make application to be admitted into the Ministry of this Church; but expresses its readiness at all times to give directions to Presbyteries in cases of practical difficulty in which the the questions may be involved; and following its course in the past, reserves to itself the right of dealing with each case of reception into the ministry of the Presbyterian Church in Canada, on its own merits, as the same may emerge.

Dissent.—Mr. Laing craved leave to enter his dissent from this decision.

Overture as to Latin Thesis.

There was taken up and read an Overture setting forth that the General Assembly had seen fit to substitute a Hebrew critical exercise for the Latin Thesis in the curriculum of Theological studies; that, as it is proper that the subjects of examination for License should correspond as closely as possible to those embraced in the curriculum prescribed by the Church; and as the production of a Latin Thesis, in the circumstances in which it must often be prepared by candidates for License, cannot be regarded as of great value in promoting their knowledge of the Latin tongue, while it is sometimes attended with much inconvenience; the General Assembly is respectfully overtured to remove the Latin Thesis from the list of subjects appointed as trials for License. The General Assembly received the Overture and decerned in terms of the prayer thereof.

Remits to Presbyteries anent Standing Committees.

Minutes, 1882, p. 13. 1. That the Committee to nominate Standing Committees be composed of eighteen members, two Ministers and two Elders from each Synod, and one Minister and one Elder from the Presbytery of Manitoba.

2. That all the Standing Committees be elected for three years, one-third retiring each year, but being eligible for re-election. In order to begin the plan equitably, each Committee shall decide by ballot as to who shall retire at the end of the first and second years.

3. That the Home Mission Committee (Western Section) shall consist of thirty members, and the Home Mission and Supplemental Committees of the Eastern Section of fifteen members, each Presbytery having at least one representative.

4. That the following Committee shall consist of not more than twenty-four members:—Foreign Mission Committee for Western Section; the Boards of Management of Halifax, Montreal, and Knox College.

5. That the following Committees shall consist of not more than fifteen members—Foreign Missions, Eastern Section; State of Religion, Manitoba College; Widows' and Orphans' Fund, Western Section; Sabbath Schools; Sabbath Observance; Aged and Infirm Ministers' Fund, Western Section and Eastern Section; Temperance; College Senates.

6. That the Boards of Examiners shall consist of not more than twelve members.

7. That the following Committees shall consist of not more than six members:—Finance; Statistics; Protection of Church Property; Record; Distribution of Probationers.

Overture, Marriage with deceased wife's sister.

There was taken up and read an overture from the Presbytery of Toronto, relating to the proposal in the last Session of the Parliament of Canada to legalize marriage with the sister of a deceased wife, and with a deceased brother's wife, and praying the Assembly to take the whole subject into consideration and adopt such measures as it deems best to avert such legislation as that recently proposed. Resolved in terms following:—Receive the overture respecting marriage with a deceased wife's sister, and appoint a committee to watch legislation on this subject, and to take such steps, by petition or otherwise, as they may deem advisable, with a view to avert such legislation as that recently proposed in the Parliament of Canada.

Overture Remitted to a Committee.

Whereas by Act of Parliament passed during last Session, marriage with a deceased wife's sister is no longer prohibited by the law of the land;

Wheress in the Confession of Faith it is expressly declared that a man may not marry any of his wife's relations nearer in blood than his own, and that such marriages cannot be legitimized by any consent of parties or law of man;

Whereas the law of the land and the law of the Church are thus at variance, and difficulties may be expected to arise from collision between them;

Therefore the General Assembly is respectfully overtured to take this matter into consideration, and appoint a Committee to investigate the scriptural authority on which the marriages referred to are condemned, and report their judgment, with reasons for it, to next Assembly.

Resolved, That a committee be appointed in terms of the prayer of the Overture.

The Committee was appointed as follows:—Principal Caven; Prof. Gregg, *Convener*; Prof. Mowat, Prof. Scrimger, Prof. Weir, Prof. Currie, Prof. Coussirat, Principal McVicar, Principal McKnight, Mr. J. Laing, D. B. Blair, E. Ross.

Remit on Theological Education.

1. That the Assembly appoint a Board of Examiners whose duty it shall be to examine students (*a*) at their entrance upon the study of Theology, and (*b*) at the completion of the Theolgical course.

2. That every Student for the ministry who is not a graduate in Arts of an approved University, shall, upon entering the Theological classes of any of our Colleges, be required to present to the Faculty thereof a certificate from the Assembly's Board of Exiners that he has passed a satisfactory examination in the literary subjects prescribed by the General Assembly.

3. That every candidate appearing before a Presbytery to be taken on trials for license, shall, in addition to the usual certificate of having completed his Theological curriculum, be required to produce to the Presbytery a certificate from the Assembly's Board of Examiners, that he has passed a satisfactory examination in his Theological studies.

4. That the examination shall be in writing, the papers being prepared and examined by the Assembly's Board, and the examinations conducted by Committees appointed by the Board for that purpose.

5. That these examinations shall be held at the College centres, and in the month of May of each year.

Resolved,—That the Report be received and sent down to the Presbyteries for consideration, and to report to next General Assembly.

Stated Collections, 1882.

Minutes, 1882, p. 57. The Assembly resolved that in congregations where there are no Missionary Associations, collections for the Schemes of the Church be taken up as follows :—

1. French Evangelization, on the third Sabbath of July.

2. Home Missions, on the third Sabbath of August.

3. College Fund, on the third Sabbath of September.

4. Aged and Infirm Ministers' Fund, on the third Sabbath of October.

5. Widows' and Orphans' fund, also on the third Sabbath of October.

6. Supplements (Maritime Provinces), on the third Sabbath of November.

7. Assembly Fund, on the third Sabbath of December.

8. Manitoba College, on the second Sabbath of January, 1883.

9. Foreigh Missions, on the first Sabbath of March, 1883.

Or on such other days as may be most convenient for the congregation. Further resolved, that all congregations and Mission Stations be enjoined to contribute to the Schemes of the Church.

Agents of the Church.

Toronto, 1876, p. 21. Resolved that the services of Rev. W. Reid, M A., D.D., and the Rev. P. G. McGregor, D.D., be retained in connection with the general work of the Church ; that the salary of each be two thousand dollars per annum.

The Duties of Dr. Reid.

Page 77. I. He shall act as General Agent and Treasurer for the several Schemes in the Western section of the Church, with the exception of the French Evangelization Scheme. In this capacity it shall be his duty—

(1). To prepare and issue notices and circulars as to the collections and contributions ordered by the Assembly, and correspond with defaulting congregations.

(2) To receive and acknowledge all sums contributed for the Schemes.

(3) To make all payments for the Home and Foreign Mission Schemes, keep the accounts and prepare periodical statements as well as annual financial reports.

(4) To manage the Ministers' Widows and Orphans' Fund and the Fund for Aged and infirm Ministers, to make investments under the advice of the Convener or joint-Convener, to collect Ministers' rates and receive interest.

(5) To receive the payments for the Assembly Fund and discharge all accounts in the general business of the Church.

(6) To attend to all necessary correspondence in connection with the financial and general business of the Church.

II. He shall act as Secretary and Treasurer of Knox College. As such, it shall be his duty to keep the minutes of Board meetings and meetings of Senate, conduct necessary correspondence, carry out the instructions of the Board of Management, act as Treasurer of the various Funds of the College, and prepare annual statements.

III. As General Agent, he shall attend to such other duties, too minute to be defined, connected with the business of the Church, as may require attention.

Dr. Reid is hereby authorized to employ whatever assistance he may require in the discharge of the above duties.

The duties of Dr. McGregor.

I. He shall act as Secretary of the Home and Foreign Mission Boards in the Eastern Section of the Church, and of the Board of Superintendence of the Theological Hall at Halifax. As such, he shall convene these Boards, keep the minutes, and conduct all correspondence connected with the same. Under Home Mission work shall be included the distribution of Probationers. He shall also prepare and submit to the Assembly the annual reports of the Boards.

II. He shall act as General Treasurer for all the Schemes, with the exception of the Ministers' Widows and Orphans' Fund, in the Eastern section of the Church. As such, it shall be his duty.—

(1). To receive and acknowledge all sums contributed to the Schemes.

(2). To take the general management of all the Funds, make investments of the same, and collect interest.

(3). To transact all the financial business of the Schemes, make all payments connected with the same, and prepare the annual accounts.

(4). To transact all the business of the Hunter Fund for church-building under the charge of the Synod of the Maritime Provinces; it being understood that this Fund shall bear its due proportion with other Funds of his salary as Agent.

Other Presbyterians in Canada.

1. The Presbytery of Stamford, Ontario, in connection with the United Presbyterian Church of North America, consisting of eight ministers and six congregations.

2. The Eastern Presbytery of Nova Scotia, in connection with the Reformed Presbyterian Church of North America, consisting of twelve ministers.

3. The Presbytery of New Brunswick and Nova Scotia, in connection with the Reformed Presbyterian Church of the United States of America, consisting of three ministers and four congregations.

4 The Synod of Nova Scotia, in connection with the Established Church of Scotland, comprising two Presbyteries, eight ministers, and corresponding congregation.

5. The Presbyterian Church of Canada in connection with the Church of Scotland, consisting of about seven ministers, and congregations.

GENERAL INDEX.

A.

B.

C.

D.

E.

F.

K.

L.

M.

www.ingramcontent.com/pod-product-compliance
Lightning Source LLC
Chambersburg PA
CBHW022257280326
41932CB00010B/895

* 9 7 8 3 3 3 7 2 0 6 1 5 4 *